The Birth of
Modern
Comedy in
Renaissance
Italy

The Birth of Modern Comedy in Renaissance Italy

Douglas Radcliff-Umstead

The University of Chicago Press
Chicago and London

#12636

Library of Congress Catalog Card Number: 69-16904

THE UNIVERSITY OF CHICAGO PRESS, CHICAGO 60637
THE UNIVERSITY OF CHICAGO PRESS, LTD., LONDON W. C. 1

To Lula Louisa with Love

Contents

Preface

It is only in recent years that American scholars have focused attention on
the comedy of the Italian Renaissance for its intrinsic value as representing
the thought and spirit of the sixteenth century. Too often mere lip service
has been paid to the influence of the Italian theater on the Elizabethan
playwrights, without any attempt to see how the learned comedy arose in
Italy after more than a century of humanistic experimentation. I have tried
to demonstrate that the Italian learned comedy did not exist in cultural
isolation but instead reflected the tastes and aspirations of a highly sophisticated society. To clarify my goals in writing this book I have included in
the Introduction a history of the critical fortune of the erudite comedy.
Readers may wonder why I have included critics like Rossi and Momigliano
to the exclusion of original figures like Croce and Russo. In the Introduction
I am especially interested in chroniclers of Italian literature; the important
critical contributions of Croce and Russo will be amply acknowledged in the
notes concerning particular comedies. Throughout the text, translations
from Latin and Italian are my own unless otherwise indicated.

Most of the research for primary material was carried out at the Florentine Biblioteca Nazionale, the Biblioteca Marucelliana, and the library of
the Faculty of Letters and Philosophy at the University of Florence while
I was on an Italian traveling fellowship from the University of California.

Introduction

ITALIAN COMEDY AS A THEATER OF IMITATION

Comedy played an important role for the "cultured" society of sixteenth-century Italy. The number of comedies written and actually performed is in itself astounding. Among the authors of comedies are such major figures of the period as Ludovico Ariosto, Pietro Aretino, and Niccolò Machiavelli. In aristocratic circles, as at Ferrara, a state event like a wedding with another reigning house would be celebrated with performances of comedies. A city like Florence, with a ruling class of merchant background, supported presentations of comedies by a notary or a shoemaker during carnival days. Distinguished artists like Raphael, Giulio Romano, and Vasari designed sets for performances. In a darkened princely hall, stage scenery with a perspective backdrop adorned the performances of comedies.

Yet, despite the glittering surface, the comedy of this period does not appear to be original or profound. Almost all these plays are in five acts with the scene set in a public square. The inspiration for this type of comedy came from the dramatic works of two Roman authors, Plautus (ca. 254-184 B.C.) and Terence (185-159 B.C.). It seems surprising that from the twenty extant plays of Plautus and the six of Terence were derived the hundreds of

1

Italian comedies written during the sixteenth century. The problem grows more complex when one realizes that Plautus and Terence were not "original" playwrights developing their own plots and character situations. They modeled their works on the Greek New Comedy of Hellenistic times represented by authors like Philemon, Menander, Diphilus, Philippides, Poseidippus, and Apollodorus of Carystus. Are the Italian Renaissance comic authors imitators of an already imitative Roman theater?

The name "erudite" or "learned" is usually assigned to this comedy, partly on account of its antique inspiration and partly to distinguish it from "popular" forms of the Italian theater active throughout the period. When, toward the middle of the century, elegant courtiers were laughing at the salacious dialogue of a learned comedy in the country's first permanent theaters since Roman times, recently formed companies of actors were touring Italy presenting not a written comedy but an improvised one. The "Commedia Erudita" would seem on superficial examination to be the antithesis of the unwritten "Commedia dell'Arte." During those same years, too, the sacred dramas of medieval origin were continuing their tradition and enlisting new authors, while the farce, with a quick satiric vein, was never more effective than at that same time. Does the superficial splendor of the Erudite Comedy fade before those examples of a popular theater? Should critics judge this formal comedy as stilted and lifeless?

The Neo-Aristotelian School of Theatrical Practice

By the second half of the century literary criticism had already arisen. When these first modern literary critics considered the comedy, they were not referring to contemporary comedies. The critics of the Renaissance wanted to see clear through to the idea of the perfect comedy. Theirs was a preceptive approach that sought the immutable schemes of art.[1]

Renaissance critics drew many of their doctrines from Horace's *Ars poetica* and Aristotle's *Poetics*. Horace's work was the only classical antique poetic to be carried down through the Middle Ages. Theories developed from his poetics were thus bound by a long tradition. Horace places emphasis on the external demands of an audience: no disorder is permitted, and disunity is considered ridiculous; certain conventions of form are to be

1 For the attitude of sixteenth-century Italian critics see Mario Apollonio, *Storia del Teatro Italiano* (Florence,1951), 2:135-41.

maintained (five acts and a limited number of performers); dramatic characters like the hero must preserve their decorum; and the style of a work must confirm to its nature. In Horace there is always a rhetorical tendency. Aristotle's *Poetics* had been entirely too intricate and confusing for the literary thought of the Middle Ages, but in 1493 Giorgio Valla published a Latin translation of the work. Alessandro de' Pazzi followed in 1536 with what became the standard Latin translation, presented along with the Greek text. These translations and subsequent public lectures by other scholars all added to Aristotle's new fame as a literary critic. In the *Poetics* Aristotle's intention is not to study nature or analyze audiences; he advances instead a general aesthetics on the ends of poetry and the nature of imitation that he uses to analyze the Greek literature known during his lifetime. Aristotle tries to see how close authors have come to attaining perfection in their art. He *does not* give rules or canons. His is not a rhetorical stand to persuade a definite audience in a particular way. The only audience Aristotle thinks of is a universal one that has all of mankind's thoughts and feelings. Renaissance critics were to take Aristotle's observations, modify them in the light of Horation tradition, and make canons of them.[2]

Giambattista Giraldi Cintio (1504-73), professor of philosophy and rhetoric at Ferrara, approached the problems of the theater in his *Discorso intorno al Comporre delle Commedie e delle Tragedie* of 1545. For Cintio both comedy and tragedy are to teach good behavior, helping the audience to gain a moral lesson through sympathy with the characters portrayed. An author must set characters in his own locality during his own times so as to give verisimilitude to their actions. Dramatic works are supposed to please the audiences, but the obscene is to be avoided, as pleasing only to an audience of sausage makers. Verse is necessary for both comedy and tragedy. The minimum time for a comedy's performance is three hours. Aristotle had made only one strong suggestion on dramatic writing: the plot action should be single. Here Cintio departs from Aristotle in preferring a double plot for its variety of episodes. One of Aristotle's observations (but in no way a rule) was that most plays completed themselves within a single circuit of the sun, a period of about twenty-four hours. Cintio codifies this observation into the rule of the unity of time: a play's action is limited to a single day. One of the major devices to resolve the plot of a comedy has been a recogni-

2 Bernard Weinberg, *A History of Literary Criticism in the Italian Renaissance* (Chicago, 1961), 1:71 and 349 f., clarifies the differences between the Horatian and Aristotelian approaches.

tion scene where parents and children find each other after having been
separated for years. Cintio justifies these recognition scenes in Aristotelian
terms:

> L'agnizione non è altro che un venire in cognizione di
> quello, che prima non si sapeva; onde ne divengono gli
> uomini di amici inimici, o di felici infelici. . . .
> Quest'agnizione, la quale è congiunta colla peripezia, è
> reputata da Aristotile più di tutte le altre lodevole,
> perchè più di tutte le altre commove gli animi degli
> spettatori. . . . Non è però l'agnizione e la peripezia
> (pigliandolo un poco più largamente) così della tragedia,
> che ambedue non siano della commedia. Ma ciò avviene
> diversamente, poichè l'agnizione e la peripezia nella
> commedia non è mai all'orrore ed alla compassione, ma
> sempre menano elle le persone turbate alla letizia ed alla
> tranquillità. . . . Che il proprio è della commedia condurre
> l'azione sua al fine, talmente che non vi rimanga persona
> turbata; il fa con la peripezia e con la cognizione a
> lei convenevole.[3]

In a section entitled "Apparato" Cintio affirms that all stage properties are
a part of the imitation of real actions. The setting must fit the subject and
genre. Cintio again breaks with tradition in saying that although the ancient
Latin grammarians gave suggestions for stage design, modern artists must
change to suit the new times. The use of foreign clothes is recommended so
as to generate the wonder of spectators. Cintio does not appear a slavishly
devoted follower of Aristotle. Rather, he uses Aristotle superficially and
alters his theories to meet the needs of audences.[4]

Further discussion on the unity of time comes from Francesco Robortello
and Bernardo Segni. Writing in his edition of Aristotle's *Poetics*, published

---

3 Cintio cited in Vincenzo De Amicis, *L'Imitazione Latina nella Commedia Italiana del XVI Secolo* (Florence, 1897), p. 159: "Recognition is just a coming into
knowledge of what was previously unknown: whereupon men who were friends
become enemies, or happy persons grow sad. . . . This recognition, which is connected with peripety, is reputed by Aristotle to be more praiseworthy than all other
practices because more than all others it stirs the hearts of the spectators. . . . Recognition and peripety (taken in a somewhat broader sense) do not therefore belong
exclusively to tragedy, for both practices are not foreign to comedy. But their result
is different since recognition and peripety in comedy do not tend toward horror and
compassion; but they always lead disturbed persons to happiness and tranquility. . . .
For it is appropriate to comedy to bring the action to such a conclusion that no character remains troubled, which is achieved through peripety and the discovery suitable to it" (translation our own).
4 Weinberg, *Literary Criticism*, 1:433 f., discusses Cintio at length.

in 1548 together with the short treatise *De comoedia*, Robortello reduced the unity of time to twelve hours, since the dramatic characters would surely be sleeping at night. But Segni, in his Italian translation of the *Poetics* of Aristotle, chose to disagree by pointing out that at night dramatic events like adulteries and murders take place. Although sleep is natural at those hours, the unjust do not act naturally. Thus, for Segni, twenty-four hours would be the proper time span for a dramatic action.[5]

Two of the foremost exponents of Aristotelian literary theories were Bartolomeo Lombardi and his student Vincenzo Maggi. In their *In Aristotelis librum de poetica communes explanationes* they displayed the same rigid doctrinaire attitude as their contemporaries by pronouncing the canon of the unity of time from Aristotle's comment: "unico solis circuitu, vel paulò longiore exprimere *debet* [italics mine]." They felt that the author must address himself to an audience that is not an elite but Aristotle's general mankind. Therefore the unity is explained by the audience's demand for credibility. Maggi later went on to write a treatise on comedy entitled *De ridiculis*. He defined the ridiculous as of body, of mind, or of circumstances. Like Cintio, he recognized the need in comedy for the audience's wonder to be excited by variety and novelty.[6]

Not all the critics of this period were erudite writers in Latin. Some were popularizers writing in Italian to diffuse major ideas on poetic composition. Important among these popularizers is Orazio Toscanella, with his *Precetti necessarii sopra diverse cose pertinenti alla grammatica, poetica, retorica, historia, loica, ed altre facoltà* of 1562. His discussion of comedy is derived from the fourth-century commentary on Terence by Aelius Donatus. Toscanella's is a moralistic approach to comedy, which he feels was invented so men could moderate their desires through the example of others and thus become better. He states that, "la commedia consiste nella imitatione, ed

---

5 Robortello's *In librum Aristotelis de arte poetica explicationes* was the first important commentary on Aristotle's text. The Italian critic felt literature should have a moral goal as well as creating pleasure. Literary characters were supposed to serve as moral examples. Tragedy, in Robortello's view, was superior to comedy since tragic plots were touching and profound. He opposed a happy ending for a tragic play as a concession to vulgar tastes. Robortello always thought of an elite audience, who would ask for more than the ridiculous actions of a comedy. Consequently his treatise *De comoedia* is disappointing. For Robortello's views see Weinberg, *Literary Criticism,* 1:66-69 and 388-406, as well as Marvin T. Herrick, *Comic Theory in the Sixteenth Century* (Urbana, 1959), *passim*. Herrick also provides a translation of the *De Comoedia* in the appendix, pp. 227-39. Joel E. Spingarn, *A History of Literary Criticism in the Renaissance* (New York, 1924), p. 92, explains Segni's position.

6 See Weinberg, *Literary Criticism,* 1:415.

uno che fa la parte del servo imita quanto può gli andamenti del servo; uno che rappresenta lo innamorato imita uno che sia veramente innamorato."[7] Toscanella presents chapters like "What Persons Are Introduced in the Comedy," "What Is the Subject of Comedy," "On Music," or "On Vocal Sections." The questions he discusses are mechanical ones. As a theatrical practice, for example, Toscanella emphasizes the development of suspense. The role of this critic was to take century-old ideas and explain them in simple fashion for a wide public.

Perhaps the most influential of Aristotelian critics is Lodovico Castelvetro, author of the first vernacular commentary on the *Poetics, Poetica d'Aristotele vulgarizzata et sposta*. He uses Aristotle as a point of departure for his own theories, placing major emphasis on an audience composed of common people to the exclusion of the learned elite. An author must consider the physical comfort and convenience of the audience. The audience's hopes must be gratified. Pleasure is the only end of poetry. An audience is pleased when it identifies itself with the dramatic characters, provided they seem real; for the audience's imagination is limited. Thus the dramatic action should hold ideally to time passed on stage. Castelvetro goes on to formulate for the first time the all-important unity of place: during a performance the place of action should not be changed. Castelvetro points out that because of Aristotle's emphasis on verisimilitude a constantly shifting scene should be viewed as highly improbable. Later theorists were to follow this new unity of place. Castelvetro does not, however, believe in the unity of action, as he feels that a multiple plot is more natural and pleasing. For him, unity of action is only the result of the unities of time and place that restrict a play's development. Castelvetro was concerned with the exigencies of state representation, realizing that the stage does not have unlimited space and time. This critic saw the stage work as scenic poetry.[8]

Not every critic was satisfied with the comic genre. Aristotle had stated that comedy did not deal with illustrious persons but with lowly ones. Bernardo Pino da Cagli in his *Discorso intorno al Componimento de la Comedia de' Nostri Tempi*, published in 1572 as an adjunct to Sforza degli Oddi's comedy *Erofilomachia*, disagreed with the attackers of comedy, feeling that erudites erred in thinking that Aristotle urged poets to imitate vile persons and their vices. He points out that the detractors of the comic

---

7 *Ibid.*, 1:167: "Comedy consists in imitation, and one who plays the part of a servant imitates as much as he can the comportment of a servant, and one who represents a lover imitates a man who is really in love" (Weinberg's translation).
8 See Spingarn, *Literary Criticism* p. 98, and Herrick, *Comic Theory*, 86-87.

genre have paid attention only to the vulgar style of a few authors. For Pino da Cagli the aim of comedy is to use the ridiculous to expose the stupidity of dishonest acts. In a Horatian manner this critic says profit and pleasure come from laughter without the causing of harm, whereas vice creates no pleasure. Pino da Cagli goes on to discuss the nature of comedy. With the change in times and customs comedy will of necessity deal with new subjects and actions, but it will always preserve the same form of five acts with an intrigue to be resolved by the play's close. Each character is to speak according to his social conditions and is to act according to the dramatic circumstances. Cagli has presented a defense of comedy based on its moral usefulness.[9]

Cagli was not alone in taking the part of comedy, for Giulio del Bene's lecture *Che la favola de la comedia vuole essere honesta et non contenere mali costumi* (1574) demonstrates why the comic genre succeeds only when it upholds the virtuous. Audiences derive no pleasure from viewing the morally ugly since the vicious moves one to disdain. The "low" characters of comedy are not vicious, but merely humble and undistinguished intellectually. A comedy has more actions and characters than a tragedy, as ordinary men are more numerous than exalted ones. Comedy is to present common objects in an exquisite manner, wherein the poet has free choice to organize dramatic material so as to show to best advantage virtuous actions. Wicked characters cannot triumph by the end of a comedy, as the audience receives joy only in the triumph of the good. Del Bene leaves the sphere of Aristotle's *Poetics* to base his dramatic theories on his own ideas about man's nature.[10]

Antonio Riccoboni became a dominant figure among critics on account of his clearly written Latin treatises. In his *Ars comica* of 1585, the first complete poetics of the comic genre to be written during that period, Riccoboni states that verse is the proper instrument of comedy as well as of all other poetic genres, as prose cannot command an audience's attention. The dance could be very effective in performances of comedy. In order to allow a single main action, a comedy's plot should run from two to twelve hours. An audience's marveling at a ridiculous deception purges it of that deception, while viewing a wicked act teaches the audience not to commit that kind of act. For certain wicked acts bring on laughter and consist in various deceptions springing from ignorance of well-known facts, from false opinion, from misunderstandings, or from sudden turning of events. Characters are

9 Weinberg, *Literary Criticism*, 1:203.
10 *Ibid.*, 1:535-38.

to be consistent throughout a play and must conform to their literary tradition: a parasite is a glutton always out to filch a meal. Like other critics, Riccoboni concerns himself with comedy's moral purposes but also considers technical problems.[11]

Still another critic, Giason Denores, feels that art is the method used by artists to please audiences. His treatise *Discorso intorno a que' principii, cause, et accrescimenti, che la comedia, la tragedia, et il poema heroico recevono dalla philosophia morale, et civile et da' governatori delle republiche* (1586) advocates the creation of a sense of wonder (*maraviglia*) in the audience so as to generate pleasure. Denores views comedy as a series of obstacle courses that the hero must overcome:

> consiste in questo, che trovandosi un huomo di bassa
> fortuna in una qualche molestia, non pare, che possa
> mai rilevarsi da quella, nondimeno i poeti, sequendo gli
> ordini de' legislatori, acconciano con le loro invenzioni sì
> fattamente questa tal poesia, che se ben nel principio egli
> è in disturbo, all'ultimo tuttavia sortisce felice fine.[12]

Plot deals with a "revolution" in a character's lot. To increase the audience's wonder, the comic poet must not allow the plot action to exceed twelve hours. Comedy, by using the pleasurable and ridiculous, purges its audience of those hardships that break the calm of their private lives. The members of the audience are brought to appreciate their private lives after seeing the love affairs of unfaithful wives, the treachery of servants, and the conspiracies of nurses and pimps. Both Denores and Riccoboni employ the Aristotelian term "purgation" when speaking of comedy's effect.

Poetic decorum is the chief concern of the Horatian critic Tommaso Correa in his *In librum de arte poetica Q. Horatii Flacci explanationes* (1587). For Correa the poet by his choice of the comic form is bound to work within its possibilities as limited by the law of decorum. Even the subject matter is determined by decorum. Correa details the content of comedies: "ut plurimum amores, nuptiae, virgines venditae, quae liberae inveniantur, cognoscuntur a patre, matre, fratre, nutrice. . . ."[13] Verse is

---

11 *Ibid.*, 1:586-88.

12 *Ibid.*, 1:622: "it consists in this, that a man of low estate finds himself in some predicament, and it does not seem that he can ever get himself out of it; nevertheless, the poets, following the orders of the law-givers, arrange this kind of poem in such a way, through their inventions, that although in the beginning he is in trouble, at the end however he achieves a most happy conclusion" (Weinberg's translation).

13 *Ibid.*, 1:217: "loves, marriages, girls sold into slavery who are later found to be free and are recognized by their father, their mother, their brother, their nurse . . . (Weinberg's translation).

absolutely necessary to all poetic compositions, and each genre has certain verses and diction proper to it. In beholding the poetic creation the audience will receive instruction (*institutio*) and pleasure (*voluptas*). All subject matter must have verisimilitude to achieve the aim of instruction, whereas variety creates pleasure. The interesting arrangement of events will hold the spectator captive.

Nicolò Rossi's *Discorsi intorno alla Comedia* of 1589 reveal themselves rather similar to Correa's theories. Comedy has two ends: the pleasure caused by imitation; and moral instruction to tame the spectators' passions. Comic imitation consists in representing "badness" in intent and deed, since certain stupid or crafty acts of badness arouse laughter. Intermezzos with music and dance are recommended for comic performances to add to a play's perfection, especially because such intermezzos delight audiences composed not so much of erudites as of "common people." The opinion of the common people is important in determining a comedy's actions, as they know just what happens in many events like a plague or a young man's love affair. Art for Rossi must change to meet the audience's new demands.[14]

Another critic intent on seeing all members of the audience pleased, even the most ignorant, was Frederico Ceruti, with his *Dialogus de comoedia* of 1593. He considered comedy a school that would give examples of life to be either followed or avoided. The actor, the musician, and the architect all could contribute to comedy's perfection. The actor in particular has a moral duty to cut out obscene passages so that the youth are not corrupted. There ought to be a prologue to awaken the audience's attention, but it should not spoil suspense by telling the story's outcome. Five acts help the memory and add relaxation, as in the intervals between acts the audience may be entertained with songs and dances. Ceruti always thought in terms of audience requirements, displaying a Horatian attitude.[15]

Whereas Cintio, Riccoboni, and Correa all defend verse as the correct instrument for dramatic and poetic writing, two other critics, Agostino Michele and Paolo Beni, advocate prose. Michele's *Discorso in cui si dimostra come si possono scrivere le comedie e le tragedie in prosa* (1592) upholds contemporary usage, as the author felt that theories must fit the new body of literature. Everything changes, art included. Genres can evolve to perfection. Dramatists should always use prose, as verse forms no part of daily life and is too artificial for the theater. Prose is as audible as verse and fully as verisimilar.[16] Beni, in his *Disputatio in qua ostenditur praestare*

14 *Ibid.*, 2:666-67.
15 *Ibid.*, 1:237-38.
16 *Ibid.*, 2:678-79.

comoediam atque tragoediam metrorum vinculis solvere, feels that the audience will not easily understand the moral lesson of a play written in the obscure and complicated form of verse:

> Ita fit ut si Comicum spectaculum detur aut Tragicum
> ac soluta oratione detur, Cives ac populares possint
> dictionem atque sententiam intelligere: inde fabulae
> mores, hoc est actorum virtutes et vitia, magna ex parte
> animadvertere: peripetiam etiam seu fortunae commutationem
> utcunque persentire: denique ad componendos mores, ad
> vitam caute prudenterque traducendam, ad familiam ipsam
> aut Rempublican commode utiliterque administrandam, institui
> et erudiri. Quod si carmine inter se actores illi agant,
> hoc est dicendi genere auditoribus plane insueto insolentique
> utantur; optandum magis est quam sperandum ut Auditores inde
> propositam utilitatem fructumque percipiant.[17]

Beni here uses an Aristotelian terminology. The end of drama is moral instruction to make persons useful to the country. Nature is a guide to the dramatist since the theater must imitate human life. People do not speak in verse, and therefore plays must be written in prose. According to Beni, language does not bring the main pleasure to the spectator; rather, the plot provides maximum pleasure. Prose will enable the audience to understand thoughts and actions and to gain moral instruction.[18] Both Beni and Michele are modern in their approach to the controversy over prose and verse.

Toward the end of the sixteenth century Italian critics had fully expressed themselves. Rarely had they addressed themselves to the theatrical practice of their era. They had engaged in various polemics, like the one over the unities, because of their desire for Italy to have a drama that would be intense and concentrated. These critics wanted to set standards for dramatists to follow so as to create a distinguished theater.[19]

---

17 *Ibid.,* 2:708: "And so it happens that if a tragic or comic spectacle is given in prose, the citizens and the men of the people can understand the diction and the thought; thence they can expend most of their attention on the moral import of the plot, that is, the virtues and vices of the actors, and feel deeply also the peripety or change of fortune, whatever it may be; and finally they can be instructed and educated to regulate their behavior, to conduct their lives carefully and prudently, to administer properly and in a useful way the family itself and the state. For if these actors use verse among themselves, that is, a form of speaking entirely unusual and unaccustomed for the spectators, it would be a simple wish rather than a definite hope that the spectators would derive from it the intended utility and profit" (Weinberg's translation).

18 *Ibid.,* 1:244-46.

19 In using Weinberg's text it was necessary to reorganize the material, inasmuch

THE CRITICAL FORTUNE OF THE ERUDITE COMEDY

Real critical evaluation of the Erudite Comedy was not to come until the eighteenth century. Giovanni Mario de' Crescimbeni, in his *Comentari intorno alla sua Istoria della Volgar Poesia* (1702), felt that study of antique Latin plays led the Italian authors of comedy to produce a theater on the level of that of Greece and Rome. This early historian of literature places those comedies, whether in prose or verse, beside sixteenth-century Italian painting and music. He contends that imitating antique plays transforms a rough native Italian tradition into a polished comic theater. Crescimbeni approves of the use of intermezzos as further perfecting this comedy.[20]

Preceptive formulas determine the judgment of Francesco Saverio Quadrio (1695-1756) in his *Della ragione d'ogni poesia,* published in several volumes from 1739 to 1752. A member of the Arcadian Academy and a Jesuit, Quadrio took the side of the Greek and Latin classical writers in the "querelle des anciens et des modernes," demonstrating the dependence of modern authors on the works of antiquity. His text starts off with a discussion of poetry in general and then examines the various genres, hoping to arrive at a universal comprehension of literature. In the second part of his third volume this critic dismisses the folk farce of medieval and Renaissance Italy as monstrous abortions of the true comic art. Not until Italian playwrights took Plautus and Terence as models did a genuine theater arise in modern times. For Quadrio the best dramatists of the comic art in Renaissance Italy were Ludovico Ariosto and Cardinal Bibbiena, who by following the ancient Roman playwrights produced "la regolata e buona Commedia nella Volgar Poesia" (p. 60). Because of his emphasis on rules, this Lombard critic preferred verse over prose for the theater, since in his opinion there was no true poetry without metrical expression of images. His study provides lists of plays in both verse and prose, with occasional brief descriptions. Quadrio, for instance, considered Machiavelli a scoundrel who deserved a life of poverty as divine punishment for his wicked thoughts; he also denied the supremacy of Machiavelli's comedy *La Mandragola* over the

---

as the author analyzes literary poetics according to Horatian, Aristotelian, and Platonic attitudes. Herrick, *Comic Theory,* definitely minimizes influence and stresses the contribution of Terence's fourth-century commentator Donatus to theatrical poetics in the Renaissance. René Wellek, *Concepts of Criticism* (New Haven, 1963), p. 24, comments that sixteenth-century Italy had only a limited degree of true literary criticism; what generally prevailed was a discussion in the name of rhetoric or poetics.
20 Crescimbeni, *Comentari* (Rome, 1702), pp. 207-10.

rest of the comic theater in modern Italy. Attacking some French critics, Quadrio affirms the contribution of Italian playwrights to the development of the theater in other countries. He points out how Molière's Tartuffe derives from the hypocritical character Dr. Bacchettone of the Italian Commedia dell'Arte. In his discussion of comedy as well as the other genres it was Quadrio's aim to instruct writers in the correct moral way to gain literary fame.[21]

One does not find a glowing description of the Erudite Comedy in the thirteen-volume *Storia della Letteratura Italiana* of the Jesuit scholar Girolamo Tiraboschi (1731-94). In this comprehensive work Tiraboschi details the history of Italian culture from the Etruscan period to his own century. He notes that the value of sixteenth-century comedies does not correspond to their number. According to Tiraboschi this comedy sought applause not for elegant style but for obscene language and lascivious stage action. These plays are cold, languid, and boring on account of antique imitation. They offend a person of integrity. For Tiraboschi, not one of those comedies is free of several faults. He judges most of the Italian authors as servile translators of the ancient Roman comedy.[22]

Early in the nineteenth century the Frenchman Pierre Louis Ginguené brought the Italian comedy to notice throughout Europe. In his *Histoire Littéraire d'Italie* he judges the Erudite Comedy imperfect because of its lewd actions. He especially objects to the way this comic theater emphasized intrigue rather than character. Its major defects arose from imitating the ancient Roman comedy. Ginguené goes on to admit that those Italian plays did constitute a real comedy as much as those of Plautus and Terence. This critic-historian is willing to grant the title of comedy to the Italian works even though many of their features do not reflect the sixteenth century. Plautus and Terence, because they imitated the Greek New Comedy,

---

21 See Francesco Saverio Quadrio, *Della Storia e della ragione d'ogni poesia* (Milan, 1744), vol. 3, part 2, pp. 53-109.
22 Tiraboschi, *Storia* (Milan, 1824), vol. 7, 1902-4. Other theatrical histories by eighteenth-century writers are Luigi Riccoboni's *Histoire du théâtre italien* (Paris, 1730-31) and Pietro Napoli-Signorelli's *La Storia dei teatri antichi e moderni* (Naples, 1777). The leading actor at the Comédie Italienne of Paris, Riccoboni, attempted to prove the arising of regular comedy in Italy even before the invention of the printing press; see the translation and adaptation of his book by Francesco Righetti, *Teatro italiano* (Turin, 183?), pp. 58-59. Napoli-Signorelli's text is a voluminous attempt to combine Tiraboschi's painstaking documentary method with the aesthetic attitudes of the French Encyclopedists; it covers American pre-Columbian, Oriental, Roman, Greek, and modern theater. Even with his defective critical system Napoli-Signorelli amassed an astoundingly informative work.

cannot be considered true comic authors in the highest degree. Ginguené criticizes on the basis of his ideas about imitation and originality, but then proceeds to forget those ideas.[23]

According to Sismondo de' Sismondi, author of *La Litterature du Midi d'Europe* (ca. 1815), most of the sixteenth-century Italian dramatists let their natural talent be destroyed by imitating Latin authors. Only a few writers of that age, like Machiavelli or Aretino, genuinely attempted to depict contemporary vices. Pedantry stifled this comedy. Sismondi points out the faults of the Erudite Comedy in this way:

> The early Italian drama comprises a considerable number
> of pieces. But the pedantry which gave them birth
> deprived them from their cradle of all originality and
> all real feeling. The action and representation of
> which the dramatic poet should never for one instant
> lose sight are constantly neglected; and philosophy and
> erudition usurp the place of the emotion necessary to
> the scene.[24]

Even the more original authors in Italy failed to portray their characters as real human beings but instead contented themselves with making their audiences laugh over the crude dialogue.

Italian Erudite Comedy did not fare any better with Giuseppe Maffei His *Storia della Letteratura Italiana* is really a compendium of the critics before him, where Maffei seems afraid to pronounce an opinion of his own. At times he even repeats the words of a historian like Tiraboschi without giving proper credit. He first published the work in 1825, and amplified editions continued up to 1864 when Francesco Rossi-Romano established the definitive text with additions of his own. Maffei felt that comedy should not copy the past but must find its material in daily happenings. The authors of the Erudite Comedy did not study the daily life of their century but turned out a learned reworking of ancient plays. For Maffei there is no spontaneity in most of the theater of the sixteenth century.[25]

The year 1860 marks the publication of one of the most significant studies on Italian culture, *Die Kultur der Renaissance in Italien* by the Swiss historian Jacob Burckhardt. He notes in the section "The Discovery of Man" that a preoccupation with scenic display retarded the growth of

23 Ginguené, *Histoire* (Paris, 1813), p. 317.
24 Sismondi, *Historical View of the Literature of the South of Europe,* trans. Thomas Roscoe (London, 1823), 2:206-7.
25 Maffei, *Storia* (Naples, 1864), p. 157.

serious drama in Italy. In the sacred plays, for instance, the Italians had early neglected dramatic values in favor of a wealth of decorative magnificence. Audiences were interested not in the plays but rather in elaborate sets and stunning costumes. With the birth of secular drama the same tastes continued in the emphasis on intermezzos performed with ballets and pantomimes. Every possibility of creating a concentrated drama was lost through those distracting intermezzos. Talking of the Erudite Comedy itself, Burckhardt makes certain important distinctions between the "genteel" comedy modeled on Latin plays and the "popular prose-comedy." He assigns Ariosto's work to the former category and states that no dramatist could have produced a play of the first order in the stilted style of "genteel" comedy. The latter category, however, includes authors like Machiavelli, Aretino, and Bibbiena. The popular prose-comedy could have developed into a distinguished national theater if its subject matter and the adverse times had not condemned it. This type of comedy satirized certain groups and classes within the society. Written in prose and taken from real life, this drama might have become very great if, by the middle of the sixteenth century, the forces of reaction with Spanish rule and the Catholic Reformation had not entered to silence every kind of criticism. For Burckhardt, drama matures late in the history of a culture; but the love of Italians for scenic splendor slowed the development of their comedy until it was too late for a promising theater to grow in a hostile atmosphere. Burckhardt's judgment is not a sweeping condemnation of the Erudite Comedy like those of the critics before him.

After 1865 Italian critics began to reexamine the Erudite Comedy. For Luigi Settembrini, a restless and polemical member of the Mazzinian *Scuola Democratica,* artistic truth was what the imagination creates and the heart feels as real and alive. Truth in art is not derived from the external world but is found within the human spirit.[26] In his *Lezioni di Letteratura Italiana* (1868-70) he points out that the Erudite Comedy is not a slavish reproduction of ancient works: ". . . non è imitata quanto si crede, ma à molte parti libere ed originali: e se ci si trova imitazione antica, questa era più nella vita che nella comica rappresentazione della vita."[27] Settembrini looks at the life of the sixteenth century and then sees the extent to which the Erudite

26 Giorgio Pullini, *Le Poetiche dell'Ottocento* (Padua, 1959), pp. 152-53, explains Settembrini's ideas.

27 Settembrini, *Lezioni* (Naples, 1870), 2:61: ". . . it is not imitated so much as is generally believed, but it is independent and original to a great extent: and if there is imitation from the ancients, the imitation was more in the way of life than in the comic representation of that life."

Comedy reflected Italian society. He feels that the authors of comedies wrote plays with lively action and well-portrayed characters. Only the novella surpasses the comedy in depicting the life of that era. To a great extent the sixteenth-century comedy succeeds in producing Settembrini's idea of artistic truth.

One can find the first rigorously demonstrated assertions about the originality of the Erudite Comedy in Alberto Agresti's *Studii sulla Commedia Italiana del Secolo XVI* of 1871. For him classical imitation in no way prevented the Erudite Comedy from presenting an accurate and masterful portrait of the sixteenth century. It is not an erudite theater but an extremely original one. The characters represented in Italian comedies are caught from the life of the century and not lifted out of Plautus and Terence. Agresti wrote with the patriotic fervor of the Italian *Risorgimento* and considered the Erudite Comedy a valuable document. As a work of art he saw it as a skillfully written satire on the social abuses of the period. The spirit of this comedy is immoral, in Agresti's view, as it is a product of a pagan Italy.[28] A patriot like Agresti would naturally attack the sixteenth century, for it was the period in which the various Italian states lost their independence. His work, though very brief, discusses how closely the Italian comedies represent the spirit and events of their age.

During those same years, 1870-71, the two volumes of Francesco De Sanctis' *Storia della Letteratura Italiana* appeared. Influenced by Hegelian theories, De Sanctis opposed rhetorical and formalistic criticism, seeing in a work of art the more or less unconscious product of the world's spirit at a given moment of its existence. The value of his history is that it rises above pedantic details toward a vision of Italian literature throughout the centuries. In reading this work, one senses the organic development of the Italian spirit, its rise and fall and resurgence. As in the case of Agresti, patriotic enthusiasm misled the critic in evaluating the sixteenth century. For him this was the period of writers like Ariosto, who lost themselves in an artificial world created by the imagination while Italy was being fought over by the French and Spanish. Only from Machiavelli is a cry of protest heard. De Sanctis finds most of the Renaissance plays to be reconstructions of Latin society and not original dramas depicting the chaos of the period. Plautine influence smothered the verve and wit of writers like Ariosto and Bibbiena. For De Sanctis the only vital element in the sixteenth-century comedy is the novellistic and satiric tradition. Machiavelli, with his play *La Mandragola*, is the one author who could give a naked portrait of the age.

28 Agresti, *Studii* (Naples, 1871), pp. 143-44.

De Sanctis' feeling of shame toward the unhappy political events of the sixteenth century prejudiced him in evaluating the works of that period.

John Addington Symonds is perhaps the most famous critic-historian from the Anglo-Saxon world to have discussed Italian culture. In his *Renaissance in Italy: Italian Literature* he regards this comic theater as overconventional and boring. Those comedies were "literary lucubrations" and not the spontaneous product of a vital mentality. Most of them deserve to be neglected, as none of the plays is original. There is no "philosophical insight" into the vices of Italian society. This is a "hybrid form of art" imposing the Latin arguments of Plautus and Terence on Italian customs, with the result that the plots are uninteresting and the characters are monotonous. Symonds objects in a Victorian manner to the "animalism of an unchecked instinct" that is the motivating force for the heroes of those comedies, persons dead to true romance and honor. He is disturbed by these characters (young lovers and their resourceful servants) lacking in loyalty and generosity. This critic notes that the wives in these comedies are just as wanton and debauched as in the novelle. The comedy reflected faithfully the political lethargy and literary emptiness of a decadent civilization. For Symonds this comedy is a product of the morally sick aristocratic courts that were to corrupt all of Italian society. Not only were language and plot obscene, but the philosophy behind those comedies was sinister. The dramatists of that epoch had no standard of goodness, no sense of "moral beauty." Italy was diseased, and the Erudite Comedy is the case history of that illness.[29] Symonds passed a very black judgment on the comedy.

De Sanctis had a German disciple in Adolf Gaspary. At the close of the second volume of his *Geschichte der Italienischen Literatur*,[30] Gaspary considers the question of why the Italians have never created a true national drama. The early decades of the sixteenth century would seem a perfect moment for a dramatic flowering, since a relative freedom of speech existed. Thus political reasons cannot have prevented the growth of comedy. Saying that imitation of Roman comedies suffocated comic breath is incorrect, because other modern genres have begun with imitation and gone on to be independent and original. Gaspary expressly states that the Erudite Comedy is not a servile imitation of the antique. He feels the authors of comedies were telling the truth in their prologues when they described comedy as a mirror of customs. According to Gaspary one can read the history of sixteenth-century customs in those comedies. For this historian, as

29 Symonds, *Renaissance in Italy* (New York, 1935), 2:271-76.
30 Gaspary, *Geschichte* (Strasbourg, 1888), 2:634-35.

for Burckhardt beforè him, drama is the last fruit of cultures. The seventeenth century was to be the great moment for the drama of continental Europe—too late for Italy, lost in full literary decadence. Italian Renaissance Comedy had a splendid appearance and a pleasing variety but lacked the maturity and depth that mark a great dramatic theater.

Toward the close of the nineteenth century Vincenzo De Amicis tried to analyze the contradictory elements of the Erudite Comedy in his *L'Imitazione Latina nella Commedia Italiana del XVI Secolo.* He first states that the Italian Renaissance comedies do not constitute a truly national theater, as imitation of Latin plays separated Italian dramatists from popular theatrical forms like the farce. The fanatic antiquity that distinguishes the Italian comedies comes from the plays' being written for performance before an elite audience of aristocrats and erudites. But at one point in his book De Amicis makes an about-face, coming very close to Agresti:

> Nelle commedie italiane . . . la scena è posta
> apertamente in Italia, i costumi posti sulle scene
> sono del tutto italiani, e vi si parla liberamente di
> principi e rettori senza circospezione e timidezza.
> I richiami ai principali avvenimenti pubbici d'Italia . . .
> vi si incontrano assai frequentemente, e servono quasi
> a dare una data istorica al quadro dei costumi, che la
> commedia pone sotto gli occhi.[31]

De Amicis continues to find many instances of Italian originality when he describes how Renaissance authors carefully portrayed domestic life in ways never attempted by Terence or Plautus. This critic concludes by drawing a table of four categories of plays, from close translations of Roman comedies to plays original in every respect but the form. De Amicis began his work with many prejudices, but the original aspects of the Renaissance comedy overcame them.

In his *Geschichte des neueren Dramas* Wilhelm Creizenach does not share De Amicis' positive views. He regards the sixteenth-century comedy as different combinations of antique plays. The comedy is original only in giving the dramatic action a background in contemporary Italy; yet imitation of antiquity penetrates throughout. The practice of setting plays outdoors in a public square is for Creizenach the kind of antique imitation

31 De Amicis, *L'Imitazione,* pp. 92-93: "In the Italian comedies . . . the scene is openly set in Italy, the customs represented on stage are altogether Italian; princes and prelates are freely discussed without caution and fear. The references to the important political events in Italy . . . frequently occur and serve almost to set a historical date for the picure of customs that the comedy presents."

that can lead a dramatist to describe ridiculously improbable scenes, like a miser's burying his treasure under a paving stone in the street. Also antique imitation prevented Italian authors from portraying character types of the Renaissance as they really were: the parasite was a part of Renaissance society, but for Creizenach this figure is no more than a stock character borrowed from Plautus and Terence, without any of the characteristics of sixteenth-century society. Creizenach does admit that there were some original creations like the characters of the humanistic pedant, the hypocritical priest, and the thieving magician; but on the whole this critic is astonished at how these comedies with their well-worn plots and characters ever succeeded in delighting audiences. He holds that novelties could never survive in the Erudite Comedy except as altered by tradition. This comedy is most original, he thinks, in its handling of dialogue and use of bright idiomatic expressions, especially in Florentine plays. For Creizenach sixteenth-century Italy produced an extremely imitative theater.[32]

Neither Francesco Flamini nor Vittorio Rossi feels that the Erudite Comedy was a pallid copy of antiquity. Flamini, in his *Il Cinquecento*, finds the imitation of classical models by the sixteenth-century authors to be very mature in its artistic selectivity. For him the comedy is generally superior to the tragedy of the period, as comic characters seem to live and breathe despite the limited repertoire of plot situations.[33] The immorality and obscenity of the Renaissance comic theater impress Rossi, who in his *Storia della Letteratura Italiana* points out that the public in the sixteenth century wanted to laugh, and playwrights thought overt indecencies or maliciously veiled double entendres were the best sources of hilarity. He distinguishes between four types of comedy: faithful translations of Roman plays; the contamination of several Latin sources; the introduction of novellistic sources; and the use of real events. Rossi believes that many of the comedies are original in their subject matter, following only the classical unities of time and place on the model of Latin plays.[34]

Perhaps the most thorough study ever made on the Erudite Comedy can be found in Ireneo Sanesi's *La Commedia*. From such points of consideration as historical exactness, critical acumen, and bibliographical richness, Sanesi's work is unequaled. Its writing stretched across the twentieth century. The first volume appeared in 1911; the second, in 1935. A revised edition came out in 1954. Sanesi was thus able to remain aware of the major research

32 Creizenach, *Geschichte* (Halle, 1918), 2:249-78.
33 Flamini, *Il Cinquecento* (Milan, 1903), pp. 264-65 and 298-99.
34 Rossi, *Storia* (Milan, 1903-4), 2:220.

work of this century. Upon starting the section on the Erudite Comedy, Sanesi points out the weaknesses of that theater: ". . . desolante uniformità del teatro comico del Cinquecento, principalmente per ciò che riguarda la tecnica, la costruzione ed ossatura del dramma, il modo di svolgere la favola e di distribuirla per i cinque atti della commedia secondo uno schema prestabilito."[35] Yet he goes on to mention the rebels who broke away from rules and those authors who, though observing rules, still created notable works of art. Later, in summing up his judgments of the comedies, Sanesi points out three currents that run throughout the sixteenth-century comedy: a conservative one of imitating antique plays; an innovating one of using novellistic material; and a bold portraying of contemporary reality. Because of this last current Sanesi considers the Renaissance comedy to be a truly national theater in its faithful imaging of Italian society.[36] Besides its importance in influencing authors in other countries like France and England, the Erudite Comedy is in Sanesi's opinion aesthetically rich.

A composite view of theatrical development in Italy is provided by the text *Storia del Teatro Italiano,* edited for publication in 1935 by Silvo D'Amico, with chapters by different critics. This book is a product of a difficult moment in Italian history, when the Fascist government controlled the theater and every other medium of expression. Thus Corrado Pavolini, in the concluding chapter "For a Theater of Tomorrow;" states that the modern stage must appeal to the great masses, showing problems of workers and explaining the responsibilities of employers. Several of the chapters, however, reflect sound scholarship uninfluenced by political pressure. In chapter 2, "The Theater of the Renaissance," Giuseppe Toffanin attempts to demolish falsehoods about dramatic writing in the sixteenth centuries. He opposes the positivistic opinion that imitation of Plautus and Terence stunted the evolution of the Italian theater out of the medieval tradition of sacred plays. He agrees with Burckhardt's observation that the emphasis on spectacle over dramatic action harmed the growth of a vital theater, but Toffanin dismisses the charge against the Catholic Reformation for suppressing the satiric prose comedy. The major weakness of the Erudite Comedy, in his judgment, is a reliance of the playwrights on conventional plots which stressed intrigue over character. Toffanin points out that Renais-

---

35 Sanesi, *La Commedia,* 2d ed. (Milan, 1954), 1:283: ". . . distressing uniformity of the comic theatre in the sixteenth century, chiefly in regard to dramatic technique, construction and arrangement; the method of developing the plot and distributing it in the five acts of a comedy according to a pre-established scheme."
36 *Ibid.,* 1:427.

sance society, especially the family, had not altered so radically from ancient Rome that the influence of Plautus and Terence led dramatists to present a distorted portrayal of life in modern Italy. He concludes by denying any antithesis between the learned comedy and the popular theater.[37]

De Sanctis' opinion that the sixteenth century was a frivolous period is not generally shared by twentieth-century critics. Attilio Momigliano, in the *Storia della Letteratura Italiana dalle origini ai nostri giorni,* comments that the authors of comedies did succeed in catching the spirit of their age. According to Momigliano, however, that spirit was often corroded by a frank rejoicing in lewd emotions. In describing the moral decay of that age, whose authors delighted in writing about sensual allurements, Momigliano comments that the comedy, along with the novelle and the poetic capitoli, was the literary genre which best depicted the filth in the life style of Italian Renaissance society. The intellectual background of many of Momigliano's thoughts lies in the aesthetic principles of the philosopher Benedetto Croce; Momigliano, for instance, feels that many comedies are "artistic" in the coldest and most formal sense of the word. He notes that there is a conventional stamp to the theater of the sixteenth century, since a comedy's fidelity to "regular" classical form tends to destroy liveliness. For Momigliano the dramatists of that century must have had great difficulty in uniting classical construction with the vivacious novellistic spirit. He does admit that the attempt to bring contemporary character types on the scene makes those comedies much less classicizing than they at first appear to be. In making an aesthetic evaluation of the Erudite Comedy, Momigliano sees it as superior to the period's novelle.[38]

Sometimes it is very difficult to understand what Mario Apollonio is trying to say in his *Storia del Teatro Italiano,* since a pseudophilosophical jargon clouds most of his thoughts. The careful reader however, will profit from his historical view of sixteenth-century formal comedy. Apollonio sees the Erudite Comedy as beginning with great innovators, then passing into mediocre hands in northern and central Italy, but to bold writers at Naples, and finally crystallizing in the material of the Commedia dell'Arte. Authors had to face the mental inertia of the public, which was content with the worn-out schemes of Plautus and Terence. Apollonio himself opposes the labeling of this theater as erudite:

37 Giuseppe Toffanin, "Il Teatro del Rinascimento," in *Storia del Teatro Italiano* (Milan, 1936), pp. 63-99.
38 Momigliano, *Storia* (Milan, 1960), p. 223.

A questa Commedia, alla Commedia del Cinquecento la
critica dell'Ottocento ha dato il nome di commedia
erudita: condannandone l'origine culta, l'imitazione
classica, la monotonia dei temi, la rigidità dello
stile. . . . La commedia erudita cessava d'essere un
mero esercizio di dilettantismo letterario . . .
diventava l'espressione coerente e concreta di quella
civiltà teatrale.[39]

For Apollonio most critics have forgotten the important role literary culture
played in sixteenth-century life. He points out that the popular Commedia
dell'Arte was not opposed to the studied Erudite Comedy but instead developed on the lines set by the "regular" comedies. Apollonio refuses to accept
critical clichés and reevaluates the comic theater of the sixteenth century
by showing how it responded to the cultural demands of the era.

As yet the most complete study in English of the Erudite Comedy is in
Marvin T. Herrick's *Italian Comedy in the Renaissance*. This work owes
a great deal to Sanesi. Herrick strikes out on his own in emphasizing the
subject matter of the comedies. According to him there arose from the
framework of the regular comedy a particular type of theater that he calls
"serious Comedy."[40] This is a romantic and sentimental theater, especially
strong in the second half of the century. The desire of dramatists to be more
modern made them turn away from Plautus and Terence to the novelle and
romances of the Italian tradition. With a serious comedy those authors could
fulfill the Horatian double purpose of teaching and delighting their audiences. Herrick's work is primarily a handbook for English-speaking students of the Elizabethan theater who wish to study the Italian influence on
British dramatists.

The Goal of this Study

In examining the birth of modern comedy in Renaissance Italy, I am
attempting to show how Italian dramatists succeeded in creating a vital
theater from the model set by ancient Roman playwrights. I am partly

39 Apollonio, *Storia*, 2:263-64: "Nineteenth century criticism has given the name of
erudite comedy to this comedy, the comedy of the sixteenth century: condemning its
cultured origin, classical imitation, monotonous themes, rigid style. . . . The Erudite
Comedy ceased to be a mere exercise of literary dilettantism . . . it became the
coherent and concrete expression of that theatrical culture."
40 Herrick, *Italian Comedy* (Urbana, Ill., 1960), pp. 208-9. Herrick has also written
a complementary study *Italian Tragedy in the Renaissance* (Urbana, 1965).

carrying on the work of Agresti, without that critic's narrow moral opinions. Sanesi, despite his amassing a great wealth of facts, fails to appreciate the aesthetic and intellectual value of several comedies because of his notions about artistic originality. For Sanesi, a comedy whose plot is strictly derived from Plautus or Terence is not worthy of critical consideration. This work will trace the development of secular drama in Italy from the early efforts in Latin by humanists to the varied careers of dramatists like Aretino and Ruzzante. I shall note how these writers often expressed the ethic of love and fortune which characterizes the Renaissance revolution in thought. Particular attention will be paid to the environments of cities like Rome, Venice, Ferrara, and Florence, to the extent that they favored dramatic productions. Throughout it will be my aim to detail those elements which can be considered "modern" in a theater that earlier critics have labeled as imitative and unoriginal. The period I shall examine extends from the middle of the Trecento to the middle of the Cinquecento. My intention is not to study every play written during those centuries, but to select those dramas which best illustrate the transition from a medieval to a Renaissance view of man and society.

1

The Humanistic Prelude

PETRARCH: THE *Philologia*

A period of intense preparation precedes the rise of a vernacular comedy. For more than a century humanists were to write comedies in Latin. Their work made possible the transition from the Middle Ages to the creative height of the Renaissance. With only a very imperfect idea of the classical theater, those Latin dramatists often turned to folktales and novelle in writing their comedies.

Petrarch made the first recorded modern effort to compose a comedy in Latin, drawing inspiration from the classics, but his work unfortunately is lost. Even the number of comedies written by Petrarch is debatable. In 1331 he alludes to a play in a letter to Giovanni Colonna di San Vito, whom he encourages not to be concerned about the future by citing a line from a drama which is entitled *Philologia*. The quotation is from a character named Tranquillinus, who declares that most men die while waiting for something to happen in the future. Several years later, in 1348 or 1349 when Petrarch was in Padua, he turned down the request of his Florentine friend Lapo da Castiglionchio for a copy of his comedy *Philologia*. The poet was unwilling to let his friend read the play, since he did not consider the work

23

worthy of the perusal of learned men. He dismissed the comedy as a product of youthful entusiasm. From the meager hints in the two letters one learns of the existence of a single comedy, but nothing more.

The possibility of a second comedy is raised by a letter to Petrarch from Francesco Nelli, the prior of the Church of the Most Holy Apostles. Nelli's letter, which dates from August 18, 1354 (or the same day in 1356), expresses a desire to read the poet's epic *Africa,* his bucolic works, his dialogues, and his comedies. Perhaps Nelli was just employing a generic plural with the word *"comediis"* when he made the request to Petrarch for copies of his works. Evidence for a second comedy comes from Boccaccio's Latin life of Petrarch. In discussing the various writings of his famous contemporary, the author of the *Decameron* speaks of a most beautiful comedy called the *Philostratus,* which Petrarch was supposed to have composed on the model set by Terence. None of Petrarch's letters refers to a comedy with the title *Philostratus.* Boccaccio may have been alluding to a character of that name in the play *Philologia,* as it was a common practice to cite the name of a play from one or more of its characters. As Boccaccio points out, Petrarch drew his inspiration from Terence. The poet once wrote a life of the Latin dramatist, and the copyist of the Ambrosian codex for that life added this marginal note: "Hoc dicit Petrarcha propter se ipsum qui comedias scripsit. Verum postea suas videns illasque comediis Terentii conferens vilissimas suas esse respectu Terentianarum, laceratas in ignem cremari dedit. Ut naravit Petrus de Parma qui admodum familiaris Petrarchae fuit; et se ab eodem Petrarcha audivisse asseveravit."[1] Peter of Parma seems to have known of the existence of more than one comedy. Petrarch himself is silent on the matter.

Today most scholars feel that at the time Petrarch composed his comedy or comedies, around 1330, he was not well acquainted with Terence's six plays. Later, toward 1345, he was able to study Terence carefully and consequently realized the enormous difference between the plays of the Roman dramatist and his own work. For that reason one senses a feeling of shame in the letter to Lapo da Castiglionchio.[2] As a youth Petrarch had

1 "Petrarch states that he wrote comedies. But in later years he looked over his own plays and compared them with Terence's comedies. Since he considered his own plays to be most unworthy as contrasted to Terence's, he tore up his comedies and threw them in a fire to be burned. Thus Peter of Parma narrated, and he was intimately acquainted with Petrarch. He claimed to have heard this from Petrarch himself." Ireneo Sanesi, *La Commedia,* 2d ed. (Milan, 1954), 1:98-100, cites the Latin originals from Petrarch, Nelli, Boccaccio, and the Ambrosian copyist.
2 See R. Sabbadini, "La 'Philologia' del 'Petrarca' e Terenzio," *Bollett. di filologia classica* 22, nos. 2-3 (August-September, 1915): 53-55.

hoped to excel Terence; but on coming to appreciate better Terence's comedies, he repented his daring. Although he had read the eight plays of Plautus that were then known to humanists, Terence was his favorite Roman playwright.[3] Already with Petrarch one sees how a modern author could suppress his own work after comparing it with antique models.

VERGERIO: THE *Paulus*

Throughout his life Pier Paolo Vergerio seniore di Capodistria (1370-1445) was a didactic figure. Most of Vergerio's career was to be passed in traveling to instruct, make orations, or to attend at courts. He was the first Italian humanist to receive foreign posts; after attending the Council of Constance in 1414 he became court poet, Latin secretary, and ambassador for Sigismund, the Holy Roman Emperor. From 1437 until his death Vergerio carried humanistic teaching to the Hungarian court.[4]

In his youth, probably as a student in Bologna,[5] Vergerio composed the only extant fourteenth-century humanistic comedy, his *Paulus, comoedia ad iuvenum mores corrigendos*. From the title itself one can note the author's didactic aim to correct youthful morals. Vergerio hoped to lead students to virtue. In the prologue he points out the irreconcilable battle between wealth and the will to study: "Quantum sit inimica bonis studiis rerum copia?" His work illustrates how bad servants can waste their masters' wealth and how greed can induce parents to lead their children to perdition. On the surface this play is classical. It is divided into five acts; the first two are called *protasis;* the third and fourth, *epitasis;* and the last act, *catastrophe.* The play is really a prologue followed by four acts. Vergerio attempts to imitate the meter of Roman Comedy, but instead of an iambic senary he produced a rhythmic prose. His language is Terentian, with special reference to the *Andria* and *Eunuchus*. From Plautus he took no more than a few words and the name "Stichus." His characters at first glance seem to be the antique types: a youthful master *(herus),* servants

3 P. De Nolhac, *Pétrarque et l'humanisme* (Paris, 1892), p. 154, mentions Petrarch's admiration of Terence.
4 A brief biography of Vergerio can be found in the preface to Amalia C. Pierantoni's *Pier Paolo Vergerio seniore* (Chieti, 1920).
5 Wilhelm Creizenach, *Geschichte des neueren Dramas* (Halle, 1918), 1:534, thought that Vergerio wrote the play in 1370 at Padua; but Sabbadini, "Il 'Paulus' di P. P. Vergerio," *Giornale Storico della Letteratura Italiana* 38 (1900), established a date of 1389-90 at Bologna.

(servi), a procuress *(lena)*, and a harlot *(meretrix)*. Throughout, classical imitation is strong.

But the content and characterization of this comedy are much more medieval than antique. The hero Paulus is a university student, and the characters around him reflect the life of Italian university towns. The procuress Nicolosa and her daughter Ursula are not at all derived from the Roman Comedy but are depicted from contemporary reality. Dramatically they are the first examples of types to be found in the sixteenth-century Erudite Comedy. Vergerio was writing from immediate experience, having lived himself in three university towns. The most modern character is the evil servant Herotes. Whereas in the ancient Roman comedies the servant is generally the best aid for his young master in securing funds for pleasure with girls, Herotes becomes an infernal figure. In the last act Herotes describes his career to the servant Papis: he boasts of having dragged many men to infamy, and of causing others to become soldiers of adventure in distant lands or to hide themselves in monasteries.This is not the speech of a slave in a Roman comedy, where the young hero is usually saved from calamity by his wily servant. Herotes' confession, dramatically inopportune, as it tends to neutralize the preceding sensual scenes, is perfect for Vergerio's moral aim inasmuch as it warns young readers to beware of the dark truth hidden under the gay surface of worldly pleasures. Along with the content and characterization, the play's structure remains medieval, without any unity of place.[6]

Vergerio's *Paulus* is the first of several plays on Italian university life. Latin is a most natural language for those comedies, as it was the language of the universities. During the fifteenth century the adventures of university students were to provide material for Latin comedies. Much later the authors of the Erudite Comedy recognized in the university environment a perfect setting for comic situations.

POLENTON: THE *Catinia*

Sicco Polenton (ca. 1376—ca. 1448) of Levico di Valsugana rose from notary to become chancellor of the commune of Padua. During his career he composed Ciceronian orations, hagiographic works, a collection of moral anecdotes, and a history of Latin writers that included more modern figures like Dante and Petrarch. In 1419 he wrote a work called the *Ca-*

6 Texts of the *Paulus* are are in Karl Muellner, "Vergerios 'Paulus,' eine Studentenkomoedie," *Wiener Studien* 22 (1900): 236-57, and Pierantoni's book.

tinia.[7] Although he gave it a classical type of title as found in many Roman comedies (e.g., Plautus' *Mostellaria* or *Asinaria*), he meant the work to be *fabula,* not a real comedy with acts and scenes but a series of dialogues divided into six parts with the refrain "bibamus, comedamus, gaudeaumus" at the end of each section. The title of "comedy" was given to the work by its unknown translator into the Trentine dialect, whose version appeared in 1482.[8]

One critic-historian has called the *Catinia* "a curious mixture of plebeian triviality and pedantry,"[9] seeing the discussion of the seven liberal arts by the five interlocutors as just a pedantic display of the author's erudition. A close study of the dialogues, however, reveals neither real pedantry nor conscious vulgarity. The five speakers never leave their character; they are not learned professors but awkward and ingenuous figures. This work is above all farcical in nature, being a burlesque discussion of academic disciplines, as for instance the passage in which dialectic arguments are defined as barbaric fights between scholars. Except for its title the work owes little to ancient Roman comedies, as its spirit is modern. The character Quaestius, a friar of the order of St. Anthony, is first cousin to Boccaccio's dealer in saints' relics Frate Cipolla (*Decameron* VI, 10). Sicco Polenton, who spent his life in Padua's university atmosphere, was writing a satire on those who abandon studies in favor of wine. His *Catinia* is a happy fusion of erudite subjects with a contemporary popular spirit.

Conquestio uxoris Cavichioli

With the *Conquestio uxoris Cavichioli* one enters fully into the world of the novella. Here, as in many novelle, a husband and wife are the protagonists. Boccaccio's last tale of the fifth day in the *Decameron* may have inspired this work, although some of its Latin phrasing recalls Boccacio's source for his novella in the ninth book of the *Asinus aureus* (chaps. 14-28) by Apuleius. Because of its form the *Conquestio* has not always been assigned to the period of the humanistic comedies. It is a dialogue in elegiac distichs between a homosexual husband and his neglected wife. This metric form seems to place it with the elegiac comedy of the twelfth and thirteenth centuries, which flourished in France and had as its most famous authors Vital de Blois, Matthieu de Vendôme, and Guillaume de Blois.

---

7 Biographical details in the preface to *La Catinia, Le Orazioni e le Epistole di Sicco Polenton umanista trentino del secolo XV,* ed. A. Segarizzi (Bergamo, 1899).
8 See Sanesi, *La Commedia,* 1:122-23.
9 Alessandro D'Ancona, *Origini del teatro italiano* (Turin, 1891), 2:148, n. 2.

Although those authors were superficially influenced by the Roman Comedy, the real subject of their works, which were not true plays, since they mixed narration with dialogue, was to provide material for later fabliaux and novelle with stories of young seducers, priests tormented by lust, or unfaithful servants.[10] Certainly the *Conquestio* appears to be an Italian example of the elegiac comedy. But other evidence would place this work in the fifteenth century. Every codex in which it is preserved is of that period. The scribe of the Vatican Codex added this note to the title of the work: "Uxor quedam conqueritur de marito sodomita cuius nomen erat Cavichiolus origine Papiensis."[11] The designating of the husband's origin in Pavia sets the comedy in the same university atmosphere as many of the humanistic plays.[12]

Cavichiolus is a far more pleasant character than Boccaccio's Pietro di Vinciolo. Both characters are homosexuals by nature. Neither one cares for women, unlike the husband in Apuleius' version. In the *Asinus aureus* the husband's one homosexual act is committed in revenge for his wife's infidelity, while in Boccaccio the husband is a depraved person, sinning against law and nature. Though a confirmed homosexual, Cavichiolus does not despise women with Pietro di Vinciolo's deep hatred. Whereas the wife in Apuleius' work is a promiscuous alcoholic, in both the *Decam-*

---

10 Vincenzo De Amicis *L'Imitazione Latina nella Commedia Italana del XVI Secolo* (Florence, 1897), pp. 57-58, gives a good historical sketch of the elegiac comedy.
11 "A certain wife complains about her Sodomite husband whose name was Cavichiolus, Pavian in origin."
12 Ezio Franceschini, *Due Testi latini inediti del basso medio evo* (Padua, 1938), p. 9, holds that the *Conquestio* is a fourteenth-century elegiac comedy. Franceschini here publishes the comedy. Sanesi, *La Commedia*, 1:114, is sure that the play is a fifteenth-century humanistic work. Manlio Pastore Stocchi, "Un antecedente Latino-medievale di Pietro di Vinciolo (Decameron V, 10)," *Studi sul Boccaccio* 1 (1963) 349-62, suggests that the *Conquestio* might very well have been a source for Boccaccio's novella. There are some elements in the tale of the *Decameron* that cannot be explained as deriving from Apuleius. Previously critics attributed them to Boccaccio's originality. But Stocchi holds that the perverted nature of the husband, the justified longings of the wife, and the close with an equivocal truce of the protagonists are to be found in the elegiac comedy as the model for Boccaccio. He cites textual comparisons between the novella and the comedy to prove a connection. He notes that Boccaccio was familiar with the genre of the elegiac comedy and that he copied some of them down in his own *Zibaldone*. He doubts that the comedy was really composed at Pavia but suspects instead some other north Italian city. No real proof is offered as to the time of composition. Stocchi is best when he points out a probable origin in Juvenal (*Sat.* 9. 70 ff.) as a source for the comedy. He also notes that Perugia was notorious in the Middle Ages for sexual perverts.

eron and the Latin comedy she appears as a sympathetic creature prevented from following the urgings of her youthful nature. The wife in the two modern versions is able to strike an accord with her husband.

A subject like that of the *Conquestio uxoris Cavichioli* is difficult to treat if the author writes with a heavy hand. The unknown author of this work, however, has a delicate touch. His use of diminutives, particularly when the husband is entreating his angry wife not to leave, brings to mind some of Catullus' lighter poems. This brief comedy of only 152 verses presents a domestic drama at a moment of crisis. It is exactly in the art of depicting family life that the humanistic Latin comedies as well as the later Italian comedies will surpass Plautus and Terence.

Comedia Bile

Another work of this period within the first half of the fifteenth century, the anonymous *Comedia Bile,* reads like a dramatized novella. It is a rapid and spirited prose dialogue between three characters.[13] Since a jolly student is the main character of this little comedy, it might appear that the work is medieval, as the goliard is usually found in writings of a period earlier than the fifteenth century. Yet the origin of this tale is antique. It was first told by the Greek Athenaeus in his *Deipnosophisti* (written about A.D. 195). This work depicts a banquet given by a wealthy Roman, Laurentius, for some of his learned friends, including Plutarch and Galen. During the banquet the friends discuss many topics. An anecdote is told about the poet Philoxenos of Cytherea and Dionysius the Elder, Tyrant of Syracuse. In this tale, instead of a jolly student one finds a court poet and instead of a town-dweller husband the mighty lord of a Sicilian city. There is no female equivalent of the stingy wife Bila. Philoxenos, at dinner with the tyrant, notices that a big mullet is placed before the ruler, while he receives only a small one. When the poet picks up his fish and raises it to his ear, the tyrant asks him what he is doing. Philoxenos replies that he was asking questions about Galatea but that the little fish answered that it was too young to know anything and the poet had better talk with the ruler's older and wiser fish. Laughing at the story, Dionysius gives the big mullet to the poet. Although the *Deipnosophisti* were not edited until 1514, this anecdote became known after the humanist Giovanni Aurispa read it in 1423 in a codex of Athenaeus' work at Constantinople. Aurispa mentioned the tale in a letter to Ambrogio

13 An edition of the *Comedia Bile* is in Johannes Bolte, "Eine humanistenkomoedie," *Hermes* 21, no. 2 (1886): 316-18.

Traversari and after this it passed to humanists all over Europe.[14] Although of classical origin and humanistic writing, the *Comedia Bile* has a decidedly medieval coloring.

ALBERTI: THE *Philodoxus*

Leon Battista Alberti wrote his Latin comedy *Philodoxus* at a difficult moment of his life. He was living with unkind relatives in Bologna. An illness caused by too much study made him interrupt courses in civil and canonical law. During his convalescence he sought to escape reality by writing a play whose subject is a dream of glory. At first the comedy seems to be a simple love story. But it becomes evident that the author intended something more than a mere amorous adventure when we read the *Commentarium* he added to the work. He expressly states his purpose in this way: "Haec fabula pertinet ad mores, docet enim studiosum atque industrium hominem, non minus quam divitem et fortunatum, posse gloriam adipisci."[15] Behind the shadowy and schematic characterizations is the moral that the studious and industrious person, no less than the rich or fortunate one, can acquire glory. Alberti explains the allegorical meaning of the characters' names: Doxia is glory; Philodoxus is the lover of glory; Fortunius is the favorite of Fortune; Phroneus is prudence and wisdom; Phemia is fame; Chronos is time, who settles everything and whose daughter is Aletia (Truth). In composing this play Alberti moved from the plane of reality to create an allegorical work.

There is a conscious effort to imitate Plautus in this comedy. Although it is written in prose, its style is archaistic. Plautine influence can also be noted in the prologue, the choice of setting, and the closing envoi. The comedy, however, is divided not into acts but into twenty scenes. Its close with a double wedding is significant, as multiple weddings were to become a typical resolution for Italian learned comedies. Alberti wrote the comedy around 1426 when only eight plays by Plautus were known to scholars. A friend, without Alberti's knowledge, took the play and showed it to several Bolognese scholars. They were amazed to behold a genuine antique comedy

---

14 Bolte describes the parallel in the *Deipnosophisti* and points out a later version by the Swabian Heinrich Bebel in his *Facetiae* of 1508. The anecdote is also told about Dante.

15 See *Opere Volgari di L. B. Alberti per la più parte inedite e tratte dagli autografi*, ed. A. Bonucci (Florence, 1843), 1:121. For the form "Philodoxios" consult L. Bradner, "The Latin Drama of the Renaissance (1314-1650)," *Studies in the Renaissance* 4 (1957): 34.

by a poet named Lepidus, reading Alberti's note on the play's origin: "Lepidi comici veteris Philodoxus fabula ex antiquitate eruta" ("the fable *Philodoxus*, by the ancient playwright Lepidus, brought to light from antiquity"). When Alberti was asked where he had found the play, he claimed that it was in a very old codex.Ten years later he wrote the *Commentarium* and revealed the true authorship. The same persons who had earlier praised an apparently antique work could only find fault with it once its modernity had been established. For some time afterward the comedy was still believed to be an ancient play. The German humanist Albert von Eyb, chamberlain to Pope Pius II, so esteemed the play that he published passages from it in his rhetorical work *Margarita poetica* (1475), erroneously attributing it to the onetime secretary of the Florentine republic Carlo Marsuppini of Arezzo. Eyb thought the *Philodoxus* worthy to be placed beside works by Plautus and Terence. Even by the close of the sixteenth century, editions of the comedy cited its author as "Lepidus."[16]

Janus sacerdos

Up to this point the comedies studied have been plays written for reading but not for real performances. There were occasions throughout the fifteenth century for performances, especially in university circles. In universities throughout Europe, the vespers ceremonies on the eve of final doctoral examinations were usually celebrated by presenting playlets in an almost bacchanalian atmosphere. Carnival time and the coming of spring were also celebrated with gay secular comedies and farces.

One Latin comedy that was probably recited by students at the University of Pavia in 1427 is the *Janus sacerdos,* which may even be taken from real events.[17] The central character of the play is the pederastic priest Janus, and the supporting characters are a band of rowdy university students. As might be expected, the setting is in an academic town. The comedy owes nothing to antiquity. It is divided into twelve scenes, without any unity of place as the scene shifts from a church to a student's bedroom, then to a cellar, and still later to the open street. The true source for a play like this is real life, as for instance in the trial scene, where the student Favius points out that the sinful priest is one of the townspeople who are forever complain-

---

16 George E. Duckworth, *The Nature of Roman Comedy* (Princeton, 1952), pp. 397-98, discusses Alberti's work as a playwright and his importance outside Italy.
17 Sanesi, *La Commedia,* 1:758-59, employs this quote from a Vatican manuscript: "vos vallete et plaudite, savucius edidit ugo recensuit. Amen." Perhaps a real Savucius wrote the play from true experiences, and his companion Ugo corrected the work.

ing that the university crowd is composed of nothing but troublemakers. Here of course, we see an example of the age-old hostility between townspeople and university students.

In portraying the homosexual priest the *Janus sacerdos* displays the same anticlerical satire to be found in the novella tradition. Boccaccio, in the second tale of the first day of the *Decameron*, describes the sexual depravity of the Vatican court as viewed by the visiting Jew Abraam, who noted the great power which young men exercised over carnally perverted prelates. Petrarch also commented on the moral corruption of clergymen. The merit of the humanistic drama is in its vivid presentation of the contemporary scene. Marred only by its unrestrainedly obscene language, the *Janus sacerdos* is a deft picture of one phase of fifteenth-century life.

BRUNI: THE *Poliscena*

In the comedy *Poliscena* we encounter a work which was deliberately inspired by antique models. Authorship is usually credited to the distinguished humanist Leonardo Bruni Aretino (d. 1444), but this attribution is highly debatable.[18] The play is about love and seduction. Its characters seem to follow the classical scheme. The servant Gurgulio gets his name from Plautus' *Curculio*. The classical contrast is made between the sober, industrious father, Macarius, and his romanic, extravagant son Graccus. These characters make dramatic asides as do those of Plautus. The scene of action is outdoors on the street, as in ancient plays. Sometimes the author confuses modern and antique elements, speaking of Jove, of Juno, and also of Jesus. Yet the comedy is a prose work without division into acts.[19] There is no regard for unity of time, the action taking place over six days, but in general the author was seeking to give a classical form to his work.

A spirit of modernity, however, is evident throughout the *Poliscena*. Bruni may have partially succeeded in imitating the form of antique drama, but the attitude toward life represented in this play is independent of the

18 See P. Bahlmann, *Die lateinischen Dramen* (Muenster, 1893), pp. 174 f., for an analysis of the play. Vittorio Rossi, *Il Quattrocento*, ed. Aldo Vallone (Milan, 1956), p. 526, notes that the play goes "sotto il nome di Bruni. . . ." Bradner, "Latin Drama," p. 34, accepts the attribution to Bruni and dates the drama around 1400. But Sanesi, *La Commedia*, 1:142, is inclined to place the work around 1433, relating it to Pisani's *Philogenia*.
19 Marvin T. Herrick, *Italian Comedy* (Urbana, Ill. 1960), p. 18, points out that the first edition (1478) is not in acts but that in editions published after 1510 there are five acts.

classical tradition. The old procuress Tharatantara is a product of the Middle Ages. Her prototype is seen very early, in the *Disciplina clericalis* of Petrus Alphonsus (1062-1110): in this collection of didactic tales (*exempla*) there are several old women like her, counting their beads and inflaming girls with love for youths.[20] A similar procuress appears in the thirteenth-century elegiac comedy *Pamphilus de amore,* sometimes compared to the *Poliscena* in its description of the history of a seduction.[21] Tharatantara is less astute than some of her predecessors, but her approach to Poliscena with a proposition based upon Graccus' love for her sharply distinguishes her from the "bawd" of the ancient Roman Comedy. When Graccus grows ill after his schemes to possess Poliscena have failed, Thartantara finally succeeds in winning the girl over with an appeal to her pity for the young man's genuine physical suffering. Only the girl's surrender to love can save Graccus. This medical opinion of love as a sickness curable once it is consummated comes from Arabic and Jewish physicians of medieval Spain and is frequently found in novelle.[22] Here the procuress's methods reflect the thought of the period.

Perhaps the most remarkably modern aspect of the play is a monologue in which Poliscena laments the harsh servitude under which unmarried girls (unlike males) are forbidden by social conventions to enjoy sexual pleasures. This monologue is part of the new ethic of love in opposition to social institutions that is to characterize Renaissance attitudes toward life; it is precisely in the moral tradition of the *Decameron.* Poliscena's monologue could not have been found in the Roman Comedy, for ancient Roman authors were not free to criticize the institution of the family. Consequently, seduction in fifteenth-century plays varies enormously from the violent act committed in antique comedies. For instance in Plautus' *Aulularia,* the lover Lyconides rapes Euclio's daughter during a drunken fit at the time of the festival of Ceres; the girl does not even know who has violated her. Similarly, Terence's *Hecyra* relates how Pamphilus ravished Philumena one dark night while he was drunk. But Graccus in the modern comedy does not have to resort to force, for Poliscena willingly gives herself to him. There is really more of Boccaccio in this comedy than of Plautus or Terence.

20 The tale "De canicula lacrimante" in the *Disciplina clericalis* presents an expert procuress.
21 A comparison between the *Pamphilus* and the *Poliscena* can be found in Creizenach, *Geschichte* 1:545, 570, 571.
22 Examples of the medical theories about love are the tale "De integro amico" in the *Disciplina clericalis* and *Decameron* II, 8 (Giannetta episode).

Although this play remained little known in Italy during the fifteenth century, it became one of the works most published and most discussed in other countries, especially Germany and Poland. Professors at the University of Cracow, admiring the play for its classical appearance, mentioned it in their lectures on ancient poetry.

Pisani: *De coquinaria confabulatione* AND THE
Philogenia

A similar revolutionary approach to the position of young ladies in society is found in the works of Ugolino Pisani. Originally of Parma, Pisani received a doctoral degree in canonical and civil law at Bologna in 1437, after previously studying at the University of Pavia. During his university years he composed two comic works: the *De coquinaria confabulatione* and the *Philogenia*. The former is a brief burlesque in which Pisani praises the art of cooking as the consoler of men in all their misfortunes and as the dispenser of exquisite delights for priests, friars, and nuns. In the course of the work a master's degree in cooking is awarded to the chef Zaninus. Pisani here wrote a lively satire on academic solemnity in university ceremonies. According to Angelo Decembrio in his *De politia literaria*, this burlesque was very cooly received by the erudites who made up the artistic and literary circle patronized by Leonello d'Este at Ferrara. To them this little work had no intrinsic value.[23]

Pisani's *Philogenia* does possess the characteristics of a comedy. Its plot is similar to that of the *Poliscena* except that the heroine is not so fortunate. Philogenia and Poliscena share so many ideas that there may possibly be some connection between the plays. Both girls feel that love is greater than social institutions. Philogenia, however, is pathetic because she is not able to achieve honorable marriage with her lover. She accepts her fate, although not in a passive way. Having once succumbed to her passion for the youth Epiphebus, she considers every following humiliation as a necessary consequence of her first fall. In Epiphebus' attempts to hide her from her parents, she is passed about among his friends, all of whom are intimate with her, much like the girl Alatiel of *Decameron* II, 7, who finally marries after having relations with at least eight men. Philogenia suffers emotionally but resigns herself to everything so as to continue her love. She is reluctant to

23 See Sanesi, *La Commedia,* 1:132-33, for details on Pisani's life and the bad reception accorded to this burlesque.

marry the peasant Gobius but concedes, giving herself over completely to Epiphebus' rule. While the young women in Roman comedies are always either correct daughters or courtesans, Philogenia, like Bruni's Poliscena, is a type of modern woman depicted in the novella tradition. Pisani knew how to make a moral and psychological study of her.[24]

The other characters also reveal the author's ability to sketch human types. Epiphebus is ruthlessly efficient in achieving his aims; he does not have to enlist a Tharatantara to persuade the girl to give herself to him. The girl's intended husband, Gobius, thinks he is the cleverest fellow in the world and does not see how others are using him in their own schemes. His brother Zabinus is a wise and dedicted farmer. The most ironic character portrayal is that of the priest Prodigius (note how names have their own satiric value), who is an example of gluttony, avarice, and casuistry. He reveals his true nature, at other times hidden by a feigned benevolent air, in the scene where he confesses Philogenia on the day before her wedding with Gobius.[25] There is a large variety of character types in this comedy, realistically drawn from Italian life.

Structurally the *Philogenia* is medieval. It is a prose play divided into ten scenes: the first three lead to the seduction; scenes four to seven deal with the flight and the girl's being passed about; the remaining scenes extend through the wedding. The conclusion with a wedding, later typical of the Erudite Comedy, is here ironic. There is no adherence to the unities of time and place: the first scene is on the street, where Epiphebus tells his friend Nicomius of his passion for Philogenia, and the second is in the girl's room, where she delivers the monologue about being a slave to social conventions. Other scenes are on the street, in Epiphebus' house, or in the room of the girl's parents. Pisani must have imagined the stage divided into different sections, each one representing a different place, between which characters could pass as the action required. This method of setting the stage for rapid change of scene is also found in the *Sacre Rappresentazioni*.

Pisani's *Philogenia* so impressed Albert von Eyb that the German humanist translated it into his native language in his *Spiegel der Sitten* (1474), along with Plautus' *Bacchides* and *Menaechmi*. This is another example of

24 Compare the heroine Melibea in *La Celestina*. Philogenia does not suffer the same tragic fate as Melibea although both of them surrender to persuasive lovers.
25 Herrick, *Italian Comedy*. p. 17, compares this priest with the arch-hypocrite and master of casuistry, Frate Timoteo, of Machiavelli's comedy *La Mandragola*.

the high esteem enjoyed throughout Europe by the Italian humanistic comedy.[26]

FRULOVISI: SEVEN COMEDIES

Writing comedies proved to be a rather hazardous career for Tito Livio dei Frulovisi (ca. 1400—ca. 1456). Born at Ferrara, he grew up in Venice. After starting to work as a notary, he soon turned to teaching at a small school near St. Mark's. Special school holidays when parents visited classes and saw programs of sports, dancing, and other entertainment suggested to Frulovisi the idea of writing Latin comedies. His first three, *Corallaria, Claudi duo,* and *Emporia,* were presented in the scholastic year 1432-33 amid a storm of controversy. Other humanists disliked his Latin style, and clerics accused him of being a heathen. A Paduan professor, Jacopo Langosco, claimed that the *Corallaria* was plagiarized from a comedy of his. Frulovisi had also satirized some leading citizens in the plays. A group of rival teachers joined together to write a play, the *Magistrea,* in hexameters, but its performance was a fiasco. After absenting himself for a short while from the stormy Venetian scene, Frulovisi returned to compose two even more satirical plays, the *Symmachus* and the *Oratoria,* during the year 1434-35. Public debate over his works, led by the adherents of traditional scholastic learning, ruined his teaching career.

Friends in England secured for him a post as poet and orator for Humphrey, Duke of Gloucester. During his English exile he composed two more comedies, *Peregrinatio* and *Eugenius.* At the duke's command he wrote *Vita Henrici V.* England did not provide the best atmosphere for him, however, and friction with members of the duke's retinue finally made him appeal for funds to leave the country in an *Encomium* to John Stafford, Bishop of Bath. After departing from England in 1438 and leaving there the only existing manuscript of his comedies, he took a medical degree at Toulouse. He finally returned to Venice to work as a physician.[27]

Theatrical activity must have been intense in fifteenth-century Venice,

---

26 Rossi, *Il Quattrocento,* p. 528, feels that the *Philogenia* is the best of the humanistic comedies. For analyses see Herrick, *Italian Comedy,* p. 17, and Bahlmann, *Die lateinischen Dramen,* p. 175 f.; Sanesi, *La Commedia,* 1:131, discusses the play's popularity.
27 Biographical details are in the introduction to *Opera hactenus inedita,* ed. C. W. Previté-Orton (Cambridge, 1932); the review of Previteé-Orton's collection by E. K. Chambers, *The Modern Language Review,* no. 4 (October, 1932), pp. 470-72; and R. Sabbadini, "Tito Livio Frulovisio umanista del secolo XV," *Giorn. Stor. d. Lett. ital.* 103 (1934): 65 f.

judging by the way Frulovisi's rivals were able to put on a play of their own. His comedies of the Venetian period were written not just for reading but for actual performance. Modern scholarly opinion on the details of performance varies. Professional actors performed the *Corallaria,* perhaps presenting the play in dumb show while a Latin *recitator* read their parts. Since Frulovisi's own students presented the following four plays, they probably spoke their Latin parts from memory.[28] Minstrels may have appeared betweeen the acts, anticipating the intermezzos of the later Erudite Comedy.

In the *Corallaria* (note the classical title) the scene is set at Pisa, although the true environment is Venice. This comedy is a series of loosely-knit scenes. Frulovisi succeeds best in depicting the ruthless police officer Ascalaphus, who was modeled from the real-life Venetian *signore di notte* Benedetto Venier, but who is made here into the classical odious character found frequently in Plautus. The girl Hernia, who disguises herself as the youth Sigismondus, is a novellistic figure, such masquerades being common in short-story collections. Similiar disguises will appear later in the sixteenth-century Italian comedies.

Frulovisi's *Claudi duo* has a moral aim in presenting the lives of two dissipated students. It contrasts scenes in heaven with the world of prostitutes and pimps. Plautus' *Amphitryon,* in which Jupiter and Mercury are among the characters, may have inspired the introduction of gods into the plot. One of the author's harshest critics, the Dominican Fra Leone, attacked this comedy because he felt that Christians should not see pagan gods on the stage. The use of allegorical figures like the Virtues and Poverty relates the comedy to the morality plays. One of the most significant characters is the pedagogue, perhaps a satire from real life, as the stock figure of the humanist pedant would figure prominently in the Erudite Comedy.

In the *Emporia* the atmosphere is more realistic and earthbound. There is a satiric note in the bargaining scene in which the hero Euthymus is sold as a slave; the notary Tremulus writes the sale contract in hexameters. The author shows some skill in contrasting characters, as he does with the dashing and reckless Euthymus and his enemy, the love-sick Leros. Aphrodite, the courtesan who is the object of Leros' impassioned attention, differs from similar figures in the plays of Plautus and Terence and seems to be taken from the mercenary prostitute world of Frulovisi's Venice.[29] All through

28 See Previté-Orton, Opera, pp. xx-xxi.
29 Jacob Burckhardt, "Society and Festivals: The Position of Women," in *Renaissance in Italy,* trans. S. G. C. Middlemore (New York, 1958), 2:394, n. 4.

the play the author attacks social abuses, as when he relates how infants are murdered in nunneries. In one extremely realistic scene, a baby is born on-stage on a balcony. Perhaps Frulovisi was inspired by offstage births in Plautus' *Aulularia* and *Amphitryon* and in Terence's *Hecyra* and *Andria*. Frulovisi was always ready to draw material from the society about him and to enrich it with his knowledge of the ancient comedy.

An open satire on Venice's patricians is found in the *Symmachus*. The author entered fully into the novellistic world with this play. Piste's disguise as a male and her trip to the Near East bring to mind *Decameron* II, 9, where Madonna Zinevra has to flee because of a false accusation of adultery and travels to Alexandria to work for the sultan. The introduction of Turk-ish characters to the stage reflects contemporary times, since the Turks were then a menace on land and sea. Symmachus, the commoner whose love for the patrician girl Piste eventually wins out over all obstacles, in part reflects the resentment of the lower classes against moneyed groups, especially since the girl's father is a usurer. A degree of social satire may be noted in the parasite Symphorus's efforts to control the older characters. The author aims to instruct his students to be polite and generous by the examples of the nobleman Eubulus, who offers to ransom the hero from pirates, and the servant maid Dula, who risks her life to save her mistress, Piste. Frulovisi tried to impress his humanistic spectators by the resounding prose of the various letters and ambassador's speeches which are declaimed throughout the play. Although the reported action of the comedy stretches over the eastern half of the Mediterranean, the scene remains at Venice.

Novellistic intrigue and characters also distinguish the *Oratoria*, in which the action occurs onstage, not only in reports of offstage activity. Several elements enter into the comedy. The love of the Neapolitan count Exochus for the patrician Hagna, whom he has never actually seen, is the traditional tale of a dream and quest. Satire on hypocritical clergymen, familiar in novelle and also seen in a comedy like the *Janus sacerdos,* is here a personal attack by Frulovisi on his enemy Fra Leone in the figure of the character Leocyon (Leo the dog), a Dominican friar. Leocyon is an oily lovemaker who wishes to use the confessional to further his amorous designs.[30] This friar even delivers a mock sermon in which he defends humanism as the fastest way to get to hell. Frulovisi also criticizes the aversion of Venetian patricians to marrying their daughters to foreigners.

It was with the *Oratoria* that Frulovisi closed the Venetian period of his creative writing. In it his satirical powers are at their best. During his

30 Compare the *Mandragola*, Act III, scene 2, with its description of lascivious friars.

English period he had to write comedies intended only for reading, not for performance. His vigor declines noticeably as the subject matter of the comedies draw away from the real world. Although in the *Peregrinatio* the scene shifts from Rhodes to Crete, Frulovisi constructed this comedy in a more orderly fashion than his earlier plays of the Venetian period, each major event being contained in a single scene. There are several echoes of ancient comedies. The bigamous marriage of the father Rhistes is similar to that of Chremes in Terence's *Phormio*; the Italian author humorously describes the marital strife between Rhistes and his second wife. Also Clerus' theft of a prostitute's cloak recalls how Menaechmus Sosicles in Plautus' *Menaechmi* walks off with the cloak that belongs to the courtesan-mistress of his twin brother Menaechmus of Epidamnus. Clerus' half sister Anapausis is a more modern figure in her intense desire to find love.

In his last drama, the *Eugenius,* Frulovisi returned to the allegorical method of the morality play. Although the comedy is set at Ravenna, the true setting is an idealized England. The author's liberal opinions are shown here when he champions the cause of the lower classes with the triumphal remarriage of the poor Macrothyma to the hero Eugenius. The eighth scene of the comedy is unique for the times because Macrothyma is actually questioned about her choice of a husband when a family council is held. Frulovisi tried to animate his heavy allegory by introducing some quarrelsome servants, and there may be an attempt at self-portraiture in the figure of the humanist Synetus, tutor to the hero.[31]

It was Frulvosis who launched the classical theater in Venice. His comedies are divided into scenes, not acts, but the author opens them with the classical argument and prologue and closes them with the envoi *Valete et plaudite.* Although unity of place is generally observed in the five comedies of the Venetian period, it is only a nominal adherence, since the scene often shifts about town. In the *Claudi duo* there are scenes in heaven with the gods. The characters of the *Oratoria* pass from the public square into the Dominican church and then out to the home of the patrician Omus. There is a conscious departure from the unity of place in the *Peregrinatio,* with its scenes in Rhodes and Crete, announced in the prologue as the author's own innovation. In no play is unity of time observed. Months pass during the various scenes of his comedies. Confusion is often frequent because Frulovisi announces an action several scenes before it takes place. Consecutive action in the scene is rarely achieved.

All his comedies are written in prose, excepting the hexameter contract

31 Previté-Orton, *Opera,* p. xxix.

of the *Emporia*. Imitating Plautus' style brought about some rhythm in his prose, especially in the later plays, starting with the *Symmachus*. The Venetian author tried his best to reproduce the ancient playwright's language. This attempt was doubtless one of the reasons his style was found objectionable by other humanists, who preferred a more refined Ciceronian style. Although he often worked with faulty manuscripts, Frulovisi was scrupulous in his effort to restore to Latin its antique form, adding the diphthong *ae,* for example, so as to avoid medieval usage. In his later years he even wrote a study entitled *De ortographia*.

His plays illustrate the technique of the early modern drama. Two doorways at the back of the stage were used as entrances to houses. Above them there was often a gallery or balcony where part of the action could take place, like the birth of a child in the *Emporia*. As a technician Frulovisi stands as a pioneer in the mechanics of the stage.[32] Like many of the humanistic dramatists, he was able to unite classical inspiration with a portrayal of the real life of his times. Especially in the first five plays, the environment represented is fifteenth-century Venice, with its overbearing patricians, scheming clergymen, and valiant commoners. The author recognized that drama is more than mere imitation of antique plays. His comedies are uneven, but this must be expected in a theater that is essentially experimental.

PICCOLOMINI: THE *Chrysis*

Another writer who suffered censure on account of one of his plays is Aeneas Sylvius Piccolomini. Piccolomini's life can be divided into two periods; before and after his ordination to the priesthood. His poetic and sensual writings belong to the earlier period, and only during the second, ecclesiastical, phase of his career did he turn to erudite and historical writings. It was in the first period that he wrote the comedy *Chrysis* in 1444, while attending the Diet of Nuremberg in the retinue of the imperial chancellor Gaspar Schlick. No sooner had he written the *Chrysis* than he was forced to defend it against charges of scandal made by the imperial protonotary Michael von Pfullendorf. From the man who was to become Pope Pius II one might have expected a more edifying play.

Although Aeneas Sylvius presents basically the same types of characters as those of earlier humanistic comedies like Vergerio's *Paulus,* in the *Chrysis* there is no didactic purpose. This comedy frankly depicts without any moralistic intent an underworld society. But in his choice of characters Piccolomini betrays his enthusiasm for classical literature. While the char-

32 *Ibid.*, pp. xx-xxi.

acters in the *Chrysis* are prostitutes and procuresses like those in ancient Latin comedies, Piccolomini is closer to Plautus than to Terence in his taste for representing crude characters and feelings. Although his play is not divided into acts, its classical derivation is obvious from the author's attempt to reproduce the iambic senary of Roman comedies. Many lines in the *Chrysis* echo passages from Plautus almost word for word. Compare Theobulus' observation that two women are worse than one,

> Proh! Verum est quod dicitur: mulieres duas
> peiores esse quam unam. Sic experior.

with this statement from the Plautine character Curculio,

> Antiquom poetam audivi scripsisse in tragoedia
> mulieres duas peiores esse quam unam: res itast.

Of all Plautus' plays, the *Curculio* is the one that provided Piccolomini with the greatest number of pithy remarks to imitate. Even the procuress Canthara, a figure worthy of being placed beside Pisani's Tharatantara, speaks lines that bear a Plautine imprint. One of the most famous of Plautus' speeches is in the *Asinaria,* when the procuress Cleaereta compares herself to a fowler (vss. 215-25); with only slight changes Canthara makes the same comparison:

> . . . questus quem facio
> similis est aucupij. In aucupio
> hec sunt: auceps, area, cibus, aves.
> Hec domus est area; cibus est meretrix;
> ego sum auceps; ac vos estis aves. . . .[33]

Plautus thus exerted a powerful influence on the Italian author. The numerous classical references tend to detract from the originality of the *Chrysis.*

But along with Plautine imitation there may be seen in the play a representation of the real world and the influence of the novella tradition. Something of Nuremberg with its houses of prostitution enters into the play, giving it a vigor that merely imitating Plautus could never achieve. Canthara, whose two sincere loves are wine and money, declares that she

---

33 ". . . what I am doing is similar to bird-catching. Bird-catching consists of a fowler, an open space, bait, birds. This house is the open space; the harlot is bait. I am the fowler; and you are the birds. . . ." Joseph Kennard, *Italian Theatre* (New York, 1932), 1:87, points out Plautine echoes. Antonio Stäuble, "Un Dotto Esercizio Letterario: La Commedia *Chrysis* di Enea Silvio nel Quadro del Teatro Umanistico del Quattrocento," *Giorn. Stor. d. lett. ital.* 142 (1965): 351-67, comments that Piccolomini was acquainted with only eight comedies by Plautus and had not seen the twelve plays recovered by Nicholas Cusanus.

never wants to drink beer; she gladly leaves it to the Germans and the Bohemians. At the time he composed the *Chrysis,* Aeneas Sylvius was leading a diplomatic career and so knew close at hand all the political and military currents in western Europe. Thus the youth Charinus delivers a long monologue in which he expresses his desire for a calm life free of worldly cares but well provided with good food and fond friends; he states that he is not at all disturbed by the hatred between Germany and France caused by a violent attack by Armagnac forces on confederated Swiss troops. Here the author has this character refer to the strife between Pope Eugene IV and the antipope Felix V.

Novellistic elements enter with the satiric description of the two corrupt clergymen Theobulus and Dyophanes, who brag about how they were born for following their pleasure in food, drink, and women, since their profession frees them from having to content themselves with one wife. In presenting these two clergymen, with their dedication to corporal pleasures, Piccolomini is not moved by any moral indignation; he is naughtily showing just how hypocritical many members of the clergy are. There is a Boccaccian echo in the cook Arthrax who, like Chichibio of *Decameron* VI, 4, wants to eat a crane's leg and thinks of covering up his act by saying that cranes have only one leg. Piccolomino was able to blend an interest in antiquity with the Italian novella tradition.

A comedy like the *Chrysis,* scabrous as it is in content, might appear out of place as the composition of a future pontiff who was thirty-five at the time of its writing. Besides possessing vast erudition, Aeneas Sylvius was fascinated with the life about him. In the *Chrysis* he presented one aspect of fifteenth-century social life and combined in the play the classical and novellistic traditions.[34]

Comoedia sine nomine

Aeneas Sylvius knew how to unite classical motives with direct observation. The unknown author of the *Comoedia sine nomine* did not possess the

---

34 For an edition of the play consult "Nuova Collezione di testi umanistici inediti o rari," ed. I. Sanesi, *Bibliopolis,* no. 4 (1941). There is another edition by A. Boutemy (Brussels, 1939), but it is definitely inferior to Sanesi's. A call for a new edition, pointing out discrepancies between those of Boutemy and Sanesi, is made by Vittorio Gelsomino, "Per Una Nuova Edizione della 'Chrysis' di Enea Silvio Piccolomini (Nel V° Centenario della Morte: 1464-1964)," *Giornale Italiano di Filologia,* no. 2 (May, 1964), pp. 162-75. The original codex is in the university library of Prague. Rossi, *Il Quattrocento,* pp. 526-27, finds the *Chrysis* to be a modern comedy despite the author's attempts at classical imitation.

same gift of fusing diverse sources and inspiration. This is without doubt the most bizarre and confusing of the fifteenth-century Latin comedies. Thanks to a scholar who has thoroughly examined its latinity and classical references in his edition of the play,[35] the author of *Comoedia sine nomine* has been identified as a Dominican frair writing between 1450 and 1460, who dedicated his work to Cardinal Prospero Colonna. In the prologue the author discusses the general corruption of his contemporaries. To correct them, he will be inspired by the ancients in his effort to renew the comedy of the Greeks and Romans. He explains the rather strange title of the "Comedy without a title" in this manner: if the play should fail at its performance, it will be easier for the anonymous author to profit from criticism and to remake his work. He admits that possible criticism about his introducing Destiny, Fortune, and pagan gods does not worry him. Although he does not believe in those pagan gods, the ancients did; and the characters of this play live in antiquity. The author calls the public's attention to the comic art, which is subtle and renews itself with every age.

Several medieval tales enter into this humanistic comedy. Different themes can be distinguished, such as the incestuous father, the persecuted daughter, and the cruel mother-in-law. The author of the comedy drew from several different tales and combined almost all the existing versions, both French and Italian. Some of the tales that may have influenced the Dominican friar are found in Ser Giovanni Fiorentino's *Pecorone* (X, 1) of 1378; the *Novella della figlia del re di Dacia* of the fourteenth century; the octave *Historia de la regina Oliva;* a Latin novella written by the secretary to the Neapolitan King Alphonso I, Bartolomeo Fazio (d. 1457); and two tales that came down in written form much later in Giovan Battista Basile's *Pentamerone* of 1637 (the tales *Penta manomazza* and *Orza*). The *sacre rappresentazioni* known as the *Rappresentazione di Stella* of the fifteenth century and the *Rappresentazione di Santa Uliva* of the sixteenth century present two dramatized versions of tales that must have inspired the author of the *Comoedia sine nomine*. French verision are the *Manekine* of Philippe de Beaumanoir, the *Roman du Comte d'Anjou* (1316) of Jehan Maillart, and the tale of *Alixandrie, roy de Hongrie qui voulait espouser sa fille* of the fifteenth century.[36] The list is staggering. The author of the humanistic comedy employed these sources or similar ones without artistic selectivity.

Although the sources of the *Comoedia sine nomine* are medieval, its

---

35 See the edition by Emile Roy in *Études sur le théâtre français du XIVe et du XVe siècle, La Comédie sans titre publiée pour la première fois* (Paris, 1902), p. xii.
36 *Ibid.*, pp. xxxii-xliv, gives the list of sources.

setting and many of its characters belong to the ancient world. The author consequently included many anachronisms. Instead of the Virgin and angels there are the oracles of Minerva and Apollo and the priestess of Delphi; medieval chivalric tourneys and jousts are held in ancient Athens. This curious mixture of ancient and modern customs arises from the author's knowledge of classical writers. In this play Cornelius Tacitus is one of the orators of the realm of the Carilles; Palinurus, "magister navis"; and Misenus, "tubicen." The author uses precise quotations from classical writers like Terence, Vergil, Horace, Propertius, Ovid, Seneca, Cicero, Statius, Lucan, Sallust, and Pliny the Younger, among many others. He also quotes Christian writers such as St. John Chrysostom, along with medieval authors such as Guillaume de Blois and Albertano da Brescia. In the *Comoedia sine nomine* every possible inspiration is sewn into the text.

Unfortunately, the Dominican friar did not know how to assimilate his material. His dominant trait is admiration for classical antiquity, which is reflected in the comedy's division into seven acts with a chorus. The canvas on which he stretches his play is too vast for the restrictive unities of time and place. It is doubtful whether the *Comoedia sine nomine* was ever actually performed, despite the author's referring in the prologue to a possible initial failure. Even though the play does not present insurmountable difficulties from a scenic technical viewpoint, its speeches are often inhumanly long. At the most someone might have read the work aloud on different occasions.[37] Antique in its form and setting, medieval in its plot, related to the sacred plays in its technique, the *Comoedia sine nomine* has no true character of its own. Erudition wrecked what could have been a fascinating fairy-tale drama.

Electoral Comedy

Bizarre fantasy withdraws from the scene, and concrete reality comes forward in a brief student play generally known as the *Electoral Comedy*.[38] This work shows a little war among students at the University of Padua. There is no imitation of the ancient theater; instead the contemporary university world is represented. The four rapid scenes are written in a vivid Latin that is sometimes brutally frank, as where the student Jacobus argues with his rival for the post as public reader of law, or delightfully sensual, as where the distraught character Conradus invokes his lady as "O

37 *Ibid.*, pp. cx-cxiv.
38 See the edition by Johannes Bolte, "Zwei Humanistenkomoedie aus Italien," *Zeitschr. f vergleich. Litteraturgesch. und Renaissance-Litteratur* 1 (1888); 79 f.

rosa bella." Its five characters are historical figures. The crafty student Pirchemer has been identified as Johann Pirkheimer, father of the humanist Wilibald Pirkheimer, and the Conradus of the comedy is Conrad Schutz, who, along with Johann Pirkheimer, took a doctoral degree at Padua in 1465. Shortly afterward, the real-life Schutz presented a legal case in Nuremberg in which Pirkheimer was to appear as a cuckold.[39] This comedy probably is taken from a true election at Padua.

Whereas the *Chrysis* of Aeneas Sylvius is a humanistic play written by an Italian who was in part inspired by Nuremburg life, the *Electoral Comedy* is doubtless the work of a German studying at an Italian university. All known copies of it are in Munich. The author might well be the copyist Hermann Schedel (1440-1516), who also wrote down the *Philogenia* and the *Philodoxus,* as well as other humanistic comedies. Schedel studied at Padua from 1463 to 1466, and the affair of the election must have occurred before 1465 when Pirkheimer and Schutz both returned to Germany. All the characters in the play are German. Certainly no Italian would have written the line from Conradus' soliloquy: "Nulla in ytalis fides est" ("There is no trustworthiness in Italians"). Even though the author of the *Electoral Comedy* is probably a German, this play is a product of the same university milieu depicted in Vergerio's *Paulus* and the *Janus sacerdos.*

Barzizza: the *Cauteriaria*

Novellistic themes are at their strongest in the five-act comedy the *Cauteriaria.* The author and the date of composition are still debatable, but one scholar attributes the work to Antonio Barzizza.[40] It appears that the author was the nephew of the noted Ciceronian grammarian Gasparino da Barzizza. As a youth Antonio traveled the university circuit between Ferrara, Venice, and Padua, where his uncle was lecturing. With this academic background, the author of the *Cauteriaria* learned to write an eloquent Latin inspired by Terence. In the prologue the author excuses himself for not writing either in Terence's meter or in any other. He does not wish to rival Terence by imitating his meter, and a choice of another meter would expose him to harsh criticism, since people would consider him pretentious to think he could create a substitute for the Terentian model. For these reasons the comedy is written in prose. All the events of the

---

39 Sanesi, *La Commedia,* 1:113, gives the full story.
40 See the preface to the edition of the *Cauteriaria* by E. Beutler, *Forschungen und Texte zur Frühhumanistichen Komoedie* (Hamburg, 1927), pp. 1-77.

play are supposed to have occurred scarcely half a month before the writing of the comedy. An examination of the plot, however, betrays that the play is basically a dramatized novella.

In the *Cauteriaria* there are three principal characters, like the usual triangle of novelle. The amorous priest Auleardus, the young wife Scintilla, and her jealous older husband Brachus are figures drawn right out of the novellistic world. The novella explores a realm of human relations not treated deeply in ancient Roman comedies: the household. Among the Romans of the Republican era there was a tremendous respect for the family as an institution; the authors of comedies knew better than to attack it. Plautus' *Amphitryon* describes a special kind of adultery between Jove and Alcmena, who was intimate with the god thinking he was her husband. According to Roman belief, relations between a deity and a mortal were an honor, not a disgrace. But in the spirit of the Italian novella, marriage is not an inviolable institution. The theories of love behind the modern spirit of the novella, especially from Boccaccio on, hold that love is greater than any social institution. This novellistic attitude toward adultery is not really immoral, since it is the reflection of a new morality of love. Adultery is the central theme of Barizza's comedy.

Like the *Poliscena,* this play displays the contemporary medical belief about love. Brachus first grew suspicious because Scintilla had fallen ill. The priest's mother Bacharinta also became concerned about Auleardus' sudden poor health and started to search the town to discover the identity of the woman he loved so as to cure him. When Brachus' porter Calmarus saw Auleardus hanging about the gate, he knew the youth was in love with Scintilla because of the way he kept on coughing as if consumed by passion. Vengeful Brachus is unique in his method of torture—applying a brand to that part of his wife's body which had sinned. In the fabliau known as *Du Prestre crucefié,* the husband and his servant make the captured priest mutilate himself. Giovanni Sercambi, writing after 1374, in his novella *De Prelato adultero* describes an angered brother who tries to remove the offense to the honor of his family by cutting off his sister's nose and castrating the monk Don Mugino. In novella 84 by Sacchetti the printer Mino notices that his wife's lover is hidden under a cloth, just like the wooden crucifixes in his shop; he takes an ax and advances toward the live crucifix to cut away the principal thing that drew him to his shop; when his wife screams out he threatens to punish her with a torch in the place where she betrayed him.[41]

41 Sanesi, *La Commedia,* 1:156, lists novellistic parallels.

Although offended husbands in novelle have taken various measures to avenge the injury committed, branding has no precedent. There is also no juridical precedent in the case of an adulterous wife. Here the juridical is contaminated by the medical practice of cauterizing a wound. Brachus' profession is never made clear; a physician would certainly have had a brand ready. Brachus is indeed the deceived husband of the novella tradition.

Tentatively dated about 1469,[42] Barzizza's comedy owes very little to the Roman theater. Its title is the classical type, and the five acts are divided into scenes. The scene where Auleardus and his friends break into Brachus' home has some antique precedent in Terence's *Adelphi* and *Eunuchus,* but events like this occurred even in contemporary life. There is absolutely no unity of place, since within a very brief time span the scene shifts from Brachus' home to the street and to the church. Within Brachus' home the scene changes from one room to another. The sacred drama never departed from the unity of place to the same extent as this play does.

In its spirit the *Cauteriaria* is a modern play. One of its main characters is a priest who is ready to use the rite of confession as a masquerade for his amorous designs. Yet the author is not at all indignant, feeling that the two young lovers have a right to see their passion fulfilled. Barzizza's play could have been highly effective as a dramatic work if the last act had not been cheapened so as to end the *Cauteriaria* as a comedy, in which the cast makes peace and gets ready for a banquet. The character changes undergone by Scintilla and her husband at the comedy's close are wholly false; she is too magnanimous in forgiving Brachus after he has branded her. The happy close with a banquet is also a trite way to conclude the drama. But with its modern attitude toward love Barzizza's play is far removed from classical comedy.

Tommaso de Mezzo: *Epirota*

In 1483 the Venetian patrician Tommaso de Mezzo published his comedy *Epirota*. He rigorously tried to revive the plot structure and characterization of antique comedy. The measure to which he succeeded can be judged by a letter written to him by Giovanni Pico della Mirandola: "Solidius nunquam me oblectatum memini, quam nuper, dum tuam *Epirotam* legerem fabellam procul dubio facetissimam, cum argumenti

42 Kennard, *Italian Theatre,* 1:87.

festivitate, tum styli eruditione priscas etiam comoedias provocantem."[43]
Despite the rhetorical emphasis common to humanists, Pico fully expresses
his admiration of a work that recalls the ancient comedy. The play derives
much of its material and some of its defects from the classical theater. Its
setting at Syracuse is perfect, as the comedies of Plautus and Terence are
placed throughout the Hellenistic world at cities like Athens, Ephesus, or
Cyrene. The Menaechmi twins are in fact from Syracuse. In the list of
characters Clitiphones is the usual young lover who needs money. There is
even a wily servant, Syrus. Clitiphones and Syrus resemble young Clitipho
and his servant Syrus in Terence's *Heautontimorumenos*. Like classical
comedies, the *Epirota* is structurally weak because much of the action is
not really performed on stage but is merely reported in the speeches of the
characters. Furthermore, the supposedly secret conversations are always
carried on in such a way that someone hidden onstage hears everything
without being seen. Tommaso de Mezzo, in his zeal to write a comedy
according to classical models, also employs some obsolete devices of the
ancient theater.

Clitiphones' relationship with the old woman Pamphila makes the
Epirota almost offensive aesthetically. She has a fortune that he would like
to possess. Even after he is enabled to marry the girl of his choice, Clitiphones
does not put his mercenary designs behind him. He convinces Pamphila
that she should marry the girl's uncle from Epirus. Although the old
woman despises the citizens of Epirus, she consents to the marriage so as
not to be permanently separated from Clitiphones. At the moment when
the young hero might be expected to be overjoyed about freeing himself
from a senile creature, he is still intent on adding to the wealth already
afforded by the dowry his beloved's uncle has granted. Clitiphones' venal
attitude detracts from the romantic mood of his love for the apparently
poor Antiphile.

Throughout the *Epirota* there are several episodic scenes which, though
they slow the action and interrupt the proper sequence of events, add
color and charm to the play. They are lively vignettes drawn with skill. The
first shows Pamphila having rouge put on her cheeks and ointments
spread over her wrinkles by her maid Lesbia. Although the scene brings
to mind one from the second act of Plautus' *Mostellaria* where the maid
Scapha attends her mistress, the music-girl Philematium, the fifteenth-

---

43 Cited by Sanesi, *La Commedia*, 1:161: "I do not ever recall being more completely delighted than recently when I read your drama *Epirota*, without doubt most
witty, summoning up the ancient comedies both for the humor of the argument and
also for the erudition of the style."

century rendering is far more effective than the ancient, since Pamphila is a grotesque creature who fools herself into thinking that she can cover up the traces of old age, while Plautus' Philematium is a courtesan who naturally uses makeup in her profession. Pamphila appears again in the fourth scene, in which she dictates to a public scribe a letter intended for Clitiphones. She wants the letter to be as charming as possible and uses delicate diminutives. The scribe objects to the address "Pamphilula Clitiphoni ocello suo ex animo salutem dicit"; he observes that the diminutive form *Pamphilula* seems to lessen the intensity of her love for the young man. It is as if she were saying: "amoris quodammodo amiculam, non amicam." She decides to have the normal form of her name restored. These two episodic scenes reveal Mezzo's ability as a caricaturist.

Perhaps the most fascinating scene of the comedy is where the Epirotan uncle is walking around town with a Syracusan citizen and sees a crowd gathered in the central plaza. A supersalesman is promoting his medicine show. The Epirotan asks his guide who the orator is. After the Syracusan answers that the man is a "pharmacopula" (a quack), a "merus sycophanta," the Epirotan stops to observe the medicine showman and makes cutting remarks to his companion. The salesman holds up some roots that he claims are from the gardens of the Hesperides. These roots uncover all thieves; no thief would be able to hold them in his hand. Anyone who carries the roots sewed up in his clothes will not suffer accidental death; therefore the salesman especially recommends them to the sailors in his audience. The roots heal scorpion stings, kidney stones, stomachaches, and heart diseases. In the portrait of the charlatan, Tommaso de Mezzo presents a modern character type. Although there are many swindling servants in the Roman comedies, even some who disguise themselves, the charlatan with a pretense to medical or scientific knowledge is a new figure. He will be seen again in the Erudite Comedy dressed up as a magician or an astrologer.

Despite the author's attempt to write a comedy on classical lines, the *Epirota* departs from the antique comedies in being written in prose and divided only into scenes. Doubtless Mezzo was working from imperfect manuscripts of classical plays. His comedy is consequently an imperfect reproduction of the Roman theater.

SLYTERHOVEN: THE *Scornetta*

In 1497 Hermann Knuyt von Slyterhoven, a Hollander from Utrecht, published in Bologna a verse comedy with the title *Scornetta*, dedicating it to his friend Nicholaus Stael, the personal physician to Philip of Burgundy.[44] Like the *Electoral Comedy,* this work was written by a foreigner living in Italy. The author's comedy praises an Italian named Blanchinus who used to invite friends to his villa Scornetta just east of Bologna. This playlet was probably read or performed at a banquet held at the villa.[45] Throughout the comedy the leading motif is the burlesque love between Blanchinus' maid Lolla and the shepherd Codrus. Thanks to a blending of classical and realistic elements, the play has a bucolic air. The scenes in which Lolla speaks of the villa's fertility or in which her mistress Corynna addresses Pan and the Amadryades recall Vergil's *Eclogues.* [46] Two tones contrast in the comedy: enthusiastic love for the countryside (as expressed in the opening lines) and the slapstick realism of the affair between the maid and her shepherd lover.

At no point are there any indications of scenes. Dialogue flows along, accompanied by marginal notes which show the person speaking or the person addressed, such as: "Codrus to the spectators; Codrus' entreaties; To the spectators; To Lolla; Lolla to Codrus; To Corydon offstage; Corydon to the spectators." The dactylic hexameter verses often make the dialogue heavy. With its pair of rustic lovers, the play is basically a pastoral comedy in skeletal form.

ARMONIO: THE *Stephanium*

Although Tommaso de Mezzo was a Venetian, his *Epirota* remained relatively unknown in his native city. For this reason the leading scholars of Venice were to hail the play *Stephanium* by Giovanni Armonio Marso as the true resurrection of the antique comedy. The author, an Abruzzese who later joined the order of the Cross-bearers and became organist of St. Mark's, was scarcely twenty-three when he took part in the first performance of his play at the monastery of Eremitani around 1502. The play had an enthusiastic reception. The erudite Marcantonio Sabellico wrote to the author that while viewing the comedy he had felt he was sitting in an ancient Roman theater watching a comedy by Plautus.[47] Another

44 Philip of Burgundy, known in Spain as Felipe el Hermoso, was the father of Charles V.

45 For a text see Bolte, "Zwei Humanistenkomoedie," 232 f.

46 Vergilian reminiscences along with a realistic portrait of shepherd folk are also found in the works of Juan del Encina (ca. 1469-1529), an initiator of Spanish drama in the Renaissance as well as a translator of Vergil's Eclogues.

47 For detailed information see E. Cicogna, *Delle Inscrizioni veneziane* (Venice, 1842), 5:551 n., where facts about Armonio's life are given. Sanesi *La Commedia,* 1:166, describes Sabellico's opinion of Armonio's play.

writer, Giovan Battista Scita, affirmed the following about Armonio:

Cecilium . . . reddit et Terentium,
Plautum aemulatur, aemulatur Nevium.[48]

Paolo Canale wrote a poem in which Thalia, the muse of comedy, rejoices before Armonio and declares that he unites in himself the souls of Plautus, Naevius, and Terence. Girolamo Amaseo composed an ode in which he held that the spirit and mind of Plautus lived again in Armonio. Finally the Augustinian friar Jacopo Battista di Ravenna said that the youthful author had been able to produce in the *Stephanium* the "total image of life."[49] The comedy was an overwhelming success.

Using the motif of kidnapped girls, the setting at Athens, and the type characters, Armonio reproduces with archeological care the Roman comedy. Both Armonio and Mezzo had the same classical models in mind and made recourse to traditional devices like the unexpected arrival of a wealthy uncle. Above all, the characters display the range of types used in Latin comedy. The youth Niceratus is kept penniless by his miserly father Aegio. Geta is the astute servant who suffers abuse from Aegio, as when in the third scene of Act IV his master scolds him and taps him with a stick. Armonio uses the same slapstick and mechanical means found in Plautine comedies. In Act IV, scene 5, there is a scuffle between Geta and the servant Palestrio that recalls a similar fight between Mercury and Sosia in Plautus' *Amphitryon.* Aegio is modeled on Plautus' miser Euclio in the *Aulularia;* in the third scene of the first act of Armonio's comedy Aegio gets ready to go out and cautions his servant Archilides to lock all the doors. Made suspicious by the servant's words, Aegio runs back into the house to see if his treasure is still untouched. Armonio has placed his characters in situations similar to those in Plautine comedies.

Structurally the *Stephanium* is closer to the antique comedy than any of the preceding humanistic plays. There are five acts divided into scenes and preceded by a prologue. Armonio wrote the comedy in the iambic senary. The spectators at the premiere were indeed justified in feeling that they were being transported back to the glories of Roman times.

48 "He brings back Caecilius . . . and Terence, he rivals Plautus, he rivals Naevius." Gnaeus Naevius (ca. 270—ca. 201 B.C.) was the first native Roman dramatist, and Caecilius Status (ca. 212-168 B.C.) as a comic writer was the transitional figure between Plautus and Terence.

49 The remarks of Scita, Canale, Amaseo, and the friar can be found in this edition of the comedy under discussion: *Johannis Harmonii Marsi Comoedia Stephanium urbis venetae genio publice recitata,* printed by Bernardino Veneto without any indication of the year.

ZAMBERTI: THE *Dolotechne*

Venice, more than any other Italian city, provided a favorable atmosphere for the humanistic playwrights, making it possible for them to
see their comedies performed. Frulovisi, Mezzo, and Armonio all worked
there. It was also at Venice that in 1504 Bartolomeo Zamberti composed
his comedy the *Dolotechne*.[50] In a dedicatory letter he says that he wrote
the play to rest himself after studying Euclid. He closely follows Armonio
and above all Mezzo in trying to re-create the spirit of the Roman Comedy.
Zamberti presents in this play the classical character types of Polycrisis,
the wise father; Mononius, the passionate son; Sfalerus, the wily servant;
Rhodostoma, the kidnapped girl fighting to avoid becoming a prostitute;
Crisophagus, the cruel procurer, and his alcoholic wife Merophila. Among
the minor characters there is even a parasite. Alitologus, the gentleman
from Athens, with his quest to recover his daughter, brings to mind
Plautus' Carthaginian Hanno of the *Poenulus*, who went traveling to locate
his lost daughters. The way the procurer is cheated of his fee for freeing
Rhodostoma recalls similar stratagems in both Plautus' *Poenulus* and his
Persa, where procurers are forced to make refunds on girls who turn out to
be freeborn citizens. Most of Zamberti's characters move about in a world
re-created from Plautine comedies.

    One of the characters, the lascivious old Bdeliria with all her wealth,
is doubtless inspired by Tommaso de Mezzo's Pamphila, in the *Epirota*.
Bdeliria desires Mononius distractedly. The author of the *Dolotechne*
even reworked the makeup scene from Mezzo's comedy. Bdeliria asks her
maid Thessala if she sees any wrinkles on her cheeks, and the maid
replies bluntly that her mistress' cheeks are full of wrinkles. Bdeliria is
highly offended, as she considers herself a fresh girl. The long and laborious
job of repairing the demage of old age then begins, the maid applying
salves, rouges, and white lead to Bdeliria's cheeks while the old woman
keeps looking at herself in a mirror after every application. Thessala grows
annoyed at her mistress's complaints and says that makeup can no more
restore the rosy complexion of youth than a salesman of medicines can
bring the dead back to life. From the *Mostellaria* to the *Epirota* to the
Dolotechne the makeup scene has increased in satiric effect. Zamberti's
Bdeliria differs to some degree from Mezzo's Pamphila. The figure in the
Epirota is a ridiculous and senile woman stupid enough to think that a young

50 See this edition: *Bartholamei Zamberti Veneti Comedia Dolotechne* (Venice,
1504).

man would want her near him, but Bdeliria is really a pathological figure, an elderly nymphomaniac determined to possess Mononius. Zamberti presents only a sketchy portrait of her. Bdeliria is the least psychologically conventional character in the *Dolotechne*.

In introducing political allusions in certain verses of the comedy's envoi, Zamberti probably had in mind the prologue made by the god Auxilium between the first and second acts of Plautus' *Cistellaria*. Auxilium proudly reminds the Romans of the defeats inflicted on Carthaginians in the Punic Wars and exhorts them to continue in that manner:

> bene valete et vincite
> virtute vera, quod fecistis antidhac.
> Servate vostros socios, veteres et novos,
> augete auxilia vostris iustis legibus,
> perdite perduelles, parite laudem et lauream:
> ut vobis victi Poeni poenas sufferant.[51]

In the envoi of the *Dolotechne* the author has the "recitator" allude to the victories of the Venetian Republic over the Turks:

> Si haec placuit fabula plausum
> date manibus. Surgite et armis potentibus
> sic Persas contundite ut extremum vobis
> linquant Venetis belligeris Tanaim.[52]

Frulovisi had first brought the Turks into the humanistic comedy with his *Symmachus*. The unrelenting struggle between the European powers and the Turkish forces was to serve as the political background for many of the sixteenth-century Italian regular comedies. Here Zamberti writes with pride of Venice's role in the conflict.

MORLINI: *Comoedia*

Political allegory is the substance of the *Comoedia* of Girolamo Morlini, who wrote at Naples.[53] This play, written entirely in hexameters except for

---

51 "Good-bye, and conquer by your constant courage, as you have done in the past; aid your allies, both old and new; render greater your resources by just laws; fall on your foes, gain praises and prizes, that the conquered Carthaginians may pay the penalties they deserve." Trans. by George E. Duckworth, *The Complete Roman Drama* (New York, 1942), 1:331.

52 "If this drama has pleased you, show your applause. Rise up and with your mighty weapons crush the Persians [Turks] so that they will surrender the outermost bank of the Don to you warlike Venetians."

53 *Hieronymi Morlini Parthenopei Novellae, fabulae, comedia* (Paris, 1855).

the prologue and envoi in the iambic senary, covers contemporary political events with an allegorical veil. The author presents a trangle where Leucasia (Naples) is loved by both Orestes (Louis XII of France) and Protesilaus (Ferdinand the Catholic). She spurns Orestes and accepts Protesilaus. Morlini is alluding to Louis XII's vain attempt to take control of the Kingdom of Naples and the Spanish Ferdinand's successful one. The author's sympathies are all on the Spanish side.

This comedy was probably presented either at the Neapolitan court or in the palace of a noble, for some verses of the prologue mention a Plautine comedy which was performed on the same occasion. In its technique the work has no connection with the sacred dramas. The classical mood sustained throughout the play relates it to some of the poems of Giovanni Pontano (d. 1503) which celebrate the beauties of Naples and the area around it. It is difficult to date the comedy exactly. The flight of Orestes seems to suggest 1503, when the French had to withdraw from the Kingdom of Naples after fierce battles at Cerignola, Seminara, and Garigliano. The references to the united forces of Spain, Germany, Britain, and Italy probably allude to the Holy League formed by Pope Julius II in 1512.[54] Morlini's *Comoedia* illustrates how the desire to write in a classical Latin style could be united with a representation of the contemporary political scene.

Aetheria

Only recently has the *Comoedia cui titulus Aetheria* been discovered and examined.[55] A glance at the text shows that it has a Terentian type of prologue, a Plautine argument, division into acts and scenes, and the meter of the iambic senary. This closeness to the form of the antique Roman Comedy places the *Aetheria* within the early years of the sixteenth century, the time when the comedies of Armonio and Zamberti were composed on strict classical lines. In the prologue, which is Terentian, since it discusses the problems involved in writing the comedy, the author declares that he would rather invent then copy. He attacks those who merely translate the ancient Greek comedies into Latin. He is an Italian writing comedy in the Roman style. The author admits that he has allowed a learned

---

54 Sanesi, *La Commedia* 1:173-74, explains the political allegory.
55 E. Franceschini, "Di una ignota commedia latina umanista," *Riv. ital. del dramma* 2 (1938): 157 f., analyzes the play at length, translating several passages from it. Later he published the Latin text in *Atti e Memorie d. R. Accad. di scienze lettere ed arti in Padova* 56 (1939-40): 107 f.

authority to examine his play, but one never learns just who the author was. All that is mentioned is his Italian origin.

Once again the characters are the antique types: young men in love but prevented for economic reasons from marrying; a wily servant; fathers who hold tightly to every cent. The three unities are observed. There is an attempt to create an ancient atmosphere by mentioning the temples of pagan gods. The Latin is archaic, with many sententious sayings in the style of Terence. The scenes in Act V in which the astute servant Margippus dresses in rich robes to masquerade as a Sicilian merchant from Agrigentum recall similar disguises by several Plautine characters: in the *Persa* the slave Sagaristio pretends to be a Persian in order to sell a free girl to the procurer Dordalus; in the *Trinummus* a sycophant is hired to disguise himself in elaborate foreign clothes and deliver letters and a dowry. Another Plautine device is repeated in this humanistic comedy when the girl Aetheria, sister of the hero Archites, never appears on the scene; this same device was continued in the Italian regular comedies.[56] The author of the *Aetheria* has carefully imitated the language and stage mechanics of Plautus and Terence.

Despite its rigorous effort to revive the classical comedy, the *Aetheria* still displays an independence of the ancient Roman theater in some characters and episodes. Paurea, the impoverished nobleman, is a fairly modern figure. His desire to save his farm by marrying a girl with a rich dowry places him in a modern world of economic competition. He has lost his fortune by being too generous, as he laments in the first scene of the third act; his complaints resemble Machiavelli's observation that generosity eventually deprives one of the means with which to be generous. In the opening scene of the play Paurea also expresses the typical Renaissance scorn for women. Paurea is a product of a declining chivalric society whose values were on trial in a world where a man's wealth counted far more than his rank upon birth.

In the fifth scene of Act II the youth Faliscus, who loves Aetheria, explains to Calmeo, the interpreter of dreams, how he dreamed of flying up to the palace of the goddess of the air; from there he was able to view the pettiness of the earth. He went through the goddess's palace and finally possessed her in her chambers. Later Faliscus saw Aetheria for the first time and recognized her as the goddess of his dream. The dream in which one is lifted up to the heavens is a widely repeated motif. In the sixth book of Cicero's *De re publica*, the younger Scipio is lifted to the heavens

56 Compare Plautus' *Casina* and Machiavelli's *Clizia*.

in a dream so that he can learn the future course of his life from his famous ancestor; in the heavens he beholds the starry sphere and all the planets. Dante, who describes many dreams in the Divine Comedy, comes to see how petty the earth is after he enters the constellation of Gemini and looks back at the sun, moon, planets, and tiny earth (*Paradise,* Canto XXII). The description made by Faliscus of the goddess's palace brings to mind the palace of Venus in the *Stanze per la Giostra* of Poliziano (d. 1494). Both Poliziano's description and that of the unknown author of the *Aetheria* are in the tradition of the Garden of Love, a subject most common in English medieval literature. The language used by Faliscus in describing his dream to Calmeo is very delicate, in contrast to the language in the comedies of humanistic writers influenced by Plautus. As it appears in the *Aetheria,* the old motif of a prophetic dream has a modern coloring.

Besides the author's delicate language, there is an effort to avoid odious characters like procurers and prostitutes. The *Aetheria* represents the humanistic comedy in its perfect form—adhering to the model of the antique theater, expressing itself in a refined style, and yet presenting characters and episodes drawn from Renaissance life and thought.

The Role of the Humanistic Comedies

More than a century and a half passed between Petrarch's unhappy attempts to write a comedy on classical lines and the completion of the *Aetheria.* Throughout this period literary currents of classical antiquity, the Middle Ages, and the early Renaissance entered into the Latin comedies. The medieval tradition, represented in part by Latin elegiac comedies and by the sacred dramas, showed a formal and technical influence in the quick shifting of scenes and the swift passing of time. In regard to content, the numerous medieval folk legends and novelle, transformed by a Renaissance spirit, inspired several of the humanistic playwrights. Contemporary life is depicted in comedies that represent the university scene or ridicule the hypocrisy of clerics. At first the comedies of Plautus and Terence provided only an initial stimulus to authors, who ended up writing plays very different from the ancient models. Sometimes the classical influence was shown only in the choice of a title, like *Catinia* or *Corallaria,* following the model of *Aulularia* or *Cistellaria.* But during the last quarter of the fifteenth century and the early years of the sixteenth the classical tradition exerted a powerful influence in plays like the *Epirota, Stephanium, Dolotechne,* and *Aetheria.* But even in those comedies, faithful to the ancient model either in form or in character types, a modern spirit is evidenced in certain characters or episodes.

Italy's Latin humanistic comedy must be considered part of a wider movement extending throughout Europe. Both the *Electoral Comedy* and the *Scornetta* had non-Italian authors. Comedies like Alberti's *Philodoxus* and Bruni's *Poliscena* were read and published in Germany and Poland. The use of Latin was itself enough to secure an international audience. Scholars all over Europe admired the efforts of Italian authors to re-create Roman Comedy. These humanistic comedies represent only in part the close of Latin tradition; their true significance is in preparing the way for the regular Italian comedies of the sixteenth century. The final adaptation of the classical form, the use of novellistic sources, and the depiction of Italian customs point the way toward vernacular comedy. Here the question is not one of direct influence of the humanistic Latin comedies on the later Italian works, but of the example set by mature imitation of classical models without excluding later traditions like that of the novella or the depiction of contemporary life.[57] The humanistic comedy is the prologue to the modern drama developed by the Italian playwrights of the sixteenth century.[58]

57 See Flamini, *Il Cinquencento*, (Milan, 1903), pp. 264-65. Bradner, "Latin Drama," pp. 35 ff., states that authors like Bruni and Alberti provided "the immediate background for Ariosto, Machiavelli, and Aretino." Rossi, *Il Quattrocento*, pp. 525-29, feels that the Ciceronian and Terentian Latin purism of the second half of the fifteenth century suffocated the realistic and satiric tendencies of the humanistic playwrights. But María Rosa Lida de Malkiel, *La Originalidad artística de la 'Celestina'* (Buenos Aires, 1962), pp. 39-43, finds the humanistic comedy an independent genre that was only externally influenced by the Roman Comedy. For her the humanistic comedy is superior to the ancient Latin Comedy due to its close representation of contemporary reality, its variety of subject matter, and its greater freedom of time and place.

58 Unfortunately texts and detailed summaries are not available to permit discussion of other Latin comedies like the *Aphrodisia* of P.C. Decembrio, the *Amiranda* of G.M. Alberto Carrara, the *Isis* of Francesco Ariosti, the *Comedia de falso ypocrita* of Mercurio Ronzio, and the *Fraudiphila*. This last comedy, usually attributed to Antonio Tridentone of Parma, is derived from the *Decameron* VII, 7. Many Latin plays are still to be found only in codices or sixteenth-century editions. Recently, however, attention is being focused on the humanistic drama; and editions of plays, even in modern translation, are now appearing. See *Teatro Goliardico dell'Umanesimo*, edited by Erminia Artese and Vito Pandolfi (Milan, 1965). Among other brief Goliardic works are included the *Conquestio uxoris Cavichioli*, the *Paulus, Janus sacerdos, Philogenia, Repetitio Zanini* (*De coquinaria confabulatione*), *Chrysis, Electoral Comedy*, and *Cauteriaria*; all of these pieces appear in Latin and Italian translation except for the *Repetitio* and the *Janus sacerdos*. In the case of the *Janus sacerdos* failure to provide a translation might be attributed to intellectual cowardice because of the obscene language of the original. Pandolfi's introduction, "Le spurie origini del nostro teatro drammatico," evaluates the humanistic comedy as a necessary apprenticeship for the vernacular theater of the sixteenth century. Pandolfi emphasizes the scholastic scene and the cult of homosexual love at the University of Pavia under the humanist Panormita, connecting this writer's collection of epigrams

Hermaphroditus with the *Janus sacerdos.* Another helpful work is provided by Alessandro Perosa, *Teatro Umanistico* (Milan, 1965). In his introduction Perosa attempts to examine humanistic drama in Western Europe, including France, England, Germany and the Low Countries. Considering Italian production, Perosa notes the difference between the more novellistic comedies in the first half of the Quattrocento and the stricter imitations of the ancient Latin comedies in the second half of the century after the rediscovery of lost Plautine plays; he points to Piccolomini's *Chrysis* as the transitional work. This book includes his own translations of the *Paulus, Cauteriaria, Philogenia, Chrysis, and Aetheria* as well as Poliziano's prologue for the 1488 production of the *Menaechmi* in Florence. To complete his panoramic presentation of humanistic plays Perosa also has added translations of an anonymous French work *Advocatus* and the *Mercator* by the German Thomas Kirchmeyer. Also cf. the review of Perosa's book by Antonio Stäuble, *Giorn. Stor. d. Lett. ital.* 143, no. 442 (1966): 266-75.

2

The Emergence of the Erudite Comedy

The Reawakened Interest in Classical Comedies

Humanistic research brought about such interest in the ancient Roman comedies that by the last quarter of the fifteenth century the works of Plautus and Terence were produced for public performances. Scholars carefully studied the ancient comedies, preparing new editions with textual criticism. Many humanists were renowned exclusively for what they knew about the Roman comic playwrights.[1]

A single event electrified the world of humanism. In the Middle Ages only eight comedies by Plautus were known; but in 1428 Nicholas Cusanus (Niccolò di Treviri) discovered in Germany a manuscript containing fourteen Plautine comedies, twelve of which had been unknown since ancient times. When the Italian humanists heard of the discovery, early in 1429, they had trouble believing that so exciting an event as that had actually taken place. Finally it became known that the precious manuscript was in the hands of Cardinal Giordano Orsini. Scholars and even rulers of

1 M. W. Wallace, *The Birth of Hercules with an Introduction on the Influence of Plautus on the Dramatic Literature of England in the Sixteenth Century* (Chicago, 1903), p. 21, discusses the Plautine vogue.

states begged the cardinal to lend the text to them. Pope Eugene IV succeeded in persuading the cardinal to let him take the Plautine manuscript to Florence. Guarino da Verona was allowed by Cardinal Orsini to copy the twelve newly discovered plays and to correct those that he already knew. Later Antonio Panormita borrowed Guarino's copy and carried it away with him. For ten years Guarino fought and pleaded to have his copy returned, even appealing to King Alfonso of Naples, for whom Panormita was official historian. Not until 1443 did Guarino retrieve his copy.[2]

Several humanists were eager to compare themselves with Plautus by filling the lacunae in his writings with their own emendations. A prologue and first scene were added to the *Bacchides;* credit for this was at first given to Panormita, but it should be attributed to Poggio Bracciolini. Codrus Urceus wrote a close to the *Aulularia,* attempting to reproduce Plautus' meter and style. Ermolao Barbaro replaced the missing portions of the *Amphitryon.* One unknown humanist even added two scenes to the *Mercator,* Act IV, which were not at all necessary to the action of the comedy. By 1472 the first printed edition of Plautus' plays had come out at Rome under the direction of Giorgio Merula. The comedies were then easily circulated to a wider reading public, creating a demand for translation into the vernacular.

This enthusiasm for Plautus did not detract from admiration for Terence. Sicco Polenton, in writing his *De illustribus scriptoribus latinae linguae* from 1419 to 1433, included a minute biography of Terence. During the same period Gasparino da Barzizza gathered sententious expressions from the six Terentian comedies, didactically drawing moral sayings from the antique writer. In July of 1433 Giovanni Aurispa discovered a manuscript of Donatus' commentary on Terence at Mayence; the copy that Aurispa brought back with him to Italy stimulated other humanists to study Terence. Copies of the Donatus commentary were soon passing from one scholar to another. When Angelo Decembrio went to Spain in 1458, he discovered some brief glosses on Terence. Between 1473 and 1477 three printed editions of the six Terentian comedies appeared. Giovanni Rufinoni prepared the edition of 1476 at Venice and the one of 1477 at Treviso, accompanying them with the Donatus commentary and his own interpretation of the *Heautontimorumenos.* Thus by 1480 the comedies of both Terence and Plautus had been made available in printed editions. The

2 Ireneo Sanesi, *La Commedia,* 2d ed. (Milan, 1954), 1:180.

language of those authors became a model for scholars desiring exercises in Latin conversation.[3]

Publication acted as an impetus to the production of ancient plays. During the pontificate of Paul II the erudite Cardinal of Teano examined the defective Plautus plays and constructed lists of characters. His example was followed by Julius Pomponius Laetus (d. 1498), whose activities were interrupted for a while when Paul II persecuted humanists because of a conspiracy against him. During the pontificates of Sixtus IV, Innocent VIII, and Alexander VI, however, Pomponius directed the production of ancient, especially Plautine, comedies, gathering around him a group of persons enthusiastic about antiquity to constitute the informal Roman academy. Pomponius led his students and associates in giving comedies in the palace of cardinals. They produced the *Aulularia* in 1484 on the Quirinal.[4] The *Epidicus* followed in 1486. Even after Pomponius' death performances of antique plays continued. On occasion of the marriage between Alexander VI's daughter Lucrezia Borgia and Alfonso D'Este of Ferrara in 1502, the *Menaechmi* was performed in the palace of the pontiff.[5]

Rome was not alone in presenting classical comedies, for in Florence several schoolmasters led their students of Latin grammer in producing ancient plays. Giorgio Antonio Vespucci had his students perform Terence's *Andria* three times in 1476: once at the school, then at the house of the ruling Medici family, and finally at the Palazzo della Signoria. Luca de Bernardi de San Gimignano, during the years of his teaching career in Florence from 1485 to 1498, directed his pupils in the performance of at least one Plautine comedy, the exact title of which remains unknown. Even church groups were willing to produce the pagan comedies. In 1478 the clerics of Santa Maria del Fiore, under the direction of Pietro Domizi, presented a Terentian comedy; they repeated their performance a year

3 Jacob Burckhardt, "The Revival of Antiquity: General Latinization of Culture," in *Renaissance in Italy*, trans. S. G. C. Middlemore (New York, 1958), 1:257. Plautus and Terence are among the most heavily published authors since the invention of printing, often in illustrated editions. See Walter Sanders, "Terence at Newberry, 1470-1700," *Research Opportunities in Renaissance Drama*, 9 (1966): 62-76.

4 R. L. Grismer, *The Influence of Plautus in Spain before Lope de Vega* (New York, 1944), p. 62, calls that production: "the first stage performance of a Latin comedy during the Renaissance."

5 For details about Pomponius' life and the activities of the Roman Academy, see Burckhardt, "The Revival of Antiquity: Fall of the Humanists in the Sixteenth Century," in *Renaissance in Italy*, 1:276-78.

later. Among the spectators at Domizi's performance was Lorenzo de'
Medici. A major production occurred on May 12, 1488, when the clerics of
San Lorenzo performed the *Menaechmi;* a special prologue in Latin
verses by Angelo Poliziano was recited, along with a letter by the director,
Paolo Comparini da Prato. In Florence the schoolmasters of Latin grammar
were eager to preserve the integrity of the Roman comedies without any
contamination by popular elements.[6]

Although the ruling classes of Rome and Florence encouraged the production of ancient plays, the real motivation came from professional scholars.
But in the city of Ferrara under Duke Ercole I (d. 1505), all channels of
popular sentiment were directed by the state. As part of his political
program the duke was determined to make Ferrara the leading theatrical
city of Italy. Besides calling on his people to attend sacred dramas during
Holy Week celebrations, the duke commanded several poets to translate
the Roman comedies into Italian for court productions. The *Menaechmi*
was performed in 1486; the *Amphitryon* in 1487; the *Trinummus* and the
Poenulus in 1499; the *Mercator, Captivi,* and *Asinaria* on three successive
days in 1501. An example of Ercole's willingness to sponsor productions
of classical comedies is the performance of the *Captivi, Mercator,* and
Poenulus at Pavia during the last days of August in 1493, when the duke
traveled there to repay a courtesy visit to the Sforza ruler Ludovico il
Moro. Ercole had costumes, actors, stage properties, and poets brought
along in his train. Theatrical productions were thus affairs of state.[7]

A deeper understanding of the love of scenic display manifested in
these Italian court productions and of the problems involved in performing
vernacular translations of ancient comedies can be gained by examining a
letter from Isabella d'Este to her husband Francesco Gonzaga, Marquis
of Mantua, dated February 3, 1502, in which she describes the festivities
celebrated in Ferrara at the wedding of her brother Alfonso to Lucrezia
Borgia. She details the production of the Plautine comedies *Epidicus, Bac-*

6 Sanesi, *La Commedia,* 1:184-85, describes the theatrical revival of ancient comedies
in Florence.
7 George E. Duckworth, *The Nature of Roman Comedy* (Princeton, 1952), p. 399,
discusses the Ferrarese productions. Antonio Piromalli, *La Cultura a Ferrara al Tempo
di Ludovico Ariosto* (Florence, 1953), *passim,* notes several negative aspects of state
control of culture. Piromalli feels that the domination of the Este family over the
nobles, intellectuals, artists, and indeed all classes prevented the true flowering of
humanism with its ideal of human dignity. He comes close to the Burckardtian
criticism about the scenic emphasis of the Italian theater when he notes (pp. 119-20)
that the ducal theatrical productions of Ferrara were arisocratic, courtly affairs set
with great splendor to please the elegant tastes of the noble audience.

chides, Miles Gloriosus, Asinaria, and *Casina* in verse translation. One hundred and ten costumes had been made for the performances. Since Isabella d'Este was rather bored with ancient comedies, the highlight of the productions for her was the intermezzos. She was delighted with the ballets, in which the performers were dressed like the soldiers of an earlier age and took part in mock battles. Why is it that the artistically sensitive marchioness found Plautus' comedies dreadfully dull? Her longing to view the intermezzos with their scenic brilliance explains her attitude to some extent. But her good taste also enters, for the Italian translations were long and tedious, killing the verve of the Plautine dialogue. Translators like Battista Guarino and Pandolfo Collenuccio felt compelled to impose upon Plautus' dialogue a metric form that stretched out his succinct language and robbed it of its quick humor; they often employed tercets in the translations. Nor were they scrupulously accurate in rendering the meaning of the dialogue in the ancient comedies. Duke Ercole himself complained that Guarino's translations were too far from the "sententia di Plauto." The discerning members of the aristocratic audiences were not content with arbitrary translations of the ancient comedies.[8]

By the early years of the sixteenth century Italian cities like Rome, Florence, and Ferrara, with their respective cultural spheres of influence, had witnessed the rebirth of the classical Roman Comedy for stage production. The technical means available for these productions indicate that the Italians were far advanced in the mechanics of the stage.

MANTOVANO: THE *Formicone*

The cultural sphere of Ferrara was exactly where the Erudite Comedy arose. In the city of Mantua, ruled by the Marquis Francesco Gonzaga and his wife Isabella d'Este, the students of Francesco Vigilio performed in November of 1503 the comedy *Formicone,* by the youthful author Publio Filippo Mantovano.[9] The subject of the comedy comes from the *Asinus aureus* of Apuleius, in fact from the same episodes that probably inspired the *Conquestio uxoris Cavichioli.* In the *Asinus aureus* (IX, 17-21) a novella is enclosed within a longer narrative in which an old confidante

---

8 A copy of her letter can be found in Sanesi, *La Commedia,* 1:188. Mario Apollonio, *Storia del Teatro Italiano* (Florence, 1951), 2:11-12, talks of the poor efforts at translation and the excuses made by some of the court poets.

9 Play published as *Formicone comedia di Publio Philippo Mantovano, con summa diligenza corretta, e nuovamente stampata* (Venice, 1534).

describes to an unfaithful wife how skillful her new lover Philetaerus is as
an adulterer; the tale of the elderly confidante provides the plot of the
Formicone.

Mantovano did not choose to write the comedy of elaborate intrigue
that was to be typical of comic productions during the sixteenth century.
His plot structure is very simple. This play, written in Italian prose, is
composed on classical lines in five acts, with the ordering of *protasis,
epitasis,* and *catastrophe.* Unity of place is maintained throughout; the
scene is set on the street before the homes of the jealous husband Barbaro
and his rival Filetero. Because the comedy is derived from a Late Latin
source, it does not present quite the same character types found in plays
inspired by Plautus and Terence. The character Formicone (ant) is not
the wily servant of the Roman Comedy; he is a bungler. The dynamic
figure is the passionate youth Filetero. One classical character is the parasite
Licopino, whose hunger leads him to aid in the youth's adulterous scheme.
Not once is Barbaro's wife seen on stage. Only later in the sixteenth century
did the heroine become a prominent stage figure. Characteristically, this
first example of the Italian Erudite Comedy deals with adultery.
Mantovano's comedy is closely related to the novellistic tradition in presenting a domestic drama.[10]

ARIOSTO: *La Cassaria*

For his entire lifetime Ludovico Ariosto was associated with the court
of Ferrara. When he was scarcely nineteen, he was in the train that Ercole I
took to Pavia to perform Plautine comedies in honor of Ludovico il Moro.
The young Ariosto may even have translated Terence's *Phormio,* writing
a prologue for it in tercets.[11] This courtier, who was to become the first
major author of the Erudite Comedy, grew up in an atmosphere where the
desire to renew the glories of the Roman theater was part of court policy.
Early in March of 1508 a prose version of Ariosto's first comedy, the
Cassaria, was performed at Ferrara. Duke Alfonso and Cardinal Ippolito
had invited the members of their retinues to compose scenic works for

---

10 Marvin T. Herrick, *Italian Comedy in the Renaissance,* (Urbana, Ill., 1960), p. 66,
tends to emphasize classical derivation over novellistic influence in the play.

11 M. Catalano, *Vita di Ludovico Ariosto ricostruita su nuovi documenti* (Geneva,
1931), 1:306-7, denies the possibility of Ariosto's writing that prologue, but Sanesi,
La Commedia, 1:221, is inclined to believe in the translation.

the carnival of that year.[12] The aristocratic audience was delighted with the *Cassaria;* the courtier Bernardino Prosperi wrote to Isabella d'Este that Ariosto seemed to surpass Terence himself. Some twenty years later the author rewrote his first comedy in hendecasyllabic *sdruccioli* verses. On either January 14, 1529, or February 19, 1531, the hendecasyllabic version received its first performance at Ferrara.[13] This was not the last time Ariosto was to write a comedy in prose and later recast it in verse.[14]

In the tercet prologue to the prose version of 1508, Ariosto declares the originality of his work:

Nova comedia v'appresento piena
  di vari giochi, che né mai latine
  né greche lingue recitarno in scena.[15]

The author was very much aware of the possibility of criticism from members of an audience well acquainted with the comedies of Plautus and Terence. He did not want his "new" comedy to appear too bold, and he was quick to recognize how superior ancient literature was to modern. The author has the actor delivering the prologue admit that the ancients achieved perfection in their literature. But although modern languages are still far from the perfection of ancient ones, human capacity remains the same. The modern author can aspire to the level reached by the ancients. Ariosto goes on to describe the manner by which a comedy can be given dramatic effectiveness:

La vulgar lingua, di latino mista,
  è barbara e mal culta; ma con giochi
  si può far fabula men trista.[16]

Those "giochi" are the various intrigues that complicate the plot of

12 Details on the first performance in Naborre Campanini, *Lodovico Ariosto nei prologhi delle sue commedie* (Bologna, 1891), pp. 46-47.
13 See Catalano, *Vita,* 1:583-86.
14 Sanesi, *La Commedia,* 1:222-25, holds that there may have been an original version in tercets. He points out how Prosperi's letter indicates the setting of the play was Taranto and not Metellino or Sibari as in the two existing versions. Prosperi also adds that the comedy was "in forma de barzeleta o sia frotola." Sanesi notes that the prologue to the prose rendering is in tercets. Thus for Sanesi the version that was produced at the first performance was a tercet play.
15 "I am presenting you with a new comedy full of diverse amusements which neither Greek nor Latin tongues ever recited on stage." Italian text in Ludovico Ariosto, *Le Commedie,* ed. M. Catalano (Bologna, 1933), vol. 1.
16 "The vernacular tongue, compounded with Latin, is barbarous and badly cultivated; but with amusements one can render a tale less boring."

the *Cassaria*. This is to be a comedy of deceptions and tricks.[17] In writing this prologue Ariosto imitated Terence's prologue to his first comedy, the *Andria*. Terence changed the nature of the prologue. By not using it to announce the argument and give the background of the comedy, he removed the link between the prologue and the drama. The Roman dramatist had already heard criticism, and his prologue served to combat his critics. Ariosto uses his prologue in much the same way, but he is trying to head off criticism. The Italian author realized that he was founding a genre in the vernacular tongue.[18]

Classical imitation is strong throughout the *Cassaria*, but it is not servile. The title is the classical type, *Cassaria* coming from *cassa* (chest). Unity of place is always maintained; the scene is a public square where several streets meet. The usual incongruity of placing the home of a wealthy merchant and a house of prostitution in the same neighborhood is found here. To sustain the unity of place Ariosto has the servant Fulcio decline to enter the house of the merchant Crisobolo at the end of the third scene of the fifth act; instead, the servant asks Crisobolo to come out and talk with him. The time span of the play is just under one day. There is unity of action, as the main point of the plot is the love intrigue. But initiative shifts from the chief servant Volpino to the united band of domestics and then back to Volpino and finally to Fulcio. Ariosto carries the intrigue to a point where it appears just about to succeed when suddenly an unexpected catastrophe occurs. In this comedy, as in all later sixteenth-century plays, there are five acts.

Ariosto modeled his characters on the ancient types. Volpino ("foxy") is the astute servant. The two youths Erofilo and Caridoro are the usual penniless lovers. Their passion is directed not toward free girls but toward two girls who are in the power of a procurer. Erofilo's father Crisobolo, determined to rear his son strictly, is like the father, Demea, of Terence's *Adelphi* in regard to his son Ctesipho. Many plot situations of the *Cassaria* are similar to those in Terentian comedies; in both the *Cassaria* and the *Andria* the schemes devised by servants sympathetic to their young masters boomerang. In the *Andria* the old master Simo orders the slave Davus bound because he has supported Simo's son, Pamphilus. Both the *Andria* and the *Cassaria* show two servants, one in favor of the old master and the

---

17 Campanni, *Prologhi*, pp. 48-53.
18 See Giovanni Zecca, *Della Influenza di Terenzio nelle commedie di Ludovico Ariosto* (Milan, 1914), pp. 15-16.

other for the young master: in Terence's comedy Davus opposes the freed-man Sosia, who is Simo's close adviser; in the *Cassaria* Volpino fights with the servant Nebbia. Crisobolo's reprimand to Erofilo (Act V, sc. 2) is very similar to the one given by Simo to Pamphilus in the *Andria* (Act V, sc. 8).[19]

Terence's *Heautontimorumenos* may have inspired some passages of Ariosto's comedy. In the third scene of the second act of Terence's play the slave Syrus explains to his young master Clitipho how he can be with his beloved mistress; but Clitipho interrupts him, saying there is too much danger. Syrus grows angry, telling the youth to solve his own problems, and Clitipho promises then to follow the slave's plans. The same confrontation occurs between Volpino and Erofilo in the first scene of the second act. Both Syrus and Volpino are concerned about the danger involved, as the responsibility for the amorous operations would really fall on them and not on their young masters. Syrus tells Clitipho: "Tibi erunt parata verba, huic homini verbera" (You'll get words; this man will get lashes"). In like manner Volpino reminds his young master of the pain that the servant may suffer: "Tu ne sentirai le grida solo, io el bastone, o ceppi, o carcere, o remo" ("You will just hear shouts; I'll feel the stick, or fetters, or jail, or the galley slave's oar"). The slave in the ancient play and the servant in the modern drama are both aware of the effort required to realize their plans.[20]

Another Terentian comedy that could have provided material is the *Phormio*. In the third scene of the third act, Phaedria, son of old Chremes, is afraid that the gluttonous parasite Phormio will not hand over the youth's beloved music-girl unless he pays a certain price. The youth, im-pelled by his great passion, begs his faithful servant Geta to obtain the necessary money; the slave, seeing that the youth is deep in despair, tries to calm him. Similarly, Erofilo almost goes mad from disappointment (Act III, sc. 6) on learning that his ladylove Eulalia has been snatched away from the friendly Trappola by a band of servants. Volpino attempts to distract Erofilo by telling him that they must recover a chest full of rich cloth, which had been left on deposit with Crisobolo but was used to pur-chase the girl's liberty from the procurer Lucrano. Both Phaedria and

---

19 Massimo Bontempelli in the preface to his edition *Ariosto: Commedie e Satire* (Milan, 1916), mentions that the reprimand scene in the *Cassaria* was modeled after a scolding that Ariosto had once received from his father.

20 Vincenzo De Amicis, *L'Imitazione Latina nella Commedia Italiana del XVI Secolo* (Florence, 1897), pp. 171-73, talks at length about the ties of the *Cassaria* to the *Andria* and *Heautontimorumenos,* comparing parallel passages.

Erofilo are motivated by ardent sensual passion. Their servants try to moderate the wild thoughts of the young lovers.[21]

Plautine influence is also diffused throughout the *Cassaria.* The unexpected return of Crisobolo from his journey and Volpino's stratagems for the new situation may be an echo of Plautus' *Mostellaria,* in which old Theuropides, father of Philolaches, comes back home while his son is having a drunken banquet. The slave Tranio keeps Theuropides away from the house by saying that it is haunted. In both the *Mostellaria* and the *Cassaria,* calamity is averted by the quick thinking of the servant loyal to the young master.[22]

One of the most Plautine figures of the Italian comedy is the Albanian procurer Lucrano, the classical odious character. Just like the pimp Ballio of Plautus' *Pseudolus,* Lucrano is ready to prostitute his still virgin charges if their young lovers do not soon purchase them. At one moment of the *Cassaria* (Act III, sc. 7) Lucrano is intoxicated with his success in obtaining the chest from the rogue Trappola, who is disguised as a merchant; the procurer describes himself in this way: "Non fu mai uccellatore più di me fortunato, che avendo oggi tese le panie a dui magri uccelletti, che tutto el dì mi cantavano intorno, a caso una buona e grassa perdice ci è venuta ad invescarsi. Perdice chiamo un certo mercatante, perchè mi par che sia più di perdita che di guadagno amico . . . ."[23] Erofilo and Caridoro were the two thin birds, and Trappola was the fat partridge about to lose the chest in purchasing Eulalia (note the pun on *perdice* and *perdita*). This speech, in which the procurer compares himself to a fowler, is doubtless derived from the *Asinaria* of Plautus, in which the procuress Cleaereta makes the same comparison. This is, of course, the same passage which inspired the fowler simile of the procuress Canthara in Piccolomini's *Chrysis.* Ariosto creates in Lucrano a portrait of a thorough scoundrel and coward.

Trappola's disguise in Crisobolo's fine clothes to fool Lucrano and help the lovers is the type of masquerade found in several of Plautus' comedies. In the *Poenulus* the steward Collybiscus is disguised as a foreigner so that he can enter the establishment of the procurer Lycus. The slave Simmia of

---

21 Zecca, *Influenza di Terenzio,* pp. 22-25, adds details about borrowings from Terentian plays, also comparing passages.

22 The parallel with the *Mostellaria* is discussed in Reinhardt-Stoettner, *Spaetere Bearbeitungen plautinischer Lustspiele* (Leipzig, 1886), pp. 482-83.

23 "Never was a fowler more fortunate than I. Although I set a trap today for two thin birds that were singing about me all day, by chance a good fat partridge came along and got ensnared. I call a certain merchant a partridge because I think he is more a friend of loss than of gain. . . ."

the *Pseudolus* is equipped as a messenger so that he can obtain the girl Phoenicium from the procurer Ballio with stolen letters and tokens. This same kind of disguise occurs in the *Aetheria*, in which the costume is assumed by the servant Margippus. Ariosto knew how to weave his intrigues with Plautine threads.[24]

Ariosto attempted to portray contemporary society in the *Cassaria*, despite its setting at Metellino; Lucrano talks with the servant Furbo in the criminal jargon of the period. The author was interested not merely in re-creating ancient comedy but also in depicting the customs of his own times, even the language of the underworld.[25] Throughout the play satiric darts are aimed at social abuses. Caridoro refers (Act I, sc. 5) to the rapacious Spanish soldiers who are billeted in the homes of private citizens. Lucrano, who came to the city of Metellino after hearing how liberal its citizens were in spending, expresses his disappointment on finding that the people spent lavishly only for elegant clothes. He remarks (Act I, sc. 7) that foreigners are more hated than the truth is hated at courts. Still later (Act III, sc. 3) Lucrano mentions to Trappola that Rome gathers into its court every kind of scoundrel. The band of servants who take Eulalia away from Trappola (Act III, sc. 5) claim that they are confiscating her because the customs duty on her as a piece of merchandise has not been paid. This is not the last time Ariosto, as well as other authors of regular comedies, will criticize the abuses of customs officers, a satiric theme which is also of the novellistic tradition. When Crisobolo is afraid that Lucrano is going to report him to the authorities for breaking into the house of prostitution to get back the chest, he declares that the magistrates of his age are lazy men who spend their time scratching their paunches and who prefer pimps to honest citizens (Act IV, sc. 2). All these satiric remarks would at first seem out of place, anachronisms in comedy supposedly set in ancient Greece. But the Greek island which provides the setting for the *Cassaria* is neither truly ancient nor an early sixteenth-century Turkish possession. Ariosto felt free to ridicule unjust practices of his age.[26]

Despite the strong influence of the Roman Comedy, the spirit of the *Cassaria* comes from the world of superior intelligence exalted in Boccaccio's *Decameron*. An example of the climate in the Italian comedy is the role

---

24 The observations about possible Plautine influence in characterizations and technique are original to the author of this study.
25 This point is discussed by R. Renier, "Cenni sull 'uso dell 'antico gergo furbesco nella letteratura italiana," in *Miscellanea di studi critici in onore di Arturo Graf* (1903), pp. 123 f.
26 Sanesi, *La Commedia*, 1:228, talks of the satire of contemporary Italy.

of servants. To be sure, Volpino owes a great deal to the astute slaves of the Roman comedies; but the number of servants in this comedy is much larger than in ancient comedies. The scenes where several servants talk together add a choral effect to Ariosto's drama, occurring at the very center of the comedy, in the fourth and fifth scenes of the third act. The high point of these scenes is the snatching of Eulalia from Trappola. This host of servants (Corbacchio, Negro, Gianda, Nebbia, and Morione) contributes a collective action to the complicated intrigues of the *Cassaria*. Their surprising dynamism interrupts the more orderly schemes invented to win Eulalia from the procurer.[27]

Two figures distinguish themselves from the choral tone of the servants: Volpino and Fulcio. Volpino devises one scheme after another to help Erofilo, acting courageously and, above all, intelligently to meet difficult circumstances. At the start of the fourth act Volpino denounces Fortune for ruining his plans by causing Eulalia to be snatched away and calling Crisobolo back from his journey: "Tante sciagure, tante aversità t'assagliono, misero Volpino, da tutti i canti, che se te ne sai difendere, te puoi dar vanto del migliore schermidore che oggi sia al mondo. O ria fortuna, come stai per opporti alli disegni nostri apparecchiata sempre! . . ."[28] This attitude toward Fortune as a negative force that swoops down to destroy man's dream of perfection is a Renaissance theme which reflects the exaltation of man's abilities. Man pits himself with all his intelligence against Fortune. By contrast the medieval vision of Fortune as an impartial power is found in Canto VII of Dante's *Inferno;* she is a special minister created by God to shift prosperity from one person, family, or nation to another so that it does not stay with any one of them for too long a time. According to the Renaissance vision typical of the fifteenth and early sixteenth centuries, there is a direct antagonism between man and Fortune. Fortune is the perpetual enemy of man in his aspirations. Poliziano, in the first book of the *Stanze per la Giostra,* describes how Fortune disturbed the Age of Gold: "Fortune envious of their peace / broke every law, and sent sadness in their midst . . . ." Castiglione comments in *Il Cortegiano* how Fortune crippled the gifted Duke Guidubaldo of Urbino with the gout: "But Fortune, envious of such great ability, was opposed with its

---

27 Carlo Grabher, *Sul Teatro dell'Ariosto* (Rome, 1946), pp. 46-47, talks of the choral role of servants.
28 "So many calamities, so many adversities assail you, poor Volpino, from every direction. If you can defend yourself from them, you should boast of being the best fencer in the world. O evil Fortune, how you are forever opposed to our plans! . . ."

entire might against such a glorious beginning" (bk. I, chap. 3). Human ability (Italian *virtù*), which distinguishes man from other animals and elevates him to the angels, struggles with envious Fortune.

Fulcio, Caridoro's servant, possesses the *virtù* that triumphs. In the eighth scene of the fourth act he comments how "mutabil Fortuna" has upset all Volpino's plans. Now it is up to him to take command of the situation and outdo Volpino, formerly his master in sly tricks. Fulcio invokes the favor of Fortune, promising to be drunk for three days straight if his schemes succeed. At the moment of his success (Act V, sc. 4) he compares his intrigue to a war: ". . . Or mi perviene il trionfo meritamente, poi che rotti ho gli nimici e disfatti totalmente; senza sangue, senza danno de le mie squadre, ho lor ripari e lor fortezze tutte spianate a terra . . . ."[29] After this military language, Fulcio calls upon Fortune, declaring that he will fulfill his vow to get drunk. It is he, the victor of the day, who closes the *Cassaria* with an envoi.

Ariosto's verse reworking of this comedy must have appeared at some Ferrarese court production between 1529 and 1531. The new prologue relates to that performance with addresses to the aristocratic gathering of courtiers and ladies.[30] In this new prologue Ariosto explains how his comedy of some twenty years before fell into the hands of pirating printers who made corrupt editions. Therefore the author was compelled to write a revised version. The beautiful ladies attending the performance are addressed, since the author would like to make them more beautiful just as he has done for his comedy. He mentions that ladies labor to make themselves beautiful with makeup, expressing his pity for women in their forties, who have lost the flower of sixteen or twenty. Then he turns to the gallant young courtiers and contrasts them with the old men who dye their hair to regain their lost youth. The author regrets that he cannot make others and himself young again as he has done for his comedy.

Indeed, the second version of the *Cassaria* is a thorough revising of the original, often a refinement. Ariosto has changed the names of some characters and modified in part the sequence and number of scenes. Some minor parts have been considerably reduced, and the role of Stamma, maid

---

29 ". . . Now victory comes deservedly to me since I have routed and totally defeated my enemies; without bloodshed and harm for my troops, I have razed their defenses and fortresses. . . ."

30 Campanini, *Prologhi,* pp. 163-64; and Anthony Gisolfi, "Ariosto's Delightful Prologue to *La Cassaria*," *Theatre Annual* 22: (1965-66): 41-47, presents a translation of the verse prologue and discusses Ariosto's career as superintendent of court spectacles at Ferrara.

to the procurer, is added. The new setting for the comedy is Sybaris, the Greek city of southern Italy. Lucrano is now called Lucramo and has come not from Constantinople but from Genoa. Ariosto elaborates many of the speeches, expanding them and sometimes giving them a different satiric slant. In the prose version Fulcio described the activity of women applying makeup in this way (Act V, sc. 3):

> . . . Spendono queste femine pur assai temp in adornarse;
> mai non ne vengono al fine: mutano ogni capello in dieci
> guise, inanzi che se contentino che così resti. E che fan?
> Prima col liscio (oh che longa pazienza!) or col bianco,
> or col rosso, metteno, levano, acconciano, guastano,
> cominciano di novo, tornano mille volte a vederse, a
> contemplarse nel specchio: in pelarse poi le ciglia, in
> rassettarse le poppe, in rilevarse ne' fianchi, in
> lavarse le mani, in tagliarse l'ugne, in fregarse,
> strusciarse li denti, oh quanto studio, quanto tempo si
> consuma! quanti bossoli, ampolle, vasetti, oh quante
> zacchere si mettono in opera! in minor tempo si dovea di
> tutto punto armare una galea. . . .[31]

The satire on women's applying makeup is quite traditional. Vignettes of makeup scenes occurred in the *Epirota* and the *Dolotechne,* as well as earlier in the *Mostellaria.* In the prose version of the *Cassaria* Fulcio's speech owed a great deal to Boccaccio—not only to the *Decameron* but to the antifeminist *Corbaccio.* Yet Ariosto's satire is not bitter; he displays a delight in making miniature portraits. In the verse recasting of his play Ariosto has Fulcio deliver the same speech in a somewhat expanded form; the author also added a whole new part on young men who imitate women in the care they take in adorning themselves. Instead of a gentle smile at the ladies, who follow their natural instinct of wanting to appear beautiful, there is a far sharper satire on the vanity of effeminate young men. During this same period Castiglione affirmed that although men and women shared many common qualities, women alone should possess a sweet delicateness and tenderness which is completely alien to men ("una tenerezza molle

31 ". . . These women spend a great deal of time adorning themselves; but they never come to an end: they change every hair ten ways before they are satisfied to leave it alone. And what do they do afterward? First with lotion (oh what great patience!), then with white powder, then with rouge they put on, take off, arrange, ruin, begin again, return a thousand times to look at themselves, to behold themselves in the mirror: they pluck their eyebrows; puff up their breasts, draw in their waists, wash their hands, cut their nails, scrub up, brush their teeth; oh how much effort, how much time is wasted! How many compacts, phials, jars, how much makeup they put into the job! In less time you could completely arm a galley. . . ."

e delicata, . . . dolcezza feminile," *Il Cortegiano,* Bk. III, chap. 4). Ariosto also takes a certain moral position as he ridicules the youths who waste their manliness (*virtù*) by performing acts that are unnatural to them. The satire is heightened by the author's skill in drawing vignettes.[32]

The verse recasting of the *Cassaria* does not possess the dynamic qualities of the original prose version. The spontaneous and exuberant freshness of the prose original is gone. In this second version Ariosto avoids facile theatrical effects, toning down the choral scenes of the associated servants. In choosing the unrhymed *sdrucciolo* hendecasyllable he was looking for the verse form closest to prose. Ariosto's reworking his comedies from prose into verse presents a practical example of the controversy over the use of prose or verse for the theater that was later to be carried on theoretically by literary critics. Although the ancient Roman Comedy had been composed in verse, the model of Boccaccio's style in the *Decameron* influenced many Italian writers to choose prose.

I Suppositi

Ariosto's second comedy, *I Suppositi,* also was written first in prose and then rendered in verse years later. Composed during 1508, this play received its first performance on February 6, 1509, at the ducal palace of Ferrara. Ten years later, on March 6, 1519, *I Suppositi* was performed at the Vatican for Pope Leo X. Raphael designed the sets for the Roman production. Between 1528 and 1531 the author wrote the verse recasting, which was probably never produced in his lifetime.[33] Bernardino Prosperi also described the 1509 production in a letter to Isabella d'Este, emphasizing how modern the comedy seemed to be: "Marti sera il R.ⁿᵒ Cardinale fece la sua, composta per D. Ludovico Ariosto, comedia invero per moderna, tuta delectevole et piena de moralità et parole et gesti da riderne assai cum triplice fallacie o sia sottoposizione. Lo argomento fo recitato per lo compositore et è bellissimo et multo accomodato a li modi et costumi nostri, perchè il caso accadete a Ferrara, secondo lui finge . . . ."[34] The setting

---

32 Grabher, *Teatro,* pp. 53-57, analyzes Ariosto's work in satiric vignettes.
33 Campanini, *Prologhi,* p. 60 f.
34 "Tuesday evening the Cardinal held his comedy, composed by Ludovico Ariosto, a play which is truly modern, totally delightful and full of morality and words and actions to arouse laughter with the triple exchange of identity or supposition. The argument was recited by the author and is most beautiful and very suitable for our customs and manners because the events occurred in Ferrara as the author pretends. . . ." Original text cited in *Commedie del Cinquecento,* ed. Aldo Borlenghi (Milan, 1959), 1:986.

is no longer in ancient Greece, but at Ferrara during the time of the author. In the prose prologue Ariosto explains that his comedy is going to be full of *supposizioni*. The author is here making a mischievous play on the meaning of the verb *supponere*, which can signify "to place under" (as in sodomitic love affairs) or "to take in exchange" (as when children are abandoned and later assigned to the wrong parents). The salacious implications of this pun are shown by Ariosto's saying: "li fanciulli per l'adietro sieno stati suppositi . . . ." Apparently no member of the Ferrarese audience was offended by the pun. Prosperi certainly felt that the comedy was "piena de moralità." The author goes on to say that children have been given the wrong identity in real life as well as in comedies. This play's novelty is that old persons are assigned different identities by the young. To let his audience know that the subject matter of his comedy is not morally objectionable, Ariosto warns that his play is not like those of the Greek authoress Elephantes, whose works often had obscene illustrations. Nor is the *supponere* of this comedy like that of philosophers in their dialectical disputes. In this comedy servant and master will exchange identities. Aristo does not wish to be accused of plagiarism and thus admits having followed Plautus' *Captivi* and Terence's *Eunuchus,* two comedies where master and slave exchange roles. The Italian author states that he is ready to imitate the Latin authors in his vernacular comedies just as those Roman writers imitated Menander and Apollodorus of Greek New Comedy. Ariosto even admits imitating the Roman comedies in the arguments and customs represented, making it very clear that his comedy is a poetic imitation, not a theft. Plautus and Terence would never be offended. He leaves final approval or condemnation to the audience.[35] Plautus' *Captivi,* one of the two classical comedies that Ariosto says influenced him, tells of the war between Aetolia and Elis. The wealthy Aetolian Hegio has been trafficking in war captives so that he can ransom his son Philopolemus from the Eleans. The well-to-do Philocrates, with his servant Tyndarus, is among the prisoners of war purchased by Hegio; Tyndarus pretends to be the master, and Philocrates claims that he is the servant. Hegio thus sends Philocrates to Elis to bargain for Philopolemus's release.[36] In Terence's *Eunuchus,* young Chaerea becomes passionately interested in the girl Pamphila, who is being held by the courtesan Thais, the mistress of Chaerea's elder brother Phaedria. Parmeno, Phaedria's slave, has been

35 Text of play in Catalano edition, Vol. 1. Also useful is the prose version in *Commedie e Satire di Lodovico Ariosto,* ed. Giovanni Tortoli (Florence, 1856).
36 Reinhardt-Stoettner, *Spaetere Bearbeitungen,* pp. 332-36.

ordered to deliver a eunuch as a gift to Thais; but Chaerea prevails upon
Parmeno to let him dress up in the eunuch's clothes to gain entrance to
Thais's establishment. Admitted there, Chaerea rapes the girl while Thais
is absent.[37] These two exchanges of roles inspired Ariosto to create the
switch in identities between the affluent youth Erostrato and his servant
Dulippo so that the master can become a servant in the household of the
Ferrarese Damone and the servant Dulippo can attend university courses.

Besides imitating Roman comedies in these two instances, Ariosto
derived a great deal more from classical sources than he admitted in the
prologue. The slave Tyndarus of the *Captivi* turns out to be Hegio's other
son who was stolen by a runaway slave. In the same manner Dulippo is
discovered to be the kidnapped son of the lawyer Cleandro. This discovery is important to the plot of the Italian comedy as Cleandro no
longer feels that he has to marry Damone's daughter Polinesta to have an
heir, thus clearing the way for Erostrato to wed the girl.

Both the *Captivi* and the *Eunuchus* provided Ariosto with models for
Pasifilo, the double-dealing parasite of *I Suppositi* who acts as matchmaker
for Cleandro as well as the false Erostrato. In ancient Athens the role of
parasite was a profession. Parasites prepared for banquets by studying
books of jokes and humorous anecdotes. Wealthy persons made it a social
status symbol to have a crowd of flattering parasites around them. In Rome
the parasites were necessarily tied to the patrician class; and the Roman
parasites were not always mere flatterers but could be useful and intelligent
servants, less adject than a slave.[38] Centuries later, when Italy was composed
of communes, a more modern type of parasite arose in the figure of a
professional jester who traveled about from one commune to another,
sometimes even taking part in political intrigues. By the sixteenth century
this jester-parasite was seen less in aristocratic circles than in bourgeois
ones.[39]

One of the distinguishing traits of the parasite as represented in the
Roman comedies is his gluttony. Already in the *Formicone* Mantovano
presented a hungry parasite in the character Licopino. Ergasilus, the parasite
in the *Captivi*, is overjoyed that Hegio has recovered both his sons and will
hold a banquet to celebrate. At the start of the third scene of Act I in *I
Suppositi* Pasifilo encounters the false Dulippo, who decides to tease the

37 Zecca, *Influenza di Terenzio*, pp. 49-50.
38 De Amicis, *L'Imitazione*, pp. 142-43, presents the history of the parasite.
39 Alberto Agresti, *Studii sulla Commedia Italiana del Secolo XVI*, (Naples, 1871),
pp. 92-93, talks of the jester-parasite.

parasite before letting him in for an early dinner with Damone, pointing out that Pasifilo has at least ten wolves in his stomach. Pasifilo is very similar to Gnatho ("Jawbone"), the parasite of the *Eunuchus*. Gnatho is a high-class flatterer attached to the mercenary captain Thraso just as Pasifilo is attached to the lawyer Cleandro. Both Gnatho and Pasifilo reflect on the miseries of life. But whereas Gnatho tends to be a rather abstract figure representing the ideal parasite, Pasifilo is a much more concrete figure, working from a very practical philosophy to achieve his ends. No less crafty, Gnatho enjoys speculating on the perfect system of the parasite's art. By comparison, Pasifilo is a superficial character, but the charm of Ariosto's character is in his quick, natural way of working on other persons to move them to benefit him. Pasifilo moves at ease within the Renaissance Italian merchant class.[40]

One of the liveliest characters of Ariosto's comedy is the servant boy Caprino. Ancient precedent for this mischievous character can be found in the Plautine "puer" of the *Persa, Stichus,* and *Pseudolus*. But this figure is too natural to be a literary reconstruction. Caprino is an impertinent child who brings a breath of fresh air into the play. He appears only in three brief scenes. The cook Dalio, exasperated by the boy's antics, draws a portrait of him (Act III, sc. 1) in which he describes Caprino as never carrying home a basket of intact eggs, and as a scamp chasing after a dog or playing with a bear—chains could not keep that boy from teasing a peasant or a porter. Caprino is a born tease, making fun of Dalio or the old maid Psiteria. The spirit of this little devil is expressed in his exclamation "Taruò!" Ariosto had real-life models in mind more than ancient ones in creating this likeable scamp.[41]

Terence provided Ariosto with more than plot situations. Pathos, a mood studied by the Latin dramatist, characterizes *I Suppositi*. Filogono is the Terentian type of father, and puts love over discipline in his treatment of his son Erostrato. The Plautine father, with few exceptions, holds his son down by granting very little money as an allowance. Filogono regrets sending Erostrato away to study, even though he has ordered study in distant Ferrara as a disciplinary measure because the youth had acted too passionately and had questionable relationships in his native Catania. But even before the youth reaches his destination, Filogono begins to miss him

---

40 Zecca, *Influenza di Terenzio*, pp. 57-60.
41 Grabher, *Teatro* pp. 71-75, talks of Caprino, quoting lengthy passages from the scamp's scenes.

greatly. The father must write the boy a hundred letters begging him to return, but Erostrato keeps replying that he does not wish to interrupt his studies. Erostrato's absence becomes such a source of grief for Filogono that he decides to brave the rough trip from Catania to Ferrara despite his advanced age. The old man does not want to die separated from his son. One Terentian father who also grieves over his son's absence is Menedemus in the *Heautontimorumenos*. His son Clinia falls in love with a poor girl and lives with her as if she were his wife. Menedemus grows so angry that Clinia runs away. Ashamed of his harsh treatment of the youth, Menedemus determines to torment himself by wearying his body with farm work from morning to night. Both the Roman comedy and the Italian represent the paternal regret experienced by sensitive men who thought they had acted correctly in disciplining their sons. Terence and Ariosto evoke the memory of a happy past, the anguish of the present moment, and the hope for a future reconciliation.[42]

Structurally *I Suppositi* follows the classical model. To maintain unity of place, the author pictures Polinesta in the first scene of the comedy as being instructed by her nurse to come outside Damone's house and talk with her on the street to avoid household spies. Ariosto tries to explain why the characters talk about their private affairs on the public street. The one-day climax of a love affair that has been going on for two years is a very crowded period. Filogono's arrival in Ferrara adds to the complications of this dramatic day. Perhaps too much is compressed into a very short time span.

This drama is not a mere reconstruction of Roman comedies, for the Italian novellistic tradition influenced the plotting and portrayal of characters. Erostrato's masquerading as a lowly servant so as to be close to his beloved has its parallel in *Decameron* VII, 7. Boccoccio tells of an Italian youth, Lodovico, in the service of the King of France, who learns of the beauty of Beatrice, wife of Egano de' Galluzzi of Bologna. Going to Bologna, Lodovico calls himself Antichino and enters Egano's household as a servant. Eventually becoming his master's most trusted servant, Lodovico succeeds in winning Beatrice's love and possessing her without

---

42 Zecca, *Influenza di Terenzio,* pp. 68-69, makes a mistake by calling Chremes the son of Menedemus. K. F. Thompson, "A Note on Ariosto's 'I Suppositi,'" *CL* 12, no. 1 (Winter, 1960): 45, fails to find Filogono a very pathetic creature and regards him as rather conventional. For an edition of the *Heautontimorumenos* see Terence, *Comédies,* ed. J. Marouzeau (Paris, 1942), Vol. 2.

Egano's ever suspecting infidelity. Both Erostrato and Lodovico renounced the comforts made possible by wealth in order to pursue their amorous designs. Their desire for love helped them to endure the humiliations of a servile position.

Erostrato does not have Lodovico's good fortune to keep his intimate relations hidden from the master of the houshold. Damone, discovering his daughter's relations with the false Dulippo, orders the other servants (Act III, sc. 2) to bind the guilty youth and imprison him in a darkened room. The offended father wishes to revenge the injury to his honor. The *Decameron* also portrays other fathers seeking revenge on a trusted servant who has dishonored the master's daughter. A tragic case occurs in the first story of the fourth day where Tancredi, lord of Salerno, has his daughter's lover, Guiscardo, strangled and his heart cut out. His daughter, Ghismonda, commits suicide after receiving the heart. Tancredi and Damone both experienced the sharp pain of shame and disappointment on seeing how their daughters willingly surrendered their families' honor to men of lowly station. A happier outcome of a similar love affair results in the seventh story of the *Decameron's* fifth day. There the servant Teodoro made pregnant the daughter of his master Amerigo Abate of Trapani in Sicily. Amerigo reported the offense to the king's captain, who ordered Teodoro to be seized and tortured into confessing. The youth was condemned to be hanged. Meanwhile Amerigo sent poison and a poniard to his daughter Violante so that she could choose the way to kill herself. He also ordered the murder of his newly born grandchild. But fortunately, just as the youth was being led to the gallows, a visiting Armenian nobleman recognized Teodoro as his son, kidnapped years before by corsairs. All tragedy was averted in time, and the lovers were able to wed. This second novella concludes with marriage just as does *I Suppositi*.[43]

In one respect Ariosto's Damone differs from the two vengeful fathers of the *Decameron*, since he feels that the blame for his daughter's being seduced by the false Dulippo was to be placed on his own blindness. Why did he ever entrust his daughter to an old nurse, who could easily be corrupted? He also made a mistake in hiring young male servants. He regrets not having married off Polinesta. During the preceding three years he had delayed the marriage from month to month, wanting his daughter wed to a person of high rank; but now he sees her in love with a servant. Damone is not like Tancredi with his rigid Norman spirit or Amerigo

---

43 Novellistic ties are discussed by Giambattista Pellizzaro, *La Commedia del Secolo XVI e la Novellistica Anteriore e Contempranea* (Vicenza, 1901), pp. 38-41.

with his Sicilian anger. This father resembles Filogono in being a pathetic character.[44]

In the prologue Ariosto had mentioned that there would be a novel *supposizione;* this occurs with the masquerade of a gentleman from Siena as Filogono to vouch for the false Erostrato's offer of a special dowry for Polinesta. Even though similar impersonations are found in the Plautine *Trinummus* and *Pseudolus,* this character owes his stupid nature to the novellistic traditions, as the citizens of Siena are usually shown as foolish figures in novelle written by Florentines. To enlist the services of the gentleman from Siena, the false Erostrato tells him that Sienese customs officials have offended Ferrarese ambassadors who were carrying gifts from the viceroy of Naples to Duke Ercole. All Ferrara is enraged and ready to strike down any Sienese visitor. This thick-skulled old Sienese gentleman accepts the story and considers himself fortunate that the false Erostrato will pass him off as his father from Sicily. Ariosto, who was Emilian, here imitated the Florentine tradition of ridiculing their Sienese rivals.

A new character appears on the stage in Cleandro, the doctor of laws. This sixty-two-year-old lawyer, who graduated from the University of Padua after fleeing Otranto when the Turks took the city, is trying to marry a young girl. Cleandro represents the type of person who is ignorant even though he has a university degree to prove how erudite he is. His thinking that he can satisfy a young girl sensually is a sign of his stupidity. A similar figure in *Decameron* II, 10, is a Pisan judge named Riccardo di Chinzica, who believes that his wealth and intelligence are sufficient to hold onto a young wife. After she is kidnapped by a pirate, she refuses to go back to her husband, as the old man is no match for the pirate's bodily strength.[45] Cleandro and Riccardo di Chinzica are both ridiculous because they ask youthful females to put aside their natural urgings.

But Ariosto's doctor of laws is a far more absurd figure than Riccardo di Chinzica. Boccaccio never mocks his character for his ability as a jurist. Riccardo is a highly talented man who make a fool and finally a babbling idiot of himself. Cleandro does not possess Riccardo's intelligence but is constantly claiming to be erudite. His pretensions show him up for the

---

44 Thompson, "A Note" pp. 44-45, thinks Damone is more a "tyrannical father who sees his mistakes too late than he is the heartbroken old man." He recognizes that Damone is better developed than the Latin *senex.*
45 Grabher. *Teatro,* pp. 35 and 68-69, compares Riccardo and Cleandro. See Aldo Scaglione, *Nature and love in the Late Middle Ages* (Berkeley, 1963), pp. 75-76, for his comments on the Riccardo novella in the light of the rights of love and nature.

pedant he is. Throughout the sixteenth century the pedant will be one of the leading characters of the Erudite Comedy, as a vain lawyer, a strutting physician, or a Latin-spouting tutor. The pedant is essentially a modern figure, a caricature of the humanists who paraded their stupid erudition. Some scholars who like to deny all originality to the Italian playwrights have tried to discover an antique example of the pedant in the tutor Lydus of Plautus' *Bacchides*.[46] Lydus, though, is merely the ancient slave who instructs and watches over his master's son. A better prototype can perhaps be found in the physician who appears in Plautus' *Menaechmi* to cure the supposed raving madness of Menaechmus of Epidamnus. At least this second example presents a character who shows off his medical knowledge.

It would really be "pedantic," however, to look for this character type anywhere other than in Italian life and literature, as Italy was the first nation where modern universities arose. Boccaccio was aware of the comic possibilities of university-trained persons vaunting their erudition. In *Decameron* VIII, 9, he speaks of the Florentine dolts who receive university degrees at Bologna: "As we see daily, our townsmen return hither from Bologna, this a judge, that a physician and a third a notary, tricked out with robes long and large and scarlets and minivers and store of other fine paraphernalia, and make a mighty brave show, to which how far the effects conform we may still see all day long" (Payne translation). This novella tells how two jolly painters succeed in casting into a trench full of sewage the physician Maestro Simone, a man richer in the goods he inherited than in the learning he received at the University of Bologna.[47] The character type of the pedant already existed on the Italian scene without Ariosto's having to reconstruct it from the ancient Roman Comedy. His contribution was to introduce the pedant as a theatrical character type.

Ariosto shows Dr. Cleandro using Latin pedantically in his conversations. When the lawyer declares to Pasifilo that his law practice has earned him more than fifteen thousand ducats, the parasite is awed, and Cleandro swells with ostentatious egotism. One of the vices commonly attributed to pedants is homosexuality, and here it is leveled at the lawyer, but wrongly so, when the false Dulippo (Act II, sc. 3) lies to Cleandro, saying that Pasifilo has claimed Cleandro wants a beautiful wife so as to lure young

---

46 See L. Stoppato, *La Commedia Popolare in Italia* (Padua, 1887), pp. 74-75, for some opinions on the origin of the pedant as a dramatic character. Although this text is rather antiquated, it still commands respect from several contemporary Italian critics.

47 See Pellizzaro, *Novellistica*, pp. 41-42.

men. The character of the pretentious pedant, sketched here in *I Suppositi,* so reflected the Italian scene that the popular Commedia dell'Arte was also to present him as a jurist or physician. Still later the comic opera was to ridicule the elderly doctor of laws. The fortune of the pedant as a comic character would alone demonstrate that there was no impassable barrier between the Erudite Comedy and popular forms of the theater.

There are no problems of anachronism in this comedy when references are made to the contemporary world of the author, since the play's mood and political setting depict sixteenth-century Italy. One of the sore points of the political division of the Italian states lay in the abuses of customs officials. Filogono complains (Act IV, sc. 3) to his Ferrarese guide that time and time again on the long trip from Catania officials tore open his luggage and upset all the contents. He feared they might flay him to see if he had anything hidden between his skin and flesh. The Holy Roman Empire had long been unable to maintain political unity in Italy. At every ford of a stream, at every mountain pass, armed guards were waiting to pounce upon travelers and demand customs duties from them.[48] Several of the authors of novelle shared Ariosto's scorn of the malpractice of customs officials in exacting duties. Ordinarily the Italian authors of the Renaissance were unable to vent their anger on princes and their chief ministers. Instead they directed their satiric darts at lesser officials.

Lawsuits are a perfect subject for satire. Lico, Filogono's servant, points out the problems involved in winning a lawsuit such as the one Filogono desires to start in order to prove his identity and prosecute his son's impostor. According to Lico, four things are needed in a legal battle: right on one's side; the man who can plead the case; favor; and the man who can decree justice. When asked to defined *favor,* Lico answers in this way: "Avere chi raccomandi la tua causa, perchè dovendo tu vincere, presto abbia fine; e così, se la conclusione non fa per te, che si differisca e meni in lungo, tanto che per il molto distrazio l'aversario stanco ti ceda, o teco pigli accordo" (Act IV, sc. 8).[49] Without powerful friends, Lico holds, no one can win a lawsuit. Ariosto presents an ironic analysis of the difficulties involved in legal battles for persons who have only right on their behalf.

In *I Suppositi* the author has carefully portrayed his own times. He refers

---

48 Agresti, *Studii,* pp. 49-50.
49 "To have someone who will plead your case so that if you are going to win, it will be over soon but if the decision is going against you, he will delay it so long that your adversary—tired from all the trouble—will either give in or come to an accord with you."

to different parts of Ferrara, mentioning monuments. The close political
and family ties between the courts of Naples and Ferrara are alluded to in
the scheme used by the the false Erostrato to enlist the Sienese to masquerade as Filogono. Later in play the real Filogono notes (Act IV, sc. 3) that
pilgrims on their way to Loreto accompanied him during part of the
journey. There are allusions to the student world of the University of
Ferrara, as the real Dulippo has been attending courses, distinguishing
himself as an excellent scholar.

A greatly feared menace to Italy was full-scale Turkish invasion. The
brief occupation of Otranto in 1480, described in this comedy as separating
Cleandro from his son, was just one of many Turkish incursions on
Italian soil. The recognition scene and recovery that occur in *I Suppositi*
between the lawyer and Dulippo are not a stilted imitation from ancient
comedies. Dulippo, whose real name was supposed to be Carino, had been
taken away on a Turkish ship when three Sicilian galleys appeared and
forced the Turks to surrender. Filogono later purchased the five-year-old boy
in Palermo. During those times thousands of prisoners were led into
slavery among the Turks. To protect the Christian realms, ships manned
by Sicilians, Maltese, and Spaniards sailed the Mediterranean on the
lookout for Turkish galleys; they often succeeded in liberating prisoners.
Ariosto was not describing a purely imaginary situation in the reunion
of Cleandro and his son. The political and social climate of this comedy
accurately reflects the early sixteenth century in Italy.[50]

The verse recasting of *I Suppositi* does not show the elaborate refinement found in the verse reworking of the *Cassaria,* for this second version
is a mere reduction of *I Suppositi* to *sdrucciolo* hendecasyllables. Only the
prologue displays considerable reworking as the author goes to great lengths
to amuse his audience with the double meaning of the verb *supponere.*
Realizing how that pun delighted the aristocratic listeners, Ariosto interrupts the prologue with a mock reprimand in which he chides them for
not being "anime sante." It must be remembered that Ariosto wrote the
verse prologue after the prose version of his comedy had been performed
at the Ferrarese court and the Vatican. He knew from actual performances
what really pleased his spectators. The author continues with a contempor-

---

50 For a discussion of the Turkish menace as viewed by Renaissance writers, see
C. A. Patrides, "The Bloody and Cruelle Turks: The Background of a Renaissance
Commonplace," *Studies in the Renaissance* 10 (1963): 126-35. Also cf. Agresti, *Studii,*
pp. 122-25.

ary reference in his prologue; he refers to the "carte belle più che oneste" that have been published in "Roma santa." Here Ariosto is maliciously alluding to the Roman editions of Aretino's lewd sonnets with pornographic illustrations by Giulio Romano that Marc'Antonio Raimondi had transferred into engravings. In this second prologue Ariosto seems sure of himself and does not acknowledge his debt to the ancient Roman playwrights. His interest is to satirize contemporary artists and authors.[51] In rendering his comedy into *sdruccioli* verses the author had to change some of the characters' names. Damone becomes Damonio; Nebbia, Nevola; and Lico, Lizio. Ariosto wanted as many words as possible with the accent on the antepenultimate syllable so he could use them to end his verses if necessary.

Ariosto's *Cassaria* extolled the quality of human intelligence that triumphs over adversity. In *I Suppositi,* however, the role of Chance is much stronger. Neither Erostrato nor Dulippo displays the same cunning that distinguished servants like Fulcio and Volpino. Erostrato and Dulippo move about like aristocrats and never really succeed in their assumed roles as servants. Erostrato takes a servile position just to pursue his amorous designs; and Dulippo, though sold into a servant's life at the age of five, easily takes up a student's career. One cannot expect from them the wiliness of arch-servants like Volpino and Fulcio.

In this comedy the denouement relies on pure chance rather than on human astuteness. Erostrato compares his setting Dulippo against Cleandro as rival for Polinesta's hand to a game of chance, using (Act III, sc. 3) the word *zara.*[52] This is the game "hazard" played with three dice. Erostrato's struggle with Cleandro will be decided by Fortune like a throw of dice. Fortune turns her wheel to decide man's fate. Erostrato fails to challenge Fortune the way Fulcio does in *Cassaria;* he does not feel that his *virtù* alone is sufficient to win his struggle against Cleandro. But other characters of this comedy do vent their anger on Fortune for attacking them. Damone, in the scene that follows Erostrato's long soliloquy, curses the "ingiuriosa Fortuna, d'insidie / piena" that brought that devil of the false Dulippo to disgrace the old man's honor. Still later in the play the real Dulippo attacks "perfida Fortuna" (Act V, sc. 3) for causing all the defeats of that

51 Campanini, *Prologhi,* pp. 98 f.
52 -Reference henceforth will be to the verse rendering. The author's picture of Erostrato's plight before the superior intelligence of Fortune recalls Dante in Purgatory, VI, vss. 1-4, where the game *zara* is described.

day with Erostrato's arrest. Damone and Dulippo can only rail at their misfortunes, considering themselves powerless to confront the disastrous situations which threaten to crush them.

Dulippo had thought to win Polinesta for his master by presenting the Sienese as the false Filogono with assurances about the special dowry. But by chance the real Filogono reached Ferrara to upset all the plans. By a chance recommendation Filogono hired Cleandro as his lawyer. When Filogono explained to the lawyer how he had purchased Dulippo, Cleandro grew suspicious and asked for more details about the servant. Finally Lico's mentioning a birthmark on the youth's left shoulder convinced Cleandro that the servant was his son Carino. This stroke of good fortune was reported by Pasifilo to Damone, who than released Erostrato. Chance brought Cleandro and his son together after many years of separation. Through Chance it was no longer necessary to continue the exchange of roles. Cleandro no longer had to marry, and the lovers could wed. Man's initiative here yields before blind Chance.

Ariosto's second comedy emphasizes sentiment. Erostrato's love for Polinesta differs from the desire of Erofilo and Caridoro for the two young women held by the procurer. The passion of the two youths in the *Cassaria* is a traditional and occasional type that merely serves as a pretext to set in motion the complicated intrigues of the comedy. Erostrato's love in *I Suppositi* starts from the point of sensual possession; he corrupted the girl's nurse so that she would convince Polinesta to surrender herself to him. But his is a profound passion, not easily sated. Even after possessing the girl, he lives in continuous fear of losing her. Erostrato has been Love's servant, and this true master has richly rewarded his service. From the very beginning of his passion Erostrato has seen that his love ought to lead to marriage. Only then could he feel sure of having Polinesta as his own. The illicit pleasures that he enjoyed during their love affair are made bitter by the fear that one day his beloved will be married off to another. Ariosto's attitude toward marriage is positive here in recognizing how that social institution could protect and stabilize an irregular relationship. *I Suppositi* is only one of many sixteenth-century Italian comedies that conclude with plans for a wedding. By the end of the play Damone and Filogono can rejoice together that their children are to wed.

In the *Cassaria* the love theme is secondary. Ariosto there described the same kind of amorous situation found in an ancient comedy. The only major debt his second comedy owes to the Roman plays is the absence of love scenes. But the love of Erostrato for Polinesta exists in a realm of sentiments far removed from the world of procurers and the slave girls in their possession that was seen in Ariosto's first dramatic work.[53]

Il Negromante

Writing a third comedy turned out to be a long and difficult task for Ariosto. This time he chose not to make a prose version and wrote solely in the *sdrucciolo* form. In a letter of January 16, 1520, the author explains to Pope Leo X that ten years before he had sketched out the plot of a new comedy, but had kept hesitating to finish it, since he was not absolutely satisfied. But at the urgings of the pontiff he was able to do in two or three days what he had not done before in ten years. He therefore sent a copy of the completed comedy to the pope.[54] Leo X had had *I Suppositi* performed at the Vatican in 1519. Obviously pleased with the work, he hoped Ariosto would write a comedy especially for Vatican performance. But the version of the new comedy, *Il Negromante,* which Ariosto sent to the pontiff failed to delight Leo X, apparently because of several satiric remarks about ecclesiastical abuses that appear in the prologue and throughout the comedy. Ariosto had to wait several years to see his comedy performed in a second version, but still in *sdruccioli* verses, at the ducal theater of Ferrara during the carnival of 1528.[55]

The prologue to the first version of *Il Negromante* begins with the mention of mythic figures famous for poetic talents: Orpheus, whose song moved beasts and stones toward him; Apollo, who built the walls of Troy; and Amphion, who played a lyre and made rocks move to form the walls of Thebes. In almost the same miraculous way the city of Ferrara came to to Rome a year before. Ariosto is of course referring to the 1519 Vatican performance of *I Suppositi,* where the sets represented Ferrara. For this performance Cremona has reached Rome in the middle of winter, as Ariosto's new comedy will represent that Lombard city. The author proceeds to throw some satiric darts by stating that no acts of homicide or other crimes were necessary to cause Cremona's moving to Rome. Even if there had been such crimes, the liberal pope would grant an indulgence. Here Ariosto alludes ironically to Leo X's wholesale business in indulgences at high prices, conducted so that the pontiff could have funds for construction projects in Rome like the new St. Peter's. The author tries to soften his

53 Grabher, *Teatro,* pp. 65-67, discusses the roles of Chance and sentiment in this play.
54 Campanini, *Prologhi,* pp. 115-16, quotes the letter.
55 See the Bontempelli *Ariosto* preface, pp. 17-18.

remarks by explaining that Cremona is in Rome solely to become acquainted with the goodness, kindliness, piety, courtesy, and virtue of Pope Leo X. All this flattery certainly did not compensate for the cutting reference to the sale of indulgences. Ariosto had enjoyed pleasant relations with Giovanni de' Medici until the latter became Pope Leo X in 1513 and failed to keep several promises of aid (see the poet's third satire). The first version of *Il Negromante* was written at exactly the time when Luther started the Protestant reformation. Leo X might laugh about a satire on the general hypocrisy of most clergymen, but he was not ready to have performed in the Vatican a comedy which ridiculed the means he took to gather revenue.

Ariosto next takes up the *questione della lingua,* the polemic then raging among men of letters as to the proper literary language for Italy. He admits that this play will not be in his native Emilian dialect. Then he states that on passing through the university town of Bologna he heard some words that pleased him and retained them for later use; later he perfected himself in Tuscan eloquence at Florence and Siena. Some traces of Lombard pronunciation remain with him, he confessess. The great literary debate of those times was whether Italian writers should choose their native dialects, make a composite language from several Italian dialects along with foreign words, or employ either the Tuscan of Boccaccio and Petrarch or contemporary Tuscan. Ariosto bowed to the authority of Pietro Bembo, who in the *Prose della Volgar Lingua* upheld the language of Boccaccio and Petrarch. Bembo's influence can be noted in the various editions Ariosto made of the *Orlando Furioso,* always polishing it according to the Tuscan masters. Here in this prologue he apologizes for any non-Tuscan words.[56]

There are two basic parts to the first prologue: the one deals with the setting of Cremona, the other with the particular occasion of the Vatican performance (which never took place). In writing the prologue for the Ferrara production, Ariosto retained the first part with few changes but replaced the remarks about Pope Leo X and the Vatican fiscal policies with comments about the present performance. The author also omitted the section on the *questione della lingua.* Ariosto emphasized that the scene of *Il Negromante* was Cremona and informed the audience not to be confused if the sets and costumes used for this comedy were the same ones that had been seen shortly before during the carnival celebrations for Ariosto's fourth play *La Lena.* The author's third comedy was thus presented after his fourth. Ariosto goes on to tell the audience to ask the loafers in shops and squares how it is that Cremona has arrived in Ferrara. Those loafers

56 Campanini, *Prologhi,* pp. 121-47, for analysis of prologue.

know more about the internal political intrigues of Rome and Venice and the calling up of Swiss and German Lansquenet troops by Spain or France than they know about what is going on in their own households.[57]

Except for the discussion on the choice of a proper language, neither prologue treats problems of literary theory or classical imitation. Both tend toward contemporary satire. Papal abuses, husbands too wrapped up in politics to watch their wives, and the military intrigues of foreign powers in Italy all come under discussion. The author's ironic remarks were not reserved for his *Satire.*

The central character in this play is the magician Giacchelino, a Jewish exile from Castile. He travels about, leading a gypsy's life. In one city he pretends to be Greek; in others he passes as an Egyptian or an African. He has a different name for every place he visits. Along with every change of name and nationality there is a change in the costume he wears. Although he is almost illiterate, he has become rich from his profession. Giacchelino is a master at advertising his arts; he claims to be able to transform men into beasts. But in reality he seeks out unhappy domestic situations and profits from people's problems by promising easy solutions. In this way threads of this comedy's complicated plot come into the hands of the necromancer.[58]

The Italian novella tradition provided the character type of the magician. Magic in the Hellenistic sense generally meant a serene interest in the miraculous. The Greeks usually did not have to turn to black arts for their spiritual needs. Plautus reflects the Hellenistic attitude toward magic in his *Mostellaria* and *Amphitryon.* Tranio in the *Mostellaria* uses the story of a haunted house to rescue his young master in a tight situation; but there is really nothing sinister about the fictitious ghost. The supernatural comes right down to earth in the *Amphitryon,* in which Jupiter and Mercury impersonate Amphitryon and his servant Sosia so that Jupiter can possess Amphitryon's wife Alcmena during her husband's absence. Thunder and lightning effects are used for this drama. The Roman Comedy did not show the evil use of magic.

But the Roman spirit was not usually so serene as in Plautus. Belief in the gods died out, at least among the members of the sophisticated upper class,

---

57 *Ibid.,* pp. 171-83. Reference has been to the second version of the play as published in Catalano's edition, vol. 1. All following plays of Ariosto will come from this edition.
58 The term *negromante* was used loosely to mean magician and not just a person who communicates with the dead in order to reveal the future.

well before the beginning of the Christian era. A sense of despair made many Romans open to black magic and superstitions. Magical practices must have come into Italy at a very early date, for the Twelve Tables include two laws prohibiting the use of spells. Despite official attempts to suppress the popular vogue in magic, the black arts continued to attract followers. The Senate decreed in A.D. 16 that all astrologers and magicians be banished from Italy. The various laws, sometimes enforced with capital punishment, point out how serious the Romans considered black magic.[59]

Witches enjoyed an even greater following than magicians and astrologers. People turned to them to win back the affections of an unfaithful lover or to ruin someone's happy love affair. One of their major functions was to inflict a disease on a person hated by one of their clients, often with a waxen image of the person to be injured. The witches also claimed to be able to recover lost articles.[60] Besides the mythic grand witches like Medea and Circe, the professional witch also is described in classical literature. Horace portrays in *Epodes* V and XVII and *Satires* I, 8, the witch Canidia; he shows her trying to win the love of the aged Varus with a love philter that she is to prepare from the marrow and liver of a boy she has kidnapped. The poet wrote an imaginary dialogue between himself and the witch, in which he complained about how her incantations made him suffer. He also describes how witches gather at the Cemetery in the Campus Esquilinus to sacrifice lambs and call up the souls of the dead. An even more frightful sorceress is found in the sixth book of Lucan's *Pharsalia,* in which Sextus Pompey asks aid from the witch Erictho in the region of Thessaly, the traditional land of black arts. Even wolves flee from her. Erictho brings a corpse to life so that he can reveal the Fates to Sextus. Although Horace and Lucan used their poetic skills to heighten their portraits of Canidia and Erictho, their works provide good pictures of witchcraft in action.

One can observe in the writings of Apuleius the transition from the classical to the medieval idea of magic. This author was once brought to trial on the accusation of having used magical means to wed the rich widow Pudentilla. To defend himself he wrote an *Apology* for the magic arts, in which he held that the titles "priest" and "magician" are equivalent terms. According to Apuleius, the gods find the magic arts acceptable, since such

59 J. E. Lowe, *Magic in Greek and Latin Literature* (Oxford, 1929), pp. 11-12, presents the legal background.
60 *Ibid.,* pp. 39-46.

arts are full of wisdom, piety, and prayer.[61] This author's *Asinus aureus* relates the misfortunes of the inquisitive youth Lucius, who went traveling in Thessaly. The wife of his host in one town turns out to be the witch Pamphile, who has an elaborate laboratory in a wooden shelter atop her roof. One night the curious youth watches Pamphile smear an ointment on her body and fly away, transformed into an owl. The youth takes the ointment and applies it to himself. Instead of a bird, he becomes an ass. Poor Lucius has to go through many painful adventures before he is able to eat some roses and regain his human shape. Although this tale of a metamorphosis reflects the Hellenistic interest in the marvelous, it also displays a marked Oriental influence; for the roses that Lucius nibbles are sacred to the goddess Isis. The sinister elements of the black arts, despite what Apuleius said about magic in his *Apology,* are prominent in the entire Pamphile episode. Apuleius wrote during the second century of the Christian era, the period when the spiritual vacuum of the Roman Empire was being filled by Oriental mystery cults.[62]

In a Christian world, with a strong fear of eternal damnation, spirits are generally seen as infernal creatures—condemned souls. Instead of the harmless ghost that was supposed to haunt a house in the *Mostellaria* there are diabolical spirits. This extremely sinister view of a supernatural that can be called up with black arts lasts through the Middle Ages and Renaissance until at least the seventeenth century. Roman antiquity gave Renaissance Europe its own superstitions. Many beliefs centered on ominous occurrences. Some humanists had faith in prodigies and auguries, as superstition was not limited to any one class. Witchcraft never died out, for the Christian view of the universe aided that profession. Witches were sought by persons who wanted to make contact with Satan to promote their schemes of greed, lust, or ambition. Witches and sorcerers were given credit for depriving men of their health and life. This was a good profession for imposters. Witchcraft thrived so much that an entire colony of witches and enchanters operated during the mid-fifteenth century at Norcia, the home of St. Benedict, in the very territories of the Church. Persecution of the practitioners of black magic grew stronger with the 1484 Bull of Innocent VIII. German Domin-

---

61 *Ibid.,* p. 6.
62 See *Opera Omnia L. Apuleii Madaurensis,* ed. G. F. Hildebrand (Leipzig, 1843); *L'Ane d'or,* trans. Paul Vallette (Paris, 1947); *Della Magia,* trans. Concetto Marchesi (Bologna, 1957); and *Le Metamorfosi,* trans. Marco Pagliano and Guido Vitali (Bologna, 1960-62). Most of the translations have excellent introductions and notes.

icans carried out the bulls against witches that were issued by subsequent pontiffs like Alexander VI, Leo X and Adrian VI. One area of their work was the Dominican province of Lombardy, even Cremona, the setting for *Il Negromante*.

Italian witches and sorcerers were on the whole very practical. The more "romantic" type of witchcraft popular among the Germans flourished only among the Italian Alpine valleys. Italian practitioners of magic did not enter enthusiastically into the realm of the marvelous, since they were merely out to make money. The marvelous deeds a magician claimed to perform were an advertising pitch to win customers. There was too much danger of inquisitors and magistrates for the Italian practitioners to run the risk of claiming to perform miraculous feats. Instead they attended to satisfying their clients' whims, especially in love affairs. They made love potions, performed abortions, made careless girls appear virgins. Witches and sorcerers were fierce competitors. But after 1500 this kind of magic became passé. Some of the leading enchanters started to journey to other countries.[63]

Authors of novelle either ridiculed magicians for claiming to perform the marvelous or poked fun at the stupidity of those who could be taken in by these impostors. The novella collections illustrate the role magicians played in contemporary Italy. In the *Novellino* three necromancers go to the court of Emperor Frederick II. Sacchetti tells (novella 201) about a certain Gonella, who tricked the gullible crowd at the fair of Salerno. In the *Decameron* X, 5, Boccaccio describes a necromancer who is much nobler than the usual type; this magician brings forth a beautiful garden in the midst of a bleak winter so that Messer Ansaldo can win the love of a married lady. Later, the magician refused to accept his fee since Ansaldo has generously freed the lady from her promise. One of the most famous of all magicians, Michael Scott, is mentioned in *Decameron* VIII, 9. There the painters Bruno and Buffalmacco make the stupid physician Maestro Simone believe that they are members of a company gathered around two followers

---

63 Gene Brucker, "Sorcery in Early Renaissance Florence," *Studies in the Renaissance* 10 (1963) 7-24, presents the latest details on Italian witchcraft. Burckhardt, "Morality and Religion: Mixture of Ancient and Modern Superstitions," in *Renaissance* in Italy, is somewhat outdated but still extremely helpful. Richard Warwick Bond, *Early Plays from the Italian* (Oxford, 1911), pp. xxxi-xxxvii, mentions that although Petrarch, Boccaccio, Piccolomini, and Poliziano all mocked magic as superstition, Aldus, Sannazzaro, Bembo, and Leo X were believers. The Inquisitors' textbook *Malleus Maleficarum* of 1487 familiarized Italians with German superstitions.

of Michael Scott. The painters claim to go twice a month to a special night of delights that the magic arts provide for them. The foolish physician believes their story and begs to be admitted to the elite circle. The necromancer was thus an established literary character well before Ariostro wrote his comedy.[64]

Ariosto does not ridicule the magician Giacchelino so much as the credulity of the many persons who accept the man's magicial powers. Nibbio, the magician's servant, points out the factor which favors his master's success: "la sciocchezza, che al mondo è in abondanzia" ("stupidity, which abounds in the world"). This common stupidity is the opposite of the Boccaccian intelligence that is held up for praise in the *Cassaria*. The magician easily gulls Massimo, the rich old Cremonese citizen; the old man's adoptive son Cintio; and Fazio, the man who allowed the youth to marry secretly the orphan Lavinia. This motif of stupidity will be developed throughout the sixteenth century by dramatists and authors of novelle.[65]

Perhaps the stupidest character is Camillo, the young man who enlists the magician's aid in an attempt to seduce Cintio's official wife Emilia. Camillo's last name is Pocosale ("Little-wit"), which describes him perfectly. He represents the type of lover who almost goes into convulsions over his passionate desires; yet he remains completely egotistical. When the magician tells him that Emilia (who has never noticed the young man's interest in her) is ready to melt in his embrace, Camillo at once thinks that the magician's arts have caused the girl to recognize his qualities. He also wants Giacchelino to intensify Cintio's apparent impotency. It is Camillo's stupidity which leads him to be hidden in a chest when the magician tells him he will be transported to Emilia. Actually Giacchelino is intent on robbing Camillo's home. This device of using a chest is novellistic; the *Decameron* contains several tales where a person is hidden in a chest for one purpose or another. In *Decameron* II, 9, the youth Ambrogiuolo has himself carried in a chest to the bedchamber of the Genoese lady Zinevra. But the youth has acted only to win a wager with Zinevra's husband, and he merely observes her bedroom and notes a significant feature of her body while she sleeps. *Decameron* IV, 10, tells about the adulterous wife of a physician and her affair with a young nobleman. One night her lover drinks by mistake a sleeping potion the woman's husband has prepared for a

---

64 Pellizzaro, *Novellistica,* pp. 46-48, lists several novellistic sources for the necromancer as a literary character. Also compare the charlatan with his medicine show in Tommaso de Mezzo's *Epirota.*
65 See Bandello, 3:29, on the distasters awaiting the credulous fool.

patient. The youth passes out as if dead. At her maid's suggestion, the woman places her lover's body in a chest outside a carpenter's shop. Later that night two usurers carry off the chest with the youth inside it. In neither of these tales is the chest used for amorous purposes. But in *Decameron* IX, 2, the abbess of a Lombard convent has her priest-lover come to her in a chest. Camillo's act is in this novellistic tradition.[66]

Only one character stands out from the crowd of the gullible: Cintio's servant Temolo. The third scene of the first act belongs to him as he makes fun of the blind faith which Fazio and Cintio place in the magician. The old man and the youth marvel at Giacchelino's being able to go about invisible; but Temolo asks them if they have ever seen the magician when he was invisible. Then they relate how Giacchelino darkens daytime and brightens the night. Temolo claims that he can do the same: at night he lights a lamp, and during the day he closes the windows. Cintio derides the servant, pointing out how little experience Temolo has had. The servant should at least recognize the power the magician has over the spirit world. Temolo replies in this manner:

> Di questi spirti, a dirvi il ver, pochissimo
> Per me ne crederei; ma li grandi uomini,
> E principi e prelati, che vi credono,
> Fanno col loro esemphio ch'io, vilissimo
> Fante, vi credo ancora. (Act I, sc. 3, ss. 413-17)[67]

The very lowly servant is the voice of common good sense that cries out against blind acceptance of nonexistent magical powers. Temolo, in his humble social position, does not share the stupid mistakes of the "great." He is not an Italian reworking of the clever slave of Roman Comedy. His attitude is one of irony.

There is no chorus of astute servants in this comedy as there was in the *Cassaria,* since cleverness is centered in only three characters: the magician, his servant Nibbio, and Temolo. It is in the play of their actions that the work comes to life artistically, and they save *Il Negromante* from being a tedious weaving of intrigues. Ariosto saw clearly how important they were to his drama when he wrote the second version. In the first working of the play Giacchelino's last stage appearance is in the final scene of the third act,

---

66 Sanesi, *La Commedia,* 1:780-81, cites the novella sources. Grabher, *Teatro,* pp. 82-90, discusses the theme of stupidity.

67 "To tell you the truth, I would have very little belief in these spirits, in my own opinion; but great men, princes and prelates, believe in them. By their example they compel me, a most lowly servant, to have belief."

and he is never seen again in the course of the drama, although Nibbio refers to him several times in the fourth and fifth acts. The author later realized the dramatic weakness of keeping the title character off the scene during the last two acts. Therefore for the second version he added three scenes to Act V so that the magician reappears at a crucial moment after all his schemes have failed. Temolo, the magician's chief antagonist, and Nibbio are also brought into this new section.

Giacchelino, a master of human psychology and a crafty Jew who recalls some of Sacchetti's novelle,[68] is deceived twice in the scenes added by the author. Temolo cheats the magician out of his cloak in the fourth scene. In the following scene Nibbio, who knows how his master has failed, frightens him into heading for the port area to find a boat so that they can escape. But in the envoi Nibbio confesses that he is going to steal all his master's goods from their room at an inn so that he can end his gypsy life of being in Italy one day and in Picardy another. By these new scenes, with their ironic close in which the master cheat twice meets his match, Ariosto shifted attention from the love story to the far more vital drama of the magician.[69]

Despite the comedy's setting in contemporary Italy and typical characters of the period such as a magican, *Il Negromante* greatly resembles three Terentian plays. The *Hecyra* provided Ariosto with the theme of an unconsummated marriage. *Phormio* suggested the device of a clandestine wedding. And the *Andria* presented a model for Camillo. This diverse classical inspiration helps account for the complicated plot of Ariosto's comedy. Terence's *Hecyra* relates how the youth Pamphilus raped and made pregnant the girl Philumena while in a drunken fit. He did not even know who she was. Shortly afterward his father compelled him to marry Philumena. But Pamphilus' affections were all dedicated to the courtesan Bacchis, and he refused to consummate his marriage. Similarly, in *Il Negromante* Cintio obeyed parental authority and publicly wed Emilia while he was already married to Lavinia. The Italian youth refused to consummate his marriage to Emilia, feigning impotency. In Terence's comedy the courtesan eventually decides to break off her relations with Pamphilus so that he will treat Philumena as his wife. Just as Cintio feared leaving Emilia, since the scandal could ruin her reputation, Pamphilus wanted to repudiate Philumena in public but realized he could bring harm to all innocent parties. The unwanted marriage in Terence's *Hecyra* is not dis-

68 Sacchetti, novelle 218 and 219.
69 Grabher, *Teatro*, pp. 95-108, compares the two versiois of the *Negromante*.

solved, since Pamphilus learns that he is the father of the baby boy delivered of Philumena.[70]

In the *Phormio* old Chremes is guilty of bigamy, having one family in Athens and another on the island of Lemnos. He wants his daughter Phanium by the wife at Lemnos to marry his Athenian nephew Antipho. But while he is on his way to the island, his Lemnian wife arrives in Athens with the daughter. The woman, worn out by neglect and poverty, dies. Antipho chances to see Phanium; learning that he cannot have her except by honorable means, he marries her. His passionate manner of appealing for her love and the girl's refusal to prostitute herself are paralleled in *Il Negromante*. Both Antipho and Cintio offered gifts of money to win the girls, who resisted the attempts at seduction. In Ariosto's comedy Cintio had to keep entreating Fazio to let him wed his ward Lavinia, since the girl would not have him other than as her husband. Neither Phanium nor Lavinia could be bought. They both refused to become a mistress and insisted on a legitimate relationship. Phanium felt confident, knowing that her father was an Athenian citizen. Lavinia did not know who her real father was, but she relied on Fazio as if he were her father. A recovery scene in each comedy removes all objections to the marriage. Phanium is the very girl intended by Chremes as the wife for his nephew. On discovering her identity, Chremes and his brother are delighted that Antipho has married her. In almost the same manner Lavinia is found to be Massimo's daughter by a Calabrese wife. The *Phormio* and *Il Negromante* present two young ladies whose virtue triumphs.[71]

An even more striking similarity in characters and plot situations may be noted between the *Andria* and Ariosto's comedy. In the *Andria* the youth Pamphilus has been treating the girl Glycerium as his wife, and during the drama she gives birth to a son. Pamphilus' father Simo knows nothing about their relationship and has arranged for his son to wed a daughter of the rich Chremes. But the youth Charinus would like to marry Chremes' daughter. Pamphilus, unlike Ariosto's Cintio, does not have to undergo an unwanted wedding ceremony because Charinus, the model for Camillo, plots with Pamphilus to have the wedding plans postponed. At one point further along in the comedy Charinus thinks Pamphilus has betrayed him. But the arrival in Athens of a relative of Glycerium's former guardian leads to the discovery that the girl is Chremes' long-lost second daughter. As in the *Phormio* and *Il Negromante* the recovery of a lost

70 See Zecca, *Influenza di Terenzio,* pp. 110-11.
71 *Ibid.,* pp. 98-101, with quotes of parallel passages.

child solves all the problems. Charinus is in a good position to become engaged to Chremes' first daughter now that Pamphilus is no longer his rival.[72]

All these Terentian influences enter into the love intrigues of Ariosto's comedy, but the Italian drama differs from the ancient plays because the young hero, Cintio, does not appeal to his servant to handle his delicate situation. Instead he hires the magician and gets the chest with Camillo inside it. The amorous situations of the Terentian comedies and Ariosto's work are similar.

Satire on official abuses and corruption is strong throughout the second version. Fazio explains (Act I, sc. 2, vss. 172-74) to a friend why he had to leave Florence five years before to live in Cremona. Members of the middle class fled from an unjust fiscal system, for Pope Leo X taxed Florence heavily with all sorts of duties so taxes could be reduced at Rome. The author does not hesitate to point out the plight of the Florentines, many of whom became exiles. Minor officials do not fare very well in this play. Since such officials usually acted like beasts, Ariosto talks about their metamorphosis from human form. When Cintio says that the magician can transform men and women into animals, Temolo answers that such transformations are not miracles but daily occurrences:

> Un divien podestade, commissario,
> Proveditore, gabelliere, guidice,
> Notaio, pagatore de li stipendii,
> Che li costumi umani lascia, e prendeli
> O di lupo o di volpe o di alcun nibio.[73]
>
> (Act I, sc. 3, vss. 379-83)

The Italian comic authors grant no mercy to rapacious officials.

A favorite subject for satire is, of course, the hypocrisy of clergymen. Nibbio holds (Act II, sc. 1) that his master is more skillful than the friars who court widows to get all they can from them. In the next scene the magician tells his servant that Cremona has more stupid fools than Rome has deceptions and wicked acts.[74] Ariosto makes his satiric thrusts boldly in this play. One sweeping condemnation occurs in the opening scene of the third act. Giacchelino is trying to convince Cintio that Emilia should

---

72 Campanini, *Prologhi*, p. 139, compares the *Andria* and the *Negromante*.
73 "One becomes *podestà*, commissioner, purveyor, customs officer, judge, notary, payer of salaries; and he abandons human customs to take up those of a wolf, fox, or vulture."
74 Campanini, *Prologhi*, pp. 118-19, talks of Ariosto's satire on the clergy.

be dishonored as an adulterous wife so the youth could break off his marriage with her. When Cintio is too scrupulous, the magician tells him that
one should harm others to help himself. Theirs is a corrupt age when
everyone is seeking his own advantage, and the powerful are especially
willing to trample over the rights of lesser persons. Ariosto portrays the
magician as a representative of a cynical age. The society that the imposter
magician preys on is infested with corrupt officials and greedy clerics.

La Lena

Contemporary Italian society comes under even sharper and more consistent study in Ariosto's fourth comedy, the *Lena*. This play, written entirely in the *sdrucciolo* hendecasyllabic verse form, appeared on the stage
before *Il Negromante,* being performed at the Ferrarese ducal palace for the
carnival of 1528. In June of that year Alfonso's elder son Ercole married
Renée de France, the sister-in-law of the French monarch Francis I, at a
ceremony in Paris. After the couple arrived in Ferrara in late December,
the *Lena* and the *Cassaria* were produced again to inaugurate the new
ducal theater. Ariosto added two new scenes to the *Lena's* last act and
wrote an entirely different prologue, which was recited by a member of the
ducal family.[75]

A carnival mood characterizes the first prologue. The actor who recites it
states that he has come wearing a mask, since such a gathering of noble persons seems to be for a ball. But some persons in special costumes have told
him that they are going to perform a comedy. The word used here to describe the nature of comedies is *sciocchezza.* Comedies were then regarded
as no more than pieces of nonsense that could divert an audience which had
nothing important to do. The actor goes on to say that the writing of
comedies is not the most difficult of all literary compositions. In fact,
Plautus and Terence were just translators of the Greeks. For these reasons
the actor laughs at the attempt of modern authors to rival ancient playwrights who were the most knowledgeable masters of stagecraft. Ariosto
and other dramatists knew how little esteem the comic genre often enjoyed.
Comedy was considered an amusing pastime. The modern playwright was
also in a delicate position because of the enormous respect accorded to ancient writers by cultured society. Ariosto does not defend here the position

75 See Borlenghi, *Commedie del Cinguecento,* 995, 997. But Sanesi, *La Commedia,*
1:226, states that the second performance may have been in 1532 and not in January
of 1529.

of the modern dramatist, but merely notes the difficulties that the Italian authors of comedies suffered. As the prologue ends the actor says that if the comedy does not provide enough amusing material, the audience can at least laugh at the author's arrogance.[76]

It is the prologue to the lengthened version of the *Lena* which decisively answers the deriders of modern comedy. Throughout this prologue the author makes one of his risqué puns. His comedy, in having two scenes tacked onto the end, is like a woman who has added a train to her dress. It really was the fashion of the day for ladies to have such alterations made. But the use of the word *coda* (tail) for the train makes clear the salacious play on meanings. "Lena" thinks she is more beautiful with her new tail and is ready to appear before the public, thinking she can please her audience again as she did in the past. She does not realize that men like variety and youth. Lena is sure she will please the youths in the audience, since new styles are always enthusiastically taken up by the young. Here Ariosto is attacking those who found fault with his attempt to rival ancient writers, the rigid old critics who accept only the antique style. But Ariosto admits that many older persons join the young in welcoming modern fashions (*le fogge moderne*). The *Lena* is being performed for them. Critics might as well leave before the comedy starts. Ariosto had held himself back in the first prologue, but in this one he sought the support of those who did not blindly worship antiquity.[77]

This play, for both plot motivation and characterization, rests on a central triangle between Lena, the inexperienced procuress; her husband Pacifico; and Fazio, their landlord and Lena's lover. Fazio is derived from the ancient type of *senex,* the old man, but in this drama he shows a greater depth of character than the tráditional type. He is a miserly lover and grants Lena only a poor home worth ten lire, soup and bread, and old shoes for her husband and new ones for herself. In addition she has to instruct Fazio's daughter Licinia in domestic arts. Fazio parades about like a very righteous citizen, but he is ready to use anyone for his own advantage. When Lena complains that he does not pay her enough, Fazio pretends to be tired of her and declares that he is going to sell her house. Crude cynic that he is, Fazio gambles on Lena's surrendering to him, since she and her husband have no money or credit, and would starve without him. Fazio does have some feelings—for himself. When the servant Corbolo

---

76 Campanini, *Prologhi,* pp. 153-59.
77 *Ibid.,* pp. 187-92. Text in Catalano edition, Vol. 2.

tells the lie that his master Flavio is also Lena's lover, Fazio is torn by rage and fear, as he has a senile passion for Lena. He is happy to learn that Flavio has been intimate with Licinia, not Lena. The author shows this character trying to reconcile his greed with his passion.

Pacifico is no rival of Fazio's. His weak nature does not let him rebel against the economic tyranny that Fazio exercises over him and Lena. His wife's prostituting herself with Fazio (and with others) provides him with a livelihood where he can at least drink to his content. Pacifico's name was doubtless chosen for its ironic overtones, since he peacefully accepts his role as a professional cuckold. But Pacifico is not a cold cynic; more than anything else, he is a poor wretch. His economic misery is paralleled by his moral wretchedness. Pacifico is not without a flash of disgust for his life. His conscience is not always easy. He merely succumbs to his passive existence.[78]

Lena, the central character, is in her middle age, but not so old that the lie about Flavio's being her lover seems ridiculous. She became Fazio's mistress to pay Pacifico's debts, but knowing how easily love is extinguished, she has decided on the career of a procuress, starting with Licinia. But in her new role Lena reveals herself a rank amateur, without the hard cynicism necessary for success. If she were more professional, she would capitalize on Fazio's senile passion for her. Her determination to sell Licinia to Flavio is made for more than economic reasons. Unlike her husband, Lena has the strength of character to rebel against Fazio. Fazio's greed drives Lena to the point where she is intent on taking revenge by prostituting Licinia. Her revolt is against the poverty that Fazio refuses to relieve with his fortune.

The dramatic focus of this play is on Lena rather than on Flavio and his love intrigue to possess Fazio's daughter. Ariosto realized Lena's importance to his comedy and made it apparent in the two scenes he added to the final act for the second performance of the work. Before those scenes were tacked on, the comedy closed with the announcement that Flavio would wed Licinia. In the first of the new scenes Pacifico reveals his moral misgivings by attacking Lena for having become a procuress for Flavio. She answers that his gluttony forced her into that career. Pacifico feels that she should act more discreetly. Lena replies that if she took on all the customers he would like her to have, she would be outdoing the professional prostitutes of Ferrara. Since she will not always be young, she must provide

78 Grabher, *Teatro,* pp. 116-17, describes Pacifico's character.

for old age just as ants prepare for winter. In the play's last scene Fazio's maid Menica invites Lena and Pacifico to Licinia's wedding. The fierce Lena, who was so intent on prostituting the girl, is really happy to see that Licinia will marry the young man she loves. Menica tells Lena there will be more than one wedding that night, for Lena is to resume her old relationship with Fazio.

By adding these two scenes Ariosto reestablished the dramatic position of the members of the triangle. Their story is a strange case of adultery, a presentation of domestic relations which could never have been found in the ancient Roman Comedy. Yet by the play's end, in the lengthened version, all three have resumed the same roles they had at the beginning of the comedy. There has been no dramatic character development. Lena's act of rebellion has failed. Fazio triumphs, and Pacifico sinks back into his passive idleness.

Ariosto's *Lena* contains several traditional character types, but the author has been able to penetrate deeply into the characters' inner nature. Flavio's servant Corbolo, for instance, is the epitome of the wily servant earlier sketched out in Volpino and Fulcio (the *Cassaria*) and in Temolo (*Il Negromante*). Of all the character types the Italian comic playwrights borrowed from the Roman Comedy the clever servant is perhaps the one imitated most closely. Corbolo, like the slave of the Roman comedies, maintains a close relationship with his young master. Despite his cleverness, he is often unsuccessful. At the start of the third act Corbolo considers his work up to then; he knows that his major task is to gain money from Ilario, Flavio's father. Such a task requires the skill of the servants in ancient comedies:

> . . . Or l'astuzia
> Bisognaria d'un servo, quale fingere
> Ho veduto talor ne le comedie,
> Che questa somma con fraude e fallacia
> Sapesse del borsel del vecchio mungere.
> Deh, se ben io non son Davo né Sosia,
> Se ben non nacqui fra Geti né in Siria,
> Non ho in questa testaccia anch'io malizia?
> Non saprò ordire un giunto anch'io, ch'a tessere
> Abbia fortuna poi, la qual propizia
> (Come si dice) a gli audaci suol essere?
> Ma che farò, che con un vecchio credulo
> Non ho a far, qual a suo modo Terenzio
> O Plauto suol Cremete o Simon fingere?

Ma quanto egli è più cauto, maggior gloria
Non è la mia, s'io lo piglio alla trappola?[79]
(Act III, sc. 1, vss. 577-92)

The force of literary tradition is made very evident here by the mention of
the names of both Roman playwrights and some of the slaves and aged
fathers in their comedies, but there is a difference in tone between Corbolo
and the traditional servant. His conception of Fortune as a power in favor
of the bold is very similar to Machiavelli's comparison of Fortune to a lady
(*The Prince,* chap. 25) who inclines to be a bit impetutous. Like Fulcio before him, Corbolo shares the Renaissance belief in human ability. In a
brief soliloquy (Act V, sc. 6), the servant states that his army of lies is going
to succeed in spite of Fortune. But it is not through his schemes that Flavio
comes to possess Licinia. Chance (or Fortune) brings about what Corbolo
failed to do. Yet in his struggle to succeed Corbolo distinguishes himself
from the schematic servant type. His liveliness has caught the attention of
several twentieth-century critics.[80]

Like *I Suppositi* and *Il Negromante,* the comedy's love intrigue concludes with marriage. Like Boccaccio, Ariosto is ready to recognize marriage as the rightful culmination of a love affair, but he does not approve of
marriages forced upon persons who feel nothing toward each other. *Il Negromante* presented two classic examples of marriage: one between Cintio
and Lavinia with Fazio's consent because of the ardor of the young couple's love; the other between Cintio and Emilia at Massimo's command.
The first was the natural conclusion of four years of entreaties from Cintio
to Fazio; the second marriage was wrong since it was imposed upon Cintio
by parental authority. For Ariosto love and marriage are not necessarily
irreconcilable.[81] Here in the *Lena* circumstances (Chance) bring the lovers
together; Flavio is hidden in a barrel which by pure accident is transported

79 ". . . Now the cleverness of a slave in ancient comedies (as I have seen on the
stage) would be required for me to use fraud and lies in order to filch this sum
from the old man's purse. So what if I am not Davus or Sosia, so what if I was not
born between Thrace and Syria, don't I have cunning in my brain? Don't I know
how to handle any intrigue that Fortune will weave? As they say, Fortune is usually
favorable to the bold. But what shall I do, for I am not involved with a credulous
old man as Plautus and Terence depict Chremes and Simo? But the greater his
caution, the greater will be my glory if I catch him in the trap. Won't it?"
80 De Amicis, *L'Imitazione,* pp. 140-42, contrasts the modern with the ancient servant types. Giuseppe Toffanin, *Il Cinquecento* (Milan, 1929), p. 163 f., states that
Corbolo is a picaresque figure who belongs with the characters in the *Orlando
Furioso.*
81 See Scaglione, *Nature and Love,* p. 98, for Boccaccio's willingness to recognize
marriage as "the logical crowning point of love," if by free choice and mutual
consent.

right into Licinia's home. The decision for a speedy wedding, once the lovers are caught together, conforms perfectly with the desires of Flavio and Licinia.

The device of a lover's hiding in a barrel to save himself from danger can also be found in *Decameron* VII, 2. Boccaccio relates how the unfaithful wife of a Neapolitan mason hears her husband knock at an hour when she had expected him to be working. After a moment of hesitation she hides her lover in an old tub. The motif of a hidden lover is found frequently in the novellistic tradition.[82] This novellistic influence is Ariosto's major inspiration. In composing the *Lena* Ariosto relied on the example of ancient plays less than in any of his earlier comedies. He reworked fewer classical devices and did not invent elaborate intrigues; no lost children are recovered. Classical influence is at its strongest in the use of soliloquies; there are nine in the play. Ariosto was seeking to follow the program of his prologue by writing in a modern style.

Ariosto's observation of the life about him, especially at Ferrara, gives the *Lena* the quality of a chronicle. In the square between the houses of Flavio and Fazio and Lena the daily life of the city passes. The hours of the day, which here maintain the unity of time without crowding the action, are heard as the townspeople pursue their occupations. People give directions to each other, mentioning monasteries and gardens in the city. Even the street where Ariosto lived is mentioned. Drunks are shown coming out of an inn while servants go out to the countryside to fetch firewood. The customs of the day are depicted on stage.[83]

Satire enters naturally in this picture of contemporary customs. Unlike Ariosto's plays, the *Lena* lends itself perfectly to satiric comments about Ferrara's society, and the satire is well integrated with the dramatic situation. The unifying theme is corruption. Corbolo relates, for instance, how he searched stores all over town to buy some game. Finally one of the duke's fowlers approached him and offered him a pair of pheasants for a good price. The servant would not need to search in the future, provided he did not expose the fowler. Corbolo is intelligent enough not to cause himself any trouble, but he cannot keep from observing (Act II, sc. 3, vss. 499–503) that the country's worst poachers are the fowlers paid by the duke to guard his game.[84]

To obtain some money for his young master, Corbolo tells Ilario that

---

82 Pellizzaro, *Novellistica*, pp. 51-53, describes the novellistic sources, Boccaccio's tale is derived from Apuleius' *Asinus Aureus*, Bk. IX.
83 Apollonio, *Storia*, 2:64-65, mentions how the Lena portrays Ferrara's daily life.
84 Agresti, *Studii*, p. 48, discusses the satire of minor officials.

Flavio has been assaulted and robbed by hoodlums. The old man does not wish to call for help from the police. Even if he went directly to the duke, the ruler would only send him to the mayor. Unless he bribed the mayor, he would be told that the police had more important matters to supervise. Ilario points out what thieves the police are. For him (Act II, sc. 2, vss. 731–35) the true criminals are men like the chief of police and the mayor, who conspire to defraud honest citizens. Like Corbolo, he uses the verb *rubano* ("they rob") to express his lack of faith in the socially appointed defenders of justice.

Police oppression is attacked in the first scene of Act IV by the messenger boy Cremonino, who curses police agents for terrorizing the poor, who cannot protect themselves. Bartolo, the creditor, utters a soliloquy in the following scene on all the trouble and expense he has borne in order to obtain a license from the mayor to confiscate Pacifico's goods for nonpayment of bills. During the last four years he has had to run to court and to pay lawyers and judges. He has gone through legal red tape with all sorts of official forms that had to be filled out and paid for before any action was taken in his case. And all his lawsuit has netted him is a favorable decision for the original debt of forty lire. Private citizens were powerless before the processes of the law unless they were wealthy and willing to pay their way. Bartolo had the funds to sustain a lawsuit but not enough to win the best legal decree.[85]

An example of the weak position of citizens who needed protection but knew they could not find it in the authorized forces of justice appears in the third scene of the final act. Here Corbolo is again trying to cheat Ilario out of twenty-five florins. Earlier in the act, the servant persuaded two of the duke's grooms to besiege Pacifico's house, where he claimed some Jews were hiding contraband cheese. When Ilario arrives on the scene, Corbolo starts weeping. He claims that the armed grooms are Pacifico's relatives, out to punish Flavio for having an adulterous relationship with Lena. Ilario first thinks of gathering friends to fight off the group, but Corbolo reminds him that the duke has severe laws against private citizens' taking the law into their own hands. The old man had better not complain to the police, since Flavio would be put on trial for adultery. Unless Ilario wants to go through an expensive trial, he would do best to bribe the grooms through Corbolo. The servant knew how easily Ilario could be frightened just by mentioning the corrupt legal system.

85 Sanesi, *La Commedia* 1:238-39, talks of the satiric thrusts at the police and the whole legal system.

Most critics have hailed the *Lena* as Ariosto's best comedy. It cannot be considered a supreme masterpiece, for the author approached the subject in a rather cold manner. Lena lacks the vitality of Celestina, that great procuress of Spanish literature. In no way can Lena's character portrait be placed beside that of Celestina. Lena seems a "constructed" character, not a figure captured fully from real life. Ariosto could have raised his comedy to the sphere of highest art if he had developed one of its unifying themes: human corruption. Lena, Fazio, Pacifico, Corbolo, the duke's fowlers, the greedy magistrates and policemen all contribute to the generally corrupt environment. Unfortunately, the author remains on the surface.

I Studenti

Ariosto left his last comedy, *I Studenti,* unfinished. He probably sketched out its plot during 1518–19. Writing it proved even more difficult for the author than composing *Il Negromante.* He started *I Studenti* in the *sdrucciolo* hendecasyllable and carried it up to the middle of the fourteenth verse of Act IV, scene 4. After Ariosto's death, both his brother Gabriele and his son Virginio, working separately, completed the comedy in slightly different manners.[86] Both Gabriele's *La Scolastica* and Virginio's *L'Imperfetta* are in the same verse form chosen by the original author. Virginio first finished the play in prose, a version still lost. Later he tried to persuade his cousin Giulio Guarini of Modena to turn the prose into *sdruccioli* verses. When his cousin declined the task, Virginio reduced the prose into verse himself.[87]

Gabriele explains in his prologue that he chose the title *Scolastica* because the comedy was about two students (*scolari*) who were more interested in girls than in their studies. He does not intend to use his prologue to give the argument (as Plautus did) or answer critics (as Terence did). Nor will his prologue offend ladies, as was often the custom among comic authors. Instead its purpose is to explain how he came to complete his brother's comedy. After Ludovico's death friends turned to one of the surviving brothers, begging him to finish the play. The friends used this argument:

86 Sanesi, *La Commedia,* 1:243, explains how for centuries Gabriele's completed version and only the prologue to Virginio's *Imperfetta* were published without anyone's being able to judge just what was Ludovico Ariosto's contribution to the play. But in 1915 Abdelkader Salza discovered the entire *Imperfetta;* he was able to compare the common parts in the two plays and determine how much Ludovico had finished.

87 Libero D'Orso, *Gli Studenti di Ludovico Ariosto* (Padua, 1929), p. 5, cites a letter by Virginio to his cousin.

all the brothers had had the same preceptor; their studies had been the same; the difference in their ages was not very great. Gabriele here replies that the study of grammar, metrics, and Horace's *Poetics* is not sufficient to make one a poet. First of all, divine inspiration is required. Gabriele recognizes that all the studying in the world will not replace poetic talent. He distinguishes himself from rigid preceptists.

Besides fearing the hard labor involved in finishing the comedy, Gabriele hesitated because poets were subject to severe criticism. Poets were often labeled as pagans because they mentioned Jupiter or Venus in their works. But then the duke of Ferrara expressed his desire to see the play completed. Four times Gabriele called on Ludovico's soul to help him, always mentioning the duke's wish. It should never be forgotten that Ludovico Ariosto was a courtier for the Este family. Finally, according to Gabriele, his brother's soul appeared to him, dressed in the costume which Ludovico used to wear at dramatic presentations. The soul spent the night dictating the rest of the comedy. Gabriele states that if the style of the close seems different from that of the first part of the comedy, the audience should not be at all surprised, since the dead write in a different style from that of the living. Except for a few weak verses, Gabriele's prologue is very well ordered. The fantastic element is introduced without any heavy rhetoric, although Gabriele is rather pretentious in claiming to have understood perfectly his brother's art and thought.[88]

Virginio is very modest, even timid, in his prologue. His main purpose is to defend the completion of the play from any criticism. He has chosen the title *L'Imperfetta* ("unfinished") because his father left the comedy in that state. To him this play is a sister. He realizes how bold he is to place his hand on a work of the unique Ariosto. At first he had hoped to give a rather tragic ending, but at length he saw that only a comic ending was possible. He should not be attacked for the work he has done any more than should a person who has added an artificial leg or hand to a disabled man. Virginio refuses to point out where his father left off and he began, since the difference between black and white is obvious to everyone. He ends by pointing out that this comedy is not similar to those of Plautus and Terence. Ariosto's son did not wish to be considered arrogant and foolhardy for tampering with his father's play. His prologue is rather prosaic,

---

88 Sanesi, *La Commedia,* 1:781, and D'Orso, *Studenti,* pp. 14-15, wage a polemic over the poetic value of Gabriele's prologue. D'Orso admires it while Sanesi finds it in bad taste.

without any flights of fancy. But his affection for his father is apparent throughout.[89]

Both completed versions conclude with an announcement of a double wedding. Like all of Ariosto's other comedies except his first, this one crowns love with marriage. One love story involves the Ferrarese youth Eurialo and the illegitimate Ippolita; they had become lovers during his student days at Pavia. Ippolita is neither a courtesan nor a slave girl like those in the *Cassaria;* her mistress, a countess, treated her very well. She is shown on stage, whereas the other heroine, Professor Lazzaro's daughter Flamminia, never appears. Flamminia voluntarily gives herself to the Veronese student Claudio when he surprises her in the house of his friendly Ferrarese landlord Bonifazio. These heroines, like Bruni's Poliscena and Pisani's Philogenia of the humanistic comedy, are modern women who wish to enjoy sensual pleasures before matrimony.

Although Virginio's prologue stated that his father's comedy was independent of the ancient Roman comic theater, a quick consideration of the plot and its mechanical expedients indicate antique influence. There are exchanges of identities, unexpected arrivals, and a recovery scene. Eurialo's servant Accursio is closely modeled on the servant of the ancient comedies. His persuading Eurialo to bring in Ippolita and the servant woman who had fled with the girl from the countess recalls a similar stratagem used by the slave Syrus in Terence's *Heautontimorumenos.* Syrus brings his young master's courtesan, Bacchis, into the home of old Chremes. The slave was supposed to fetch the girl Antiphila, mistress of the recently returned son of a neighbor befriended by Chremes; Syrus tells his master that Bacchis is the woman he was supposed to bring and that Antiphila is her maid. In the Terentian comedy, as well as in the Italian play, the deception is uncovered. Chremes threatens to punish Syrus. When Eurialo's father Bartolo learns that Ippolita and the old woman are not Flamminia and her mother, he orders Accursio to be bound and made prisoner (*Scolastica*, Act IV, sc. 6). This recalls not only similar scenes in ancient plays but, more specifically, the imprisoning of Volpino in the *Cassaria*. Gabriele doubtless had his brother's first play in mind. In Virginio's completion, Accursio escapes punishment.[90]

---

89 The Catalano edition, vol. 2, contains the texts of *I Studenti, Scolastica,* and *Imperfetta.*

90 Sanesi, *La Commedia,* 1:194, makes the comparison with the *Heautontimorumenos.*

The Italian play is much more complicated than Terence's, since it presents still another masquerade in which Bonifazio tries to pass as Bartolo in order to receive Lazzaro. To help the lovers, Bonifazio is willing to play all the tricks of the servants in ancient comedies:

> Né mi vergognerò d'ordire e tessere
> Fallacie e giunti, e far ciò che son soliti
> Gli astuti servi in l'antiche comedie:
> Che veramente l'aiutar un povero
> Innamorato, non mi par ufficio
> Servil, ma di gentil qual si voglia animo.
> Non so perché la Chiesa non l'annoveri
> Per l'ottava opra di misericordia.[91]
> (Act IV, sc. 1, vss. 1246-53)

Bonifazio may resort to the intrigues used by servants in Latin comedies, but his attitude is modern, since he considers helping lovers a noble act and, indeed, part of religious charity.

One does not note novellistic influence in mechanical expedients like hiding a lover in a barrel or a chest. But the comedy does share several motives with the novella tradition and the humanistic comedy, for instance the representation of the university world. Bonifazio rents rooms to students. When he learns that Claudio is thinking of going to Venice, Bonifazio says (Act II, sc. 1) that he will ask the university porter to help him find new boarders among the students. Claudio and Eurialo started their legal studies at Pavia, the scene for several of the humanistic comedies. Lazzaro is a university lecturer who has to change institutions because of political upheavals. Ariosto depicted the academic atmosphere far more effectively in this play than in *I Suppositi*.

But Claudio is much more than a student who neglects his academic work to pursue a love affair. Right from the first scene he appears melancholy and disturbed, fretting constantly about Flamminia. Eurialo does not tell him about the scheme to pass Ippolita and the servant woman off as Lazzaro's family because Accursio is afraid that the secret will be discovered. Claudio flies into a rage in the fourth and fifth scenes of the second act when he believes that Eurialo has betrayed him. His jealousy is almost pathological. He is sickened by his friend's remaining silent about the

---

91 "I shall not be ashamed to tell lies and weave intrigues and do what clever slaves in ancient comedies usually do: for truly to help a poor lover does not seem a servile task to me but a generous act. I do not know why the Church fails to list it as the eighth work of mercy."

women's arrival. To add to his torture the maid Stanna tells him in the fifth scene of Act II that Eurialo and the girl are doing more than exchanging formal greetings. The maid describes how she hid behind a large desk and watched the lovers in a passionate embrace. She delights in describing the ardor of their kisses. Every word is a knife thrust into Claudio's heart. He wants the old woman out of his sight. Bonifazio tries to calm him by saying that there are other women in the world. Claudio is desperate; he feels abandoned and betrayed by everyone. He declares that he will give up his legal studies and burn all his textbooks; he curses the day of his birth. Claudio is the most jealous character in Ariosto's comedies. Erostrato of *I Suppositi* never felt secure in his love affair as long as he was unmarried; yet he did not doubt the faithfulness of his beloved. Claudio also wanted to marry to secure his position; his passion was all the greater because he had never been intimate with Flamminia. The fear of being betrayed by Eurialo temporarily destroyed his mental equilibrium.[92]

This comedy shares another character with the novella and the human-istic comedy: the hypocritical clergyman. A preaching friar appears in two scenes: Act II, scene 6; and Act IV, scene 4. Bartolo confesses to him his remorse for not helping the mistress and daughter of a friend who had en-trusted a fortune to him before going into exile. Bartolo enjoyed the money without trying to locate the friend's family. The friar understands men's consciences very well; he knows that Bartolo is wavering between remorse and greed. So he finds a way to set Bartolo's conscience at ease and also make a profit. Instead of going to Naples to find the family of his dead friend (a long journey far too strenuous for a man of his age), all Bartolo has to do is give the money he would have spent for the trip to the friar, who has a papal bull granting him the power to absolve people from their vows. Bartolo, in words that Ariosto charged with ironic overtones, answers that he is impressed by the friar's holy "odor" and exemplary life. The friar assures him that his vow to search for his friend's family can be transformed into a pious work, an act of charity. In the second of the two scenes in which he appears (the second finished by Ludovico Ariosto) the friar hands the papal bull to Bartolo so that the old man can read about the extent of the friar's power to absolve vows. Accursio calls this friar an "ipocrita/Gag-lioffo," "a loutish hypocrite" (Act IV, sc. 3, vss. 1425–26). The adjective does not do justice to the cleric's ability to work on men's feelings. Ariosto's study of the friar is not profound for the cleric's character is barely sketched

92 Apollonio, *Storia,* 2:69, compares Claudio with the *Misanthrope.*

out in these two scenes and is never well integrated into the play's running action. The friar remains a lateral, episodic figure.[93]

Despite its borrowing from the antique comedy, Ariosto's last play reflects the customs of contemporary Italian society. A favorite subject of satire was the court of Rome. When the countess's agent Riccio accuses Accursio of aiding Ippolita and the servant woman in their flight, Accursio denies the charge and says that the women probably went to Rome, where life was very easy:

> . . . in Roma, dove intendono
> Che 'l sangue de li Apostoli e de' Martiri
> È molto dolce, e a lor spese è un bel vivere.[94]
>   (Act III, sc. 4, vss. 1022-24)

Ariosto never missed an opportunity to slur the Roman court. Apostles and martyrs died so that the clerics of the Roman court and their friends could live on a grand scale. The mention of women who want to try their luck in Rome recalls contemporary stories and comedies of other ambitious persons going to the Vatican court to make their fortunes.[95]

The force of politics and wars is felt in Ariosto's play. Professor Lazzaro (Act I, sc. 1, vss. 110–14) lost his salary at Pavia and had to transfer to Padua because of the wars raging in northern Italy. Bartolo's wealthy friend Gentile, Ippolita's father, went to Germany during the exile of Ludovico Sforza. Later, Bartolo alludes (Act III, sc, 6, vss. 1191–93) to the way Swiss troops brought Duke Ludovico back to Milan but later betrayed him at Novara.[96] Ariosto was not entirely lacking in political conscience, for here as elsewhere in his writings he criticizes political abuses or betrayals.

It is difficult to pass a definitive judgment on this comedy, since Ludovico Ariosto left it unfinished. Also, the dating of the original sketch, 1518–19, raises problems as to where to place this comedy in relation to the other four. Accursio is closer to servants like Volpino and Fulcio than to Corbolo. The emphasis on a complex intrigue keeps the play like the traditional classic models. Sentiment is strongest in Claudio, with his raging jealousy. The world represented in this play is not a revived ancient one like that in the *Cassaria* but is Italy at the start of the sixteenth century.

93 Grabher, *Teatro,* pp. 137-41, discusses the friar.
94 ". . . in Rome, where they hear that the blood of the Apostles and the Martyrs is very sweet, and at their expense there is a glorious life."
95 Agresti, *Studii,* pp. 71-76, describes the satiric literature aimed at the Roman court.
96 *Ibid.,* p. 58, gives the historical background of the betrayal.

Ariosto's comedies became known throughout Italian cultured circles. Although many admired their wit and courtier charm, others found fault with either the style or the satiric subject matter. Early in 1532 Ariosto sent his first four comedies to the Marquis of Mantua, who had requested copies of the works and promised possible performances. The marquis replied on the twenty-fifth of March in this manner:

> Per il cameriere che mandai a Ferrara ho ricevute con
> la lettera vostra . . . le quattro commedie vostre che
> me havete mandate, quale mi sono state gratissime e per
> la bellezza loro et per la prestezza che ho vista in voi
> de mandarle subito che in mio nome ve state rechieste, de
> che vi rengratio molto; et avenga che l'inventione de
> tutte sieno belle, et scritte benissimo, nondimeno a me
> non piace de farle recitare in rima. Però ve le remando. . . .[97]

Ariosto's answer to the marquis is one of his coolest letters. The marquis expressed interest in reading the prose versions of the comedies, but he thought that the use of the *sdrucciolo* made plays unsuitable for actual production on stage.

In his *Discorso intorno al comporre delle Commedie e delle Tragedie,* Giraldi Cintio places the *Cassaria* ahead of Ariosto's other comedies because of its involved plot, which resembles the Terentian double intrigue. The *Lena,* today regarded as the author's best comedy, ranks second for Cintio because of its single plot. Since there was some lack of verisimilitude in the relationship among the characters of *I Suppositi,* Cintio gave it third place. He criticized *Il Negromante* for an even greater lack of verisimilitude, placing it last among the comedies. He would not consider *I Studenti,* since the author did not complete it.[98]

One can speak of an evolution in the comedies of Ariosto. In an almost linear fashion he freed himself from rigid imitation of the Roman comic theater and moved toward an artistic equilibrium between realistic observation of life and classical influence. He followed certain definite steps in his

---

97 "Through the chamberlain I sent to Ferrara I received along with your letter the four comedies that you forwarded to me. They have pleased me a great deal both for their intrinsic beauty and for the promptness you showed in sending them to me immediately after they were requested in my name, for which I am very grateful. And although the invention of all is beautiful, and the plays are very well written; nonetheless, I do not want to have them acted in verse renderings. Therefore I am returning them to you. . . ." Italian original cited in Borlenghi, *Commedie del Cinquecento,* 1:999, n. 43.

98 Herrick, *Italian Comedy,* pp. 67-68, talks of Cintio's opinion of Ariosto's comedies.

career as a dramatist. Ariosto started by translating from ancient comedies, and his first effort at an original play closely followed the classical model. But by the close of his career the only major influence of the ancient theater was the technical form of the five-act play with scenes. His theatrical career is a story of artistic progress and gradual independence from strict imitation.

Nardi: *La Commedia di Amicizia*

During the long period of Ariosto's activity as a comic poet, other dramatists in different parts of Italy were writing comedies according to the classical scheme. Although Florence lost its cultural preeminence in Italy after 1492, the strong example set by il Magnifico influenced the continuance of several traditions. Sacred plays were still given. Poets often cast the sacred legends in new dramatic form. The "trionfi," public parades with floats and carnival songs, continued for a time. Church groups still presented rather academic performances of the Roman comedies. But much more significant for the future was the formation of amateur dramatic companies that gave plays at banquets and in private gardens.[99]

Jacopo Nardi deserves the credit for initiating the Erudite Comedy in Florence. Whether production of his first comic work, *La Commedia di Amicizia,* preceded the performance of Mantovano's *Formicone* and Ariosto's *Cassaria* remains a disputed point. Most likely this comedy was performed during 1502–12 when Pier Soderini was gonfaloniere of Florence.[100] Like Mantovano and Ariosto, Nardi attempted to reproduce the spirit and form of the ancient comic theater, but he lacked their artistry.

Boccaccio's *Decameron* X, 8, is the source for the *Commedia di Amicizia.* This is the story of two perfect friends who, in the fashion of Damon and Pythias, made great sacrifices for each other. Since Boccaccio's tale requires a long period of time and a shift of scene from Athens to Rome, Nardi, in his desire to imitate ancient plays strictly, trimmed down the action to the last twenty-four hours of the crisis over a murder involving

---

99 Apollonio, *Storia,* 2:28-33, describes the theatrical scene in Florence at the start of the sixteenth century.

100 Herrick, *Italian Comedy,* p. 65, dates the play as early as 1497, working from an edition also viewed by the author of this study. But that edition does not indicate the date or place of publication or the printer's name. Sanesi, *La Commedia,* 1:247, upholds the period 1502-12 because of the play's dedication to Lorenzo Strozzi (d. 1482). In 1497, according to Sanesi, Lorenzo Strozzi would have been too young to merit dedication.

both friends. The scene is set at Rome. Events which occurred at Athens are related to Lucio (the Roman friend) and the servant Lico. A new character is added to the tale to make it appear classical: a parasite with an insatiable appetite. Boccaccio's tale of two loyal friends lent itself perfectly to Nardi's attempt to reproduce antiquity. The story in the *Decameron* portrayed a golden past when Octavian ruled Rome. But the spirit of the novella and of Nardi's comedy is far more tied to the Middle Ages than to antiquity.[101] The *Commedia di Amicizia* is the first example of what one historian has labeled the "serious" comedy of sixteenth-century Italy.[102] Sentiment predominates over intrigue. Anguish and suffering are the mood of this work, up to the happy conclusion.

Technically, this play displays a mixture of dramatic devices and meters. Even though it shows the classical five-act division, it recalls the *Sacre Rappresentazioni* in Act III, scene 5, in which two thieves argue over their loot. Such episodes were found in sacred dramas. Usually the meter goes from tercets to octaves, but inserted here and there throughout the comedy are short stanzas of seven-syllable verses or songs with seven- and eleven-syllable lines. This metric variety may have been suggested by the translations of Roman comedies which were used for performances.[103] In his first dramatic composition Nardi wavered amid several literary traditions, but lacked the talent to fuse them. Even the title of his play suggests a morality drama. Artistically, the *Commedia di Amicizia* is inconsistent and uneven.

I Due Felici Rivali

After Soderini's removal from power and the restoration of the Medici family in 1512, the once fervent republican Nardi switched his political and cultural allegiance to the winning party. On February 17, 1513, his second comedy, *I Due Felici Rivali,* was performed at the Medici palace before the leading members of that family and perhaps even Ludovico Ariosto. Allegiance to the new regime made possible such performances.[104]

Once again the dramatist turned to Boccaccio for inspiration. The argument of the comedy carefuly follows *Decameron* V, 5. To make the play

---

101 Two sources for Boccaccio's tale are the exemplum "De integro amico" of Petrus Alphonsus and the twelfth-century French verse novel *Athis et Profilias* of Alexandre de Bernay. See Letterio di Francia, "Alcune novelle del 'Decamerone' illustrate nelle fonti," *Giorn. Stor. d. lett. ital.* 44 (1904): 33-56.
102 Herrick, *Italian Comedy*, p. 165, expresses this opinion.
103 See Sanesi, *La Commedia*, 1:248.
104 For details on the first performance see the introduction to *I due felici rivali, Commedia inedita di Jacopo Nardi*, ed. Alessandro Ferraiolo (Rome, 1901).

seem more classical, Nardi switched the setting from Faenza, where the Boccaccian tale takes place, to Athens. The Boccaccian names of thirteenth-century merchants are replaced with classical ones such as Carino, Callidoro, Tindaro, Cremete. The play is carefully constructed along classical lines, with regular exposition, complication, and resolution. The author even reminds the audience of the care with which he follows classical schemes. Just at the end of the fourth act, after the two rivals have been arrested for their unsuccessful attempt to kidnap the lady they love, the servant Strobilo addresses the audience, declaring that the knot of intrigue has to be loosened before another day passes. The unity of time will thus be maintained.

Just as in the *Commedia di Amicizia,* the author introduces into the Boccaccian plot character types from the ancient Roman Comedy: a parasite and a braggart warrior. Saturio, the parasite, has a sententious manner of quoting ancient writers. As a matter of course he is hungry, although not so voracious as the parasite in Nardi's first comedy. Saturio works within the plot action, for one of the rivals engages him to plan the kidnap attempt.

Nardi created the first braggart warrior of the Italian comic theater—the soldier Trasone. This character is enlisted to fight, if necessary, in the abduction scheme. True to his nature, he orders a retreat at first sight of the enemy's arms. The character of the braggart warrior was first developed in the Greek New Comedy, in which he was modeled on the mercenary soldiers who had returned home wealthy with booty gained in Eastern wars under Macedonian generals. Those officers paraded their riches before the civilian population. They strutted about, blustering about their military records. With their treasures they were able to maintain courtesans, parasites, and a household staff of servants, as well as to give grand banquets. They thought they were the greatest masters in love affairs. But all they accomplished with their opulence was to win the scorn of the Greek civilians.

Comic playwrights reflected that scorn by ridiculing the braggart soldiers in their dramas. Menander satirized them in several of his comedies. Captain Bias of the *Kolax* rose from a poor infantryman to high position thanks to a bribe for betraying a city. His one truly valorous distinction is his capacity to drink wine. The name of the braggart in Menander's *Misoumenos* (*The Hated Man*) is carried down to Nardi: Thrasonides, from *thrasos* for "boldness" or "foolhardiness." Thrasonides is always boasting about his social attainments, claiming he is a favorite of the King of Cyprus. The braggart soldier as he appears in Menander is a ridiculous parvenu.

Although only twenty-six Roman comedies have come down to us, they provide eight examples of the braggart captain. This is all the more remarkable when one considers that during the times of Plautus and Terence, Rome did not employ mercenary soldiers but had its citizen militia. The Romans felt contempt for the mercenary captains, who often sold out the very cities they were hired to defend. Southern Italy had suffered from Pyrrhus and his sons. Roman citizens were to fight and defeat mercenary troops throughout the realms held by Macedonian rulers. Plautus created the most famous example of the boastful military adventurer in the title character Pyrgopolinices (Tower-town-taker) of his *Miles gloriosus*. With his thundering voice this officer proclaims how he has fought in the Field of Weevils under General Battleboomski Mightimercernarimuddlekin (Bumbomachides Clutomistaridysarchides). He claims to have slaughtered seven thousand men in one day. Once he smashed an elephant's leg to amuse himself. Every woman who beholds him falls madly in love with his beauty; his illegitimate children live a thousand years. Helped along in all this highly exaggerated boasting by a parasite, the captain hopes to hold a lofty position in the society of Ephesus, the setting for the comedy. He is a kind of dandy, all perfumed and curled and dressed in a striking military cape. Yet despite all his swaggering, he is taken prisoner by the play's end after he tries to commit adultery. Easily overcome and cudgeled, this "brother of Achilles" shivers with fright when threatened with castration, the usual way of punishing adulterers. Instead he receives a flogging, pays off his tormentors, and expresses his gratitude for the beating. In this comedy Plautus presents the fullest portrait ever made of the braggart, with all his pretension to valorous exploits, high social standing, and success in love affairs. Six other braggart warriors appear in Plautine comedies.

Nardi's chief model for his Trasone is the officer Thraso of Terence's play *Eunuchus*. The Latin playwright does not present so much a swaggering lout as a social boor in his braggart Thraso, whose name is of course derived from Menander just as Nardi was to take it from Terence. Thraso refers only briefly to his battle experiences, for he is really interested in cutting a fine figure amid the elite of Athenian society. He thinks he is a past master at repartee. The truth of the matter is that the parasite Gnatho always finishes his patron's inept remarks. Thraso relates to Gnatho his success at conquering women, but he falls apart before the courtesan Thais. Terence included a scene in this play which was to provide Nardi and other Italian dramatists with an example of the braggart's cowardice when forced into battle. To regain a slave girl he has given to Thais as a gift, Thraso

besieges the courtesan's establishment with a band of his servants armed
with kitchen utensils. The courtesan and a youth outmaneuver him and
get him to retreat. Not a single blow is struck. During this mock battle
Thraso has been issuing commands from the safety of the rear.[105]

Sixteenth-century Italy possessed a modern equivalent of the braggart
warrior. For some time the Italians had been hiring mercenary armies.
Petrarch attacked this practice in his canzone *Italia mia,* since the city-states
which possessed many mercenary soldiers had the greatest number of enemies ready for treachery. Those mercenary troops had become accustomed
to fighting great battles and taking thousands of prisoners without one
man's being left dead on the battlefield. Courage was not necessary to these
soldiers, many of whom lived to be old. Machiavelli was convinced that
the use of mercenary armies was one of the major causes of Italy's enslave-
ment. He advocated the creation of a citizens' army recruited from all
classes. To this end he wrote a treatise on military science, the *Arte della
Guerra.* In the proem to this work Machiavelli describes how the braggart
warrior of his day tried to frighten civilians by growing a fierce beard and
cursing; the modern mercenary soldier considered refined manners to be a
sign of effeminacy. These living examples of the braggart warrior aided
the Italian comic playwright in depicting the swagger and cowardice of the
mercenary captains.[106]

Nardi had a wide background from which to find inspiration for his
Trasone. This braggart speaks in pretentious literary language about his
profession as an assassin. Trasone is to some extent a caricature of the pedant, since he shows himself to be a humanistic braggart. He is writing a
little treatise on the six hundred kinds of death he has invented. Temples,
graveyards, and gardens have been fattened by his work.

There may be another important source for Trasone besides the Roman
Comedy and contemporary military conditions in Italy: the *rufián* (pimp)
Centurio of the Spanish dialogue novel the *Celestina.* This character was
not in the 1499 edition of the novel but appeared in the Seville edition of
1502. Trasone and Centurio have a great deal in common. Both praise their
swords and relate how armorers, surgeons, and gravediggers have paid

---

105 Daniel C. Boughner, *The Braggart in Renaissance Comedy* (Minneapolis, 1954).
passim, provided the material for the preceding history of the braggart warrior as a
dramatic character. The translations of humorous Plautine names are on p. 12.
106 De Amicis *L'Imitazione,* pp. 144-45, talks of the military conditions in Renaissance Italy and quotes from Machiavelli, who in other works like *Il Principe* repeats
his condemnation of the use of mercenaries.

their respects to these weapons for the wealth they have brought them. These two hoodlums are very content with their professions, Centurio with his *oficio* and Trasone with his *mestiero*. Thanks to their work hundreds have perished; they claim that the world is talking about their exploits. Centurio can offer any client 770 forms of death, outdoing his Italian counterpart. Just as Trasone reveals his cowardice by taking to his heels when faced by enemy arms in the abduction scene, Centurio fails to kill a young lover named Calisto as he has been entrusted to do by two of his prostitute clients. Instead he turns the job over to the lame thug Traso (note the name). One of Trasone's confederates in the Italian comedy is lame. Seven years before the production of Nardi's comedy Alphonso Hordognez translated the *Celestina* into Italian. This translation (Rome, 1506) provided still another literary model of the braggart warrior for Italian authors to use. The opulent recruiting officer of the ancient comedies has been reduced to an assassin and pimp, but the old swaggering is still there.[107]

Although written in the traditional five acts with scenes, Nardi's second comic work displays the same variety of meter that distinguished the *Commedia di Amicizia*. The prologue is in seven-syllable verses. Most of the work is in octaves and tercets. But at three points in the comedy some rhyming couplets of seven-syllable verses appear. Boccaccio's tale is here transformed by Nardi into a "serious" comedy in which the two rivals suffer frustrations and express their melancholy. Throughout the play the rival lovers lament their subjection to the God of Love. In the first scene of Act I, Carino blames the blind god not only for his personal unhappiness but also for mankind's general misery. He recognizes that he is a prisoner of

107 Boughner, *The Braggart*, pp. 182-83, is strongly inclined to accept the theory that the *Celestina* influenced Nardi in molding the figure of Trasone. But María Rosa Lida de Malkiel, "El Fanfarrón en el teatro del Renacimiento," *Romance Philology* II, no. 3 (February, 1958): 268-91, does not even accept Boughner's assertion that Centurio is modeled after the braggart warriors of ancient comedy. She feels that Centurio is completely independent of the *Miles gloriosus*. She admits that the figure of the braggart was adapted to the realities of Renaissance life. According to her, classical imitation, imitation from Spanish literature, and satire of Spaniards in Italy all contributed to the creation of the braggart in the Italian Erudite Comedy. She feels that Trasone in Nardi's play has little to do with the title character of the *Miles gloriosus* or with Terence's Thraso except the name. Her judgments are partly based on the following article: Pietro Mazzei, "Per la Fortuna di due opere spagnuole in Italia," *RFE* 9 (1922): 384-86. Mazzei quotes passages from the *Celestina* and *I Due Felici Rivali* in an attempt to demonstrate that Nardi was merely translating Centurio's speeches in writing Trasone's part. Boughner's main contention that Trasone is the first example of the braggart in the Italian Erudite Comedy remains valid despite all attacks even though the character is not a professional warrior.

love. Carino calls himself stupid and foolhardy because he will not flee the evil he sees menacing him. He keeps following the enemy he hates. His reason and his senses are perpetually at war with each other. Carino is like a ship being willfully run onto a rock.

In the second scene of Act III the other rival, Callidoro, indulges in the same kind of self-analysis. His lament is expressed in paradoxes. Love has brought him joy and sorrow, not at different times but at the same moment. The reward granted for his long service to love has caused Callidoro happiness, but his release from the duties of a lover has made him sad. In a flash he swings from one extreme to the other. This taste for amorous self-analysis in paradoxes follows a tradition that is modern and Italian. The type of lament found in Nardi's comedy derives from the Petrarchan tradition, as it was defined by Pietro Bembo's dialogue *Gli Asolani* of 1505. In this dialogue Bembo presented a modified version of Petrarchan love thought expressed in a mildly Neoplatonic spirit. Bembo's interlocutor Perottino discusses the paradoxical situation in which love brings the lover both happiness and utter misery. Instead of ridiculing the Petrarchan love attitude with its *innamorati* swooning from melancholy or joy, Nardi seriously accepts the tradition.[108]

The language in *I Due Felici Rivali* never slips into the obscene, but Nardi's style is heavy and pedantic. The drama moves along slowly, although Boccaccio's novella could have provided a better playwright the opportunity for swift, animated stage motion. Once again Nardi failed to fuse different sources into an artistic whole.

MACHIAVELLI: *La Mandragola*

With Niccolò Machiavelli the Florentine comic theater, and indeed the comedy of all of Italy, reached its highest point artistically and intellectually. He applied to drama the same investigating thought he displays in his letters and political works. In his two major comedies this statesman endeavored to find the same effective truth (*verità effettuale*) about how people really do live, not how they ought to live, that he sought in his masterwork *Il Principe*. In composing the comedies Machiavelli did not forget his mental discipline as a political scientist. Yet he is such an artist that his two important comedies are not merely a series of maxims set in dialogue

---

108 Herrick, *Italian Comedy*. pp. 170-71, compares Nardi's work to Bembo's dialogue and the Petrarchan tradition.

form. Machiavelli was able to study and re-create drama, in both the political and the domestic spheres.[109]

Before reaching the high level of his comedies *La Mandragola* and *Clizia*, this author produced some dramatic exercises. Toward 1504 he composed a work called *Le Maschere* in imitation of Aristophanes' *Clouds*, but unfortunately it is lost. His nephew Giuliano de' Ricci alludes to the reasons why the work was never copied down: "because under fictitious names he works over and badly treats many citizens who were alive in 1504."[110] Sometime afterward, at a date not yet fully determined,[111] Machiavelli translated into prose Terence's *Andria*. Although he stayed close to the Terentian text, Machiavelli rendered the play in a rather colloquial Florentine. His language was much more colorful than that of other translators of the ancient comedies, such as Pandolfo Collenuccio.

Scholars are still debating the date of the composition of *La Mandragola*. Around 1518 a first edition by a minor Florentine printer appeared with the title *Commedia di Callimaco e di Lucrezia*. Several schools of thought exist as to the possible date of the writing. One puts the comedy around 1504, the date mentioned as the time of action for the plot. Another school paces the comedy after 1512 but before 1520, arguing from a passage in the prologue in which the author laments because major tasks are denied to him. He doubtless refers to his exile after 1512 to a farm at San Casciano. But in a sonnet to Giuliano de' Medici the author appeals for release from prison and mentions that he is the writer of a comedy. This sonnet is most likely the product of the author's short imprisonment after the Medici restoration. Although in the sonnet Machiavelli fails to mention the comedy's title, the work could well be *La Mandragola,* since most of the author's contemporaries always referred to that play as "la commedia." If this were the case, the comedy would have been written between 1504 and 1512; and the prologue would have been added to the work sometime afterward during Machiavelli's exile from political life.[112]

109 The recognition that Machiavelli's comedies can be judged along with his political works is due in part to the critical contributions of Bendetto Croce and Luigi Russo. See B. Croce, "Intorno alla commedia italiana del Rinascimento," *La Critica* 28, no. 1 (January, 1930): 5; and L. Russo, *Commedie Fiorentine del Cinquecento* (Florence, 1939), pp. 15-16.

110 Cited in Sanesi, *La Commedia,* 1:253.

111 A date of 1517 is suggested by A. Gerber, *Niccolò Machiavelli: Die Handschriften, Ausgaben und Übersetzungen seiner Werke im 16. und 17. Jahrhundert mit 147 Faksimiles und zahlreichen Auszügen* (Gotha, 1912), p. 9.

112 Text of plays in *Commedie e Belfagor di Niccolò Machiavelli,* ed. L. Russo (Florence, 1943). F. D. Colimore, "The Date of Machiavelli's 'Mandragola,'" *MLN*

Recently the debate has been settled to the satisfaction of most critics. In the third scene of Act III are mentioned an imminent Turkish invasion of Italy and the use of prayers to ward off the attack. In 1504 there was no fear of the Turks, as the peaceful Sultan Bajazeth II had a truce with the Venetians. But early in 1518 the fear of Turkish invasion became wide-spread in Italy because of the military successes of Sultan Selim, and the Pope asked that special prayers be said. The scene in the third act would certainly seem to indicate composition in 1518.[113]

Machiavelli wrote *La Mandragola* for one of the amateur acting groups that were active in Florence. The work may have been first read in the Orti Oricellari. Around 1520 the members of the Campagnia della Cazzuola acted out the comedy in Florence, with sets by Andrea del Sarto and Aristotele da San Gallo. Domenico Barlacchi, Florentine municipal herald, was the chief actor.[114]

---

55 no. 7 (November, 1940): 526-28, upholds the 1504-12 writing. But Sanesi, *La Commedia*, 1:254-55, places the comedy after 1513. Borlenghi, *Commedie del Cinquecento*, 1:23, puts it at 1518. As a possible solution to this rather unclear problem, it should be kept in mind that Renaissance playwrights often added prologues to plays long after the original composition. Just consider the double prologues for some of Ariosto's comedies.

113 Roberto Ridolfi, *The Life of Niccolò Machiavelli*, trans. Cecil Grayson (Chicago, 1963), pp. 301-3, n. 19, has established 1518 as the definitive date. Alessandro Parronchi, "La Prima Rappresentazione della 'Mandragola,'" *La Bibliofilia* 64, no. 1 (1962): 37-86, accepted Ridolfi's findings and attempts to demonstrate that the *Mandragola* was written for performance at the Palazzo Medici in Florence early in September of 1518 as part of the festivities honoring the return of Lorenzo de' Medici, Duke of Urbino, from France with his wife Madeleine de la Tour d'Auvergne. But Ridolfi, "Composizione, Rappresentazione, e Prima Edizione della 'Mandragola,'" *La Bibliofilia* 64, no. 3 (1962): 285-94, places the period of composition between the middle of January and the middle of February 1518 because of the references to the wintry season and the short days in the comedy as well as the fact that plays were usually written for performance during the carnival season; the *Mandragola* might have been given around February the sixteenth (the last day of carnival) for Lorenzo, who was still a bachelor. Ridolfi has now published a definitive edition of the *Mandragola* (Florence, 1965); in the preface, pp. 7-50, the editor discusses the recent finding of a manuscript copy of the play in the Laurentian Library's Rediano Codex 129, hidden along with copies of works by Lorenzo il Magnifico. The codex displays the haste and mechanical inaccuracies of the copyist; it dates from 1519 and mentions the author's name, which is not to be found in the Florentine printed edition. Rather surprisingly, Ridolfi bases his edition on the Florentine printed version and uses the Rediano codex merely to make emendations. He feels that the spelling in the codex differs too greatly from Machiavelli's own. Roberto Tissoni, "Per una nuova edizione della *Mandragola* del Machiavelli," *Giorn. Stor. d. lett. ital.* 143, no. 442 (1966): 241-58, expresses astonishment at Ridolfi's reliance on the printed version and states that the Rediano codex will prove not only to offer a more correct version of the play but a substantially different edition.

114 Details of early performance in Borlenghi, *Commedie del Cinquecento*, 1:23.

A prologue in the canzone form precedes the comedy. The actor who reads it greets the audience and announces that this comedy deals with a new event which has occurred recently in Florence. Another time the setting could be Rome or Pisa. Machiavelli chose to confront the contemporary world in his comedy, and did not select an ancient Greek setting like Ariosto in *La Cassaria* or Nardi in *I Due Felici Rivali*. The scene the public square by the Via dello Amore. Although the classical unity of place is maintained, the setting is the world that was known to the author. After pointing out the homes of the leading characters, the actor pauses to make a sad comment:

> E se questa materia non è degna
> per esser pur leggieri,
> d'un uom che voglia parer saggio e grave,
> scusatelo con questa, che s'ingegna
> con questi van pensieri
> fare el suo tristo tempo più suave,
> perch'altrove non have
> dove voltare el viso;
> ché gli è stato interciso
> monstrar con altre imprese altra virtue
> non sendo premo alle fatiche sue.[115]

The attitude expressed here on the levity of comic subjects reminds one of the first prologue of Ariosto's *Lena*. Machiavelli's prologue grows increasingly bitter as it continues, but the author is ready to receive harsh criticism and knows how to return it. The argument is not given.

This prose comedy follows the classical pattern. The author adheres strictly to the three unities. The time is just less than twenty-four hours. Some of the characters, especially the parasite Ligurio and the cunning priest Frate Timoteo, refer to the passing of the hours. Just after the nocturnal kidnapping of a supposedly drunk youth on the streets, Frate Timoteo addresses the audience in this way: "E voi, spettatori, non ci appuntate; perché in queste notte non ci dormirà persona, sì che gli Atti non sono in-

---

115 "And if this material is not worthy
   of a man who wishes to appear sage and serious,
   because it is frivolous;
   pardon him, for he is endeavoring
   to make his sad hours more pleasant
   with these empty thoughts,
   since he has no where else
   to look; for he has been forbidden
   to display other abilities with different enterprises,
   there being no other reward for his efforts."

terrotti dal tempo" (Act IV, sc. 10).[116] Machiavelli displays a remarkable skill in re-creating the classical structure. There is no looseness in *La Mandragola;* the play is unified with transition's between scenes and between acts.[117] Just before the prologue and between the acts are brief songs which act as intermezzos and allude to the phase of the drama reached in each act; at the opening of the play is a scene in which nymphs and shepherds sing a *carpe diem* theme; between the first and second acts, a song on the power of love; later, one on the stupidity of the lawyer Messer Nicia Calfucci; then a song on the force of deception; finally an intermezzo on Night as the friend of lovers. The same meter and stanza form (eleven- and seven-syllable verses) is used in these intermezzos as in the prologue. The author avoided the mistake made by several Italian comic dramatists who wrote long and involved intermezzos that often had nothing to do with the plot of the main comedy.[118]

Some folk legends enter into Machiavelli's plot, which is not derived from any particular ancient comedy or modern novella. The two major legends are those of the poisoner girl and of the medicinal virtues of the mandrake plant. An Arabian book of the twelfth century, the *Secretum secretorum*, tells of a girl who was nourished all her life on the venom of extremely poisonous serpents. Coming to adulthood, this beautiful girl was able to poison males in several different ways, but especially in the sexual act. This tale of the poisoner girl came down in several Italian renderings. The mandrake plant, which lends the title to the comedy, has an even longer history. Its powers are mentioned in the *Physiologus* text of the Dark Ages. It was supposed to be both a narcotic and an aphrodisiac; the person who possessed the mandrake plant could win anyone's love.

116 "And you, spectators, don't complain to us; for nobody is going to sleep tonight because the action will be continuous."

117 The unities in the *Mandragola* are discussed in these articles: Charles Singleton, "Machiavelli and the Spirit of Comedy," *MLN* 57 no. 7 (November, 1942): 585-92; Edwin J. Webber, "The Dramatic Unities in the Mandragola," *Italica* 33, no. 1 (March, 1956): 20-21. The Singleton article is particularly shallow. Ridolfi, "Composizione, Rappresentazione," pp. 291-92, talks about Machiavelli's care in having Frate Timoteo address the audience about the necessity of not interrupting the temporal sequence of the acts; even though Machiavelli was writing before the period of Aristotelian dogmatism over the unities, he followed the model of ancient comedies to write a structurally perfect classical play.

118 These canzoni were written for a performance of the play in Faenza, which failed to take place in 1526. Guicciardini, who was then president of Romagna, had encouraged the production. Ridolfi's edition places the canzoni in an appendix since he does not consider them a true part of the drama.

The plant could control spirits and genies: whoever owned the mandrake was protected from demons and from illnesses caused by Satan. Thieves and assassins would not dare come near the mandrake plant, since anyone who tried to uproot it would surely die. To pull it up, safely, it was necessary to tie a hungry dog to the plant and then excite the animal with a piece of bread. Important in *La Mandragola* is the plant's power to free women from sterility; its roots were supposed to have a human shape. Thus in Machiavelli's play Messer Nicia believed the story of the false Dr. Callimaco about the mandrake potion which would make the lawyer's wife Lucrezia fertile and about how the first man who slept with her might die from poisoning. Machiavelli had this background of popular superstitions, and he used it to advance Callimaco's love intrigue.[119]

Many of the characters of *La Mandragola* can be labeled as types. But the author gives his characters a history. He places them in the Florentine society of his times. Allusions to the political events of the period provide the comedy with a contemporary atmosphere. Messer Nicia is the new Renaissance type of the pedantic doctor of laws. Despite all of his book learning Nicia is described by Callimaco as "el più semplice e el più sciocco omo di Firenze" ("the most simple and stupid man in Florence," Act I, sc. 1). He is the object of a trick (*beffa*) that Ligurio and Callimaco play with the scheme of the mandrake plant. This use of trickery relates Nicia to an old novellistic tradition. He has a rather Boccaccian air about him, not that of the intelligent hero who triumphs through his wits but that of a fool who credits himself with great intelligence. Nicia is closest to Boccaccio's Calandrino (*Decameron* VIII, 3 and 6; IX, 3 and 5). Neither character is an absolute simpleton, although both are simpletons who think themselves cunning and witty. Theirs is a rather ambitious stupidity; they become comic especially when they fall into the traps that truly cunning persons set for them. Nicia and Calandrino are both proud of their sex appeal. Calandrino lets a prostitute (*Decameron* IX, 5) make a fool of him because he thinks she has fallen in love with him. When asked if he is impotent, Nicia laughs and declares that he is "the most virile and robust man" in Florence.[120]

The lawyer believes he is a man of the world. Callimaco's first scheme

119 Popular legends behind the play are treated by A. Borgognoni, "Ancora della 'Mandragola,'" *Domenica Letteraria*, December 17, 1882.
120 Russo, *Commedie Fiorentine*, pp. 31-32, compares Calandrino and Nicia at length. Compare Nicia's tasting bitter aloes (Act IV, sc. 9) to the pills Calandrino is fed in *Decameron* VIII, 6.

was to get the parasite Ligurio to persuade Messer Nicia to go in May to a warm springs area where Lucrezia could receive hot-bath treatments for her supposed sterility. The young man hoped to meet her there and overcome her resistance. Seeing that the lawyer was hesitant about leaving town, Ligurio made fun of him by pointing out that Nicia was not accustomed to losing sight of the cupola of Florence's cathedral. The lawyer was offended and hastened to prove what a great traveler he had been: "Tu erri! Quando io ero più giovane, io sono stato molto randagio. E non si fece mai la fiera a Prato, che io non vi andassi, e non ci è castel veruno all'intorno, dove io non sia stato: e ti vo' dire più là: io sono stato a Pisa e a Livorno, oh, va!" (Act I, sc. 2).[121] Prato is just a few miles from Florence. Pisa and Leghorn are both in Tuscany. Nicia swells with his importance as a traveler. Ligurio leads him on and asks if the sea at Leghorn is much greater in size than the river Arno. The lawyer laughs and answers in a way meant to show what a Christopher Columbus he is: "Che Arno? Egli è per quattro volte, per più di sei, per più di sette, mi farai dire: e non si vede se non acqua, acqua, acqua."[122] Nicia's expressive manner of speaking about his travels gives one the impression of distant countries; the repeating of *acqua* three times suggests an unending stretch of ocean. But on realizing how narrowly circumscribed his travels are, one truly understands what a comic figure Nicia is.

Like every pedant Nicia adores the Latin language. Knowing that Callimaco has studied in Paris, Ligurio instructs the youth to display his Latin before the lawyer so as to be convincing in his pose as a physician. Callimaco succeeds in outlatinizing the lawyer (Act II, sc. 2), who is blindly devoted to Latin rhetoric. In his use of Italian, or rather his native Florentine, this doctor of laws also reveals his inner emptiness. He speaks a special idiotic language, employing idiomatic expressions and proverbs to show off his erudition. Along with the proverbs Nicia mixes many extremely obscene words. He is a lawyer who has "cacato le curatelle per imparare due hac.' He is always spouting proverbs like: "Ho più fede in voi che gli Ungheri nelle spade" ("I have more faith in you than Hungarians have in their swords"); or "Come disse la botte all'erpice" ("As the barrel said to the harrow"). A person who frequently uses proverbs could be very wise, but Ni-

121 "You're wrong. When I was young, I had a wanderlust. Whenever a fair was held in Prato, I went there; and there isn't a castle in the area that I haven't visited. And I'll tell you something more: I've been to Pisa and Leghorn. There now!"
122 "Than the Arno? It's four times—more than six—I might even say more than seven times greater; all you can see is water, water, water."

cia's proverbs are trite and silly. Along with his obscenities, Nicia employs childish words like *bomba* (home base). Machiavelli creates character portrayals through language.[123]

But the lawyer is not such an idiot that he never offers any resistance to those who are playing tricks on him. When Callimaco suggests that Nicia place some other male with Lucrezia to draw away the mandrake's poison, the lawyer flatly states that he does not want to make his wife a harlot and himself a cuckold. His revolt ends when Callimaco says that the king of France and many French nobles have agreed to that treatment so their wives could conceive. Who is Messer Nicia beside the sovereign of France? In agreeing to make himself a cuckold, Nicia is mainly concerned that the Florentine Council of Eight not learn of his actions. Later Nicia experiences a few moments of remorse because the kidnapped youth will have to pay for his one night of pleasure with his life. Nicia recognizes his part in a murder plot, but Ligurio quickly calms these feelings of remorse. Messer Nicia's feelings may not go very deep, like his intelligence, but Machiavelli has not presented him as a mere puppet that others manipulate.[124]

Whereas Nicia speaks in an idiotic and obscene way, Callimaco uses an elegant language. This youth is like the princely figure the author studies in his most famous political work. The youth possesses the *virtù*, understood here as active ability, with which to achieve his goals. Callimaco is an ardent lover; he is neither a swooning Petrarchan lover nor a cynical conqueror of women. He was ten and orphaned when his guardians sent him to Paris. At the age of twenty, in 1494, Callimaco decided to remain in France, since Italy was just beginning the period of being invaded by foreign nations; he needed security and found it in France. He created his own little state, a happy position where he divided his time between studies, business, and amusements. But Fortune (the continual enemy of man's peace) caused him to hear of Lucrezia's beauty and to return to his native city.

Callimaco thinks by the same analytical process that Machiavelli uses in *Il Principe*. He studies the situation in which he finds himself. The youth enumerates the various obstacles to his winning Lucrezia's love and counters them with the factors to his advantage. Like one of the rulers studied in *Il Principe*, Callimaco takes Ligurio as his ally. But he is not always a lucid calculator; at times a desperate feeling sweeps him along:

123 In his edition of the play Ridolfi cites, pp. 205-6, a letter by Machiavelli to Guicciardini where the dramatist explains some of the traditional proverbs.
124 Croce, "Intorno alla Commedia," p. 7, analyzes Nicia's sentiments.

Ma come ho a fare? Che partito ho a pigliare? Dove mi ho
a volgere? A me bisogna tentare qualcosa, sia grande, sia
pericolosa, sia dannosa, sia infame. Meglio è morire che
vivere così. Se io potessi dormire la notte, se io potessi
mangiare, se io potessi conversare, se io potessi pigliare
piacere di cosa veruna, io sarei più paziente ad aspettare el
tempo; ma qui non c'è rimedio; e se io non son tenuto in
isperanza da qualche partito, io mi morrò in ogni modo; e
veggendo di avere a morire, non sono per temere cosa alcuna,
ma per pigliare qualche partito bestiale, crudo, nefando.[125]
(Act I, sc. 3)

In moments of extreme desperation, when he does not listen to the voice of
reason, Callimaco is restrained only by Ligurio, his rational counselor.
This youth is similar to two characters in the *Decameron* who became
fired with passion on merely hearing of a woman's loveliness. In *Decameron* I, 5, the French king Philippe le Borgne learns that the Marchioness
of Monferrato is renowned as the fairest lady in his realm. On his way to a
crusade the monarch rushes to visit the lady and makes an unsuccessful attempt to seduce her. Callimaco's situation is even closer to that of young
Lodovico in *Decameron* VIII, 7, already recalled in connection with *I Suppositi*. Like Callimaco, Lodovico is a Florentine youth living in France.
Hearing praise about Madonna Beatrice of Bologna, Lodovico travels to
that city and he succeeds in winning the lady's love.[126]

Callimaco sometimes attempts to check the force of his passion. In a
soliloquy (Act IV, sc. 1) he calls himself mad. Once he has fulfilled his
aim, will it be worth all his efforts and suffering? The rational element is
strong enough that he sees himself waver from hope to despair. Callimaco
tries to talk himself out of his passion:

Non sai tu quanto poco bene si truova nelle cose che
l'uomo desidera, rispetto a quelle che l'uomo ha
presupposte trovarvi? Da l'altro canto, el peggio che
te ne va è morire e andarne in inferno; e' son morti
tanti degli altri! e sono in inferno tanti uomini da
bene! Ha'ti tu a vergognare d'andarvi tu? Volgi el
viso alla sorte; fuggi el male, e, non lo potendo

---

125 "But what can I do? What course must I take? Where can I turn? I have to try
something, whether it's grandiose, dangerous, harmful, or scandalous. It's better to
die than to live this way. If I could sleep at night, if I could hold a conversation, if I
could enjoy anything—then I would be patient and bide my time. But there's no
remedy here; and if I lose all hope, I'll die in any case. And since I have to die, I won't
fear anything, but I'll take a course of action that will be bestial, violent, criminal."
126 Sanesi, *La Commedia,* 1:260, mentions the ties with the novella tradition.

fuggire, sopportalo como uomo; non ti prosternere, non
ti invilire comme una donna.[127]

This willingness to go to hell and join the worthy persons already there
brings to mind Aucassin's heretical answer to the viscount in *Aucassin et
Nicolette.* Callimaco becomes comical through the excess of his passion.
His physical composure is so upset that he trembles. He feels on the brink
of suicide.

The youth's actions are not dictated by a passing whim for sensual enjoyment. In Act V, scene 4, Callimaco relates to Ligurio that the pleasure
he first experienced in possessing Lucrezia did not seem good to him. He
was ill at ease until he revealed himself and captured her love. The joy of
conquest meant nothing to him unless the physical pleasure was accompanied by her affection. Callimaco promised to marry her if Messer Nicia
should ever die; he is no cynical scoundrel out to make cuckolds of husbands. Compare him with the lover Filetero of Publio Filippo Mantovano's
Formicone, who is an accomplished adulterer out to gratify his sensual
urgings. Callimaco enjoys a complete victory. Nicia feels indebted to him
(as he really is) for seeing to it that the lawyer will have an heir. Nicia
hands the youth a key so he can visit his ground-floor room as often as he
likes. Callimaco's *virtù* has triumphed fully, since the love affair will continue. Machiavelli's Callimaco is far from being a cardboard lover. He remains faithful to his passion throughout the play.[128]

Lucrezia says very little. Knowledge about her is generally gained from
other characters. Her name is ironic, as it recalls the Roman matron Lucre-
tia. Machiavelli does not emphasize the comparison, since Nicia is not de-
described as the comic Renaissance equivalent of Collatinus. She is a rather
rigid and fanatic character, ready to go from one extreme to the other. Lucrezia is married to a man who is old but not elderly; their relationship
could not have brought much sensual pleasure. Yet she was never disposed

---

127 "Don't you know how little profit one finds in the things that he desires compared to what he expected to find? On the other hand, the worst that can happen to
you is to die and go to Hell; so many persons have already died! So many worthy
persons have gone to Hell! Are you ashamed of following their example? Look fortune straight in the eyes; avoid trouble, and, if you can't avoid it; face it like a man.
Don't grovel, don't shame yourself by acting like a woman."
128 Leo Strauss, *Thoughts on Machiavelli* (Glencoe, Ill., 1958), pp. 284-86, points
out that in matters of state and love men must be made to "operate well." In the
Mandragola the triumph of forbidden love is the parallel of the political triumph of
forbidden desires to oppress or rule. Callimaco's natural good comes first but coincides with the common good of all parties concerned. Strauss does not divorce the
comedy's content from the political content of Machiavelli's treatises.

to be unfaithful to her husband. Nicia understands his wife's rigid nature and knows how difficult it will be to persuade her to accept Callimaco's idea of giving herself to a stranger; he describes (Act II, sc. 6) how his wife spends hours kneeling and saying her prayers in spite of great cold. She is not an easy, passive type.

Frate Timoteo also recognized the difficulties involved in making Lucrezia agree to lie with a kidnapped youth. Knowing that she was "savia e buona," he hoped nevertheless to overcome her objections by playing on her feminine nature. In her first stage appearance, going with her mother to see the priest, Lucrezia is horrified that her husband wants her to take such action because of his desire for a child. Her two main objections are these:

> Ma di tutte le cose che si son tentate, questa mi pare
> la più strana, di avere a sottomettere el corpo mio a
> questo vituperio, ad essere cagione che un uomo muoia per
> vituperarmi; che non crederrei, se io fussi sola rimasa
> nel mondo, e da me avessi a resurgere l'umana natura, che
> mi fussi simile partito concesso. [129]
>
> (Act III, sc. 10)

The priest attempts to convince her to obey her husband by arguing that she will be released from any sin and will provide for the maximum good. Lucrezia yields to his casuistry but feels that she will not live until the following day. Even while her husband puts her to bed, after she has taken the mandrake potion, she keeps on objecting to the scheme.[130]

Lucrezia occupies a solitary position between those who desire the birth of a child and the conspirators who want to deliver her over to Callimaco. Her decision to give herself willingly to Callimaco is like a fanatic's swinging from one position to the opposite. Callimaco reports to Ligurio (Act V,

---

129 "But of all the things that have been tried, this seems the strangest to me. That I have to subject my body to this outrage and that a man should die for committing the outrage against me. For if I were the only woman left on the earth and the whole human race had to be reborn from me, there would be no justification for my taking this course of action."

130 Giulio Levi, "Difesa di Madonna Lucrezia," *Giorn. Stor. d. lett. ital.* 86 (1925): 105-12, describes her resistance. Readers might object to our character analysis of Lucrezia as being fanatical. She reminds us of Molière's Orgon in *Tartuffe*, switching from one extreme action to the opposite. It is true that her modesty and honesty would seem fanatical to the vitiated society in which she lives. Machiavelli would ironically find fault with the corrupt society and not with her; nevertheless, hers is a rather severe character.

sc. 4) the speech she made to him after he had revealed his identity and professed his love for her:

> Poi che l'astuzia tua, la sciocchezza del mio marito la
> semplicità di mia madre e la tristizia del mio confessore
> mi hanno condotta a fare quello che mai per me medesima
> arei fatto, io voglio iudicare che e' venga da una celeste
> disposizione che abbi voluto così, e non sono sufficiente a
> recusare quello che'l cielo vuole che io accetti. Però io ti
> prendo per signore, padrone, guida; tu mio padre, tu mio
> defensore, e tu voglio che sia ogni mio bene; e, quello che'l
> mio marito ha voluto per una sera, voglio ch'egli abbia
> sempre. . . .[131]

Lucrezia realized that she had been tricked. Her husband and mother had betrayed her, but not out of evil intent; the friar had used her for his personal gain. But she saw in Callimaco one who had labored to win her love. Lucrezia would never have sought sensual satisfaction from a stranger, but her acceptance of Callimaco as a lover implies her experiencing sexual pleasure for the first time.

Precedent for this type of conversion can be found in various novelle, especially those of Boccaccio. *Decameron* III, 6, is an outstanding example. There the Neapolitan noble Ricciardo Minutolo makes several fruitless entreaties for the love of Catella, wife of Filippello Fighinolfi. Knowing how jealous Catella is about her husband, Ricciardo tells her that Filippello has arranged an assignation in a "bagnio" with Ricciardo's wife. Catella angrily goes to the meeting in place of Ricciardo's wife and is intimate with the man she believes to be her husband. The man is, of course, Ricciardo. On learning his identity, Catella feels outraged and swears to take vengeance, but Ricciardo keeps entreating her with sweet words and turns her rigor into a love-liking for him. Catella, like Lucrezia, commits adultery involuntarily, as the victim of a ruse. But both women adjust themselves to the fait accompli and do not deny themselves the chance for more enjoyable amorous relations.[132]

---

131 "Since your cunning, my husband's stupidity, my mother's gullibility, and my confessor's wickedness have led me to commit what I would never have done on my own, I must judge that divine will has brought this about; and since I should not oppose what Heaven desires, I give in. Therefore I take you for lord, master, guide; you will be my father, my defender; and I want you to be everything for me; and what my husband wanted for a single night, I want him to have forever. . . ."
132 Pellizzaro, *Novellistica*, p. 90, cites the Boccaccian novella.

There is no hypocrisy in a direct creature like Lucrezia. When she decides to maintain her relationship with Callimaco, part of her motivation is a desire for revenge on her husband and the others who forced her to lie with a stranger. But in accepting Callimaco she is rising to a new *virtù* understood as the intelligent way of reacting to new circumstances instead of the conventional idea of virtue. Lucrezia would have been stupid to lose the chance for happiness with a loving and handsome man. Her speech to him proclaims an adulterous faith.[133]

It is not only in connection with the plot to win over Lucrezia that anticlerical satire appears. A neighbor once told Lucrezia that she would conceive if she fulfilled a vow to hear morning mass forty times at a certain church. She attempted to fulfill that vow, but a friar kept after her with obvious erotic intentions. She was freed from the vow by special dispensation. Nicia deplores how men who ought to set good examples behave like that friar.

Ligurio makes a sharp stab against the morality of convents when he tests Frate Timoteo to see if the friar will help Callimaco. The parasite says (Act III, sc. 4) that Nicia and another worthy citizen are ready to contribute several hundred ducats to charity if the priest will aid them in a delicate matter. According to Ligurio's fiction Nicia's nephew went to France on business and left his daughter in a convent for safekeeping. But the following occurred: ". . . o per straccurataggine delle monache o per cervellinaggine dela fanciulla, la si truova gravida di quattro mesi; di modo che, se non ci si ripara con prudenzia, el dottore, le monache, la fanciulla, . . . la casa de' Calfucci è vituperata. . . ."[134] Ligurio pretends he wants the friar to persuade the convent's abbess to let the girl have an abortion. Satiric attacks on convents and monasteries where vows of virginity were broken are frequent in novella collections, as in *Decameron* III, 1, in which Masetto da Lamporecchio claims to be mute in order to be hired as the gardener of a convent. He becomes the lover of all the nuns, including the abbess.[135] Machiavelli was not alone in finding fault with the moral life of convents.

<hr>

133 Apollonio, *Storia,* 2:72, speaks of her adulterous rebellion. Parronchi, "Prima Rappresentazione," pp. 56-62, suggests that the *Mandragola* is a political allegory where Lucrezia represents Florence; Callimaco is Duke Lorenzo; and Nicia is the ill-fated gonfaloniere Soderini; he calls the play (p. 80) an "allegoria del ritorno dei Medici in Firenze."
134 ". . . either because of the nuns' carelessness or because of the girl's stupidity, she is four months pregnant; so that, if the situation is not handled prudently; the lawyer, the nuns, the girl, . . . the Calfucci household will be disgraced. . . ."
135 Pellizzaro, *Novellistica,* p. 88, mentions the novella in the Decameron.

Scholars are still arguing over Frate Timoteo's character. Some consider him a good devil. One finds him a crude cynic, an imposter like Molière's Tartuffe. Another calls him an arch-hypocrite without any religious sense.[136] Machiavelli makes no outright polemic against him. As a result the friar is an ambiguous figure. Frate Timoteo has a coherent moral character with two goals: to maintain his reputation as an upright clergyman; to appease his greed for money. Before others, the friar always preserves his dignity. He first appears in Act III, scene 3 (mentioned above as providing the best clue to the play's date), in which he consoles an unnamed widow, assuring the lady that her husband is probably in Purgatory, since God's clemency is great if the sinner repents. The friar is the perfect priest in the way he answers the widow. When Ligurio and Nicia approach him with their propositions, Frate Timoteo strains to hold onto his sanctity. His answers and questions are brief phrases of two or three words so that he will not betray himself. He lets Ligurio do the talking and agrees to aid in the abortion scheme only because he can do some work of good with the money promised in Nicia's name.

Only in his soliloquies does this seemingly impeccable friar reveal himself. He realizes (Act III, sc. 9) that Ligurio has ensnared him with the story about the pregnant girl. Still, he intends to profit now that he has learned from the parasite what Callimaco's true intentions are. Everything must remain secret because the friar does not wish to see his reputation ruined. Frate Timoteo employs a pre-Jesuitic casuistry (Act III, sc. 11) to convince Lucrezia to lie with a stranger. On greeting Lucrezia and her mother he declares that he has been studying his books for hours to find if there are any good factors in favor of the proposed action. When Lucrezia asks him if he is bantering or speaking seriously, the friar acts offended and answers that she should know what kind of man he is. He enumerates the various factors in her case: although a man may die from lying with her, it is certain that she will be able to bear a child. When there is a choice between a certain good (the birth of a child) and an uncertain evil (the man's death), as a general rule the certain good must be sought. The friar is scrupulously correct in seeking the greatest good. Knowing that Lucrezia does not wish to sin, Frate Timoteo points out that the act of being intimate with a stranger is not a sin since only Lucrezia's body is involved. One sins

---

136 Francesco De Sanctis, *Storia della Letteratura Italiana*, ed. Niccolò Gallo (Turin, 1958), 2:595-604, finds Frate Timoteo cynical. Arturo Graf, *Studi Drammatici* (Turin, 1878), pp. 151 f., calls him a good devil. Sanesi, *La Commedia*, 1:264, considers him as deprived of every moral sense.

with the will, not with the body, which is merely the instrument of the will. This fine distinction between body and soul is typical of many clergymen who wished to twist religious doctrine to their own ends. Boccaccio also tells, in *Decameron* III, 8, of an abbot who was truly a saint except in regard to women. The abbot promised to cure a lady's husband of jealousy if she would love him. When she reproved him for not behaving like a holy man, the abbot replied that holiness dwelt in the soul and he was merely asking her to commit a sin of the body. Although Frate Timoteo has no lecherous intentions of his own, he makes a similar argument so Lucrezia will remain assured about the salvation of her soul.[137]

To prove that he has been studying her problem in the sacred texts, the friar mentions to Lucrezia the story of Lot's daughters, who thought they were alone in the world and were intimate with their father to continue the human race. Since their intention was good, they did not sin. Making his final supreme effort, Frate Timoteo swears on his *petto sacrato* that Lucrezia will be committing a sin no worse than eating meat on Fridays, a sin easily washed away with holy water. The priest actually takes the name of his holy profession and uses it to persuade Lucrezia to commit an adulterous act.

This friar has his twinges of conscience, knowing that his involvement in the affair could ruin his reputation. His strongest doubts are expressed in a soliloquy in Act IV, scene 6. He is ready to join in the kidnap plot, having falsified his identity by disguising himself as Callimaco to remove any of Nicia's suspicions. The friar comments on how bad company will lead one to the gallows; his one fault was in being too good and too easy rather than in being bad. He did not seek trouble; it came to him: "Dio sa che io non pensavo ad iniurare persona, stavomi nella mia cella, dicevo il mio ufizio, intrattenevo e' mia devoti, capitommi inanzi questo diavolo di Ligurio, che mi fece intignere el dito in uno errore, donde io vi ho messo el braccio, e tutta la persona, e non so ancora dove io m'abbia a capitare . . . ."[138] Frate Timoteo does recognize that he has erred; at most he is an immoral figure, but not amoral. This priest is not actively sinful. When the opportunity comes for gain by sinful means, he responds, as long as scandal can be avoided; but Frate Timoteo is not a diabolical figure who loves sin as a category of life.

---

137 Pellizzaro, *Novellistica,* pp. 88-89, draws the novellistic parallel.
138 "God knows that I had no intention of harming anyone; I was in my cell, saying my office; I took care of the devout parishioners. Then this devil of Ligurio unexpectedly came to me; he made me dip first a finger, then an arm, and finally my whole body into trouble—and I don't know where I'll end up. . . ."

This soliloquy also points out one of the priest's chief traits: his devotion to the formal aspects of religion. In one respect he is profoundly devout. The first scene of Act V is his most revealing soliloquy. To pass the night when the lovers are together, he has been saying his morning prayers, reading a saint's life, lighting a lamp in the church, changing a veil on the miracle-working image of the Madonna. Frate Timoteo places emphasis on the exteriority of religion, living for rites and practices. He is disgusted that the other friars fail to keep clean veils on the Madonna. Once there were five hundred images in the church, but now there are only twenty. Public support is lacking because the friars have failed to maintain their reputation. In his opinion, the religion of his times is decadent: "Noi vi solavàmo ogni sera doppo la compieta andare a processione, e farvi cantare ogni sabato le laude. Botavànci noi sempre quivi, perché vi si vedessi gli uomini e le donne a botarvisi. Ora non si fa nulla di queste cose, e po' ci maravigliamo se le cose vanno fredde! Oh, quanto poco cervello é in questi mia frati!"[139] The priest worries less about causing a virtuous wife to commit adultery than about going to processions, attending to images, and saying prayers.[140]

Although he is tricked by Ligurio to aid Callimaco, Frate Timoteo is one of the comedy's victors. He overhears Nicia talking with Ligurio and realizes that the danger is past. The friar rushes off to meet the others at the church, where he declares: "my merchandise will be more valuable." The church is his place of business; and now that his reputation is left intact, he stands to make a great profit. It is Frate Timoteo who makes the comedy's envoi. All the principal characters are going to attend church, where he will say prayers. The friar can now be happy, as he is performing his favorite task, religious ceremonies.[141]

There is one person who can outwit Frate Timoteo: Ligurio, the parasite and master of intrigue. Machiavelli rose above the schematic character type in portraying him. Although Callimaco once mentions the parasite's gluttony, Ligurio himself never refers to his hunger. He is ruthlessly efficient, but is loyal where his advantage lies. This onetime marriage broker is the real plotter of the comedy. Ligurio, in his close relationship to Calli-

139 "We used to go in procession every evening after compline, and have lauds sung every Saturday. We always made our own *ex votos,* to encourage men and women to follow our example. Now none of these things are done, and we are astonished if affairs are going along so cold! Oh, how stupid my brother monks are!"
140 Sanesi, *La Commedia,* 1:264-65, sees this scene as proof of the priest's lack of any religious sense. For him the priest has a twisted mind. Sanesi states that Machiavelli surpasses Dante and Boccaccio at depicting wicked clergymen. Timoteo applies his own specious reason and logic to himself as well as to others; herein lies Machiavelli's art.
141 Russo, *Commedie Fiorentine,* pp. 44-56, talks of the priest's coherent character.

maco, resembles the cunning servant of ancient Roman comedies. The youth's servant Siro is a very pale figure beside this parasite. It is Ligurio who rejects the plan to have Nicia go to the hot baths in May. Instead he dreams up the mandrake scheme. If Callimaco can be thought of as a princely figure, then Ligurio ought to be considered his prime minister, who restrains the youth's emotional outbursts. This parasite understands Nicia and the friar perfectly. Just before approaching the priest about convincing Lucrezia to lie with a stranger, Ligurio ironically informs Nicia that he, Ligurio, will be the sole negotiator. In the scene where he tests the priest with the story of the pregnant girl, Ligurio displays almost as much skill at casuistry as the friar, presenting a logical argument on how Frate Timoteo can do good by assisting in the abortion and thus saving the honor of a family and a convent.

This parasite actually defeats Frate Timoteo in the duel of wits. Ligurio is careful to advise Callimaco to satisfy the priest only with ducats and not sweet prayers. As long as the friar fulfills his part of their bargain, Ligurio wants to keep good faith. This parasite is not a thorough scoundrel.[142] Ligurio becomes almost a military commander in Act IV, scene 9, as he assembles his forces to make the kidnapping: "Io voglio essere el capitano, e ordinare l'esercito per la giornata. Al destro corno sia preposto Callimaco, al sinistro io, intra le due corna starà qui el dottore, Siro fia retroguardo, per dare susidio a quella banda che inclinassi. El nome sia San Cucù."[143] Along with the military terms Ligurio mentions horns and San Cucù (whom he explains to Nicia as the most honored saint in France) to point out the lawyer's being made a cuckold. The irony of Ligurio's relation with Nicia is that the parasite does act like a friend by helping the lawyer to have an heir. All principal characters see their wishes fulfilled, thanks to Ligurio's skill at intrigue.[144]

142 But De Sanctis, *Storia,* 2:599, finds Ligurio the worst (morally) character ever created by Machiavelli.
143 "I want to be captain and command the army for the campaign. Let Callimaco take the right horn, I'll handle the left, between the two horns will be the lawyer. Siro will be the rearguard to aid whatever side may waver. The password will be Saint Cuckoo."
144 Theodore Sumberg, " 'La Mandragola' : An Interpretation," *The Journal of Politics,* no. 2 (May, 1961), pp. 320-40, sees in Ligurio the able counselor who lacks ambition with no desire for power or fame and thus fails to be a princely figure like Callimaco. For Sumberg the play is an allegory where a new social order rises through fraud and conspiracy to control Italy. Ligurio possesses the natural cleverness that enables Callimaco to win Lucrezia (who represents the body politic) from Nicia, the representative of a corrupted Florence.

Although Machiavelli was economical in composing this play, he succeeded, nonetheless, at creating a sense of local texture for this stage representation of Florence in 1504. Two scenes are especially significant in this respect: Act II, scene 3, and Act III, scene 3. In the first, Siro and Nicia are going to fetch a specimen from Lucrezia for Callimaco's inspection. Nicia comments that Callimaco did well to establish a medical practice in Paris, since his merits would never be appreciated in Florence. If the lawyer did not have independent means, he would be in serious financial difficulties, as his legal career does not provide him with sufficient earnings. Professional persons who had no friends in the city government cannot find clients. All they are good for is attending weddings and other social gatherings and sitting on the bench outside the building of the "Proconsolo" to size up the girls who pass by. Nicia gives a glimpse into the professional life of a city rapidly becoming provincial.

Machiavelli's power to focus on the local environment is even more apparent in the third scene of Act III. This is the first time Frate Timoteo comes on stage. With him is a character merely identified as "una donna" (a woman), who remains dramatically an unattached figure. She stands outside usual ancient and Renaissance character types. This woman is not a protatic character, as she contributes nothing toward the plot exposition. Yet the accent of the entire scene is upon her. This stray figure is not a farcical, ridiculous portrayal. The woman chatters on in her rich Florentine and rarely lets the friar get a word in edgewise. She gives the priest a florin so that masses will be said for the soul of her dead husband, who was a very lascivious man, as she explains. Later she asks if the Turks will invade Italy, fearing those barbarians would impale her. Finally she runs off to talk with a lady she sees in the church. Without any excess detail Machiavelli has introduced this woman to present the "local texture" of life in early sixteenth-century Florence. She makes the spectators think of the society to which the principal characters of the drama belong.[145]

The author's contemporaries recognized the comedy's merits. After its performance at Florence, other productions followed at Rome and Venice. Giovanni Mannelli informed the author that on the same evening the *Mandragola* was performed in Venice, a company of gentlemen recited the *Menaechmi* in an Italian translation. Although the beauties of the ancient play were appreciated, it was considered dead in comparison with Machiavelli's work; so the producers of the Plautine comedy invited the other ama-

145 Singleton, "Machiavelli and the Spirit of Comedy," pp. 582-95, discusses the role of local texture in the play, in a superficial manner.

teur acting company to recite the *Mandragola* for them.[146] Already the Erudite Comedy was gaining in respect over the ancient comic theater. The amateur companies which performed works by Plautus and also the Machiavellian comedy realized how vitally *La Mandragola* reproduced the Renaissance spirit.

La Clizia

Encouraged by his success as a comic dramatist, Machiavelli turned to Plautus' comedy *Casina* for inspiration in writing the *Clizia*. Jacopo Fornaciaio had asked Machiavelli if he could have *La Mandragola* performed for a gathering of leading Florentine citizens. The author decided instead to compose a new comedy. The first performance of the *Clizia* was on January 13, 1525.[147]

The comedy's prologue, written in prose like the rest of the play, starts by presenting a cyclical view of history. If the same men ever returned to the world, they would do the same things they did before. The author goes on to mention the setting and plot of the *Casina,* fictitiously claiming that the events of the ancient comedy have really occurred again in modern Florence. He chose Florence ". . . because Athens is in ruins: the streets, the squares, the landmarks can no longer be recognized. Besides, those citizens used to talk in Greek; and you wouldn't understand that language." Machiavelli has decided to present his own environment and times: the Florence of 1506. The author pretends he has merely changed the names of citizens who really experienced the events that the spectators are to behold. After introducing the leading characters and pointing out that the girl Clizia will never appear on stage, Machiavelli attempts to head off his critics by listing the two general aims of comedy: to benefit people and to delight them. The author is ready to accept the didactic function attributed to the comic genre by literary theorists. He admits that youths can benefit from portrayals of greedy misers, disturbed lovers, thieving servants, gluttonous parasites, and enticing courtesans. He has included this traditional view of

146 Cited in Sanesi, *La Commedia,* 1:266.
147 For details see Borlenghi, *Commedie del Cinquecento,* 1:23-24. R. Ridolfi, "La *Clizia* del Machiavelli," *Il Veltro* 9 (1960): 5-8, holds that the *Clizia* is a product of Machiavelli's declining years, the period of the *Storie* and of a senile love for a young woman. Ridolfi is about to bring out a critical edition of the *Clizia*; he intends to use the Colchester manuscript by the Vicentine copyist Ludovico degli Arrighi, which the editor dates at about 1526; the copy may have been a wedding gift from Machiavelli to Lorenzo Ridolfi on his marriage to Maria Strozzi. See Ridolfi, "Contributo a un'edizione critica della *Clizia*," *La Bibliofilia* 69 no. 1 (1967): 91-101.

comedy to defend himself from those who might attack him for being a scabrous writer.

In speaking of the comic genre's second purpose, Machiavelli makes a more original point. Spectators are delighted when they are moved to laughter. According to Machiavelli, it is language that makes characters ridiculous. Serious, grave language does not excite laughter; the words which make people laugh are stupid, injurious, or amorous ones. This author was very much aware of linguistic problems, since he knew the effects different words could produce. Machiavelli expresses similar opinions on the comic genre in his *Discorso intorno alla Nostra Lingua,* the dialogue which deals with the problem of the Italian language; there he repeats the ancient definition by Livius Andronicus and Cicero of comedy as a mirror of private life. The comic genre is a study of human passions. As Machiavelli affirms in his treatise, only a Tuscan author can avoid serious words and know which words will move audiences to laughter. Ariosto's comedies are weak since they mix Ferrarese and Tuscan expressions. The prologue to the *Clizia,* which discusses the three comic qualities of words, is not isolated in Machiavelli's thought but is connected with his linguistic theories.[148]

Not wishing to use injurious words or to present stupid characters in the play, the author announces that his comedy will deal with love and the problems connected with it. It is evident that there will be no character like messer Nicia with his stupid language. Machiavelli claims that ladies will be able to listen to the comedy without blushing. In this prologue the author has combined the Plautine method of preparing for the plot with the Terentian defense against critics.

This play is a thorough reworking of Plautus' *Casina,* not a mere translation. The first two acts of the *Clizia* are very different from Plautus. From the third act on, Machiavelli moves closer to the *Casina* in scenes and dialogue, but Plautus merely provides material for the Italian author, who transforms the spirit of the comedy.[149] Plautus describes the girl Casina as having

---

148 Borlenghi *Commedie del Cinquecento,* 1:968-71, gives a selection from the *Discorso intorno alla Nostra Lingua* and compares it to the prologue of the *Clizia.*
149 A detailed act by act listing of Plautine influence is in Reinhardt-Stoettner, *Spaetere Bearbeitungen,* pp. 375-83. The *Casina* was one of the ancient comedies most imitated by Renaissance dramatists; seven plays that are modeled on it are Gerolamo Berardo's *La Cassina* (1530), Lodovico Dolce's *Il ragazzo* (1541), Giovan Battista Della Porta's *La fantesca,* Cornelio Lanci's *La Ruchetta* (1584), Giovan Maria Cecchi's *I rivali;* the anonymous Sienese play *Il Capriccio* (1566-68), and of course Machiavelli's comedy. See Beatrice Corrigan, "*Il Capriccio:* An Unpublished Italian Renaissance Comedy and its Analogues," *Studies in the Renaissance* 5 (1958): 74-86. These plays range from romantic melodramas to coarse popular comedy.

been exposed to die in infancy but fortunately having been turned over to Cleostrata, wife of the Athenian Stalino. Since babies were not exposed in Renaissance Italy, Machiavelli wrote a convincing story about the way Clizia was separated from her family in Naples during the period after Charles VIII of France invaded Italy in 1494. According to the play's fiction, the French gentleman Beltramo di Guascogna lodged with the family of the Florentine merchant Nicomaco during a pause in the French march to Naples. Later, because the Pope, the Holy Roman Emperor, the Venetians, and the duke of Milan threatened to imprison the French monarch in Italy, Charles rapidly retreated. Beltramo, on his way to the battle of Taro, sent the five-year-old Clizia to Nicomaco. Nothing was ever again heard of Beltramo, who probably died in the battle. This description, in the play's opening scene, is like a page from *Il Principe*.

In Plautus' *Casina* Euthynicus, Stalino's son, never appears; his father has sent him away on business to get rid of him. But Machiavelli introduces Nicomaco's son Cleandro and thereby creates the role of a suffering lover. In the *Clizia* Cleandro does not reveal his amorous designs to his mother, Sofronia, whereas Cleostrata of the *Casina* actively supports her son against Stalino. Along with character changes, other important modifications are made in the Italian comedy to gain economy. Machiavelli eliminated a scene in the third act of the *Casina* where a thieving hired cook (a character common to Plautine plays) appears. The drawing of lots between Pirro, Nicomaco's candidate for marriage with Clizia, and Sofronia's candidate Eustachio occurs in Act III, scene 7, of the *Clizia,* because it is a central event of Machiavelli's drama. But in the *Casina* the drawing takes place in the second act. Parallel scenes of the *Clizia* come later than those of the *Casina,* usually for structural reasons.

Machiavelli also changes the plot of the *Casina* to produce a more concentrated dramatic effect. In the last act of the *Casina,* Olympio (the model for Pirro) decides to enjoy his bride before Stalino arrives to possess the girl. Thus Olympio is the first one to be beaten up by the male bride who has been substituted for Casina; although he recognizes the bride's true sex, Olympio does not warn Stalino; so the old man suffers a similar fate. It is the servant who relates what has happened to his master and himself. Machiavelli chose to keep Pirro in his servile position and pictured him as faithful to his pact with Nicomaco. The old man alone goes to bed with the male servant. Pirro has nothing to lament and joins in the general laughter over Nicomaco's disastrous love encounter. Every ridiculous effect of the act is centered on Nicomaco, who himself describes his stormy night. The Machiavellian version is concerned with the old man and the painful way in which he comes to recognize his folly.

Although most of the characters of the *Clizia* are the same as those in the *Casina,* they seem to be living individuals, whereas those of Plautus are no more than types. Sofronia, made unhappy by her husband's infatuation for Clizia, is very different from the Xanthippe-type shrews of the Roman Comedy. She is a natural creature, feared a little by her husband but respected by him and by the son. She is concerned for the honor of the entire family. Whereas Plautus' Cleostrata is always finding fault with her husband, insulting him at every occasion, Sofronia attacks Nicomaco only because of his failure to preserve the dignity of his age and because of the bad example he has set for his son. Sofronia is never jealous; Cleostrata is jealous even when there is no cause. The wife in Machiavelli's play is alone in her struggle to protect the family ward from both Nicomaco and Cleandro; she does not wish to see her husband lose the respect of the family and servants because of his frenzied love. Cleostrata forgives her husband only because of the technical necessity of ending the comedy, but Sofronia pardons her husband because of her affection for him. All the efforts of the wife in Machiavelli's play are made to shock Nicomaco out of his amorous madness; Sofronia has to use brutal means to wake him from his dream of sensual delight. When he surrenders, she is ready to forget everything. Machiavelli has depicted this woman as a thoughtful and loving wife.[150]

Nicomaco is a capable Florentine merchant suffering from a senile passion. His obsession with Clizia recalls the classical idea of love as a grand deviation, an aberration from the norm. He is not vulgar and stupid like Stalino, who is a thoroughly ridiculous figure, deprived of all ability. Stalino is so love-struck that he tells his wife of his intention to possess Casina; Nicomaco is admired by Cleandro and Sofronia for keeping his desires secret. Machiavelli suppresses the outright suggestion of homosexual relations between master and servant that Plautus makes about Stalino and Olympio; the salacious in the Italian drama is reserved for Nicomaco's description of his night with the male bride. Nicomaco never loses his prestige as head of his household. Sometimes his anger flashes when he makes his

---

150 Russo, *Commedie Fiorentine,* pp. 81-85, discusses Sofronia's character. Corrigan, "*Il Capriccio,*" p. 82, points out that the termagant was never a popular figure in the Italian theater.

authority felt, as when he threatens Cleandro and Eustachio (Act III, sc. 1):
"Ma te e lui caccerò nelle Stinche; a Sofronia renderò io la sua dote o manderolla via: perché io voglio esser io signor di casa mia; ed ognuno se ne sturi gli orecchi: . . . non arò altro rimedio, caccerò fuoco in questa casa . . . ."[151] He is ready to do anything to remain lord of his home, even to destroy it. No servant makes fun of him. Only Pirro, because of the pact, speaks to him ironically. But Nicomaco never excites contempt in Pirro as Stalino is degraded before Olympio. After his frightening humiliation Nicomaco comes to his senses and surrenders to his wife's rational authority. But Stalino displays no such heroic resignation; caught in his amorous folly, he runs away, leaving his cape behind. Then he starts to rave, calling himself a victim of the Bacchantes and screaming: "Bacchae! ergo hercle, uxor." The other characters answer him with disbelief, and Stalino tries to defend his lie. Finally he asks Cleostrata to tie him to a beam and lash him. The husband in Plautus' play is a coherent farcical character, but Nicomaco is a man of great ability who becomes grotesque because of his amorous obsession.

Even minor figures take on new characters in the Italian drama. Clizia is respected as a ward even though she is penniless. Casina, however, is regarded as a slave. Although Pirro is just about as depraved as Olympio, frequenting taverns and not above procuring, Eustachio is described as a dedicated farmer, who preserves his mental health. This steward genuinely wants to marry Clizia and is sorry when he loses to Cleandro. Machiavelli restricts the role of the servants, whereas the slaves in the *Casina* are very prominent.

In taking over the plot of the ancient comedy, the Italian dramatist introduces some of the weaknesses of the classical theater. Cleandro's friend Palamede appears only in the first scene of the work, as a protatic character to whom Cleandro relates the drama's background. It should be remembered that protatic characters were conventional in the classical theater. The sudden arrival of the Neapolitan gentleman to find his daughter who had been lost for twelve years is extremely artificial, but the recovery scene in the *Casina* does not require such a mechanical arrival since the girl turns out to be the daughter of a neighbor. Once again the problem concerns stage conventions that were acceptable to the artistic tastes of Renaissance Italy but are today considered artifical and contrived. Machiavelli was a dramatist of

---

151 "But I'll put you both in jail; I'll return Sofronia's dowry or send her away; because I want to be the master in my own home; and everyone better pay heed to me . . . if nothing else works, I'll set fire to this house. . . ."

his times, using a theatrical form which was developed from the humanistic interest in ancient Roman Comedy.[152]

This play studies the intimate life of Italian society with an attention to detail that cannot be noted in the ancient Roman theater. In discussing her husband's romantic frenzy (Act II, sc. 4), Sofronia gives a picture of their middle-class mode of living:

> Chi conobbe Nicomaco, uno anno fa, e lo pratica ora,
> ne debbe restare maravigliato, considerando la gran
> mutazione ch'egli ha fatto. Perché soleva essere uno
> uomo grave, resoluto, respettivo. Dispensava el tempo
> suo onorevolmente: e' si levava la mattina di buon'ora,
> udiva la sua messa, provedeva al vitto del giorno; dipoi,
> s'egli aveva faccenda in piazza, in mercato, a ' magistrati,
> e' la faceva; quando che no, o e' si riduceva con qualche
> cittadino tra ragionamenti onorevoli, o e' si ritirava in
> casa nello scrittoio, dove ragguagliava sue scritture,
> riordinava suoi conti; dipoi con la sua brigata desinava,
> e desinato, ragionava con il figliuolo, ammunivalo,
> davagli a conoscere gli uomini, e con qualche esempio
> antico o moderno gl'insegnav'a vivere; andava dipoi fuora,
> consumava tutto il giorno n in faccenda o in diporti gravi
> ed onesti; venuta la sera, sempre l'avemaria lo trovava in
> casa; stavasi un poce con esso noi al fuoco, s'egli era di
> verno, dipoi se n'entrava nello scrittoio a rivedere le
> faccende sue; alle tre ore si cenava allegramente. . . .[153]

Along with sharp psychological observation in Nicomaco's portrait, there is portrayal of the domestic sphere. Not even Terence provides a similar study of Roman domestic life. Some critics have contrasted the *Clizia* with

152 Sanesi *La Commedia,* 1:268-69, makes these and other objections about the *Clizia,* feeling ashamed to put this play beside the *Mandragola.* He fails to recognize how originally Machiavelli treats the plot material from the *Casina.*

153 "Anyone who was acquainted with Nicomaco a year ago and should meet him now would be astonished by the tremendous change in him. Because he used to be a serious man, resolute, dignified. He followed a worthwhile schedule: he got up early in the morning, heard Mass, provided for the day's food; afterward, if he had business in the public square, in the market, at the magistrates', he took care of it. If not, he took part in conversations on respectable topics with his acquaintances or he stayed home in his study to go over his correspondence and balance his accounts. Later he would dine with the household; after dinner, he would talk with our son and advise him so that the boy would understand people. Citing some ancient or modern example he taught the boy how to get along in life. Then he would go out to spend the whole day in business or in some serious and respectable activity. After evening fall, the avemaria always found him at home. If it was winter, he would stay with us by the fire. Afterward he would return to his study to attend to his business again. Toward nine o'clock he would dine with us quite happily. . . ."

the *Mandragola,* seeing Machiavelli's second comedy as a healthy portrait of Italian family life, in contrast with the first comedy, in which adultery triumphs.[154]

Certain themes prominent in Machiavelli's political writings appear in this comedy, not as passing insertions but as forces working in the dramatic crisis. In the struggle between Nicomaco and Sofronia, the wife's greater *virtù* wins out. The seventy-year-old husband is no Messer Nicia or Calandrino who stupidly lets others manipulate him. But since Sofronia is a match for him, their home becomes a battlefield. Nicomaco realizes (Act II, sc. 1) that he is declining physically; still, he is determined to have a last fling with Clizia. Cleandro feels lost in the struggle; his youth is no match for his father's intelligence. He describes his rivalry with Nicomaco as a war (Act I, sc. 2):

> . . . lo innamorate e il soldato si somigliano . . .
> El capitano vuole che i suoi soldati sieno giovani; le
> donne vogliono che i loro amanti non sieno vecchi. Brutta
> cosa è vedere uno vecchio soldato: bruttissima è vederlo
> innamorato. I soldati temono lo sdegno del capitano; gli
> amanti non meno quello delle loro donne. I soldati dormono
> in terra allo scoperto; gli amanti su per muriccioli. I
> soldati perseguono insino a morte i loro nimici; gli amanti
> i loro rivali. I soldati per la oscura notte nel più gelato
> verno vanno per il fango, esposti alle acque e a' venti, per
> vincere una impresa che faccia loro acquistare la vittoria;
> gli amanti per simili vie, e con simili e maggiori disagi,
> di acquistare la loro amata cercano. Ugualmente, nella
> milizia e nello amore, è necessario il secreto, la fede
> e l'animo: sono e' pericoli uguali, e il fine più delle
> volte è simile. Il soldato muore in una fossa, lo amante
> muore desperato. . . .[155]

All the youth can do is to rely on his mother's ability.

154 See G. Tambara, *Intorno alla "Clizia" di Niccolò Machiavelli* (Rovigo, 1895), p. 36; Flamini, *Cinquecento,* pp. 279-80. De Amicis, *L'Imitazione,* pp. 158-59, makes some very penetrating remarks on Machiavelli's study of the domestic sphere in the *Clizia.*
155 ". . . lovers and soldiers resemble each other . . . Captains insist on young recruits; women don't care for old lovers. It's an ugly thing to see an old soldier; it's an even uglier thing to see an old lover. Soldiers fear the scorn of their captain; lovers hate the contempt of their mistresses. Soldiers sleep on the ground out in the open; lovers, stretched out on a wall by the ladies' home. Soldiers pursue their enemies to death's very door; lovers likewise pursue their rivals. On icy winter nights soldiers tramp through the mud, exposed to the water and wind, in order to win a decisive victory; lovers seek in similar ways, with similar or greater discomforts, to conquer

One of the major themes of Machiavelli's thought is the role Fortune plays in human affairs. He did not take a fatalistic attitude, and recognized that men must be impetuous sometimes in order to succeed; but at other times, he felt, they ought to proceed cautiously to avoid disaster. In the twenty-fifth chapter of *Il Principe,* Machiavelli concedes the outcome of half our actions to Fortune; the other half is left to man. The old husband of the *Clizia* is able to combine the force of a lion and the guile of a fox, as Machiavelli recommends for the ruler in the eighteenth chapter of *Il Principe.* Nicomaco resembles Pope Julius II, studied in *Il Principe,* chap. 25, in being impetuous like a youth. His fury pushes him to suggest drawing lots in the last scene of Act III when he expressly states that he is placing his fate in the hands of Fortune. Nicomaco is honest throughout the drawing and is apparently victorious.

This victory plunges Cleandro into full melancholy. He angrily laments the cruel trick Fortune has played on him:

> O fortuna, tu suòi pure, sendo donna, essere amica
> de' giovani; a questa volta se' stata amica
> de' vecchi![156]

His lament echoes the last paragraph of the twenty-fifth chapter of *Il Principe:*

> Io iudico bene questo, che sia meglio essere, impetuoso
> che respettivo, perchè la fortuna è donna: ed è
> necessario, volendola tenere sotto, batterla e urtarla.
> E si vede che la si lascia più vincere da questi, che da
> quelli che freddamente procedono. E però sempre, come
> donna è amica de' giovani, perchè sono meno respettivi,
> più feroci, e con più andacia la comandano.[157]

The trouble with Cleandro is that he does not possess his father's active

---

the beloved lady. Secrecy, faith, and courage are equally necessary for love and war. The dangers are the same, and most times the outcome is similar. The soldier dies in a ditch; the lover perishes in despair. . . ."

156 "Oh Fortune, since you're a lady, you're generally a friend of young men; this time you have befriended the old!"

157 "I conclude that it is better to be bold than cautious because Fortune is a lady: and it is necessary, for anyone who wants to keep her under control, to beat her up and trample over her. And it can be observed how she permits herself to be conquered more readily by the bold than by those who proceed coldly. And therefore, always, as a lady she is a friend of young men because they are less cautious, more ferocious, and order her about with more audacity."

virtù. Nicomaco is the impetuous character; his son is sometimes sentimental, sometimes cross.

In the chapter on Fortune, however, the author realizes that there are weaknesses in human nature which prevent one from winning all the time. A man who always acts boldly will one day ruin himself. The cautious person will let his opportunities for success pass him by. No one can always know just when to be bold and when to be cautious. When he wins at lots Nicomaco is absolutely sure of himself, not at all doubting that his wife will accept his victory honestly. Nicomaco still has the chance to win out when he notices that something is strange about the bride being led to the nuptial chamber. His failure to inspect the bride is his one mistake. Nicomaco is like Cesare Borgia, a figure studied with great care in *Il Principe,* who made his one mistake in trusting the wrong person. For both Cesare Borgia and Nicomaco one mistake cost them victory.

Nicomaco's mistake makes him a grotesque figure. In the opening scenes of the fifth act the servant woman Doria and the neighbor Damone keep repeating forms of the verb *ridere* (to laugh) like *risi, risa, rideva, ridi, rida, ridersene,* since the old man has become thoroughly ridiculous. While describing the way the bride received him, Nicomaco expresses all his pain in the exclamation "Uh! Uh! Uh!" With those three cries he indicates how much he has to suffer on account of his one mistake. The old man is completely defeated. Machiavelli noted in the chapter on fortune in *Il Principe* that there are almost always defects in a man. Just as *La Mandragola* represents the victory of those who possess active *virtù,* the *Clizia* presents the defeat of a person who possessed ability but trusted others too much to win.

The *Clizia*'s drama reflects the author's original thoughts on human actions and destiny. Machiavelli penetrates the inner characters of the persons in the play. Nicomaco is the fullest psychological study. In presenting him the author did not use obscene expressions as he did with Messer Nicia; only in the passages where Nicomaco tells of the sexual acts the male bride performed on him does the comedy contain anything that could cause ladies to blush. The salacious does not appear just to excite the audience; the lewd, even the disgusting, enters only as a dramatic force. The theater of Niccolò Machiavelli, obeying the conventions of classical comedy, stands apart from all other examples of the Erudite Comedy in presenting more than a few hours of pleasant entertainment. His dreams reflect his vision of the world, where he studies men as they really act. The Machiavellian theater is an intellectual as well as an artistic experience.

BIBBIENA: *La Calandria*

Authors such as Nardi and Machiavelli were products of Florence's bourgeois spirit. A more courtly atmosphere characterized the duchy of Urbino. Theatrical activity in Urbino usually centered in state-promoted allegorical-mythological spectacles. Raphael's father, Giovanni Santi, was an author of dramatic pageants presented to celebrate major state occasions. To honor the arrival of Elisabetta Gonzaga in Urbino on February 13, 1488, a spectacle with all the gods of Olympus in allegorical costumes was held; Juno and Diana debated the virtues of married and virgin life. When Isabella d'Este stopped over at Urbino in 1494 while returning from a pilgrimage to Loreto, the Seven Virtues came forth on a decorated float to greet her. These Urbino court productions did not always deal with abstract, allegorical themes. Upon the return of Duke Guidobaldo and Elisabetta to power in Urbino and the fall of the usurper Cesare Borgia, a spectacle was performed, on February 19, 1504, representing the events connected with the flight of the legitimate rulers and their efforts to regain the throne. This is an example of historical drama. Despite the court sponsoring, the theater in Urbino was not a rigid attempt of the state to control public sentiment, as at Ferrara.[158]

Under the rule of Giudobaldo's nephew Francesco Maria della Rovere, several comedies were performed during the carnival of 1513 to celebrate the acquiring of Pesaro. A boy of fourteen, Guidobaldo Ruggeri, saw his comedy produced. The *Eutichia* of the Mantuan Niccolò Grassi was among the works presented. But the high point of the festival occurred on the sixth of February with the performance of the *Calandria* of Bernardo Dovizi da Bibbiena.[159] Bibbiena combined the careers of courtier and cleric with charm and political ruthlessness. Famous for his wit, he dashed off the comedy with his usual humorous vivacity.[160]

Castiglione, who portrayed the court life of Urbino in *Il Cortegiano*, describes the sets for the *Calandria* in a letter to Lodovico Canossa, bishop of Tricarico. There was the usual street scene with churches and palaces set in

158 Sanesi, *La Commedia*, 1:199-201, gives the background of the allegorical and historical theatrical productions at Urbino.
159 Documented evidence on the date of the first performance, with proof that the play was not produced before 1508, is presented by G. L. Moncallero, "Precazioni sulle rappresentazioni della 'Calandria' nel Cinquecento," *Convivium*, no. 6 (1952), pp. 819-34.
160 Biographical information in Giuseppe L. Moncallero, *Il Cardinale Bernardo Dovizi da Bibbiena umanista e diplomatico* (Florence, 1953), *passim*.

careful perspective. All the sets were painted with brilliant colors. This letter reveals the joy taken by cultured Italian audiences in scenic display, as Castiglione repeats again and again the adjective "bellissima." The play's stage mounting seemed to mean more than the work itself. Castiglione continues to tell about the intermezzos which were performed along with the major comedy. First there was a Moorish ballet in which Jason acted out the story of the Golden Fleece. Then came a float carrying Venus accompanied by small Cupids; they set fire to a gate, from which nine dancers rushed forth to give another ballet. In the third intermezzo Neptune rode out in a chariot drawn by sea horses. So skillfully had the artists worked that everything seemed real. Castiglione explains that the intermezzos were allegorical representations of the wars which were raging in Italy. These intermezzos show that the taste for historical allegory was still carried on, along with the encouragement of regular comedies. The way the various intermezzos were linked together to form a continuous allegory separate from the main comedy shows the danger to the development of drama in Italy. Dramatic values were being sacrificed in favor of spectacular effects.[161]

Because Bibbiena sent his prologue too late for an actor to memorize it, Castiglione composed a shorter prologue that was recited at the Urbino performance. Here the author of *Il Cortegiano* writes the canons of Italian comedy. He announces that the spectators are going to behold a "new comedy entitled *Calandria:* in prose, not in verse; modern, not ancient; vernacular, not Latin." No sooner has he started than he is taking a stand for the independence of modern comedy. After pointing out that the title is the classical type, taken from the unbelievably stupid character Calandro, Castiglione defends the author's choice of prose over verse, since people speak in prose. Castiglione, who advocates in *Il Cortegiano* a courtly language composed of words from different Italian dialects along with some foreign words, argues from realistic principles that the language of comedy should be as close as possible to daily speech. He holds that since comedy deals with "things familiarly done and said," prose is the only acceptable vehicle. Although he recognizes that ancient subjects are not displeasing to persons of good taste, Castiglione upholds Bibbiena's setting his comedy in contemporary times. Castiglione indicates that modern fashions are always more delightful than ancient customs, which have grown stale through long use.

161 Castiglione's letter cited in Apollonio, *Storia,* 2:20-21. Burckhardt, *Renaissance in Italy,* 2:313-15, speaks of the detrimental effect of the intermezzos on the regular comedy.

Castiglione explains that the author of the *Calandria* wrote in Italian, not Latin, since the comedy was to be given before many who do not understand Latin. This advocate of "lingua cortegiana" goes on to affirm that the Italian language has as much grace as Greek, Latin, or Hebrew; he contends that the vernacular would not be at all inferior to the ancient tongues if Italian writers polished their style with the diligent care ancient writers took. According to him, a person who scorns his native language is his own enemy. But it must be remembered that some of the most interesting products of the Latin humanistic comedy, such as the *Aetheria,* were written in the early sixteenth century just a short while before the *Calandria;* and Castiglione recognized the strength of the Latin tradition even though he defended the choice of the vernacular. To head off possible criticism, Castiglione admits that Plautus influenced the writing of Bibbiena's comedy. But the author of the *Calandria,* Castiglione holds, is no thief, since Plautus has lost nothing. Castiglione is ready to accept an author's being inspired by ancient writings as long as he does not slavishly imitate antique models. To him, this modern comedy is an intelligent imitaton of Plautus.

Bibbiena's own prologue is not at all academic or rhetorical. It is an imaginative sketch in which the actor delivering the prologue claims that the stage director has awakened him from a pleasant dream. The actor relates how he dreamed of finding Angelica's ring, which makes people invisible. He first thought of visiting the shops of misers and robbing them. This desire to be invisible in order to rob was doubtless inspired by *Decameron* VIII, 3, in which Calandrino goes to the stream Mugnone searching for the heliotrope stone that makes one invisible; he would like to rob the money changers' table. The prologue takes an erotic turn when the actor tells how he wanted to view all the ladies of Florence as they rose from their beds. He mentions then that on recalling an evening party to be held in town, he decided to visit the homes of the ladies who were invited. A series of vignettes follows in which the actor describes domestic scenes. In one a husband pushes his wife out of the house, supposedly so she will arrive at the party in time but really so that he can enjoy their maid. But in another home a jealous husband refuses to let his wife leave the house. On flying over to a third home the actor discovers that not all wives are innocent, for the lady of this house pinches her baby to make him cry and then tells her husband to go to the party while she cares for the baby; actually, she is expecting her lover. The actor leaves and beholds a lady at home who is scolding her maid for not pinning her up from underneath to make her bosom protrude. In the last home he visits a lady who is applying makeup before the mirror. There is a very detailed description of the excesses she goes to in adorning herself. This vignette recalls satiric sketches in Plautus' *Mostellaria*, Tommaso de Mezzo's *Epirota*, Zamberti's *Dolotechne*, and Ariosto's *Cassaria*. The actor's dream was brought to an abrupt end because the stage director Ser Fiuliano wanted him to excuse the poor comedy before the gracious ladies in the audience. There is no discussion of comic theory in Bibbiena's prologue. He does not try to counter any criticism. A Boccaccian sprightliness penetrates throughout, with a delight in sketching people in humorous situations.[162]

Unlike many vernacular comedies, the *Calandria* includes a formal argument. This is an obvious imitation of classical practice. Its setting is Rome, once the ruling city of the world but now so small that it can appear on stage without aid of magic. This reminds one of the prologues to Ariosto's *Il Negromante*, in which Cremona comes on stage without the work of a magician. The story is about the Greek twins Lidio and Santilla, who when dressed alike were exactly identical. To convince the audience that such a resemblance can exist, Bibbiena mentions the contemporary Roman twins Antonio and Valerio Porcari, whom no one could tell apart. The author thus appeals to contemporary reality to show that his work is lifelike. This device of presenting twins, with all the possible scenes of mistaken identity, comes, of course, from the *Menaechmi*. A series of errors leads up to a recognition scene. Bibbiena's original touch is to make one of the twins a female. His *Calandria* is not a direct imitation of Plautus. The chief borrowing is the twins' resemblance to each other.[163]

Throughout the comedy the major inspiration is Boccaccio. The name and stupidity of lady Fulvia's husband Calandro come from the four tales of the *Decameron* in which Calandrino is the central figure. Calandro's belief that a young girl like Santilla has fallen in love with him especially recalls *Decameron* IX, 5, in which the prostitute Niccolosa leads Calandrino to an assignation that turns out disastrously for him. The scheme of Lidio's servant Fessenio to place Calandro in a darkened room with a prostitute instead of Santilla may have come from *Decameron* VIII, 4, where the widow Piccarda humiliates the lecherous rector of Fiesole by luring him into a darkened chamber where he lies with the lady's hideously misshapen

---

162 Text in Borlenghi, *Commedie del Cinquecento* vol. 1.
163 See Reinhardt-Stoettner, *Spaetere Bearbeitungen*, pp. 510-14. Moncallero *Bernardo Dovizi*, pp. 544-60, closely examines the Plautine influences and concludes that Bibbiena was more interested in depicting the comic mood of contemporary life than in resuscitating antique comedy.

maid, Ciutazza. Besides being caught by the bishop, the rector is to suffer ridicule for the rest of his life because of his intimacy with the maid. The prostitute hired by Fessenio was just as ugly as Ciutazza. When Calandro saw her for a brief instant, he was told by Fessenio that she was Death. A foolish man with too many pretensions, either in Boccaccio or in Bibbiena, falls into humiliating situations.[164]

Fulvia's dressing up as a male to go in search of her lover Lidio has its parallels in the novellistic tradition and the humanistic comedy. The daughter of the king of England (*Decameron* II, 3) goes to Rome disguised as an abbot. A classic example would be *Decameron* II, 9, the story of Zinevra. Frulovisi's *Symmachus* shows Piste dressed as a male. Bibbiena had several literary precedents for the disguise scenes.[165] Fessenio's resourceful substitution of Santilla for Lidio, after Calandro discovers the lovers and runs for his brothers to denounce the adultery, recalls *Decameron* VII, 8, in which Boccaccio tells of Arriguccio Berlinghieri's jealous attitude toward his wife. Despite his vigilance she managed to receive a lover in her own home while Arriguccio was sleeping. But one night her husband surprised the lover and started to pursue him. Fearing for herself, his wife placed the maid in bed. After he returned from unsuccessfully chasing the lover, Arriguccio soundly thrashed the maid and cut off her hair, thinking she was his wife. He did not notice the substitution, and went out for her brothers with the hair as proof. When he came back with his wife's brothers and mother, all were astonished to find the lady untouched, sitting and sewing. She denounced her husband as a drunk who had probably thrashed a prostitute. Her brothers beat him up and warned him to treat their sister with full respect. After that, the lady could meet her lover without fear. In both the Boccaccian novella and Bibbiena's comedy the wife's innocence and chaste conduct are established through a cunningly devised substitution.[166]

Other Boccaccian ties are suggested by the way Fessenio convinces Calandro that he can die, be placed in a chest, and then come back to life in Santilla's arms. An abbot in *Decameron* III, 8, already compared to Frate Timoteo for his casuistry, gave the jealous but stupid Ferondo a sleeping

---

164 The first critic to note the influence of *Decameron* IX, 5, was Richard Wendringer, "Die Quellen von Bernardo Dovizis 'Calandria,'" in *Abhandlungen Hrn Prof. A. Tobler zur Feier seiner fünfundzwanzig jährigen Thätigkeit als ordentlicher Professor an der Univ. Berlin von danckbaren Schülern in Ehrerbietung dargebracht* (1895), pp. 168 f., Pellizzaro, *Novellistica*, pp. 65-66, points out *Decameron* VIII, 4.
165 Sanesi, *La Commedia*, 1:271-72, draws attention to the novelle in the *Decameron*.
166 *Ibid.*, 1:272-73, for novellistic parallels.

potion that made him appear to be dead. After Ferondo was entombed publicly, the abbot, in the disguise of a ghost, was able to visit the dolt's wife. Meanwhile Ferondo was kept in a cell and told that he was in Purgatory. Both Fessenio and the abbot cause others to think they have died but can return to life.[167]

The device of transporting a lover in a chest, also used by Ariosto in *Il Negromante,* has several novellistic precedents; and the surprise appearance of customs officials to intercept the porter carrying Calandro recalls still another Boccaccian tale. Madonna Francesca of *Decameron* IX, 1, rids herself of two bothersome would-be lovers by telling one to entomb himself in place of a dead kinsman of hers and by commanding the other to rob the tomb for her. Both candidates for her affections fulfill the orders, but the second is frightened by the night watchman into dropping the live corpse. Once again, for amorous reasons, a person pretends to be dead. Calandro in Bibbiena's play is willing to be carried about as a corpse just so he can reach the lady he loves; lovers in the Boccaccian tradition will risk anything.[168] As happens often in novelle and in other regular comedies, like Ariosto's *I Suppositi,* customs officials are a great nuisance for the major characters. The chest scheme would have succeeded perfectly if the customs officials had not tried to confiscate the property for the duties which could be levied on it. The porter, adding an extra comic note by replying in the Venetian dialect, informs the officials that silks and other fine cloths are in the chest. Satire on contemporary abuses by greedy officials, novellistic motives of a false death, and perilous transportation in a chest are among Bibbiena's major plot devices.

Whereas *La Mandragola* exemplifies comedy of intense dramatic concentration, Bibbiena's play lends itself to a farcial game in which complications develop, like a lady's disguising herself as a male, a lover's hiding in a chest, the arrival of the husband's brothers at the wrong moment. The preceding examination of some possible novellistic sources for the *Calandria* demonstrates that variety is the keynote of the comedy. But is there a unifying theme? Not every critic has thought so.[169] Perhaps the spirit of this comedy can be seen in its exalting the theme of love. Thoroughly inspired by the Boccaccian love rebellion of the *Decameron,* Bibbiena writes his comedy as a hymn in praise of love.

---

167 See Pellizzaro, *Novellistica,* p. 63.
168 *Ibid.,* pp 63-64.
169 Graf, *Studi,* p. 113, holds that the play's structure is completely fragmented, with no unifying element.

All the major characters come under Love's sway. An amorous fever inflames them all. Early in the comedy, Lidio pronounces his belief in Love as a positive force that controls everything, in answer to his preceptor's reproofs. The student knows that he is young and that it would be unnatural for him to lose his chance for Love:

> Polinico, io son giovane; e la giovinezza è tutta
> sottosposta ad Amore. Le gravi cose si convengono a'
> più maturi. Io non posso volere se non quello che Amor
> vuole: e mi sforza ad amare questa nobil donna più che
> me stesso. Il che, quando mai si risapessi, credo che
> io ne sarò da molti più reputato. . . .[170]
> (Act I, sc. 2)

Love is an ennobling force. Lidio's answer recalls how Tito in *Decameron* X, 8, tried to calm his conscience when he fell in love with the fiancée of his friend Gisippo: ". . . io son giovane, e la giovanezza è tutta sottoposta all'amorose forze: quello adunque che ad amor piace a me convien che piaccia. L'oneste cose s'appartengono a' più maturi: io non posso volere se non quello che amor vuole. . . ."[171] Both Tito and Lidio point out that they are subjects of the God of Love, ready to accept whatever pleases that divinity; they recognize that surrendering to Love is natural at their youthful age. Lidio goes on to affirm that Love is the great vital force that perfects the whole world: "Alla sua potenza ogni cosa è suggetta. E non è cosa alcuna perfetta nè virtuosa nè gentile."[172] These lines could have come right out of the *Decameron*. Bibbiena, a disciple of the love theories in Boccaccio's modern Bible, regards love not as a grand abberation from the norm, but as a sentiment that lifts one to a more perfect state.

Even Calandro, childish as he may be, grows passionately interested in Lidio when the youth is disguised as a girl. Fessenio is surprised (Act I, sc. 7) that such a dolt is capable of amorous passion: "Or vedo ben che ancor li

---

170 "Polinico, I am young, and youth is entirely subject to Love. Serious matters are fitting for older persons. I can wish only what Love wishes: and it compels me to love this noble lady more than myself. So that, if my love were ever reported to other persons, I believe that many of them would highly respect me. . . ."
171 ". . . I am young and youth is altogether subject to the laws of love; wherefore that which pleaseth Him, needs must it please me. Things honorable pertain unto maturer folk; I can will nought save that which Love willeth . . ." (Payne trans.). Borlenghi, *Commedie del Cinquecento,* 1:70-71, n. 6, compares Lidio's speech with Tito's.
172 "Everything is subject to His power. And there is no greater sweetness than to win what one desires in Love, without which nothing is perfect or valorous or noble."

dei hanno, come li mortali, del buffone. Ecco, Amore, che suole inviscare solo i cori gentili, s'è in Calandro pecora posto, che da lui non si parte; che ben mostra Cupido aver poca faccenda poi che entra in sì egregio babuasso. Ma il fa perchè costui sia tra gli amanti come l'asino tra le scimie."[173] At times Calandro abandons himself to a comic lyricism which contrasts with Lidio's eloquence. Carried along by the miracle of love, he defends his passion for Santilla when Fulvia surprises him at her lover's home: ". . . Fastidiosa! Tu non vali le scarpette vecchie sue, che la mi fa più carezze e meglio mi bacia che tu non fai. Ella mi piace più che la zuppa del vin dolce; e luce più che la stella Diana. . . ."[174] The gross images are consistent with Calandro's backward mental state. Yet these are the words of an ardent lover.

His wife suffers because of her affection for Lidio until she is ready to use any means to secure his love. She is an intelligent woman but is led by her passion to place herself in compromising and even dangerous situations. Fulvia is a mature woman, the mother of a son old enough to marry Santilla; her lover's age must be close to that of her son. She sees in Lidio her last chance to enjoy love before old age cuts her off from every amorous pleasure. She has become an enthusiastic slave of Love: "Nulla è, certo, che Amore altri a fare non costringa, Io, che già sanza compagnia a gran pena di camera uscita non sarei, or, da amor spinta, vestita da uomo fuor di casa me ne vo sola. Ma, se quella era timida servitù, questa è generosa libertà. . . ."[175] This speech, coming in the seventh scene of Act III, near the center of the comedy, expresses the author's positive attitude toward Love.

Bibbiena excells at portraying feminine psychology in all its dramatic contradictions. Fulvia goes into a searing rage on discovering Calandro in Lidio's home. Along with her surprise there is the disappointment of not finding her lover, as well as jealousy toward her husband. The way she reproaches Calandro recalls how Catella of *Decameron* III, 6, complained to

173 "Indeed I now see that the gods, like mortals, can be buffoons. Behold Love, who usually ensnares only noble hearts, has entered in that fool Calandro and is staying there; which goes to show how unoccupied Cupid must be if he takes up with such an outstanding simpleton. But Cupid is doing that because Calandro may stand out among lovers as an ass does among apes."
174 ". . . Bothersome woman! You're not worth her old shoes. For she caresses me more than you do, and her kisses are better than yours. I like her better than the soup of sweet wine, and she is more resplendent than the star Diana. . . ."
175 "There is nothing that Love does not compel others to do. Once I would have hardly left my chamber without a companion; now, impelled by Love, I am going out of my house alone and dressed as a man. But, if that was timid servitude, this is noble freedom. . . ."

the man she thought was her adulterous husband.[176] Fulvia did not let surprise betray her even though her disguise in men's clothes was enough to make Calandro suspicious. Instead she turned savagely on him, declaring that she had disguised herself to check up on his faithless activities. The impetus of love has not impaired her resourcefulness; indeed, Fulvia has grown sharper through her amorous passion. As he sees Calandro being led home in shame and defeat by the triumphant Fulvia, Fessenio sings the praises of Love as the power that enabled the lady to avoid the danger threatening her: ". . . O Amore, quanto è la potenzia tua. Qual poeta, qual dottore, qual filosofo potria mai mostrare quelli accorgimenti, quelle astuzie che fai tu a chi séguita la tua insegna? Ogni sapienza, ogni dottrina di qualunche altro è tarda rispetto alla tua. Qualaltra, sanza amore, averia avuto tale accorgimento che di sì gran periculo escita fusse come costei? . . ." (Act III, sc. 13).[177] Fulvia's ability to save herself is very similar to that of lady Ghita in *Decameron* VII, 4, with her jealous husband Tofano; Boccaccio shows how Love lends an otherwise defenseless lady the means to triumph over a man. Lauretta, who tells the tale of the well, introduces it with this apostrophe to Love:

> O Amore, chenti e quali sono le tue forze, chenti
> i consigli e chenti gli avvedimenti! Qual filosofo,
> Qual artista mai avrebbe potuto o potrebbe mostrare
> quegli accorgimenti, quegli avvedimenti, quegli
> dimostramenti che fai tu subitamente a chi sèguita
> le tue orme? Certo la doctrina di qualunque altro è
> tarda a rispetto della tua, sì come assai bene comprender
> si può nelle cose davanti mostrate. Alle quali, amorose
> donne, io una n'aggiugnerò da una semplicetta donna
> adoperata, tal che io no so chi altri se l'avesse potuta
> mostrare che Amore.[178]

176 Sanesi, *La Commedia,* 1:276, refers to the Boccaccian novella.
177 ". . . O Love, how great is your power. What poet, what professor, what philosopher could ever demonstrate the devices, the clever subterfuge that you create for those who follow your banner? All the wisdom, all the learning of anybody else is faulty compared to yours. What other woman, without Love, would have had the alertness to get out of such great danger as she has done. . . ."
178 "O Love, how great and how various is thy might! How many thy resources and thy devices! What philosopher, what craftsmen could ever have availed or might avail to teach those shifts, those feints, those suberfuges which thou on the spur of the moment suggestest to whoso ensueth in thy traces! Certes, all others' teaching is halting compared with thine, as may very well have been apprehended by the devices which have already been set forth and to which, lovesome ladies, I will add one practiced by a woman of a simple wit enough and such as I know none but Love could have taught her." (Payne trans.)

Fessenio seems to be repeating Lauretta's words. Love, not just innate ability, inspired Fulvia to attack Calandro as the adulterous party, just as Ghita reversed the situation with her husband.[179]

Fulvia and her maid Samia work closely together. The maid is much more than a servant; she is her mistress's chief adjutant in the love affair with Lidio. Samia is shown running about the streets to deliver Fulvia's messages, often taking the initiative, as in the scene in which she approaches Santilla, who is disguised as a male. Her close working relationship with Fulvia recalls the ninth tale of the seventh day in the *Decameron*, where the maid Lusca assists her mistress Lidia in a love affair with a youth.[180] At first Samia is amazed by the way Fulvia surrenders to her passion; the lady's disguise upsets the maid and causes her to reflect on woman's weak state once Love takes hold. But Samia comes to envy her mistress for her courageous determination to follow Love. Once again Bibbiena shows his understanding of feminine psychology. After all her worrying and lamenting, Samia watches Fulvia hurry away to find Lidio and decides that it would be madness not to give way to Love's impetus. Samia follows Fulvia's example and calls for her free-spending lover, Lusco.

In Bibbiena's vision of life the natural law of love is supreme. The lovers' success in the *Calandria* is expressed in a spirit of jubilation, with no concern about the sin of adultery, since the two feel that they have acquired the greatest good to which humans can aspire. Fulvia rejoices: "Whoever is happier than I am cannot be mortal." The *Calandria* is inspired by an ideal of love—not Christian spiritual love or an irrational kind of love, but the force which sharpens the intelligence of lovers so they can be victorious over every obstacle.[181]

This comedy does more than carry the Boccaccian love tradition to the stage. It introduces new character types and elements which reflect Italian Renaissance life. Lidio's preceptor Polinico, who makes his one appearance in the second scene of Act I, is a typical Renaissance pedant. Although Ariosto anticipated this type in Dr. Cleandro of *I Suppositi*, Polinico is a more professional pedant, as he is a tutor. This preceptor attempts to turn Lidio away from his passion for Fulvia. His demands that the youth use

---

179 Croce, "Intorno alla Commedia," pp. 3-4, speaks of the power of Love in Bibbiena's play.
180 Sanesi, *La Commedia,* 1:272, points out the novella.
181 Moncallero, *Bernardo Dovizi,* pp. 572-86, states how organically Bibbiena integrates the Boccaccian material, making it his own; (pp. 560-61) he discusses the revolutionary nature of adulterous love.

moderation are unreasonable, since he asks Lidio to act against his nature. One of the pedant's chief traits is his determination to distort nature according to some formalistic scheme. Polinico acts as a foil for Fessenio, who calls the unnatural demands "pedagogarie." The play's loose structure, with its emphasis on variety, easily accommodates the pedant, although he does not participate in the main action.[182]

A figure who is better integrated into the comedy is the magician Ruffo, who may have inspired the title character of *Il Negromante*. Ruffo is not the most highly skilled practitioner of black magic, and he really believes that Santilla is a hermaphrodite. The imaginary change of sex, supposedly brought through the magical arts but in reality effected by substituting a man for a girl who had been disguised as a male, has parallel's in the *History of the Seven Wise Masters of Rome*, in a continuation of the *Huon de Bordeaux*, and in the *Camilla Bella* and the *Reina d'Oriente*. There is a contemporary parallel in an episode of the *Orlando Furioso*.[183] One critic has noted that Ruffo brings a certain "surrealistic" element into the comedy.[184] This magical atmosphere can also be found in works like the *Orlando Furioso*, with its flying hippogryph, and Cellini's *Vita*, in which the artist is imprisoned in Castel Sant' Angelo and the governor of the castle is a madman who thinks he can fly like a bat. The use of magic always carries with it a sense of the vague and fantastic. Boccaccio was Bibbiena's master in portraying hallucination, as in *Decameron* V, 8, in which Nastagio degli Onesti beholds ghosts in an enchanted forest, or VII, 9, in which the husband Nicostrato is made to believe he is the victim of a bewitched pear tree. Ruffo, however, does not enter actively into the magical world and is little more than a lowly swindler, without the flair for appearing a master sorcerer that distinguishes Ariosto's Giacchelino. Although he claims to have power over spirits, Ruffo laughs at Fulvia's belief in him. This magician turns out to be a rather cold figure.

Fessenio is the brightest character of the comedy, with a superior intelligence that saves everyone in difficult situations. His importance to the drama is made evident in a long monologue which takes up the entire first

---

182 *Ibid.,* pp. 539-40, mentions that since Polinico suffers from the humanistic vice of sodomy, he does not join in the play's festival of natural love; (p. 564) Moncallero notes that Polinico has been compared to the pedagogue Ludus in Plautus' *Bacchides,* but the classical character is not a vicious hypocrite.

183 P. Rajna, *Le Fonti dell'Orlando Furioso* (Florence, 1900), *passim,* gives part of the background on the switch in sex.

184 Russo, *Commedie Fiorentine,* pp. 185-88. He compares the mood of the play with writings of Cellini, Ariosto, and Boccaccio.

scene of Act I. He points out how hard it would be for any servant to serve two masters, while he has to attend three: Lidio, Calandro, and Fulvia. Fessenio has a heavier load than the servant in Goldoni's *Servo di due padroni*. Bibbiena's character is more capable than any servant in ancient comedies. He loves to play tricks, just like Boccaccio's two capricious painters, Bruno and Buffalmacco; Calandro is the puppet with which Fessenio plays. This servant uses magic far more enthusiastically than Ruffo. In Act II, scene 6, Fessenio pretends to teach Calandro how a man's body can be taken apart limb by limb, placed in a chest, and later reassembled by saying the magic word "Ambracullac." Calandro, unable to repeat the spell, cries out in pain when the servant almost twists off his arm; and Fessenio scolds him for ruining the spell. This scene brings to mind *Decameron* IX, 10; in the novella, Donno Gianni claims he can transform the wife of the peasant Pietro da Tresanti into a mare. When Pietro screams out against pinning a tail on his wife, Donno Giani reproaches him for destroying the conjuration.[185] Calandro even receives a lesson from Fessenio on how to die. Whenever they appear together, Calandro is the target of Fessenio's tricks. The comedy's envoi is rightfully delivered by Fessenio, as credit goes to him for resolving all the intrigues.[186]

In relating how Lidio and Santilla were separated by a Turkish raid on the Greek city of Modon, Bibbiena draws from contemporary political and military events to provide a background for his comedy. Ariosto does the same in *I Suppositi*, in which he brings up the Turkish occupation of Otranto. The Turkish menace was real to sixteenth-century Italians, since pirate raids on the Italian coast were common. Cellini, in chapter 5 of the *Vita*, tells how he barely escaped from a Turkish ambush near Rome. Islands like Elba and Ischia were struck again and again, and thousands of Christian prisoners were carried away to be made slaves or to be ransomed. Women often ended up in harems, while kidnapped boys were trained to become Janizaries. Thus the purchase of Santilla and her servant Fannio by the merchant Perillo in the slave market of Constantinople was a typical occurrence of that period. The reunion of the twins, even with the influence of the *Menaechmi*, could have taken place in that politically unstable century.[187]

185 Sanesi, *La Commedia*, 1:272, compares the novella with the scene in the play.
186 Moncallero, *Bernardo Dovizi*, pp. 518-19 and 525-26, discusses Fessenio as the epitome of intelligence reacting against circumstances. Calandro is needed as a contrast of a stupid quest for sensual love. Fessenio holds contempt for the necromancer just as Temolo does in the *Negromante*.
187 Agresti, *Studii*, pp. 122-27, mentions how the Italian comedy reflects the Turkish threat.

The Urbino performance of the *Calandria* was so successful that Pope Leo X had the play produced at Rome in 1514 and 1515.[188] Since that time critics have attacked the play as an immoral work, an obscene vehicle of the author's lewd wit, an ugly farce, and a realistic portrait of the corrupt life of sixteenth-century Rome. But recently scholars have recognized both Bibbiena's debt to Boccaccio and the courtier charm of his style. This comedy does take a moral stand—on the side of Love as an invincible natural force. Bibbiena does not possess Machiavelli's insight into human relations, and often he does no more than rephrase passages of the *Decameron*. But the comedy sparkles with the author's rejoicing in the rights of Love.[189]

THE CONTRIBUTION OF THE EARLY DRAMATISTS

With the discovery of the lost Plautine comedies and the subsequent publication of ancient Roman plays during the fifteenth century, the classical theater began to reawaken in Italy. Toward the last quarter of the century the comedies of Plautus and Terence were performed, usually in translated form, but the audiences were often dissatisfied with the translation's fidelity to the Latin texts. The cultural centers which led in reviving the ancient comedies were those in which the Italian Erudite Comedy was to be born. Mantua, Ferrara, and Urbino formed a cultural triangle whose courts were related by state marriages, while Florence was distinguished from other theatrical centers because of its bourgeois atmosphere.

Of these early playwrights Ariosto had the longest career, from 1508 to nearly 1530. All these authors adhered to the three unities of the classical theater. Although they sometimes set their plays in ancient times, the more daring placed their works in contemporary Italy, relating the events of the comedies to the political conditions of the age. In these early years the leading comic character types, including those original in the Renaissance, like the magician and the hypocritical priest, appeared for the first time in the vernacular theater. Alongside the influence of Plautus and Terence, which was common to all these playwrights, was the novellistic tradition. Boccaccio, more than any other author of novella collections, inspired the early playwrights of the regular comedies. By 1525 a new genre had been fully created, which was to provide comic situations and characters as well as a dramatic form for both innovating and academic playwrights.

---

188 Moncallero, "Precisazioni," pp. 836-51, mentions the various performances, all of which attest to the comedy's success. He points out that the play was even produced in Munich.

189 Russo, *Commedie Fiorentine*, pp. 188-95, gives the comedy's critical history.

3

Rebel and Academic Comedies

ARETINO: *La Cortigiana*

In 1513 the champions of a comedy in the Italian language still felt at a disadvantage before the Latinists, but by 1530 theatrical tastes had changed. Paolo Giovo, the humanist, expressed his sorrow over the decline in the popularity of the Latin comedies: "The plays of Plautus and Terence, once a school of Latin style for the educated Romans, are banished to make room for Italian comedies."[1] The defense of the Italian language which Castiglione had made in his special prologue for the *Calandria* marked one step in the battle for a vernacular theater.

Few writers have been more antitraditional than Pietro Aretino. A despiser of pedantry, he turned to writing plays shortly before the Sack of Rome in 1527. During the last thirty years of his life he continued to compose plays in the comparative safety of Venice, the only Italian city that could offer him asylum. Between February and July of 1525, Aretino wrote the first version of his comedy *La Cortigiana*. After leaving Rome he reworked the play in his Venetian retreat, and in 1534 the second version ap-

1 Cited in Jacob Burckhardt, *Renaissance in Italy*, Trans. S.G.C. Middlemore (New York, 1958), 1:246.

peared in print. In the second version he toned down bitter expression about his disappointing years in Rome, the comedy's setting. He particularly rewrote the prologue, since the original was extremely vitriolic; Aretino had alluded to his enemies in Rome while threatening the spectators with a smear campaign if they did not remain silent. He also eliminated some pessimistic remarks about the politics of the day. Venice's healthier political climate seems to have freed him of the desperate feeling he had expressed in the comedy's first draft.[2]

Aretino's prologue to the second version is a dialogue between a stranger and a nobleman. It is in prose, like the rest of the comedy. The stranger wanders onstage and marvels at the deluxe setting for the play that is to be performed. He asks the nobleman who the author is. Several authors are mentioned, with ironical remarks about their writings. As is often done in Aretino's works, a Latin phrase, here "quae pars est," is inserted to mock pedantic authors, with their pretense of being grave and learned. The stranger comments that poets are flooding the land like Lutherans. He adds that Petrarch is being crucified by those who write glosses for his poems. There follows a list of kings, high nobles, and prelates, with appropriate praise. The nobleman informs the stranger about the comedy's plot, explaining that the action takes place in Rome, now purged of its sins by the Spaniards who sacked the city. The nobleman gives this warning: ". . . do not be surprised if the comic style is not observed in the customary way, because we live in Rome according to a different fashion than people used to live in Athens." Here Aretino is defending the author's right to be faithful to his own times, since sixteenth-century Rome is not ancient Athens. Aretino wished to be a modern author, and asserted that comedy had to be found in the life of his own times.[3]

Although Aretino was a partisan of modern comedy, he did not break with traditional schemes. *La Cortigiana* is a five-act comedy obeying the unities of time and place, but the use of a double plot causes the characters to

2 A copy of the original version of the *Cortigiana* exists in a codex of the National Library of Florence. A. Luzio, *Pietro Aretino nei primi suoi anni a Venezia e la corte dei Gonzaga* (Torino, 1888), p. 2, dates the first version. Mario Baratto, "Commedie di Pietro Aretino," *Belfagor* 12, no. 4 (July, 1957): 372-74, speaks of Aretino's unsettled life from 1516 to 1536, filled with the patronage of the banker Agostino Chigi and betrayal from two popes (Leo X and Clement VII), a brief and adventurous relationship with Giovanni de' Medici, and a mixed reception from Federico Gonzaga. Baratto points out how Aretino, in his prologues and in the plays, addressed the outside world, never forgetting his contemporary audiences.
3 Text in *Le Commedie e l'Orazia*, ed E. Camerini (Milan, 1897). This edition will henceforth be used for all five comedies.

rush on and off stage at a dizzy pace that breaks with most theatrical traditions. In order to weld the two plots together Aretino accepted the exterior
form of the classical comedy. But he never reflected on the functions of
classical stage convention. The comic playwrights before him had established the unchanging stage scene set on the street and the subject matter of
suffering lovers.

Despite its adherence to classical formulas, Aretino's play has a vibrant
quality which comes from the mad pace of the comic action. There is a
rapid running from scene to scene, from one episode to another. The author
recaptures the local color of life in Rome during the first third of the sixteenth century. His style is essentially impressionistic, with one vivid sketch
following another. In one episode the protagonist Messer Maco sends his
servant Sanese out to buy a book on courtiership. A bookseller comes on
scene shouting: "Histories. Fine histories, histories, the Turkish war in
Hungary, the sermons of Fra Martino, the Council, histories, histories! The
affair in England, the pomp of the Pope, the circumcision of Voivoda, the
sack of Rome, the fall of Marseilles with its aftermath, histories, histories."
Sanese runs after the itinerant salesman to purchase *La Vita de' Turchi* of
Paolo Giovio, since he thinks courtiers are barbarians like the Turks. After
these scenes in Act I the salesman is never seen again; yet he has brought
onstage part of the animated movement of life in Rome.

Sometimes these local-color characters appear in several scenes throughout the play. One character who returns again and again is a fisherman,
who was once a Florentine gambler but is now reduced to selling fish
to support his five children. Rosso, servant to the other protagonist Parabolano, cheats the fish seller out of ten lampreys by pretending to be the
Pope's official purchaser. Instead of paying the fish seller, Rosso turns him
over to a priest with the story that the man is possessed by evil spirits. The
priest has the fisher tied to a church column and lashed to exorcise him. The
wretch grieves more about the money he has lost on the fish than about the
pain he has suffered. Besides Rosso's art in outwitting the fisher, Aretino
depicts the economic fears of the poor wretch. Along with the delight the
author takes in the trick played by Rosso, there is a flash of sympathy for the
fisher.[4]

Still another of Rosso's victims is Romanello Ebreo. As a Jew he is
compelled by law to wear a red sign on his clothes, thereby becoming a
target for ripe fruits thrown by street urchins. Romanello is also an itinerant

---

4 Ireneo Sanesi, *La Commedia,* 2d ed. (Milan, 1954), 1:287, lists novella parallels
for the trick on the fisher in Sacchetti, Morlini, Straparola, Sozzini, and Arienti.

salesman, calling out, "Ferri vecchi, ferri vecchi," as he wanders the streets. When Rosso pretends he wants to purchase a cloak, Romanello displays the excellent points of his merchandise in the name of his religion (Act IV, sc. 15) : ". . . Put your arm in here. May I never see the Messiah if it doesn't seem custom made for you; the finest in fashion . . . God take me to the synagogue on Sabbath if it isn't a perfect fit" But Rosso runs away; and when Romanello catches up with the thieving youth, Rosso denounces the Jew to the constable and has him arrested. The portrait of Romanello is only a sketch; yet Aretino has captured his main points. Romanello might be considered a character type, but he is a modern type that the author drew from the world around him.

Aretino's *Cortigiana* surpasses even the *Lena* of Ariosto in showing the movements of a city; both comedies are like the chronicle of a city's daily life. A crowd of varied characters caught from life moves across the stage. Ladies of high class wink at their would-be lovers from windows while courtiers pompously parade about with trains of servants. Tradesmen such as bakers go about their business. A constable with his rough-and-ready policemen patrols the streets. Clergymen pass. Low-life characters are seen coming out drunk from inns of ill fame. All these figures seem to have stepped onstage from Roman society. Through them Renaissance Rome becomes the most important character in the comedy.[5]

This comedy reflects much of the author's own disillusionment with Rome. Maco's story could have been Aretino's own in that it is about a provincial's coming to the great city to make his fortune, where instead of success he encounters a crowd of opportunists ready to swindle him. The Roman court is the favorite target for Aretino's hatred. Valerio, one of Parabolano's few loyal servants, comments on how to succeed in Rome: "Whoever wants to do well at Court must come here deaf, blind, mute, an ass, an ox, and a kid. . . ." The first act closes with an imprecation against Rome by the fisher, just after he has been lashed. In the sixth scene of Act II the old man Sempronio wonders if he should send his son Camillo to serve in the Roman court; the servant Flamminio advises against it. There follows a contrast of ages. When Sempronio was young, the court was a

5 Aulo Greco, *La Vita Romana nella Commedia del Rinascimento* (Rome, 1945), p. 409, describes how Aretino recreates the movement and color of Rome. Baratto, "Commedie di Pietro Aretino," pp. 378-79, comments that the essential intuition of the *Cortigiana* is the street inasmuch as it coincides with the stage; Aretino according to Baratto breaks the purely fictitious structural unity of the erudite comedy. This critic talks of a *vocalità* of the street characters who lose their individuality to become theatrical instruments that recapture the life of Rome.

gathering place for liberal patrons and happy courtiers. But in Flamminio's time the court is full of petty masters and starving servants. The court is no longer a fit place for the virtuous but suits thieves and murderers. Women are now in charge of prelates' households. In Flamminio's opinion, Camillo would be better off in hell, where only the soul is injured, than in the Roman court, where both body and soul are injured.[6] Aretino's bitter feelings reach their high point in the tenth scene of Act II, in which Valerio explains to Parabolano that the times are favorable to lovers because wars, pestilence, and famine in Italy have broken family ties and upset the older morality. If one recalls that this second version of *La Cortigiana* is far more gentle and optimistic than the first, one is astonished by Aretino's intense hatred for the Roman society that rejected him. The play takes on autobiographical value.[7]

In the entire play there are twenty-four characters, an almost confusing number if one compares the eight characters of *La Mandragola*. At least two of the characters are historical figures: Maestro Andrea, the swindling painter who makes a fool of Messer Maco; and Rosso. Both of them are mentioned in Aretino's *Ragionamenti,* also published in 1534.[8] Doubtless, other characters were modeled from real-life figures. But Aretino does more than write a documentary comedy, since even the historical characters are dramatic figures.

Maco da Siena has a close cousin in the Sienese gentleman of Ariosto's *I Suppositi*. Both Aretino and Ariosto worked within the Florentine novellistic tradition in which the Sienese are depicted as buffoons,[9] and Maco has the mental acumen of Messer Nicia or Bibbiena's Calandro. He begins to reveal himself in the twenty-second scene of Act I, in which he receives his first lesson in courtiership from Maestro Andrea. He is told that a courtier must be envious, ignorant, and flattering. Above all a courtier must make himself into a nymph. Andrea says that one becomes a nymph by spending hours by the mirror to make curls and perfume his hair. The nymph must go about with a copy of Petrarch's love poems in his hand; kissing hands and speaking Tuscan are prerequisites. Maco answers that he is the perfect man to play a nymph. In fact he is a poet, and he recites unintelligibly eight Latin verses he has stolen from Vergil and Ovid but which he claims are his own. There is something of the pedant in Maco, who is also a vain per-

6 See Sanesi, *La Commedia,* 1:286, for an identification of Flamminio as Aretino.
7 Greco, *Vita Romana,* p. 5, mentions the play as a document of the author's life.
8 Cf. Aldo Borlenghi, ed., *Commedie del Cinquecento* (Milan, 1959), 1:32.
9 *Ibid.,* 1:32.

son striking a ridiculous Petrarchan pose as a suffering lover. In the eleventh and twelfth scenes of Act II he composes a bad Petrarchan letter and a worse strambottino for his fair Camilla Pisana. Maestro Andrea plays on Maco's vanity to win his way. After drawing Maco out of a kettle, Andrea hands him a counterfeit mirror with a portrait of a handsome courtier on it, and Maco believes that he has been transformed. The Sienese dolt actually does reach Camilla, but Andrea and a confederate rush on the scene dressed as Spaniards and make the fool jump from a window. In Maco the author has portrayed the misadventures of a vain bumpkin.

The other protagonist, Parabolano, differs from Maco, for this Neapolitan character is a cultured aristocrat. But Parabolano has the Neapolitan excess of romantic ardor and has taken on many Spanish affectations. He is the very type of the nymph-courtier that Andrea describes to Maco. Parabolano's servants make fun of the way he carefully puts on his stockings and cleans his teeth. His letters are perfumed. Parabolano is not popular with most of his servants, since he often hires on a two-month trial system in which the servant has to donate his work free. At the end of the first month the servant is dismissed without receiving any salary. Parabolano is much more cunning than Maco, but when involved in a love affair, he is a slave of his emotions. He constantly laments in Petrarchan paradoxes over his beloved Livia, wife of Luzio Romano. In the fifth scene of Act II he delivers a soliloquy about Good Fortune and cruel Love. On the way to a tryst with the false Livia, he invokes in the last act *notte, fronte, petto, occhi.* The trick played on him by Rosso and the procuress Alvigia in substituting a prostitute for Livia recalls the *Calandria,* with Fessenio's scheme to place Calandro in a darkened room with a harlot; there is also the novellistic precedent of *Decameron* VIII, 4. Aretino does not portray Parabolano as a thorough buffoon; he is an affected noble whose good sense has been lost because of his amorous interests. On realizing that he has possessed the prostitute and not Livia, he does not act vindictively. Aretino shows how this aristocrat becomes ridiculous with his Petrarchan mannerisms but finally recovers his equilibrium.

Alvigia is the most fascinating character of the comedy a procuress, a witch, and a religious hypocrite. She is a figure from the criminal world of that age. As a literary character she owes little or nothing to the procuresses of the ancient Roman Comedy. She is much closer to a character in *Decameron* V, 10, (the Pietro di Vinciolo story) who is also a religious hypocrite. Boccaccio describes this go-between as ". . . an old woman who showed like Saint Verdiana, that giveth the serpents to eat, and still went to every pardoning, beads in hand, nor ever talked of aught but the lives of the Holy Fathers or of the wounds of St. Francis and was of well nigh all reputed a saint" (Payne translation). Aretino had behind him a novellistic tradition in which the figure of the procuress was associated with pretended religious devotion. Alvigia is thus a modern character, not one imitated from Plautus or Terence.[10]

When she first comes onstage, Alvigia is on her way to perform a sad duty. The woman who had been her instructress in the arts of procuring and magic is to be burned alive for almost no reason, as Alvigia explains to Rosso (Act II, sc. 7). Her instructress had merely poisoned her lover and done a lady-friend a favor by throwing a baby into the river. It was not enough for the procuresses of Aretino's time to arrange meetings for lovers; they had to prepare love potions, ointments, and other medications for persons in love. Members of this profession had to visit graveyards and remove pieces of flesh from corpses, because victims of the gallows offered magically effective limbs. In this scene Algivia gives a list of the instruments that witches used.

Even though she is shown as very poor, Alvigia has had a glorious past. In Act III, scene 6, she describes her youth, when she was the toast of Italy. No other woman could compare with her. Men treated her like an empress; noble lords presented her with fine homes, parrots, monkeys, servants, clothes in the latest fashions. She was able to mock a bishop by snatching his miter and putting it on one of her maids. One of her patrons was a sugar merchant, so she seasoned all her food with sugar. But she caught the "French disease"; thanks to the disease and the medical treatments she received for it, Alvigia lost her youth, becoming an ugly old woman. Aretino gives a sympathetic portrait of her as he evokes the elegance of her past. For a moment she forgets her present poverty and enthusiastically recalls that happy, beautiful youth. The author here writes an elegiac passage.

This criminal never fails to observe the exterior rites of her religion. In the twelfth and thirteenth scenes of the third act she talks with her father confessor d'Araceli, who is a rather casuistic priest, interested in worldly affairs. Alvigia cannot understand how paradise can hold the souls of all the persons who have died repentant for their sins. The priest explains that souls are like lies; they do not occupy space. This conversation may have been modeled on the third scene in the *Mandragola's* third act; Alvigia's questions about whether her instructress will go to heaven and the menace of a Turk-

10 Sanesi, *La Commedia,* 1:289, mentions the procuress in the Pietro di Vinciolo story.

ish invasion are similar to those that a lady asks Frate Timoteo in Machiavelli's play. Guardiano does not appear as impeccably pious as Frate Timoteo does. This passage illustrates that a dramatist like Aretino was aware of the theatrical activity of the period.[11] The procuress's talk with the priest reveals her concern about the salvation of the soul. But for Alvigia one need only observe the forms of religion. Even in the midst of her professional activities this hypocrite is careful to say her prayers. In the eighth scene of Act IV she approaches the prostitute Togna to inform her of the ruse they are going to play on Parabolano. As she speaks, the procuress recites her "Pater Noster" along with the news:

> Alvigia: E tu savia.—Pater noster—(verrai vestita da
> uomo perché questi palafrenieri,—qui es in
> celis,—fanno di matti scherzi la notte)—
> sanctificetur nomen tuum,—e non vorrei che tu
> scappassi in un trentuno,—adveniat regnum
> tuum—come incappò Angela dal moro,—in celo et
> in terra.[12]

She even manages to slip in an "Ave Maria." This woman sees no contradiction between her criminal life and her religious practices.

Religious superstition is the strongest character trait of the witch Alvigia. On seeing that her scheme to fool Parabolano has failed, she starts to make vows of fasts and good works in the hope that Heaven will save her from tragedy. She vows to visit the seven main churches of Rome ten times every month, to go barefoot, to boil water for the sick and work in a church hospital for nothing. Alvigia calls for help from the Angel Raphael, San Tobia, and Messer San Giuliano. In a way she is not a hypocrite; for her religion is only an exterior matter. She differs from Frate Timoteo, since the Machiavellian priest was aware of his sinful actions in supporting an adulterous affair. But for Alvigia religion is similar to the magical arts she practices in her professional career as a witch. She leaves theological problems to her father confessor.

Aretino's portrait of a procuress brings to mind the *Lena* of Ariosto and the Spanish *Celestina*. Lena does not belong in Alvigia's class, for Ariosto's character is an unfortunate creature whose circumstances have forced her to

11 Arturo Graf, *Studi Drammatici* (Turin, 1878), p. 147, connects the *Cortigiana* with the *Mandragola*.
12 "And you're wise.—Pater noster—(you will come dressed as a man because these grooms—qui es in celis,—play some crazy jokes at night)—sanctificetur nomen tuum,—and I wouldn't want you to get into trouble—adveniat regnum tuum—as Angela had,—in celo et in terra."

become a procuress. Alvigia is much closer to Celestina, who is also a witch. Celestina, like Alvigia, delights in describing a happy past when she was treated like a queen. Both Alvigia and Celestina have had high-ranking clergymen as patrons. The relationship between Alvigia and Parabolano, with her demanding and receiving an expensive gift, is similar to the one between Celestina and Calisto, a noble lover in the Petrarchan manner. Alvigia is opposed by Parabolano's loyal servant Valerio just as Celestina is at first hindered by Calisto's servant Pármeno. Apparently procuresses in Spain and Italy worked in the same way, since Celestina and Alvigia have a great deal in common.

The language of *La Cortigiana* illustrates Aretino's sensitivity to every level of the life about him. Rome was much more than an Italian city; it was the center of church activities, attracting persons from all over the world. Consequently, there is a mixture of tongues in Aretino's comedy. Besides Alvigia's recitation of Latin prayers, Spanish is frequently used. Often Italian is mixed with the Spanish. Throughout the play one notices expressions like these: "Senza lei non si può far *nada*"; "tocca a pagar a *nosotros*"; "mucciaccia"; "mozzo mui lindo et agradable"; "muccio appassionado Don Sancio"; "vigliacco, higio de putta, traidor"; "ti chiero, ombre civil, tomar la capezza"; and "aorca, aorca." The Spanish influence in sixteenth-century Italy, reinforced by occupying troops, was widespread, and was reflected in language, literature, and dress.[13] Although Aretino does not hesitate to use crude, vulgar, rough words that reveal perfectly the inner characters of the figures in his play, some characters speak an affected, artificial Petrarchan language. The fullness of life's experience, from coarse criminal circles up to ultrarefined lovers, shows itself in the language of the play.

Structurally, this comedy is out of proportion, with its 106 scenes. The author himself recognized that the drama's construction was loose, and he makes an attempt to bring together the various threads at the play's end. All the main characters are onstage; some minor figures like the fisher and Romanello Ebreo are also there. Parabolano has everyone make pardons and arranges for a banquet in his house so that the comedy will not end in tragedy. Rosso gives a little speech in which he apologizes for the play's length and rambling, blaming it on faithfulness to nature. The final impression one has in viewing *La Cortigiana* is that the play's structure is fragmentary. Narrative, documentary, lexical, and satiric elements enter into the author's theatrical technique, as nothing imprisons his creative freedom.

13 B. Croce, *La Spagna nella Vita Italiana durante la Rinascita* (Bari, 1949), p. 156, lists Spanish expressions in this play and in other writings by Aretino.

The only nucleus of the comedy is the portrait of the city of Rome. Every dramatic fragment recaptures an instant of Renaissance Roman life.[14]

Il Marescalco

Structurally, Aretino's second comedy, *Il Marescalco,* is the opposite of *La Cortigiana.* Literary discipline, even at the cost of dramatic vigor, distinguishes his second play. Aretino probably first sketched out *Il Marescalco* in Mantua between the end of 1526 and the spring of the following year. He may have polished the rough sketch after going to Venice, where the work was published in 1533.[15]

In the prose prologue an actor comes on stage and tells of his embarrassment in performing before such an illustrious audience of leading nobles. He admits being afraid he might deliver the argument in a clumsy fashion, but the presence of noble persons compels him to act. As he continues, the actor grows more confident, finally declaring that he is worth more than all his theatrical company. He makes a prolonged attack on pedants, first dropping the Latin expression *cuium pecus.* The actor imagines himself in various dramatic roles. First he dresses up in a toga and gives this speech: "Spettatori, snello ama unquanco, e per mezzo di scaltro a sé sottragge quinci e quindi uopo, in guisa che a le aurette estive gode de lo amore di invoglia, facendo restìo sovente, che su le fresche erbette al suono de' liquidi cristalli cantava l'oro, le perle e l'ostro di colei, che lo ancide." For Aretino, as the passage illustrates, Petrarchism and pedantry are closely bound, and this speech is a playful caricature of pedantic and Petrarchan terms. The actor goes on to imagine himself as a procuress dressed in gray, going about to visit churches while counting beads; in this role he would try to ensnare a

14 Marvin T. Herrick, *Italian Comedy* (Urbana, Ill., 1960), p. 86, and Mario Apollonio, *Storia del Teatro Italiano* (Florence, 1951), 2:100, discuss this comedy's structure. Especially note Giorgio Petrocchi, *Pietro Aretino tra Rinascimento e Controriforma* (Milan, 1948), pp. 222-26. Giuliano Innamorati, "Lo Stil Comico di Pietro Aretino," *Paragone* 14, no. 162 (1963): 6-28, speaks of the primitive energy of Aretino's style in his first comedy with its verbal violence and impassioned satire of the Roman court; for Innamorati the author succeeded in creating a sensation of environment in a play lacking any plot development so that the audience would imagine the life of the dramatic characters continuing beyond the scenic presentation. Innamorati feels that the *Cortigiana* expresses a moment of crisis and bitterness which Aretino was to lose during his luxurious retirement to Venice, so that his later plays display an elegant but enervated mannerism.

15 Luzio, *Aretino e la corte dei Gonzaga,* p. 88, believes that the play was written at Mantua since there are many allusions to historical Mantuan figures. His placing the date of writing before 1530 is debatable as a reference is made in Act V, scene 3, to Agostino Ricchi's play *I Tre Tiranni* first performed at Bologna in 1530.

married lady. Then the actor sees himself taking the role of the married lady as she is handed a letter from her would-be lover, at first appearing angry but later preparing to inflame his love while planning to hold down scandal. The actor switches over to the lover's role, a Neapolitan or Spaniard dressed in dandy fashion, quoting Petrarch and serenading. He could also play a jealous husband keeping lovers away. Other possible roles are a miser, a braggart warrior, a parasite. It would take a tremendous effort for him to play a lord since nobles are faithless and ignorant. Aretino did not hesitate to insult the nobles with his prologue, since he was proud of being known as the "scourge of princes." Along with attacks on nobles and prelates, this prologue presents the whole gamut of character-types.

Above all *Il Marescalco* is an intentional satire on court life. Scenically, all the action takes place in the court environment of Mantua, as the setting is an esplanade between the stables and the ducal palace. In the eighth scene of Act I the official farrier, who is the play's title character, regrets that he did not become a shopkeeper, because treachery and envy are the powers which hold sway in the court. Old Ambrogio shares the farrier's disenchantment with courtly life. Another character, Count Nicola, warns (Act IV, sc. 3) the farrier that the worst thing in the world is to displease a lord; the farrier should marry the girl the duke has designated for him. Along with a large dowry the duke has offered the farrier a title as knight if he consents to marry; but the farrier declares (Act V, sc. 2) that the knightly title is absolutely empty.[16]

The trick played in this comedy by which a boy is substituted for the bride in a false wedding recalls Plautus' *Casina*. Aretino doubtless had Machiavelli's *Clizia* in mind.[17] But in the *Marescalco* the recognition of the bride's true sex is not accompanied by a painful beating. There is a strong misogynic sentiment in this comedy. In the Middle Ages and well into the Renaissance misogynic literature was rather highly developed in Italy, on learned and popular levels. The speeches of the old nurse to persuade the farrier of the virtues of married life and the attack by Ambrogio on the marital state are an echo of the medieval *contrasto,* a kind of debate. One

---

16 Vincenzo De Amicis, *L'Imitazione Latina nella Commedia Italiana del XVI Secolo* (Florence, 1897), pp. 110-12, talks of satire of the courtly circles in Aretino's first two comedies. Baratto, "Commedie di Pietro Aretino," pp. 347 and 400, discusses the author's difficult relationships with the historical Duke of Mantua, alternating from friendship to threats, and that the duke himself never appears in the comedy. Instead characters like the pedant, the count, the knight and, the nurse create the courtly environment.

17 Apollonio, *Storia,* 2:88, mentions the classical source.

of the outstanding misogynous works that may have influenced Aretino is Boccaccio's *Corbaccio*. Early in the sixteenth century, probably before the writing of the *Marescalco,* there appeared a *Farsa contro il tôr moglie* in the folk tradition, in which a youth is dissuaded from marrying by an argument an old man makes with the aid of Fortune against women and family life. Using this traditional motif of mysogynic literature and uniting it with the trick of the male bride, Aretino was able to sustain the comedy for the entire five acts without any straining.[18]

Although the farrier is the play's central figure, he is dramatically weak. This horse doctor is the principal victim of the duke's trick. Such a trick, to be artistically effective, must be based on the psychology of the victim. Machiavelli was careful to portray Messer Nicia's stupid vanity. All the play's main action ought to be developed around the psychological circumstances of the tricked character. But one learns little about the farrier and his reasons for wanting to remain a bachelor. He refuses to marry and curses the very idea of marriage. Why is he a misogynist? As he appears in this play, the farrier is little more than a dramatic sketch. But since he is the main character, his reasons for despising matrimony should be clarified. The author has paid too much attention to painting the outward details of this character. With an effort, made by following every hint, one can see in the farrier a perverted nature. When the nurse tells him to marry, she warns him that the time has come for him to give up certain vicious habits. The boy Giannicco urges the farrier to marry since he could use his wife to decoy "bei giovanetti." The farrier insists that he wants to live in his own way, sleep with whom he pleases, eat whatever is to his taste, all without a wife's scolding. Without a doubt this man is a pederast, but the theme of his perversion is merely hinted at, never developed as it should be to explain fully his misogynous attitude. The farrier is a character constructed from without but never revealed from within.[19]

Aretino is more successful in portraying the minor figures of the play than in presenting the title character. One of the most natural characters is

18 Petrocchi, *Pietro Aretino,* p. 231, gives the background of the *contrasto, Corbaccio,* and the misogynous attitude of many humanists, Sanesi, *La Commedia,* 1:291, compares the *Marescalco* with the *Farsa contro il tôr moglie.* This farce was published as *Un'antica farsa fiorentina,* ed. F. Pintor (Florence, 1901).

19 Baratto, "Commedie di Pietro Aretino," pp. 392-93, talks of the farrier's vice and his pederastic relations with the boy Giannicco. He mentions that the vice was common to the period, especially in court circles. Aretino was not supposed to be free of this vice. For further discussion on the farrier's nature see Petrocchi, *Pietro Aretino,* pp. 232-34.

the boy Giannicco, who is in the same class with the scamp Caprino in *I Suppositi*. Giannicco is an impertinent creature with an exuberant nature, who loves to tease. Aretino makes this boy representative of popular life and has him sing genuine folk songs, like this one in the comedy's first scene:

> Il mio padron to' moglie,
> il mio padron to' moglie in questa terra,
> in questa terra.
> La torrà, non la torrà,
> ei l'avrà, ei non l'avrà in questa sera,
> in questa sera.[20]

When he is with the farrier, Giannicco repeats over and over the word "moglie" since he knows how much the farrier hates the duke's command to marry. The boy takes delight in infuriating others, impudently addressing his superiors with the familiar "tu." On seeing a Jewish jewel merchant, the boy wants to throw a stone at him; but the ducal law prevents him from carrying out his caprice. The author has depicted the boy as full of childish mischief.

Whereas Giannicco is totally unrestrained, the official pedant is a stilted, solemn, and ridiculous character. This orator in the worst Ciceronian tradition is just as artificial as the boy is natural. The pedant tries to be a grave figure, strutting about full of pride in his learning. Scornful of everyday speech, the pedant intersperses Latin phrases in his Italian, often quoting the Bible and classical Roman authors. He even tries to coin his own Latin words, abusing pet names with absurd diminutives. His erudite pose fails to win him respect; others mock him. Giannicco and a page tie firecrackers to the pedant's toga. He swells up in offended dignity (Act II, sc. 11): "Questi temerari adulescentuli, questi effeminati ganimedi infamano istam urbem clarissimam; a capestri sine rubore, a gli sfacciati cineduli subiaceno gli erarii de le Vergiliane littere. . . . Honorem meum nemini dabo. Un presuntuoso, uno inetto ladrunculo mi ha posto dietro alcuni scopiculi di

---

20 "My master is taking a wife,
   my master is taking a wife in this town,
   in this town.
   He will take her, he won't take her,
   he will have her, he won't have her this evening,
   this evening."
Sanesi, *La Commedia,* 1:291-92, cites a carnival song by Lasca and a *capitolo* of the Sienese Francesco Linaiuolo to prove that Giannicco's songs are genuine examples of those that sixteenth-century Italian street urchins used to sing. Sanesi also provides here character analyses of Giannicco and the pedant.

pagina, e datogli lo igne, mi ha combusto i capegli, et inzolfato lo indumento, idest la toga cum sulphure." One of the major functions of humanists was to give Latin orations on behalf of the state. Aretino's pedant tries to carry on that tradition by delivering the wedding oration. But after the duke's trick has come to light, the pedant makes an envoi in which he speaks against marriage even though he had praised it before. He is a character without convictions, always ready to parade his nonsensical erudition.

It is not known if Aretino was acquainted with the comedy *Il Pedante* by the Roman author Francesco Belo, who published his work around 1529. Belo's title character is much like Aretino's pedant; he also goes about sputtering Latin while attending to his profession as a schoolmaster. Since there were many real-life pedants, Belo and Aretino probably had no influence on each other but found the models for their characters in the society about them. According to Paolo Giovio, Aretino's model might have been the scholar Giambattista Pio, infamous in his times for inserting Latin phrases into his Italian conversations. Whatever the source, Aretino's pedant is a far more complete dramatic figure than the preceptor Polinico in the *Calandria*.[21] Aretino here exploits all the comic potential in the figure of a pedant.

A few of the minor figures in the play serve only to express certain attitudes, without ever being true individuals. The old nurse and Ambrogio belong to this category. This nurse, who mumbles Latin prayers with her gossip, describes in Act I, scene 6, a prophetic dream about a fig tree and a bird, applying it to the ducal command that the farrier should marry. She is also a practitioner of the magic arts, as she later promises the farrier to enchant the duke so the horse doctor will be released from the command. The farrier repeats a spell, but to no avail. Ambrogio hates married life just as much as the nurse believes in it. He seems to despise everything connected with women, especially the care they take in putting on makeup (Act II, sc. 5): "Pensando ai visi che elle hanno la mattina quandro si levano, non ti vo' dire altro, i polli, che mangiano ogni sporcheria, si farebbeno schifi d'esse. Sia pur certo che non hanno tanti bossoletti i medici da gli unguenti, quanti ne hanno loro, e non restano mai d'impiastrarsi, d'infarinarsi e di sconcacarsi, e taccio la manifattura loro nel viso, ritirandosi

---

21 The date of the Roman publication of Belo's play is uncertain. Herrick, *Italian Comedy*, p. 93, says 1538; but Sanesi, *La Commedia*, 1:292, indicates 1529 mentioning the Giovio suggestion. Baratto, "Commedie di Pietro Aretino," p. 399, n. 53, thinks that the pedant's language is a subtle parody of the maccheronic style in Folengo's *Maccheronee*.

prima la pelle con le acque forti, onde innanzi al tempo, di sode e morbide diventano grinze e molli, e con i denti di ebano."[22] This is the same kind of satire on women's making up that appeared in Plautus' *Mostellaria,* in two humanistic comedies, and in both versions of the *Cassaria;* but here the description is not lighthearted, since it is sharpened by a misogynous attitude. According to Ambrogio, wives are the ruin of husbands, wasting all their funds to dress like duchesses. For him a wife is like syphilis.

Although the picture of Mantuan court life in *Il Marescalco* is not especially vicious, like that of the Roman court in *La Cortigiana,* Aretino has shown how persons attached to courts lose their freedom. The author has carried his hatred from his first to his second comedy.

Lo Ipocrito

For some years Aretino's comic vein seemed to have dried up. But at the end of 1541 and early in 1542 he composed two plays: *Lo Ipocrito,* written in only a few days, and the *Talanta,* completed in just a week. In the first of these comedies he failed to achieve the structural control which distinguished *Il Marescalco.* Aretino was in the mood to experiment with literary themes new to the learned theater.[23]

For the *Ipocrito* Aretino wrote one of his angriest prologues. Two actors are speaking. The first is full of hate, and attacks miserly princes, scoundrels, pedants, the envious, the greedy, and French and Spanish partisans. This actor wants courts to be good, and rails at all sinners. The second actor is a less violent figure who desires, nonetheless, to do away with criticism and gives a list of insolent types of criticism. The only noteworthy part of this prologue is when the first actor implies that the poet Francesco Berni sinned in reworking Boiardo's *Orlando Innamorato* in the Tuscan dialect. Boiardo's work influenced the plot of the *Ipocrito.*

In this work Aretino displays a greater debt to the ancient theater than he did in his first two comedies. Once again Plautus' *Menaechmi* has sug-

22 "In regard to the way women look when they get up in the morning, all I can say is that chickens which eat every kind of filth would be sickened by their sight. You can be certain that physicians do not have as many unguent jars as they do. Women never stop plastering themselves over, powdering their bodies, or messing themselves up. I'm going to pass over in silence the way they ruin their faces, first by drawing off their skin with hard water so that before their due time they change from firm and delicate to flabby and wrinkled, and with black teeth."

23 Baratto, "Commedie di Pietro Aretino (II)," *Belfagor* 12, no. 5 (September, 1957): 522, declares that these two plays mark an artistic crisis in Aretino's career. The author was trying to be recognized by the arbiters of official culture, like Daniello Barbaro. He hoped to rival playwrights like Alessandro Piccolomini.

gested the comic device of presenting identical twins, here Liseo and Brizio Rocchetti, thus providing the chance for several scenes of mistaken identity. The situation of a wife deserted by her husband and urged by her father to marry another man is also presented by Plautus in the *Stichus,* in which there are two daughters, Philumena and Pamphila, whose husbands have been absent for three years making commercial journeys. The girls' father Antipho asks them to take new husbands, but they remain faithful and are rewarded when their husbands come back wealthy from their travels. Liseo's daughter Tansilla never demonstrates a similar faith in her husband Artico, who has set off on a trip around the world; she is willing to comply with Liseo's request to marry the youth Tranquillo. Sophocles' *Electra* may have suggested the trick Prelio plays on Liseo's daughter Porfiria after the young man's return from Arabia.[24] Disguised as a pilgrim, he pretends that he is bearing an urn with Prelio's ashes. In this way he is able to see how relieved Porfiria feels.

These possible imitations of dramatic expedients from an ancient tragedy illustrate the pathetic mood of the love stories in the *Ipocrito.* Although the earlier authors of erudite comedies, like Ariosto or Bibbiena, wrote love stories, none of them, with the exception of Nardi, presented such a tearful atmosphere. Romantic sentiments pour out of the mooning little heroes and heroines in the *Ipocrito;* their speeches and letters have a sweetly sad, plaintive tone about them. But Aretino's fault is that he does not enter emotively and artistically into the romantic scenes. As a consequence, the romantic language is highly artificial and precious, to the point of being ridiculous. Troccio, servant to the youth Zefiro, prepares a letter in his master's name for Liseo's daughter Annetta, using Neoplatonic terms about Love's being the desire for beauty. The letter turns out to be a burlesque of Petrarchan terms. Annetta's reply repeats the medical idea of love as an illness that can be cured only by consummation. Aretino plays with the traditional love language, not taking it seriously.

In the heartbreaking triangle of Porfiria, her new lover Corebo, and her old fiancé Prelio, Aretino pushes the amorous element to the utmost. In the second scene of Act II Porfiria stands on a balcony and talks to Corebo below. The technique, if not the spirit, of the Romeo and Juliet story is already here. Dialogue here and elsewhere in the comedy between Corebo and Porfiria is affected and often tedious. On seeing how Corebo is suffering, she tells him of her own agonies: "Io mi dorrò più, se voi cominciate a

---

24 Possible derivation from the *Stichus* and *Electra* is pointed out by A. Salza, "Le Commedie del Secolo XVI," *Giorn. Stor. d. lett. ital.* 40 (1902): 435.

dolervi del mio dolore, che non farò, perché mi dolga nel modo, che nel suo essere egli mi duole." All this repetition of forms of the verb *dolere* (to suffer) is a precious way of stressing love's pain. Prelio also suffers: after he has succeeded in the test of love by traveling across seas and deserts to find the feathers of the phoenix, he returns to see that she loves another. When she tells him of the suicide pact with Corebo, Prelio declares that he will also take poison. Porfiria is joyful at the idea of a triple suicide in the name of love. The author of the comedy delights in buliding up the love situation to achieve a mock emotional intensity. His lovers are comical because they take themselves so seriously. Prelio holds (Act V, sc. 5) that: "to the one who loves the impossible is easy to achieve." These romantic characters live in their own special heroic world.

Aretino most certainly drew the story of this triangle from the twelfth canto of the first part of the *Orlando Innamorato,* the story of the two Saracen friends of Babylon. The nobleman Prasildo fell in love with Tisbina, wife of his friend Iroldo. To save him from his nearly suicidal passion, Tisbina sent Prasildo to the wilds of Barbary to fetch her a bough of the Tree of Wealth. Despite all the perils of the journey Prasildo performed the task. Iroldo and Tisbina decided to take poison so as to avoid dishonor. On learning of their act Presildo intended to join the suicide pact, but an apothecary informed him that he had given the couple only a harmless drink. Telling the good news to the couple, Prasildo so impressed Iroldo with his generosity that the latter resolved to exile himself forever from Babylon and grant Tisbina to his friend. Later Prasildo learned that Iroldo was in a dangerous situation, and he immediately left Babylon to rescue his friend. Boiardo reflects a chivalric tradition in which questions of love and friendship were debated.

Although the love story in the *Ipocrito* and the episode from *Orlando Innamorato* are similar up to the happy outcome of the poisoning attempt, Aretino resolved the love intrigue by Prelio's freeing the girl with a kiss from her obligation to him. This different conclusion may go back to *Decameron* X, 5, a source, in fact, for Boiardo's episode. Boccaccio narrates how the lady Dianora requested Messer Ansaldo to bring forth a beautiful garden in January. With the aid of a magician, Ansaldo succeeded. Dianora's husband told her to do Ansaldo's pleasure, but this act of generosity so moved Ansaldo that he freed the lady from her promise. Neither Ansaldo nor Prelio took advantage of the debt his beloved lady owed him for performing a quite impossible task. Another similar version of this tale is in the Thirteen Questions of Love in Boccaccio's *Filocolo*. Aretino had this literature behind him, but he did not use it in an artistically "sincere" way.[25]

Besides the amorous relationships of the play there is also the relationship between Ipocrito and Liseo. Ipocrito is a religious hypocrite who assumes a pious air to win Liseo's confidence. His control of Liseo is similar to Tartuffe's influence over Orgon in Molière's comedy. Ipocrito speaks in a manner that is "sì adagio e sì pensato" and walks with his head down, a book of prayers under his arm. He frequents churches and is always talking about charity and obedience. Liseo feels he cannot live with Ipocrito. This hypocrite has his own philosophy of life, declaring simulation to be his shield and chief weapon. Questioned by Liseo about the many suitors for his five daughters, Ipocrito finds fault with every profession and class. This hypocrite is a parasite, with the gluttony typical of his kind. His true qualities are known to the procuress Gemma. When approached to be the go-between for Zefiro and Annetta, this old procuress pleads that she is worn out by the expenses of maintaining a large establishment with several servants; she recommends Ipocrito as the person best qualified to be a go-between. Ipocrito handles the love letters for Zefiro and Annetta, tempting the girl with a diabolical cunning that finally wins her over. It is never made clear whether Ipocrito himself is lascivious. One of the servants, Perdelgiorno, comments that he does not care for the hungry looks Ipocrito throws at Liseo's wife Maja. The play's happy outcome, with multiple weddings and a reunion, does not please Ipocrito. In a brief soliloquy (Act V, sc. 16) he expresses his chagrin at the peaceful conclusion: "In fine noi altri Ipocriti siamo scellerati per natura più che per arte. Questo dico a proposito di quel non so che, il quale mi arrabbia l'animo ne lo aver male i successi buoni, che mi escano di mano, mentre mi sono isforzato che i loro esiti siano pessimi."[26] Ipocrito wears a mask of piety to work chaos in Liseo's household.

Liseo is too weak to run his household by himself and needs a stronger figure like Ipocrito to hold onto in the face of domestic problems. At the play's start Liseo is genuinely concerned about his family, but he undergoes a character change when Ipocrito explains to him his idea of Lady Fortune's true nature. Ipocrito contends that people are wrong to consider Fortune an impartial power which gives and takes. Instead Fortune, according to him, is like a prostitute who torments the lovers that are passionately interested

25 Petrocchi, *Pietro Aretino*, p. 238, mentions the sources in Boccaccio and Boiardo.
26 "In conclusion we hypocrites are scoundrels more by nature than by profession. I am saying this in regard to a certain delicate matter which irritates me because of my hating happy outcomes that slip away from my control while I have worked hard for them to turn out very badly." Apollonio, *Storia*, 2: 89-95, discusses Ipocrito's character.

in her and favors the lovers who are indifferent. On hearing Ipocrito's theory Liseo reflects on it and decides to live by it. No matter what happens, good or bad, he is to remain indifferent. His supremely impassive attitude is undisturbed when Maja argues with him. Annetta's flight, the return of his twin brother and Tansilla's husband—nothing moves him. Not even wedding plans stir Liseo, for he has voluntarily made himself a block of wood. In his own words he has closed his ears to pleasant or unpleasant news. This lack of any concern comes out in the envoi Liseo makes: "todos es nada, y nada es todos." Aretino portrays in Liseo a troubled man shielding himself from his problems by accepting indifference as a way of life.[27]

Aretino's servants are not direct heirs of the clever slaves of the Roman Comedy. Liseo's servants Malanotte, Guardabasso, and Perdelgiorno do not possess the superior intelligence of some servants in the theatrical works of Ariosto and Bibbiena. Instead the servants in *Lo Ipocrito* are background figures who comment on the action that develops around them. They are a crowd of clowns, whose one weapon is slandering those they serve by creating verbal caricatures of their employers. They describe Maja as a religious fanatic and a gossip. When Brizio's servant Tanfuro enters the household, he and Guardabasso make a mutual advantage alliance to exploit the twin brothers. Despite this pact, all the servants remain in a subordinate position, never affecting the play's outcome.[28]

Rarely is a play as confusing as *Lo Ipocrito*. This comedy begins as another version of the errors of identification caused by twins. Then an extremely complicated love story is added. The number of Liseo's daughters contributes to making the play even more complex. Since the author has observed the unities of time and place, the work's structure is weighted to the breaking point with the return of Brizio, Prelio, and Artico in less than twenty-four hours. If the hypocrite were dominant in the play, the various elements of the work could be held together. But Aretino failed to develop the hypocrite's character to its fullest psychological extent; so, unfortunately, the portrait of the hypocrite is lost amid the involved love intrigues, recovery scenes, and surprise encounters. The author's desire to write a full-length comedy caused him to neglect the central figure of the play. Its many characters are too uniform; instead of acting they merely pronounce grandilo-

27 Baratto, "Commedie di Pietro Aretino (II)," pp. 528-32, comments that the conversion of Liseo is the height of unreal absurdity in Aretino's art. B. Croce, "Intorno alla commedia italiana del Rinascimento," *La Critica* 28, no. 1 (January, 1930): 18 also discusses the change in Liseo.
28 Apollonio, *Storia* 2: 93-94, describes these nonclassical servants. Petrocchi, pp. 239-40, mentions their use of slander.

quent speeches. The hypocrite ought to be at the comedy's nucleus. He makes some suggestions as to what Liseo could do, but his schemes are rarely carried out. Most of the time he is giving long monologues that interrupt the comedy's dramatic rhythm. Internal unity is completely lacking.[29]

Despite its structural defects, *Lo Ipocrito* is a milestone in the Italian theater. For the first time an author of prime magnitude has introduced serious romantic elements in a stage comedy. Aretino's predecessor Nardi did not possess poetic talents. Tearful emotional intensity, moral conflict between love and friendship, examples of high-mindedness—all these elements anticipate the change in theatrical taste which took place in the second half of the sixteenth century when the Erudite Comedy passed into the serious comedy. Aretino, while turning back to Boiardo's chivalric epic, created a romantic drama.[30]

Talanta

After setting *Lo Ipocrito* at Milan, Aretino once again places a comedy in Rome with his *Talanta*. This play shows a greater classical imprint than any of the first three comedies. Its situation is very close to that of Terence's *Eunuchus;* in the Latin comedy the courtesan Thais has two lovers: the youth Phaedria and the braggart captain Thraso. Aretino was aware of possible criticism about the Terentian influence and has Orfinio, one of the three lovers of the courtesan Talanta, distinguish himself from Phaedria: "Io che non son Fedria di Taide, se ben paio, perchè anch'egli non è di Terenzio, benchè sia tenuto. . . ."[31] Thraso gives a slave to Thais just as Captain Tinca does for Talanta. There is a recognition scene in the *Eunuchus,* just as in the *Talanta*. But although he borrowed some themes, character types, and situations from the Terentian play, Aretino did not slavishly imitate the Roman author.[32]

Another classical play that may have influenced the Italian author is

29 Petrocchi, *Pietro Aretino,* pp. 235-41, goes in great detail over the structure.
30 Baratto, "Commedie di Pietro Aretino (II)," p. 530, calls the love episode of Porfiria and Prelio a degeneration of the chivalric tradition. The love speeches are just verbal tours de force. The *Ipocrito* was one of the most frequently reprinted of Aretino's plays in the second half of the sixteenth century and in the first quarter of the seventeenth. Since Aretino's works passed on the Index, the plays were often reprinted under the name of Luigi Tansillo or with changed titles. A discussion of Aretino's place in the history of the Italian theater can be found in Louise George Clubb, *Giambattista della Porta Dramatist* (Princeton, N.J., 1965), p. 137, n. 3.
31 "I am not Thais' Phaedria, even if I appear to be, for he also does not belong to Terence although he has that reputation. . . ."
32 Petrocchi, *Pietro Aretino,* p. 242, talks of the Terentian influence.

Plautus' *Truculentus*. This Plautine comedy presents the courtesan Phronesium besieged by three lovers: Dinarchus, a dissipated young Athenian; Strabax, a youth from the country; and Stratophanes, an officer in the Babylonian army. The courtesan's relationship with Dinarchus is especially similar to Talanta's with Orfinio. Although both females try to get expensive gifts from these lovers, they tolerate Orfinio and Dinarchus even when penniless because of the youths' wit. The *Truculentus,* perhaps because its dramatic situation is not fully realized and its text is corrupt, has rarely been noted by critics; but its portrait of a scheming courtesan playing one lover against another to her greater profit has its parallels in the *Talanta.*

One of the most obvious classical influences comes from Plautus' *Menaechmi.* In the *Talanta* there are triplets, Antino, Lucilla, and Oretta (children of Messer Blando of Castro), instead of twins. But the disguise of Lucilla as a Saracen male slave and of Antonio as a Moorish slave girl may have come from Lidio and Santilla in Bibbiena's *Calandria.* The youth Armileo was particularly fooled by the resemblance between Antino and Oretta; at one point of the drama he tries to kidnap Oretta, believing her to be the false slave girl. This is the second time Aretino has employed the device of identical twins, having used it in the *Ipocrito.*[33]

Although the example of the Roman Comedy is rather strong in this play, the author took considerable pains to set the work in sixteenth-century Rome. Talanta's Venetian lover Messer Vergolo has come to Rome to find a court position for his son. While there he wants to see the famous monuments. His friend Ponzio gives him a guided tour (Act I, sc. 3). Like most Venetians, Vergolo is not accustomed to horseback riding, and in this scene he is shown trying to keep from falling off a horse during his tour of the *antichità del Senatus et populusque Romanus.* On sighting one building he asks: "Say, what is that big oversized place?" He learns that it is the Pantheon, then called the Rotunda. Vergolo goes on to see the Colosseum, Trajan's column, and the arch of Septimus Severus. The guide explains that under the arch passed "Giulio Cesare con le sue genti trionfanti." Vergolo, overwhelmed by the sights, is unable to note the historical error. To clinch the effect of wonder, Ponzio points out the Templum Pacis, relating a medieval legend that says the temple was partially destroyed at Christ's birth,

33 Sanesi, *La Commedia,* 1: 297, compares the *Talanta* to the *Calandria.* Another influence of Bibbiena's may be in the prologue to the *Talanta* where the reciting actor tells how in his sleep he flew to the gardens of the learned and then to the heavens; he was allowed to take the form of Cupid and to go and spy on various love affairs. There is a series of vignettes similar to those that Bibbiena included in the prologue he wrote for his play.

just as the ancient Romans had prophesied would happen after a virgin gave birth. All during the tour Vergolo continues to compare the Roman ruins with landmarks of his native Venice, even mentioning Titian and Sansovino. In this scene Aretino has given an archeological view of Rome.[34]

Elsewhere in the comedy Aretino has his characters allude to artists working in Rome. Orfinio's friend Pizio refers (Act II, sc. 3) to Michelangelo's work on the *Last Judgment* and to the activities of Sebastiano dal Piombo. Messer Blando, who is visiting the metropolis for the first time, praises Raphael's paintings (Act IV, sc. 21) and goes into the Pantheon to see his tomb. The Rome which Aretino presents to the audience is not the city of itinerant salesmen and venal clergymen that appeared in *La Cortigiana*. Here in the *Talanta* the author works from a different angle, creating a vast panorama, which taxed the perspective stage setting of his time to its limits, of the city that had preserved the glories of antiquity and inspired the most distinguished artists of the Renaissance.

To explain the separation of Blando and Oretta from the rest of their family, the author refers to the Turkish menace. Blando relates that when his children were nine years old, the Turks of Soliman raided Castro. He and Oretta were held in prison for four years. The Turks sold Lucilla and Antino to an Italian merchant in Ancona. During her whole imprisonment Oretta had remained disguised as a male. This disguise of a female in masculine clothes is of course common in novelle like *Decameron* II, 9, and in comedies like the *Calandria*. Aretino's reference to Turkish raids not only sets the play in the Renaissance period but also provides a modern background for the classical device of a recognition scene.

Even though several characters are drawn from conventional types, Aretino succeeds in making them belong to his own times. Talanta is more than an Italian reworking of the Terentian Thais or the Plautine Phronesium, since the author could have found models for her in contemporary society. Many Renaissance courtesans were cultured, enjoying a social role close to that of the *hetairae* of Hellenistic Greece. Imperia, the Roman courtesan, was expert at composing sonnets and had musical talent. Her clients were intelligent and distinguished persons who demanded more than sensual satisfaction. Talanta belongs to Imperia's class; she is so sure of her accomplishments that she laughs at the way Vergolo kept a servant with him for two years in order to learn the Tuscan tongue. Pedantic affectations

---

34 Greco, *Vita Romana*, pp. 10-11, describes Vergolo's tour. Also see Jacob Burckhardt, "The Revival of Antiquity: Rome, the City of Ruins," in *Renaissance in Italy*, trans. S.G.C. Middlemore (New York, 1958).

disgust Talanta. She sings delightfully, accompanying herself on the harp. This courtesan fits perfectly into an elevated society.[35]

A strange coldness can be detected in Talanta's aristocratic nature. She possesses a certain superior haughtiness, as if she were following her profession out of intellectual daring rather than out of economic necessity or the attraction of vice. Her movements are slow and studied. She knows what men are worth; the clients that long for her and finally obtain her succeed only after she has interviewed them and carefully examined their characters. The comedy opens with a scene in which Talanta is talking with her maid Aldella, the only person in whom she confides. It is a quiet moment in her busy day, which is usually spent receiving lovers and their messengers. The courtesan runs down the list of her lovers, laughing at their credulous way of thinking that they are truly beloved by her. With her cold logic Talanta knows how to deceive men, but she never deceives herself about their intentions. When Aldella declares that Orfinio truly loves Talanta, the courtesan disagrees, making fine distinctions: "Orfinio ama non me, ma il suo trastullo, e spende non in mio pro, ma a suo piacere. Ecco, un ghiotto compra una starna, non per amor che gli porti, ma per la voglia ch'egli ha di mangiarsela. . . ."[36] This woman is a realist who does not intend to look out for the benefit of her clients to her own disadvantage. At one time she grows concerned since she knows that the day will come when she will no longer please men: "Ne viene la vecchiaia, Aldella, e come la fronte comincia ad incresparsi, le borse si serrano e gli amori si freddano."[37] Talanta is determined to provide for her future and avoid poverty.

Few master the art of handling men as well as Talanta; she knows when to pretend interest or indifference. In her relationship with Orfinio she plays cat to his mouse. Talanta uses a classical phrase (Act I, sc. 8) to explain how she first wounds, then heals her lover. When Orfinio threatens to leave her, she plays on him until he is ready to purchase her an expensive gift. Her superior detachment from her lovers is evident in a scene where she learns that two of them have just fought a duel on her account. She bursts out in laughter. When the messenger scolds her, Talanta does not

35 Burckhardt, *Renaissance in Italy,* 2:394, speaks of the position of highly cultured courtesans in Italian Renaissance society.
36 "Orfinio does not love me but his own pleasure, and he does not spend money on my behalf but for his own delight. Look, a glutton buys a partridge not for the love that he holds for it but for the desire he has to eat it up. . . ."
37 "Old age comes, Aldella, and as your face begins to wrinkle, purses start to close and love grows cold."

lose her calm for a second but explains that she is not to be held guilty for the jealous quarreling which her beauty excites in her admirers. She sees herself as a high-priced commodity, but recognizes that she cannot claim too much from others. By the play's end Captain Tinca and Vergolo present her with two slaves, yielding their claims to Orfinio. Talanta, seeing clearly her inferior social position, thanks them for their noble act in words that are almost humble. This portrait of a courtesan is not at all stereotyped. Aretino has pictured fully both Talanta's character and her social role.[38]

In contrast with Talanta, who lives by exciting men's passions, there is Orfinio's friend Pizio, a "positive" character who tries to combat the courtesan's bewitching attractions. Pizio attempts to rein in Orfinio. For a while Pizio thinks he has succeeded, but the illusion does not last long. He attacks lascivious youth, for he has an ideal of love as pure and not sullied by contact with courtesans. Pizio is always delivering soliloquies, like this one: "Veramente l'amore per donna da bene è un piacere che partecipa della gioia divina: ecco che io la figuro sul balcone mezzo dentro a mezzo fuori; intanto io passo e passando la veggo, e vedendola ne godo, e godendone dico:—E non val più questa contemplazione che qualunque possesso ci dessero di lor medesime quante cortigiane fûr mai?"[39] Aretino is often a depraved writer who ruins the higher flights of his imagination. But a few times, such as in a letter to Titian about the play of clouds over the Grand Canal, he was able to escape from his usually base attitudes and write in a delicate and sincerely moving manner, without any false rhetoric. Pizio is a sensitive character who genuinely desires to save his friend from his mad passion for Talanta. When he sees that his efforts have failed, Pizio courteously helps Orfinio in every way possible.[40]

Captain Tinca is more than a servile reproduction of Terence's Thraso. A product of the Italian scene, he has had a hard soldier's life during the wars of mercenary armies in Italy. He mentions real battles in which he participated, such as Cerignola of 1503 and Marignano of 1515, whereas the braggart captain of the *Miles gloriosus* describes purely fanciful battles with exaggerated names. Tinca is a seasoned veteran with precise military knowl-

38 Petrocchi, *Pietro Aretino,* pp. 245-46, and Croce, "Intorno alla commedia," pp. 14-15, analyze her character.
39 "Truly love for a good lady is a pleasure that participates in divine joy: behold how I imagine her on a balony half indoors and half outdoors; meanwhile I walk by and in passing I see her and in seeing her I receive enjoyment, and in enjoying myself I say: 'And isn't this contemplation more worthwhile than the possession which courtesans have ever granted of themselves.' "
40 Petrocchi, *Pietro Aretino,* p. 246, describes Pizio.

edge about siegecraft and fortifications, in contrast with Terence's Thraso, who has hazy ideas about warfare. One of the ways Renaissance authors changed the braggart type was to make him very poor, whereas the braggart captains of the ancient comedy were ostentatiously wealthy. Tinca does not have large estates with many servants, and has had to sleep on his horse during wars—rarely in a bed. He has the responsibilities of husband and father. His greatest desire is to marry his daughter Marmilia to a wealthy suitor. On learning that Marmilia has given herself to a lowly slave, Tinca is ready to roast the lover since he sees his dream of money destroyed. He is weary of battle, declaring that soldiers win more wounds than riches. Marmilia has proved troublesome in his efforts to gain rest from his battles.

But Tinca shows his inheritance from the ancient character type in maintaining a parasite, Branca, to listen to his boasts of military glory. Branca, whose parallel is the parasite Gnatho of the *Eunuchus,* is far more clever than Tinca and constantly ridicules his patron's claims. This flatterer holds (Act II, sc. 4) that religious hypocrites are the new class of parasites. Tinca uses the parasite as his sounding board to compare himself with Hector. He says that he wants to hire a poet to sing his glories. The captain is proud of his sword, comparing it to Roland's Durlindana. Tinca feels that he has a place beside the heroes of chivalric literature. He is ready to duel with Orfinio. Renaissance comic playwrights developed the duel scene for its most ridiculous effects, revealing how cowardly the braggart warriors were. Tinca fails to punish Antino for seducing Marmilia; instead the slave catches Tinca riding on a mule and gives him a beating. This captain is a real philosopher on self-defense and would always rather flee than fight. Although ancient comedies provided a model for a braggart warrior like Tinca, Aretino rendered him as a figure right out of Italy's unstable political and military circumstances. Tinca does not seem to be a product of a "learned" comedy imitated from Roman plays. This Neapolitan lover and boaster anticipates the vain captains like Matamoros and Vallinferno who belong to the Commedia dell'Arte. The author employs expressive elements that also characterize the popular theater.[41]

The most surprising character in the comedy is Armileo's preceptor, Peno. One would expect him to be like the pedant Polinico of the *Calandria*

---

41 Daniel C. Boughner, *The Braggart in Renaissance Comedy* (Minneapolis, 1954), pp. 49-52, talks of Tinca and his professional manner. Croce, *La Spagna nella Vita Italiana*, p. 220, discusses the captain as a figure from Naples. Petrocchi, *Pietro Aretino*, p. 244, comments on this character as anticipating the captains in the *Commedia dell'Arte*.

with his bothersome sermons about the evils of passion. Instead Peno philosophizes in favor of Love, feeling that it would be mad for him to try to suppress his student's amorous feelings. He believes that Love cannot be avoided. In the lessons he gives, Peno recognizes that torment is often bound up with Love, pointing out (Act II, sc. 10) the paradoxes of Love: "La somma della sua natura è duolo allegro, torto giusto, stoltezza saggia, timidità animosa, avarizia splendida, infermità sana, asprezza agevole, odio amicabile, infamia gloriosa et iracondia placida."[42] Love is thus a union of contrary elements. Peno also suggests how one can live once Love has penetrated his soul. The solution is to live amid those contrary forces: "Imita la prestanzia di quegli che ciechi veggono, pentiti perseverano, languendo godono, gridando tacciono, perduti si trovano, negando consentono, partendo restano, prigioni son liberi, digiunando si saziano, e morti resuscitano."[43] Peno constantly speaks of Love in these Petrarchan paradoxes. He reveals his pedantry by his superior air before his student. Just as he vindicats Love, he justifies philosophy as being bound up with the existence of reason, without which one could not speak. Only in matters of religion does he submit to a voice higher than his own. Aretino created in Peno a pedant who does not fit the conventional mold.[44]

Two of the liveliest figures in the play are Costa, Orfinio's servant, and Fora, another servant. They are hungry scoundrels whose masters pay them little. In one scene they discuss how poverty and desire are at war in them. Poverty takes away their chance to buy the food they want, but it can never take away their desire. Costa recalls a day when he was in the fish market; he saw a sturgeon and pretended to himself that he could buy it. On hearing him Fora starts to chew as if he had the fish himself. Both servants are stirred by the sound of the fish's name, *sturione;* they have a poetic gluttony. Fora and Costa are not passive sufferers, but try to alleviate their animal hunger. Joining with Branca, the two servants succeed in tricking the pedantic lawyer Dr. Necessitas over a painting. In the last act, Fora and Costa

42 "The sum of its nature is happy pain, just wrong, sage idiocy, courageous timidity, extravagant greed, healthy infirmity, easy harshness, friendly hate, glorious infamy, and placid wrath."
43 "Imitate the excellence of those who though blind see, though repentant persevere, though languishing enjoy, though shouting are silent, though lost are found, though denying agree, though departing remain, though prisoners are free, though fasting sate themselves, and though dead arise once more."
44 Petrocchi, *Pietro Aretino,* pp. 246-47, contrasts Peno with Polinico. Croce, "Intorno alla commedia," p. 16, notes Peno does not fit the usual pattern for a pedant.

turn to violence. They approach a delicatessen owner, who is a usurer and cheat. One claims he has been commissioned to purchase a large food order, and the other is disguised as a porter to carry away the food. When the dealer asks for payment, he receives a blow. The dealer screams and starts chasing the fleeing servants, but one rogue is a quick-change artist and confronts the dealer with a disguise as a lame and one-eyed man. He warns the robbed dealer not to continue his pursuit at the risk of facing greater violence. At last the two rascals can begin to rejoice. Fora and Costa do not belong to the comedy's main action, but remain lateral figures. Even though they are very cunning, they differ from the sly servants of Ariosto's comedies, who combine the astuteness of slaves in ancient comedies with the resourceful intelligence of Boccaccian characters. Fora and Costa contribute little or nothing to the love intrigue; yet the author has been able to fit them into the play's loose structure.[45]

By introducing triplets who had been separated and forced into disguising their true sexes Aretino made the plot highly involved. If he had followed the model of the *Eunuchus* closely, the structure would have been compact; but to the story of the courtesan and her three lovers he joined a tale derived from the *Menaechmi*. The rather realistic picture of the courtesan's world is upset by the burlesque element of the triplets, whose close resemblance causes errors in identification. Focus on the main subject is lost amid the side arguments. There seems to be an attempt to represent Talanta allegorically: she, the courtesan of Rome, is sought after by the Venetian Vergolo and the Neapolitan Tinca, just as the Roman court is frequented by persons from all of Italy seeking favors. Unfortunately the allegory is merely hinted at, being lost in the comedy's various intrigues. Much of the old material used in the *Cortigiana* is here again, but what is lacking in the *Talanta* is the spirited commotion that welded together the various elements in Aretino's first comedy.[46]

Il Filosofo

Structural control distinguishes Aretino's last comedy, *Il Filosofo*. On finishing it, in December of 1544, he sent a copy of the work to the Duke of

45 Croce, "Intorno alla commedia," pp.17-18, describes the servants and their poetic gluttony.

46 Petrocchi, *Pietro Aretino*, p. 243, and Apollonio, *Storia*, 2: 101-2, analyze the play's structure. Baratto, "Commedie di Pietro Aretino (II)" p. 523, feels that Aretino was close to exhausting his artistic abilities in constructing this play; consequently he had to lean heavily on ancient sources. For Baratto this comedy, along with the *Ipocrito,* is marred by an extreme degree of falseness.

Urbino, to whom he had dedicated the play. Its Venetian publication took place in 1546. The dryness which marred both the *Ipocrito* and the *Talanta,* with their complicated plots, is gone. Scenically *Il Filosofo* is the most experimental of Aretino's comedies.[47] Two plot lines run independently through the play. The first tale of the jewel merchant Boccaccio obviously comes from *Decameron* II, 5. Aretino begins his "Argomento e Prologo" by having the actor who delivers the prologue describe how on the preceding night he had seen in a dream the elaborate stage sets and the presentation of the drama: "e più vi dico, che non solo ho udito recitare in foggia di Commedia la baja del Perugino Andreuccio in sul Cento novelle, ma la chiacchiara di un filosofastro."[48] The author acknowledges his debt to the *Decameron* by even giving his hero the name Boccaccio.

Aretino does more than render the tale of Andreuccio of Perugia in dialogue form. He introduces a series of underworld characters who dash across the stage almost with daggers drawn to fight off police agents. Tullia the prostitute is far below Talanta; the great courtesan of Aretino's fourth comedy does not have to resort to criminal means to separate her clients from their moneybelts. Tullia is a she-wolf, in the words of her maid Lisa, with a ruthless determination to prey on others. She has a staff of servants and protectors. Her pimp Cacciadiavoli (note the name) chases Boccaccio away from her establishment. The merchant's night on the streets brings him into contact with a group of cutthroats like the three thieves who unwittingly release him from a tomb. Their names, Mezzoprete, Sfratato, and Chietino, are a naughty slap at the clergy. As in the *Cortigiana,* the low life of Italian society is depicted in the theater; the author had no ancient model for these figures. A particular novellistic source, along with Aretino's skill at making his characters seem real, provided the material of the first tale in this comedy.[49]

Although the author indicates no particular source for the parallel story of the philosopher Plataristotile, its plot line and characterization are overwhelmingly Boccaccian. The tale most similar to this one is *Decameron* VII, 8, discussed above as a possible influence on the *Calandria.* Just as an ass is substituted for the lover Polidoro in Aretino's comedy, Sismonda in

47 Baratto states (*Ibid.,* p. 533) that by the time of the writing of the *Filosofo* Aretino had passed his creative crisis, renouncing his cultural pretensions.
48 "And I'll tell you more, not only did I hear the pleasant nonsense of Andreuccio of Perugia from the One Hundred Tales turned into a comedy, but also the chattering of a dull philosopher."
49 Petrocchi, *Pietro Aretino,* p. 253, hints at Aretino's portrait of the modern criminal world.

the Boccaccian novella substitutes her maid for herself. The way Arriguccio Berlinghieri, in Boccaccio's tale, fails to prove his wife's infidelity closely parallels the inability of Aretino's philosopher to demonstrate the guilt of his wife Tessa. In the comedy and in the novella a young wife takes a lover because her husband neglects his marital duties. Both works use a substitution scheme.[50]

The philosopher's very name reveals Aretino's scorn for useless metaphysical studies. This character would love to unite the knowledge of Plato and Aristotle in himself. Plataristotile is the target for the author's polemic, and is presented as a man who has spent his life outside the world of intense human passions. Aretino, as usual, does not try to penetrate the character's inner spirit. The author's comic power does not rise from a complete, precise psychological portrait of the philosopher; instead Aretino condemns an entire category of individuals. The pedant, with his pretense of profound knowledge and understanding, can be a Latinizing orator like the one in *Il Marescalco* or a vain would-be philosopher. Plataristotile understands so little that he cannot see that his wife is sexually starved while he withdraws to his study. Although he has married a younger woman, the philosopher holds the opposite sex in contempt. He explains (Act I, sc. 5) his antifeminist opinions to the servant Salvalaglio; this "erudite" follows the tradition of many humanists who wrote misogynic works. His inability to appreciate Tessa's sensual desires makes him similar to the Boccaccian Ricciardo di Chinzica (*Decameron* II, 10); but whereas Ricciardo di Chinzica was a truly learned judge, Plataristotile is merely an intellectual pretender. His pompous strutting recalls still another Boccaccian character, the incredibly stupid Maestro Simone of the *Decameron* VIII, 9. The philosopher's blindness to his domestic problems makes him similar to the many duped husbands of the novellistic tradition.[51] Aretino's presentation of Plataristotile as a caricature of the archpedant reaches its culmination in the scenes of Act IV in which the philosopher fails to prove his wife's faithlessness. The discovery of an ass in his study, instead of the lover, is symbolic and satirizes the uselessness and stupidity of Plataristotile's metaphysical researches. This scene has a parallel in one of the fragments of the *Rinaldo Ardito,* some-

---

50 Novellistic parallels are treated of by A. Salza, "Commedie del Secolo XVI," p. 437, and by Enrico Perito, "Il 'Decamerone' nel 'Filosofo' di P. Aretino," *Rassegna Critica d. lett. ital.* 6 (1906): 17-25.

51 Perito, "Il 'Decamerone' nel 'Filosofo' di P. Aretino," p. 19, compares the philosopher to Gianni Lotteringhi (*Decameron* VII, 1) and Tofano (*Decameron* VII, 4).

times attributed to Ariosto. In the *Rinaldo Ardito* Malagigi uses a disguise as Orlando to enjoy the love of Queen Gallicana; to escape he substitutes an ass for himself.[52] Plataristotile, with his pretensions to vast wisdom, is an asinine figure.

Monna Tessa rebels against her husband's preoccupation with pseudo-philosophical questions. Since she cannot get love from her husband, she is determined to take a lover. This woman is not a passive, mild creature like the Monna Tessa who is married to the simpleton Calandrino in the *Decameron*. The Tessa of Aretino's comedy resembles more closely her namesake in *Decameron* VII, 1, in which the faithless wife devises a complicated system of signals so her lover can meet her in safety. Tessa's triumph over the philosopher's attempt to discredit her before her mother recalls Ghita of *Decameron* VII, 4, the story of the well, in which the wife proves her false innocence before her relatives and neighbors. In the tenth scene of Act IV Tessa declares the rights of her youthful sensual drives in a speech that begins: "Nature which resides between the thighs. . . ." Before Aretino, Boccaccio had presented numerous examples of women who were sexually starved, like Pietro di Vinciolo's wife. Tessa is like all of them, with one exception; although the troubled wives of the *Decameron* seek sensual pleasure, they appeal to a higher ideal of Love. Fulvia in the *Calandria* repeats Boccaccio's message of the natural right to love, but Tessa fails to refer her desires to a higher ideal and remains on an animal level.[53] Tessa's mother Monna Papa displays the same concern for her daughter as the mother in *Decameron* VII, 8. At first she pleads with the philosopher not to punish her daughter severely. But when the ass is discovered she turns on him; her meekness becomes ferocity to defend her daughter. This woman is drawn from the popular level, as is evident from a conversation she makes in the sixth scene of the first act with her neighbor Donna Druda (note the irony of the name). The two attack mean confessors, vulgar husbands, and the many abuses wives have to suffer. This defense of wives is the opposite of the misogynic comments made by the philosopher. Something of the spirit of *Il Marescalco* is also in this comedy, with its debates on the pros and cons of relationships between husbands and wives. Monna Papa intends to plead the case of wives against their cruel husbands.[54]

---

52 Salza "Commedie del Secolo XVI," p. 437, mentions the *Rinaldo Ardito*.
53 Salza and Perito list the novellistic ties. Apollonio, *Storia,* 2: 103, contrasts Calandrino's wife to the Tessa of the *Filosofo*.
54 Petrocchi, *Pietro Aretino,* pp. 252-53, discusses the scene between Donna Druda and Monna Papa. Salza and Perito compare her to the Boccaccian mother.

Even the servants of *Il Filosofo* are swept up in the love intrigues. One of the active figures in arranging the assignation between Polidoro and Tessa is the maid Nepitella. This girl is young and lusty, and enjoys a love affair with Polidoro's servant Radicchio. In the ninth scene of Act II she makes a speech urging all women to snatch the chance to love while they can. Nepitella clears away her mistress's doubts and hesitations.[55] The maid's lover Radicchio is a representative of rustic life. He has a naive style of talking, as when he praises a "camisciotto bianco" (white shirt), a "guarnello azzurro" (blue petticoat), and a "pianelluzze rosse" (red slippers). He is an earthy figure with a healthy appetite for life and a predilection for thickset women like Nepitella. Radicchio feels that Polidoro is making a major mistake in not loving his servant maids, but going after another man's wife. He could easly fit into the *Nencia da Barberino* and some of Luigi Pulci's writings. Radicchio is in the literary tradition of portraying the awkward simplicity of peasants.[56]

Plataristotile's servant Salvalaglio may be derived from Cesena's legendary swineherd Giovanni Salvalagli. This legend, mentioned in the *Notabilia temporum* of Angelo de Tummulillis, tells how the swineherd kissed a serpent that had promised to transform itself into a beautiful woman and to give him a great quantity of riches. There is also a poem, entitled *Sonetto di Salvalagli fatto per llo ischambrilla*, about this character's wealth. In Act II, scene 12, Salvallaglio relates to the servant Garbuglio how he has been out with witches on Mount Taborre under a magic walnut tree. When Garbuglio mentions that he is ready to go to the wars in Hungary, Salvalaglio says that he has had enough military campaigns. With the background of a soldier's life, Salvalaglio is a small-time braggart who boasts of military exploits. Knowing about those boasts, Plataristotile decides to arm Salvalaglio to police Polidoro. In this character Aretino displays an ability to fuse popular and learned literary elements.[57]

Although the novellistic, and especially the Boccaccian, element is strong in this play, the author makes this work his own and not a theatrical reduction of several novelle. The key to Aretino's success with this comedy is its structure. Despite the fact that the two actions of the work are never woven

---

55 Perito, "Il 'Decamerone' nel 'Filosofo' di P. Aretino," pp. 24-25, talks of her character.
56 Salza, "Commedie del Secolo XVI," p. 437, makes the comparison with the *Nencia da Barberino*.
57 Sanesi, *La Commedia,* 1:301, mentions the *Notabile temporum.* Salza, "Commedie del Secolo XVI," p. 437, gives the background and details of the legend. The sonnet can be found in *Giorn. Stor. d. lett. ital.* 5 (1885): 327.

together, the unities of time and place are carefully maintained. Technically the play is well-balanced, since the author subordinates the tale of the jewel merchant to that of the philosopher with his domestic problems. In this way the philosopher's tale is enlivened by a series of spirited scenic movements as the jewel merchant passes from one misadventure to another. The comedy's linear progress reaches its high point by the end of the third act, in which both actions seem catastrophic: Boccaccio has been abandoned inside a tomb; Plataristotile has overheard his wife's plans and has armed Salvalaglio for the attempt to imprison the lover in the study. But the most comic effects are reserved for the last two acts, with the substitution of the ass and Boccaccio's jumping out of the tomb like a demon to frighten away a group of thieves. Not once do the two plots ever come in conflict.

Thanks to its solid construction, *Il Filosofo* offers the spectator a varied entertainment. This artistic variety is principally expressed in the great number of characters in the parallel actions. Definite psychological traits distinguish each character in the philosopher's tale, in contrast to the flat, uniform quality which marred the five sisters and their lovers in *Lo Ipocrito*. The author draws the maximum humorous effect from each character. Aretino's comic art was always aimed at capturing life's vibrancy; he has created the impression of reality in *Il Filosofo* by two independent actions that run side by side within the classical scheme of five acts.[58]

The Contributions of Aretino to Italian Comedy

As a whole, Aretino's comic plays have certain organic weaknesses. Often the various dramatic actions within a comedy are not well integrated, and the final effect is sometimes inharmonious. The hilarity of the comic scenes is at times not sufficiently restrained for the play's total good, and the succession of scenes that break away from a work's nucleus results in formlessness. One reason for the lack of a firm technical construction is that Aretino's comedies anticipate the popular theater of the late Renaissance. Aretino excels in sketches, either of characters or environments. This tendency to emphasize sketches is caused by his desire to present a chronicle of daily life. The comedy's classical form is merely a literary scheme that Aretino accepts as part of Renaissance culture. Although the five-act scheme helped him to contain formless reality in his work, Aretino never truly questioned the meaning and function of the classical formula. Consequently he never mastered the form, and left his comedies disconnected.

58 Petrocchi, *Pietro Aretino,* pp. 248-49, describes the subordination of the jewel-merchant's tale and the variety of psychological sketches.

The classical tradition set the scene for him, along with the various character types. Despite this literary heritage, Aretino sought for creative liberty, and in the development of particular episodes he forshadowed the Commedia dell'Arte.[59]

RICCHI: I Tre Tiranni

Agostino Ricchi was an even greater professed rebel than Aretino against academic restrictions of theatrical form and content. Both writers were Tuscans who produced major works outside their native province. They were acquainted with each other's literary activity, for in the prologue to *La Cortigiana* and in a scene of *Il Marescalco* Aretino expressly refers to Ricchi's sole comedy. One of Aretino's most famous letters, "Le delizie dell' inverno," is addressed to Ricchi. Aretino was amused by the youth's attempt to create a serious comedy.

Born at Lucca, Ricchi was not even eighteen years old when he wrote his comedy *I Tre Tiranni*. He was attending courses at the University of Bologna in 1530, just at the time when the Holy Roman Emperor Charles V and Pope Clement VII met in that city to draw up an alliance. On the fourth of March Ricchi's comedy was performed, to commemorate the emperor's coronation, at a public palace in the presence of the two rulers; so the youthful author had the singular honor of seeing his play premiered at a state festival. The comedy was dedicated to Cardinal Ippolito de' Medici, with a commentary by the erudite Alessandro Vellutello. No official pomp was lacking at the play's performance.[60]

After a brief argument, the verse prologue begins when the god Mercury explains that he has been sent down from Olympus at Jupiter's order to help the earth's sadly neglected poets and philosophers. The audience is warned that if they do not attend to the needs of creative persons, the wrath of Aretino will come thundering down. But since he sees that a comedy is to be performed, Mercury agrees to give up his mean job and deliver the prologue. A *new* comedy, not one imitated from the ancients, is to be presented. Mercury explains that the three tyrants of the title are Love, Fortune, and Gold. Then comes the most rebellious declaration in the prologue, as the god points out Ricchi's intent:

59 Petrocchi considers (*ibid.*, p. 217-20) the structural weaknesses and the foreshadowing of the Commedia dell'Arte. Apollonio *Storia*, 2:85-87, talks of Aretino's accepting but never really understanding the classical form.
60 Details of the performance in Sanesi, *La Commedia*, 1:324-25, and Apollonio, *Storia*, 2:167.

Ma, perchè ben sappiate la sua mente,
gli è piaciuto scostarsi cosí alquanto
dal modo e da l'usanza degli antichi:
ché, dove han sempre usato essi che il caso
e tutto quel che pongono in comedie
possa essere in un tempo o in un dí solo,
questi ora vuol che la presente scena,
sicondo che richiede la sua favola,
servi a più giorni e notti in fine a uno anno.
E, benché si potesse aperto dire
che gli è cosí piaciuto, ha pur in vero
qualche ragione in sé: perché, sí come
si vive or con la vita del dí d'oggi
e non di quegli che fûrno giá un tempo,
e son vari i costumi, pare onesto
con questi le poesie, le prose, i versi,
li stili e l'uso ancor del recitare,
sicondo i tempi, si mutino e innovino.[61]

Although Machiavelli and Aretino sought to portray their own period, both accepted the unity of time. Ricchi was determined to break with the ancient tradition on the principle that modern times with their changed customs require a different kind of poetry and theater. The one concession the author makes to tradition is the use of Greek-style names for the characters, although the setting for the comedy is Bologna at the time of the play's writing.[62]

Throughout the play there is an attempt at allegory. The commentator Vellutello explains the symbolic roles of the three rivals for the girl Lúcia: "in old Girifalco, Love; in young Filocrate, the harmful and severe persecutions of Fortune; and in the noble Chrisaulo, the supernatural power of Gold." The commentator relates this use of allegory to Aristophanes' com-

---

61 Italian text in *Commedie del Cinquecento,* ed. I. Sanesi (Bari, 1912), vol. 1. "But, in order that you may indeed know his mind, it has pleased him to break away somewhat from the custom and practice of the ancients: for, while they have always been in the habit of having Chance and all that they place in a comedy occur in the time span of a single day, the author now wants the present scene to take up many days and nights over an entire year as his tale requires. And although one could say openly that he has done so merely for his own pleasure, he still has right truly on his side since we are living today's life and not that of persons who lived long ago and our customs are different, so that it is fitting for poems, prose, verse, style, and practice to be changed and renovated just like the times."

62 Emilio Goggio, "Dramatic Theories in the Prologues to the *Commedie Erudite* of the Sixteenth Century," *PMLA* 68 (1943): 322-36, comments on Ricchi's deliberate violation of the unity of time and his defense on the principle of changed times and modern customs.

edy *Plutus;* but whereas true symbols and personified abstract concepts are the characters in the Greek play, this comedy deals with human characters who acquire symbolic value either because of their moral qualities or because of their dramatic circumstances. Ricchi's allegory is not altogether successful. Although Girifalco is dominated by Love and Filocrate is tormented by Fortune, Crisaulo is not torn by a passion for gold. This nobleman merely uses gold to satisfy his desires. The one true tyrant in the play is Love, which holds sway over all three rivals.[63]

Although the comedy is written in eleven-syllable verses without rhyme, the author avoided the *sdrucciolo* verse and prefered one with the final accent on the penultimate syllable. Crisaulo sings a madrigal in the fifth scene of Act II, and there in a series of tercets (Act IV, sc. 4) Filocrate begs forgiveness from God. For every scene there is an introductory prose summary. Scenes and acts are interlocked; the last verse of one section is completed at the start of the following section. The parasite Pilastrino appears in the last scene of every act, which helps to unify the play. Even with its many episodic scenes, *I Tre Tiranni* is so carefully constructed that all parts easily hold together.[64]

Ricchi never lets his desire to give the characters allegorical value interfere with presenting them as individuals. Filocrate is shown throughout the play as a fanatic, maintaining his mental equilibrium with the greatest difficulty. This youth sees in his love for Lúcia the meaning of his life. He is constantly afraid that she will reject him. In Act I, scene 7, he goes to the girl's home at night. He thinks that a large pot covered with a sheet on the windowsill is Lúcia, and he pleads with the cooking-pot to talk to him. When there is no answer, Filocrate believes that he has lost her love. One of the play's incongruities is his mention of Jove's wrath; Ricchi at times forgets that he is representing contemporary Bologna. This cooking-pot scene illustrates Ricchi's art well by combining the pathetic and the ridiculous. Pilastrino and the maid Fronesia witness Filocrate's actions and laugh at his mistake; but for the youth the apparent silence of his beloved is heartbreaking. Every way he turns, Filocrate is frustrated. Fronesia tries to persuade

63 Sanesi, *La Commedia,* 1:325-26, makes the quotes from Vellutello and paraphrases his commentary. He also points out how superficial the influence of Aristophanes is.

64 Goggio, "Dramatic Theories in the Prologues," p. 334, discusses Vellutello's defense of the use of verse in the play. For Vellutello prose was the medium of expression for history and rhetoric while a natural-sounding proselike verse is ideal for the theater. This erudite commentator, however, did not altogether dismiss prose for plays with totally modern subject matter.

Lúcia to take Crisaulo as her lover. Deceived by her maid, the girl insults (Act IV, sc. 1) Filocrate before his friends, telling him never to come near her again. The tension the youth has barely suppressed explodes, and he goes mad and starts to strip himself. His decision to become a pilgrim brings ridicule from Pilastrino. Soon after his return from Spain, Filocrate witnesses Crisaulo's successful entry into Lúcia's house. He pours out the anguish that Fortune has caused him: "Quest'empia che dichiam Sorte o Fortuna" (Act V, sc. 7). His last hope was to have revenge on Crisaulo by taking the noble's place one night with Lúcia, but he succeeds only in fooling Fronesia. The mutual mistake between Filocrate and Fronesia recalls the scenes of *qui pro quo* in the *Calandria* and the *Cortigiana*, which had novellistic precedents.[65] On learning the truth, Filocrate feels that God's will has forever separated him from Lúcia. Adverse fortune has made a fatalist out of the youth.

His rival Crisaulo is a whining, Petrarchan type of lover who greatly resembles the hero Calisto in the *Celestina*. Like Calisto, this noble maintains a large staff of servants, not all of whom approve of their master's amorous schemes. Although Crisaulo is associated with gold, he despises greed as a great sin. He is sick with a love fever. After he sings his Petrarchan madrigal, he faints. On reawakening he describes a beautifully lyrical vision:

Mi pare aver sentito apparir, dentro
ne le tenebre mie dell'intelletto,
luce d'immortal guardo che gli oscuri
e dogliosi pensieri in parte m'abbia
rinconfortato. E m'è venuto in mente,
quando si truova un poverino ignudo,
nel tempo de le nevi, essere, in luogo
diserto, sí aggelato che giá l'alma
si sia partita, pur restando alquanto
nel cuore ancor del caldo naturale,
che, venuto un allegro e ardente sole,
li porta, insieme con un dolce caldo,
la vita giá perduta.[66]

(Act II, sc. 5)

65 Sanesi, *La Commedia,* 1:327.
66 "Within the darkness of my intellect, there seemed to appear the light of an immortal countenance which comforted to some extent my dreary and painful thoughts. And I thought of a poor naked wretch standing in a snowy wasteland, so frozen that his soul has already fled; yet some of the natural warmth still remains in his heart so that after a cheerful shining sun has come, together with a sweet warmth it restores to him the life that he had lost."

Crisaulo finally reaches Lúcia by climbing into her window on a ladder from the garden around her home. He is more fortunate than Calisto, who falls from a ladder and dies after visiting his beloved lady. In all the ecstasy of his triumph Crisaulo hails (Act V, sc. 5) God, Venus, the Moon, Kind Stars, his tired Heart, Eyes, and Tongue. He and the girl belong to different classes, and he never seriously intends to marry her. But the accomplishment of his sensual desires does not satisfy him. The force of love wins over his social prejudices, making Crisaulo wed her. He falls victim to his own emotion.

Part of Crisaulo's success is due to the eloquence of the procuress Artemona, whom he engages to plead his love with Lúcia. This woman is a religious hypocrite like Aretino's Alvigia, dressing in sackcloth and going about town reciting prayers. But she keeps a large crowd of girls about her, fattening them like capons for a higher price when she sells them. Artemona is also a witch like Alvigia and Celestina, with her own laboratory. Crisaulo's servant Fileno describes to his master how the girls assist the witch in her magic work:

> . . . Ivi tutte hanno
> il lor proprio esercizio: una pesta ossa
> e piú cose bizzarre; una crivella
> le polveri e sementi; un'altra l'erbe
> mette ne le strettoie e cava il sugo;
> questa fa medicine; un'altra unguenti,
> penso, da gambaracci e simil cose;
> una è in lavar la trementina; e l'altra
> falserá sollimato e, con salnitro
> e solforo, fará puzzar la casa.
> e vedi poi, d'intorno, mille fatte
> di lambicchi e campane da stillare,
> bocce di vetro le piú contrafatte
> del mondo. Ivi fornaci, scaffe e stufe,
> orci, fiaschi, arbarelli e tarabaccole.
> Per le fenestre fiori, erbe e sementi,
> radici, zucche, zucchelle e pignatte,
> laveggi, pignattini e speziarie
> e cose strane. E ci vedrai d'augelli
> piú membra; e piú animali scorticati;
> e pelle e grassi e sangui come inchiostro;
> unghie e capei morti.[67]

---

67 ". . . There they all have their own job: one pounds bones and several bizarre things; one sifts powder and seeds; another puts herbs in a blender and extracts their juice; this one makes medicine; another unguents from crayfish (I believe) and

Artemona is skilled at a very personal kind of magic, as is shown when she tries to fire Lúcia's imagination with the name of Crisaulo. This is dangerous work, but the procuress understands feminine psychology and knows that girls mean "yes" when they answer "no." Upon her success she receives a golden necklace from Crisaulo. Artemona rejoices in a speech on the godlike powers of gold.

One of Artemona's enemies is the parasite Pilastrino, who is more than the traditional type. Pilastrino is the kind of gay scoundrel that Luigi Pulci created in the character of the half-giant Margutte in the *Morgante*. In a special argument that follows the prologue Pilastrino actually compares himself to Margutte while describing his chief interests:

> . . . c'ho piú fede
> ne' tordi e nel buon vino e nel pan bianco
> che i frati al campanel del reflettorio.
> E certo, se vivesse oggi Margutte,
> mi adoreria sí come adoro lui.[68]

These words partly reproduce what Margutte says to himself (*Morgante* XVIII, 115): "Io non credo piú al nero, ch'a l'azzurro; / ma nel cappone, o lesso o vuogli arrosto; / . . . / ma sopra tutto nel buon vino ho fede."[69] Gluttony has become a religion for this parasite. In the special prologue he explains that he was going to be a friar but reflected on the fasts he would have to make. His realm is the most holy kitchen, since heaven for him would be eating well and drinking in a high fashion. Pilastrino admits that he goes mad upon thinking that in paradise no one eats; he would rather go to hell or limbo where he could eat. Realizing that Girifalco is torn by a violent passion in old age, Pilastrino enlists a confederate, Listagiro, to pose as the necromancer Maestro Abraham. To win a good meal out of the miser,

---

similar things; one is working on turpentine and another is falsifying metals and with nitre and sulfur she makes the house stink. All around, you see a thousand kinds of retorts and distilling glasses, the most counterfeit decanters in the world. There you see furnaces, shelves, stoves, jugs, flasks, paint-pots, cauldrons. Along the window sills you see flowers, herbs, seeds, roots, gourds, garbanzos, saucepans, jars, cooking-pots and tubes full of chemicals and strange things. And you'll see the limbs of birds and many flayed animals; and skin and fat and blood as black as ink, talons and dead hair."

68 ". . . I have more faith in thrushes and good wine and white bread than monks have in the bells of the refectory. And certainly, if Margutte were alive today, he would adore me just as I adore him."

69 "I do not believe more in black than blue; but in capons, or boiled meat, or rather a roast; . . . but above all I have faith in good wine." Sanesi, *La Commedia,* 1:795, cites the passage from the *Morgante*.

Listagiro reads Girifalco's palm (Act II, sc. 3), relating the lines of fortune on the hand with favorable stars. Girifalco is so impressed that he gives a sumptuous supper; Pilastrino comes out reeling from intoxication and babbling incomprehensible sounds. The parasites have their moment of triumph in the opening scene of Act III, in which Listagiro recites an unintelligible spell, which he claims will enable the old man to enjoy Lúcia that evening. They blindfold and bind Girifalco so he will not be terrified by the devils which are to appear in response to the magic spells. Instead the scoundrels rob Girifalco's house and beat him up, making the old man believe that devils are carrying him away.

After this robbery Pilastrino is increasingly obsessed with greed. He closes the third act by going out to bury his sack of gold coins, but afterward Crisaulo compels the thieves to restore all but a third of the money to Girifalco. The appetite Pilastrino felt for food and drink is now directed to gold. After Artemona receives the golden necklace, Pilastrino tries unsuccessfully to wrest it from her. At the play's end, when Pilastrino delivers the envoi, a delicious aroma is coming from a kitchen, recalling the parasite to his usual gluttony. Pilastrino differs from the conventional parasite by belonging to the criminal world; he has his confederate play the same type of imposter role as Giacchelino in *Il Negromante*. Greed is not usually a character trait of parasites—not to the point where the character turns into a miser. Ricchi portrays Pilastrino as cutting across traditional character schemes.

In its own times *I Tre Tiranni* was enthusiastically received. Charles V expressed his pleasure by naming Ricchi a knight and one of his familiars. Part of the author's success is due to his adjusting to rapidly changing political conditions. In the version of the play that was presented at Bologna, Filocrate sings the emperor's praises upon his return from Spain:

> Ciertamente sus grandes vitorias
> y empresas honrosas y magnanimos
> hechos muy felices dexaran
> tal fama de Su alta Maiestad
> que, sin scrittores o poetas, haran
> que su nombre siempre viva, sin
> falta alguna, despues de mil mondos.[70]
>
> (Act I, sc. 5)

---

70 "Certainly his great victories and his honorable enterprises and magnanimous deeds will happily leave behind such fame of His Majesty that, without writers or poets, they will cause his name to live forever, without fail, beyond a thousand worlds."

The youth mentions the emperor's defeating of the Turks at a battle in Hungary, and he predicts that another Golden Age is to come. This notion of the emperor's greatness, evoked with the Vergilian theme of a Golden Age, was common in that period; for example, the Spanish poet Fernando de Acuña wrote a sonnet, *Al Rey nuestro Señor*, in the hope that Charles V would unite the world under Christianity. But Ricchi's attitude seems to be no more than an effort to ingratiate himself with the emperor when one compares a manuscript of this play that is in the town library of Lucca. In this other version praise for Charles V and Pope Clement VII is replaced with complimentary words about Francis I and his allies, Sultan Soliman and the prime minister Ibraim. Instead of Spanish, the author uses Greek.[71] Ricchi, like Aretino, courted all sides in the military and political battles of the day.

This drama is distinct from most sixteenth-century learned comedies because of its bizarre, original quality. Filocrate does not fit the general theatrical pattern of a lover, as he neither delivers a Boccaccian defense of the natural right to love nor pours out his heartbreak in Petrarchan paradoxes. This could be called a serious comedy, although it cannot be listed along with other serious comedies, like those of Nardi or Aretino's *Ipocrito*, that had a decisive influence on the Italian theater in the second half of the sixteenth century. Ricchi did not write of swooning lovers and magnanimous heroines; the pathetic strikes a genuine human note in *I Tre Tiranni*, not a false "literary" one as in most serious comedies. This play is a remarkable work, propelled by the author's youthful force. The episodic scenes move from lyric to obscene as the dramatic rhythm demands. In many respects, for some characters and scenes, *I Tre Tiranni* is like the *Celestina*; but the Italian comedy avoids a tragic conclusion. Yet the close, with the typical multiple wedding plans, differs from the conclusions of many learned comedies in that the three male rivals agree to marry only to adjust to their circumstances. Girifalco saw that his amorous folly almost caused him to lose his fortune, while Filocrate bowed before the harsh decisions of Fortune; and Crisaulo surrendered to an emotion he could not control. Ricchi was a rebellious playwright who saw new dramatic possibilities in the learned comedy.

THE INTRONATI: *Gl'Ingannati*

While Aretino and Ricchi were writing outside their native province, theatrical activity was continuing in Tuscany. Siena had a more closed at-

71 See Codex 1375 of the Biblioteca di Lucca.

mosphere than Florence. The theater developed rather slowly there, but in the opening decades of the sixteenth century semiprofessional actor-playwrights from the artisan class inaugurated a folk farce. Two prominent figures were Salvestro Cartaio (known as "il Fumoso") and Niccoló Campani (called "lo Strascino"), whose plays were performed in Rome and Naples as well as in their native Siena. Then on October 1, 1531, a group of Siense artisans founded the Congrega dei Rozzi, a nonacademic theatrical company whose activities continued throughout the century, except for brief interruptions because of the precarious political situation in Tuscany. The fragmentary plays of the "Rozzi" had pastoral, rustic, or urban themes. Although some of the farces were intended as mythological allegories, they usually presented sympathetic satires of peasants. Looking benevolently at the silly love affairs of peasants, the "Rozzi" playwrights often used trivial or obscene language. These dramatists were also sensitive to the local scene, satirizing political corruption, clerical decadence, and the conflicts between peasants and city authorities. Among these playwrights were Francesco Mariani (known as "Appuntato"), Angelo Cenni ("Resoluto"), and the tailor Giovan Battista Sarto ("Falotico"). They usually called their plays "commedie" or even "Mogliazzi," and often wrote in tercets.[72]

At the same time that the folk plays were flourishing, the Erudite Comedy was cultivated by members of the Siense "Accademic Intronati," founded in 1525 or 1527. In 1531 the "Intronati" presented an allegorical farce called the *Sacrificio*, in which members sacrified to Minerva the dearest souvenirs of their beloved ladies. Amid music and verse recitations, the festival's high point was the performance of the comedy *Gl'Ingannati*. Although the play's author remains unknown, he is sometimes identified as Lodovico Castelvetro. Since the play is set at Modena, with accurate references to landmarks and streets, the author must have been from there or have lived in the city long enough to become well acquainted with it. Although Castelvetro was born in Modena, a problem occurs as to his whereabouts in 1531. He may have stopped off at Siena on his way from Rome to Modena that year, and he could have let his comedy be produced by the academicians as a friendly gesture toward them. He let the play remain anonymous because it contained some sharp anticlerical attacks about the corrupt life of monasteries and convents. In a letter of 1536 Castelvetro men-

---

72 The activities of the "Rozzi" are discussed by Franca Angelini in the *Enciclopedia dello Spettacolo* 8 (Rome, 1961): 1978-79. Also consult Apollonio, *Storia*, 2:158-59, and Borlenghi, *Commedie del Cinquecento* (1959 ed.) 2:905-6; and the introduction to *Commedie del Cinquecento*, ed. Nino Borsellino (Milan, 1962), 1: xxix.

tions a stay at Siena, describing theatrical ceremonies that could fit the *Sacrificio*. But as yet there is no sure documentary evidence that Castelvetro was in Siena in 1531. It is also doubtful that such a heavy-handed writer as he could have written a serene comedy like *Gl'Ingannati*, even though he was rather poetic in his youth, composing Latin verses. Most likely the comedy is the fruit of collaboration among the members of the academy.[73]

A great many of the academicians' interests were amorous. Thus the prose prologue is addressed to "nobilissime donne," as it is supposed to be an ambassador entrusted with the task of maintaining good relations for the academicians. The actor who recites the prologue explains that it took three days to write the comedy and that the title was chosen because most of the characters end up being deceived. He goes on to defend the play's originality, holding that it is wholly the product of the academicians' imagination. This actor explains that the performance is not for men who are not members of the academy. He adds that the academicians want the grace of fair ladies to declare which of them are the most witty and pleasing. He then states that a lesson can be learned from attending the comedy: that patience with good advice can triumph in love. This prologue is rather like a jester's monologue; it illustrates the original way Renaissance dramatists developed the prologue to do more than introduce the argument or answer possible criticism. It sets its own mood.[74]

73 Mario Verdone, *Enciclopedia dello Spettacolo* 8 (Rome, 1961): 1979, examines the contributions of the Intronati to theatrical tradition in Siena. Edmund V. De Chasca, "Early Editions of *Gl'Ingannati*: The Problem of Overlapping Dates," *MP* 50 (1952): 79-87, speaks of the four early editions of the play between 1537 and 1538 and mentions how printers often listed its title as *Sacrificio*. G. Cavazzuti, "Lodovico Castelvetro e la commedia *Gl'Ingannati*," *Giorn. stor. d. lett. ital.* 40 (1902): 343-65, upholds Castelvetro's authorship; but Pietro Mazzamuto, *Letteratura Italiana: I Minori* (Milan, 1961), 2:1226-27, does not accept Cavazzuti's evidence. Borsellino, *Commedie del Cinquecento,* 1:197-98, believes in a collective authorship. Robert Melzi, "From Lelia to Viola," *Renaissance Drama* 9 (1966): 67-81, identifies Castelverto as the play's author; he cites a "Canzone nella morte di una civetta" (Canzone on the death of an owl) at the close of the fifth act. The owl along with an upturned urn and the word "kekrika" ("I have judged") always appeared on the colophon of Castelvetro's books. See R. C. Melzi, *Castelvetro's Annotations to the Inferno: A New Perspective in Sixteenth Century Criticism* (The Hague, 1966), p. 11. We are still not convinced about the authorship.

74 Beatrice Corrigan, "*Il Capriccio*: An Unpublished Italian Renaissance Comedy and its Analogues," *Studies in the Renaissance* 5 (1958): 76, mentions that in order to be admitted as one of the Intronati the candidate had to compose a comedy; almost all the Intronati comedies are addressed to the ladies making up the audience. Borsellino, *Commedie del Cinquecento,* 1: xix-xx, notes the similarity between Boccaccian proems and the prologues to Renaissance comedies. Text of play in Borlenghi, *Commedie del Cinquecento,* vol. 1.

Although Plautus' *Menaechmi* suggested the plot line for the errors caused by the close resemblance of the twins Lelia and Fabrizio, Bibbiena's *Calandria* with its set of twins of different sex was doubtless the most significant influence for the author or authors of this play. The same argument as in *Gl'Ingannati* can be found in a novella by Bandello (II, 36). The comedy probably provided the author of the novella with his material.[75]

One of the major attempts of the "author" was to make the characters seem as natural as possible, with traits taken from real life and not from ancient comedies. The old suitor Gherado is an example of this attempt. At first he seems to be no more than the stage *senex,* gone babyish in his passion for the girl Lelia. In the first scene points out that he feels just as robust as he did when he was twenty-five, asserting: "And, if I have this white beard, in the tail I am as green as the Tuscan poet." The Tuscan poet is Boccaccio, who in the proem to the *Decameron's* fourth day defended his work against the detractors of the book who felt that the author was too old to be interested in love; Boccaccio answered in this manner: "As for those who go railing anent mine age, it would seem they know ill that, for all the leek hath a white head, the tail thereof is green. . . ." (Payne translation). This love frenzy has made Gherardo ridiculous in the eyes of his servant Spela, for the old man carefully combs himself, walks about town like a dandy, and sings while playing a lute. To Spela his master has become another Calandrino; but this elderly man is never entirely deprived of his good sense. Little by little Gherardo's amorous passion dies. Serious doubts about his actions begin as soon as he learns of Lelia's flight from a convent. On discovering his daughter Isabella with Fabrizio, he entirely forgets his love and concentrates his energy to revenge the outrage to his family honor. He locks the youth up and is going to denounce him to the governor. Gherardo resembles Nicomaco of the *Clizia,* but is not so wholly absorbed in his passion and consequently not so much in need of a great shock to free him of senile love.

The Spanish occupation in several parts of Italy weighed heavily on the natives, but the Spaniards strongly influenced the fashions of Italian life. In dress, in taking noble titles, even in language the Italians copied from the Spanish. Yet the Spaniards arrogantly considered the Italians a nation of shopkeepers. In retaliation the Italians ridiculed the Spanish for their effeminate ways, such as kissing hands, perfuming themselves, and posing as deli-

75 Apollonio, *Storia,* 2:160, contrasts *Gl'Ingannati* with the *Calandria.* Cavazzuti, "Gl'Ingannati," pp. 364-65, feels that Bandello derived the novella from the plot of the comedy.

cate cavaliers. The lowliest Spanish soldier boasted of being of noble stock. Here in *Gl'Ingannati* the anti-Spanish satire is centered in the character Giglio.

This Spaniard, who mixes Italian words with Spanish ones, is haughty, mean, and conceited; he is one of the first of his type in the Italian comedy. Although he claims that noble ladies are ready to fall into his arms, he continues to pursue Gherardo's maid Pasquella. Giglio wants her to win over Isabella and also to provide him with hose, doublets, and shorts by robbing Gherardo; but Pasquella does not wish to become involved with him, as she declares in the third scene of Act II: "Non mi voglio impacciar con spagnuoli. Sete tafani di sorte che o mordete o infastidite altrui; e fate come il carbone: o cuoce o tegne. V'aviam tanto pratichi oramai che guai a noi! E vi conosciamo bene, Dio grazia; e non c'è guadagno coi fatti vostri."[76] The maid is ready to outsmart this fraud, and she promises to have a rendezvous with him provided he gives her his rosary. While going to the meeting Giglio is very sure of himself, babbling in this way: "Harta gana que tiene de ser conmigo! Ya sabe la maldita quanto valen los spagnolos en las cosas de las mugeres! Oh como se holgan de nosotros estas putas italianas!"[77] In this scene, the sixth of Act IV, Pasquella persuades Giglio to turn his rosary over to her, since she knows better than to accept the promise of money from a Spaniard. She approaches the door of the house and starts to call out as if to gather in the fleeing chickens. And while the slow-witted Giglio looks around saying, "Donde stan estos pollos? Aqui non veo ni gallos ni gallinas," she slips into the house and slams the door. The maid repeats the conjuration from *Decameron* VII, 1, modified here to fit the new circumstances: "Fantasima, fantasima, che dí e notte vai, se a coda ritta ci venisti, a coda ritta te n'andrai. Tristi con tristi, in mal'ora ci venisti e me coglier ci credesti, e' ngannato ci remanesti. Amen."[78] In arguing with him over the rosary, Pasquella calls Giglio a "marrano," the Spanish term for a Jew or Moor recently converted to Christianity but not sincerely taking the new

---

76 "I don't want to meddle with Spaniards. You are lice that either bite or bother other persons; and you work like coal: either it burns or it sends up smoke. We've had so much to do with you that it's now to our own undoing! And we really know you well, goodness sake; and there's no profit from dealing with you."

77 "She'll gain a great deal from being with me! Indeed that damned creature knows the great excellence of Spaniards in pleasing women! Oh, how these Italian sluts enjoy themselves with us."

78 "Phantom, phantom, you who go by day and night, if you came here with tail upright, you'll go away with tail upright. Nasty with the nasty, in an evil hour you came here and thought to snatch me, and you were deceived. Amen."

faith. The Italians thought of the Spanish as heretics. The maid douses Giglio with water to cool his passion. When Gherardo rushes on the scene, Giglio runs away, with these cowardly words: "Meior es de fuir" ("It's better to flee"). The braggart always avoids a conflict if he can.[79]

Along with the ridiculous Spanish lady-killer is Fabrizio's pedantic instructor, who cannot refrain from mixing Latin phrases in his daily conversation. Messer Piero is constantly careful to preserve his doctoral dignity, treating every minor subject as if it were an important affair, and he loosens up only with the servant Stragulcia. Their major scene is the second of Act III, where Fabrizio is trying to decide whether he should stay at the inn Specchio, owned by Agiato, or at the Matto, owned by Frulla. The two innkeepers scream out the good points of their respective establishments in the hope of gaining the youth's patronage. Piero examines each of the innkeepers; he likes the name Specchio since "Speculum prudentia significat iusta illud nostri Catonis 'Nosce Teipsum.'" But the abundance of food promised by the innkeeper does not please him: "Omnis repletio mala, panis autem pessima." When Fabrizio asks him what to do, the pedant answers solemnly: "Etiam atque etiam cogitandum." By this the servant's patience is at an end, causing him to mock the preceptor's Latin: "Bus asinorum, buorum, castronorum, tatte, batatte, pecoronibus!" But Stragulcia convinces the pedant to go to the Matto by firing his interest: "Maestro, I saw there the innkeeper's son, who is as handsome as an angel." He alludes here to the vice generally attributed to pedants during the Renaissance. Messer Piero is really no more than a sketch caught in all the traditional lines.[80]

Structurally, the comedy is built on a series of deceptions. Lelia fools Flamminio and Isabella with the disguise as Fabio, and Pasquella leads Giglio on to rob him. Fabrizio, when mistaken for Lelia, lets Isabella believe he is the page so that she will surrender herself to him. The exposition is somewhat too obvious in the opening scenes, and the scenes are sometimes excessively prolonged. But on the whole the play is harmoniously balanced.

Gl'Ingannati is the comedy of youth. A spontaneous, impetuous, even insolent spirit dominates the play. Youthful love pushes the characters along in spite of every obstacle set by elderly parents. Although Virginio places

---

79 Boughner, *The Braggart,* pp. 23-27, speaks of Spanish influence in Italian life and then describes Giglio. Also see Croce, *La Spagna nella Vita Italiana,* pp. 181-82 and 224. V. I. Milani, "The Origins of the Spanish Braggart in Strozzi's *Commedia erudita," Italica* 42, no. 3 (September, 1965): 226, points out that the first Spanish braggart is the soldier Castiglia in Strozzi's play *La Nutrice,* dated 1512-19.
80 Apollonio, *Storia,* 2:163, discusses the pedant.

his daughter Lelia in a convent while he arranges for her wedding with Gherardo, she manages to slip away. Lelia is the modern heroine, as in the novella tradition, who disguises herself in men's clothing.[81] Her beloved Flamminio has the same ebullient nature. He cannot believe his ears when the servant Crivello informs him that Fabio has kissed Isabella, and he almost kills the servant. Flamminio is ready to cut off Fabio's lips, ears, and an eye, promising to put them on a plate and send it to Isabella. The vehemence of the threat indicates the energy of this character, so carried along by the force of his anger that he wishes to commit a violent crime. The play possesses a farcical dynamism and an erotic fervor.[82]

Alessandro Piccolomini: *L'Amor Costante*

One of the possible collaborators in the writing of *Gl'Ingannati* and the director of the whole *Sacrificio* festival was Alessandro Piccolomini (1508-78). Among the "Intronati" he was known as "Stordito." In 1536 the first and most significant of the three comedies attributed to him, *L'Amor Costante,* was performed at Siena in the presence of the emperor Charles V.[83] Piccolomini had to fit a great deal within the limits of the regular comedy. The flight of two lovers from Spain, their imprisonment by the Turks, their separation, their assumption of false identities—all this material is perfect for a narrative genre like the novella. Boccaccio would have had no difficulty in arranging the various elements, developing them with no limits of space and time. But this comedy obeys the unities of time and place; the scene is always the street in Pisa. Many actions are squeezed into a twenty-four-hour period.

One of the devices used to bring together the parts of the plot is the pro-

81 Melzi, "From Lelia to Viola," p. 70 and *passim,* describes Lelia's psychological complexity, demure yet anguished, self-sacrificing and self-assertive all at the same time. He finds the characterization of this heroine to be unique in the Italian tradition and does not appreciate the similar feminine figures in Boccaccian novelle, humanistic comedies, and Bibbiena's *Calandria.*

82 Croce, "Intorno alla commedia," speaks of the impetus of youthful love as displayed in this work. Borsellino, *Commedie del Cinquecento,* 1:xxix, analyzes the play's erotic fervor. Hyperbole may perhaps characterize Flamminio's threat and consequently render it more amusing than terrifying.

83 Florindo Cerreta, *Alessandro Piccolomini, letterato e filosofo senese del Cinquecento* (Siena, 1960), pp. 14-15, raises some doubts as to the emperor's attendance at the performance; in any case, the play was composed for Charles V's official visit to Siena. Borsellino, *Commedie del Cinquecento,* 1:293-96, talks of the role that Piccolomini played in the Sienese academy.

logue. Piccolomini may have had the prologue to the *Cortigiana* in mind, since in both plays the prologue is really a dialogue; here it is between the actor called "Prologo" and a Spaniard who wanders on scene and is amazed by the stage properties. "Prologo" tells the argument while the Spaniard translates it into his language. The translation must have served a practical purpose, since many members of the audience were surely Spanish. By this means the audience could know the comedy's background action.[84]

Every effort is made to secure the maximum theatrical effect, for the author was sensitive to the spectacular side of the theater. The first three acts are built up to the point where the lovers' plot to flee and perhaps kill Lucrezia's guardian Guglielmo is uncovered. By the end of the third act everything is apparently catastrophic, as Guglielmo has ordered poison for the lovers. Terrible suspense is created, as the spectators must look forward to the last two acts to see the catastrophe averted. Piccolomini was aware of the effects that stage movement could bring about, and the opening scenes of Act V are full of grouped movement when the amorous priest Giannino-Ioandoro and his followers are going to fight Guglielmo, causing the intervention of the police captain. Swords flash on stage. These stage movements are like those in a comic opera, with the chorus broken up strategically. The warring parties make peace by joining in a dance, and Guglielmo orders a party in honor of the double wedding of Ferrante with Ginevra and Ioandoro with Margarita (daughter of the physician Guicciardo). A *Moresca* dance is struck up, and drums start playing. The dance finale illustrates the author's interest in spectacle.[85]

L'Amor Costante is a serious romantic comedy. The lesson of the work is announced in the prologue: "quanto un amor costante . . . abbia sempre buon fine e quanto manifesto error sia abbandonarsi nelle aversità amorose: perché quel pietosissimo dio che si chiama Amore non abbandona mai chi con fermezza lo serve."[86] The trials of Ginevra and Ferrante are a Romeo and Juliet story with a happy ending. Ferrante had to marry Ginevra secretly and flee with her, since her uncle Consalvo distrusted the young man's

84 Text in Borlenghi, *Commedie del Cinquecento*, vol. 1. Apollonio, *Storia*, 2:165, comments on the function of his prologue. Emilio Goggio, "The Prologue in the *Commedie Erudite* of the Sixteenth Century," *Italica* 18 no. 3 (September, 1941): 124-32, remarks on the service that the prologue to *Amor Costante* rendered to the foreign spectators. Riccardo Scrivano, "Alessandro Piccolomini," *Rass. d. Lett. Ital.* 68 no. 1 (January–April, 1964): 63-84, refers to Aretino's influence on the Sienese author.
85 Borsellino, *Commedie del Cinquecento*, 1:293-96, describes the dance finale.
86 "To what a degree constant love always comes to a happy outcome and what a manifest error it is to lose hope in the adversities of Love: because that most merciful god who is called Love never abandons those who serve him without swerving."

family because it had implicated Ginevra's father in a political plot which caused his exile. Youthful love has to combat family authority and political interests. A struggle like this has pathetic, even tragic overtones. Here the plot is not reproduced from an ancient comedy with a cunning slave who helps his young master obtain a slave girl against his father's wishes; this story of feuding families reflects the Italian scene. With its modern subject matter, it has parallels in *novelle*.

Ginevra is a sentimental creature who always remains faithful to Ferrante. When death threatens, she wants to be the only one to take the poison. On entering Guglielmo's household she begged him not to force her to marry, claiming she had made an irrevocable vow. Neither Giannino with his expensive gifts nor the false Lorenzino could win her from the love she felt for Ferrante. As a dramatic figure Ginevra is almost unique for the period in which Piccolomini wrote the play, since she anticipates the heroines of Italian comedy in the second half of the sixteenth century. But she rarely appears on scene; consequently the author did not realize her full dramatic potential. Most of what is learned about her noble character comes from what others say about her. Her great scene is the fourth of Act V, where she appears in chains, expiring from the drink she thinks was poisonous. Guglielmo curses her for the murder plot, but in talking with her he learns she is his daughter. The recovery scene is at first heartrending, for Guglielmo is full of anguish for ordering his daughter to be poisoned.

Ferrante is straight out of the novella tradition, sharing some literary precedents with the hero Erostrato of the *Suppositi;* both became servants to be near the girls they loved. The hero of Piccolomini's play has known a life of tears and regret, having suffered imprisonment in a foreign land. In talking to a friend (Act II, sc. 3) he expresses his scorn for the cruel way Fortune has treated him: "Ma la fortuna, che sempre s'oppone ai bei disegni de li inamorati, volse che, come fummo nei mari di Pisa, fussemo assaliti da quattro fuste di mori. . . ."[87] But in all his misfortune he has never forgotten his beloved. The one jarring note in this pair of faithful, noble-spirited lovers is the plot to kill Guglielmo, for the old man had treated the girl kindly, respecting her false vow; and he has trusted Ferrante-Lorenzino as a loyal servant. Their readiness to murder reflects the violence of the age as well as the intensity of their love.[88]

---

87 "But Fortune, which always opposes the fine plans of lovers, willed that when we were in the sea of Pisa, we were assailed by four Moorish galleys. . . ."
88 The character of Ferrante and Ginevra is discussed by Maria Rossi, "Le opere letterarie di Alessandro Piccolomini," *Bullett. senese di storia patria* 17, no. 3 (1910): 292-93.

A secondary plot deals with the love of Margarita for Giannino. The young man is oblivious to her passion for him. His unrequited love for Lucrezia has disrupted his career in the church. Clement VII had befriended him, and with the ascent of Pope Paul III he could have hoped for an even more brilliant career. He gave up everything to attempt to win Lucrezia. Her refusal of his gifts and messages upset his health. His servant Vergilio describes (Act I, sc. 2) Giannino's moral and physical suffering: sleeplessness, inability to eat, continual weeping; the pains of love have carried the youth close to death. But once he learns that the object of his passion is his sister, from whom he was separated early in life, he is willing to marry Margarita. On learning of Giannino's change of heart, the maid Agnoletta points out (Act V, sc. 9) how Margarita is being rewarded for her true love: "Or coglierai el frutto di tanta perseveranzia e fermezza; or porrai fine a tanta miserabil vita quant'hai fatto sino a oggi; ora i sospiri e le lagrime si convertiranno in dolcezze e abbracciamenti; ora il tuo amor costante sarà esempio a tutto il mondo. Imparate, voi amanti, a non abbandonarvi nelle miserie e soffrir le passioni per fin che venghino le prosperità. Imparate, donne, da costei a esser costanti nei pensieri vostri; e non dubitate. . . ."[89] There are really two tales of constant love in the play, presented as examples from which troubled lovers can learn. The success of the suffering parties is supposed to encourage the spectators or readers in their own love affairs; the play is an example of amorous didacticism.[90]

Love touches even the minor characters such as the Spanish Captain Marrada, an undistinguished veteran of the imperial liberation of Tunis and the siege of Florence. Duke Alexander has now assigned him as captain of Pisa's military guard. This captain is fairly modest in talking of his military exploits; according to him, his greatest victories have been with women. He brags (Act II, sc. 9) to the Spaniard Consalvo about his miraculous love

89 "Now you will pluck the fruit of so much perseverance and constancy; now you will put an end to the wretched life that you have led up until today; now your sighs and tears will turn to sweetness and embraces; now your constant love will be an example to everyone. Learn, you lovers, not to surrender to misery and to endure suffering until good times come. Learn, ladies, from her example to be constant in your thoughts; and not to doubt. . . ."
90 Scrivano, "Alessandro Piccolomini," p. 77, speaks of the derivation of the central love theme from the prevalent Neoplatonic theories of Pietro Bembo in his *Asolani*. By ironic contrast Piccolomini's masterpiece *La Raffaella, overo della bella creanza delle donne* (ca. 1539) relates how an accomplished procuress teaches a young wife to take good care of her husband, to make him content, to be an excellent homemaker, and to be a social success. Yet the wife is to choose an ideal lover, who is the procuress' client. This work upholds an ideal of adultery.

adventures: "Tengo muchos passatiempos, maxime con estas gentiles damas; y, por dezir os la verdad, muchas andan perdidas por mi, y aun de las primeras de la tierra."[91] Marrada is the "capitano innamorato," a Renaissance variation of the *Miles gloriosus*. He claims to conquer two thousand ladies annually. He is a fop, dressing in dandy clothes, using cosmetics and perfumes. The captain bows grandly like a regular cavalier. But his one true conquest is Margarita's maid Agnoletta, who will accept any man that wants her. When the maid apologizes for having to meet the captain in a cellar (a place hardly worthy of such a distinguished person as this braggart), he pours out thanks to her, declaring that she is the only woman he has loved since leaving Spain. Only once in the comedy does the captain have to fulfill his police functions, and then he does not even succeed in keeping down the street brawl between Giannino's supporters and those of Guglielmo. The languishing captain agrees to act as presiding judge over the fight, turning it into a chivalric contest, since the Spaniards made dueling fashionable in Italy. But a civilian like Consalvo is able to settle the differences without any fighting. The captain fails both in love and in war.[92]

Yet the captain hardly seems a fop beside the Neapolitan Ligdonio, Margarita's suitor. This ceremonious poetaster is a social climber, frequenting Pisa's high circles to find a girl with a large dowry. He is not interested in any particular girl and is ready to switch from one to another. In the third scene of Act I he explains his philosophy of life to the servant Panzana: "Sapientis est mutare propositum." Ligdonio will not imitate the lovers described by Vergil and Ovid, with their dedication to a single person. Speaking in his comic Italianized Neapolitan dialect, he makes his servant understand the relationship they must maintain in public view: "Mo te lo dico per sempre. Quanno me vedi infra la gente, sforzati de star remiso e non parlare, se non te parlo; non ridere, non responnere, se non te chiamo: e sta' che sempre para ch'abbi paura de' fatti miei. Quanno po' sarimmo infra nuie, pazzeia, burla, baciami, e fa' chello che vuoi, ce non me ne curo."[93] If

---

91 "I have many pastimes, especially with these noble ladies; and, to tell you the truth, many are mad about me, even among the first of this town."

92 Boughner, *The Braggart,* pp. 28-29; Rossi, "Alessandro Piccolomini," p. 295; and Croce, *La Spagna nella Vita Italiana,* pp. 182-83, consider the captain. Frederick R. Bryson, *The Point of Honor in Sixteenth-century Italy: An aspect of the Life of the Gentleman* (New York, 1935), *passim,* discusses the duel in Italy and chivalric virtues.

93 "I'm telling you this for good. When you see me with other persons, try to stay quiet and don't talk except when I speak to you; don't laugh, don't answer if I do not call you; and act if you are afraid of me. When we're alone together, play the madcap, joke, kiss me, and do what you want, for then I don't care."

Ligdonio is too familiar with his servant in public, his social image will be jeopardized. This pretentious suitor is, in his servant's description, a forty-eight-year-old roué. Ligdonio has hired the hypocritical procuress Monna Bionda to carry his messages to Margarita. Since he thinks that he is a great poet, Ligdonio has written a madrigal for the girl, in which her name is spelled out by the first letter of each line. The words of the poem are "murtifere" in Ligdonio's opinion. He decides to change "baldanzosi guai" with "sollazzosi guai" as the second rendering is better Tuscan, since Boccaccio had never used the word "baldanzosi" in the *Decameron*. But when this abortive Don Juan meets Margarita on the street, he can only mumble a few incoherent words.

On one of his promenades Ligdonio encounters an old acquaintance, the Perugian courtier Roberto, whom the poetaster had known in Naples. After his training as a courtier, with special emphasis on pleasing ladies, Roberto is now with the prince of Salerno. He is another version of Ligdonio, exaggerating his amorous adventures, but he holds that Pisa is devoid of gracious ladies. Ligdonio counters that one can have a very pleasant time in Pisa. His poetic gifts, he claims, have made him most successful. Once, Ligdonio relates, a lady requested a composition from him. After he sent her a novelletta, she became so bestially fired with passion for him that she granted her favors immediately. Ligdonio is a far greater or far more imaginative braggart than the captain. One of the bad poet's character traits is his flexibility. When offered Giannino's benefices, he is quite happy to become a priest, as he can have the riches a good dowry would bring without having to marry. Ligdonio is also a glutton, and priestly benefices would enable him to feast to his fullest content. His experiences as a master liar would also be an advantage in the new career; a holy appearance would hide his vanity. Ligdonio's chameleonlike qualities have brought him success.[94]

This poetaster is not the only glutton in the play; he shares an insatiable appetite with his servant Panzana and with Giannino's parasite Sguazza (the feaster). Neither the servant nor his parasite friend can understand why gentlemen are interested in love affairs. In the eighth scene of Act II they confer with each other. Sguazza thinks that an interest in love makes a man effeminate, and draws a vignette of the fops of that era as miserable creatures who walk about in tight pants and hose, with starched shirts, suf-

94 Rossi, "Alessandro Piccolomini," pp. 293-95, analyzes Ligdonio's character. Scrivano, "Alessandro Piccolomini," p. 78, discusses the parody of Petrarchan treatises on love and precious language.

fering for a kiss or sigh from a lady fair and looking more like puppets than men. For Sguazza and Panzana all pleasures are vain except gluttony: music is nothing but air and cannot fill the stomach; money is a help only when one uses it to buy food. If Sguazza had to take a wife, he would want her plump and young, just like a little pig; and he would like to see her roasted, set on a spit. The greatest pleasure for these two is eating good food. Although they play a minor part, the parasite and his servant friend provide a comic commentary on the actions of the more important characters.[95]

Piccolomini has made every effort to place his characters in a contemporary seting. Pisa was a fairly international city, not only because of the Spanish soldiers stationed there; it was also a center of studies, attracting scholars from all parts of Europe. Among the men who join Giannino in attacking Guglielmo's house is a student from Germany who speaks barbaric Italian with a few words of his native language mixed in: "Torto fare, messer Iannin. Stare noi amici. . . . Affettare el vecchio, io, Vist, conz, sacrament! . . .; Far fette de el" (Act V, scs. 10 and 11); "Troppo supportar tu superbia. . . . Tutte star parole. o mazzarme de mano mia, se non fo star stil com'olio, se aver tutti en torn" (Act V, sc. 12). Usually the Italian Renaissance theater portrays Germans as great drinkers, and the student here is no exception, as he shows when the wedding festivities start: "Far danze; far far danz, messer Iannine; ballar, ballar per miglior trinch" (Act V, sc. 12). The other languages heard in the play are Ligdonio's Neapolitan and the Spanish of the captain and other visitors from Spain; entire scenes are in Spanish. The mixture of different languages and dialects, used before in the *Sacre Rappresentazioni,* is a standard means of provoking laughter. At times the comedy must have been difficult for the Italian spectators to follow, but the author succeeds in reproducing the sounds of a city that drew foreign soldiers and students.[96]

Contemporary politics have their part in this comedy. Guglielmo went into exile because he allied with other Spanish nobles, in Ferrante's family, shortly after the death of Pope Hadrian. The most important political figure mentioned frequently in the play is the emperor Charles V, as in the twelfth scene of Act I, in which Guglielmo and Guicciardo discuss the emperor's visit to Siena. Although their city is poor, they state, it loves the emperor. Later Ferrante and his friend Corsetto talk of the imperial liberation of

95 Rossi, "Alessandro Piccolomini," p. 297, cites Sguazza's portrait of a fop.
96 Sanesi, *La Commedia,* 1:393, talks of the comic effects of a multilingual dialogue and its use in the *Sacre Rappresentazioni.*

Tunis; Ferrante tells his friend: ". . . aresti visto una quiete d'esercizio, una contentezza di soldati, una diligenzia di capitani, un'imagine verissima di antica e bene ordinata milizia, e, sopra tutto, una divina cortesia e incredibile providenzia e fortuna maravigliosa d'uno imperadore. . . ."[97] The emperor was the greatest hope the Christian nations had in the war against the Turks. Even Ligdonio has composed a poem entitled the *Trionfo d'Italia nella venuta de l'imperatore.* The period's political climate is felt here.[98]

These were also times of religious unrest, when many persons looked to the emperor as a possible reformer of the church. Although Piccolomini was one day to become an archbishop, he did not hesitate to satirize clerical abuses. He admired Aretino and imitated him in flaying the church for its corruption. In the play's first scene the servant Vergilio is trying to talk Giannino into forgetting Lucrezia and going back to his church career; the servant reminds his master that the city of Rome has much to offer priests: ". . . E, se pur sete inclinato ad amore, in Roma non mancaranno donne, no, molto più belle che Lucrezia non è, delle quali voi n'arete il mele e gli altri le mosche: perché i vezzi, i basci, gli abbracciamenti, le dolci conversazioni, le saporose parole, le carezzine delle donne son di voi preti; e le spese, i rimbrotti, le vilanie, i tagliuzzi, lo impaccio, le corna sono dei lor mariti. . . ."[99]

A common attack against clerical corruption concerned the licentiousness of monastic and convent life. Since Margarita's father plans to go to Rome after the emperor leaves Pisa, she is to stay at a convent during his absence. The girl tells Agnoletta (Act III, sc. 4) that the conversation of nuns must be very boring, but the maid answers that nuns of their day know more about worldly affairs than the sisters of earlier generations did. This maid had lived in a convent for two years, and according to her the rulers of the church would be scandalized by the activities of nuns. Satire on convent life is frequently found in novelle; the adventures of Masetto da Lamporecchio (*Decameron* III, 1) with the sisters of a convent illustrate the atti-

97 ". . . you would have seen the orderliness of the army, the contentment of the soldiers, the diligence of the captains, a very authentic image of ancient and well-disciplined soldiery, and above all, the divine courtesy and incredible providence and marvelous fortune of the emperor. . . ."

98 Apollonio, *Storia,* 2:164, discusses the references to contemporary politics in the play. Also see Scrivano, "Alessandro Piccolomini," pp. 76-77.

99 ". . . And, if you are still inclined toward love, women are not lacking in Rome, much more beautiful than Lucrezia, from whom you'll have honey while others will have flies: because the endearments, kisses, embraces, sweet conversations, loving words, caresses of ladies belong to you priests; and the expense, rebukes, insults, barbs, trouble, and horns belong to their husbands. . . ."

tude of many writers toward the lack of holiness in those who ought to have been exemplary.

This dramatist was writing during the pontificate of Paul III, who ascended to his post in 1534 and later called the Council of Trent in the hope of holding the church together. In the concluding scene of Act I, Guicciardo states that he is traveling to Rome to see if its court is still as corrupt as before. Guglielmo feels that nothing has as yet reformed Rome. He and the doctor both express their hope that the emperor will undertake the reform of the church. Scenes like this reflect the anxiety of the period when the unity of the church was being shattered.[100]

Late in his career Piccolomini became the commentator of Aristotle's *Poetics* and *Rhetoric,* still upholding the use of prose for comedies but advising against the use of several languages in one dramatic work, contrary to his practice in *L'Amor Costante.* He then saw literary imitation of life as an artistic transformation of reality. But in writing his first comedy this author did not have strict canons in mind. Instead he fashioned a serious romantic comedy in which the pathetic is felt along with the ridiculous.[101]

RUZZANTE: *the Formative Period*

Angelo Beolco is without doubt the most puzzling figure among the playwrights of the Erudite Comedy, since he does not fall into any easily drawn category. Known as the actor-playwright Ruzzante (1502?-42), he united the folk and learned comic traditions as no Sienese writer was ever

100 Rossi, "Alessandro Piccolomini," p. 296, and Borsellino, *Commedie del Cinquecento,* 1:295, talk of the period's religious climate and its reflection in Piccolomini's thought.

101 Scrivano, "Alessandro Piccolomini," *passim,* sees Piccolomini's *Annotationi nel libro della poetica di Aristotele,* as a sign of creative decline in the author. Cerreta, *Alessandro Piccolomini,* pp. 154-60, examines the dramatist's theories on theatrical practice; how the unity of time restricted the action to twelve or thirteen hours; the emphasis on the social nature of comedy to illustrate the errors in everyday common life. Also consult the review of Cerreta's book by G. Fatini, *Nuova Antologia* 95 (1960):403-4. Toward 1544 Piccolomini composed another comedy, *Alessandro,* which has recently appeared in a critical edition by Cerreta (Siena, 1966); we have have chosen not to include a study of it since it did not have the international impact of *L'Amor Costante.* For some time Piccolomini was credited with a third comedy, *Ortensio;* but Cerreta in "Clarifications concerning the Real Authorship of the Renaissance Comedy *Ortensio,*" *Renaissance News* (Summer, 1957), pp. 63-69, establishes the play as the work of collective authorship by the Intronati without assistance from Piccolomini. The *Ortensio* was first performed in 1561.

able to do. He worked outside the Tuscan sphere, unlike the other sixteenth-century dramatists studied here. Ruzzante was the illegitimate son of the rector of the faculty of medicine at the University of Padua and was only eighteen when he founded a dramatic company with several of his friends. Performing under the peasant names of Menato, Vezzo, and Bilora, they soon drew favorable attention. They were not true professionals but were superior amateurs. It was Beolco's good fortune to win the patronage of the wealthy Venetian patrician Luigi Cornaro. Ruzzante's company was able to perform at Cornaro's town house in Padua and at his many villas, such as the one at Codevigo. From 1520 until 1526 Ruzzante went to Venice each year with his fellow actors for the carnival season, and they appeared in the homes of patrician families like the Foscari. In 1529 Ruzzante was at Ferrara, singing for the Este family in a festival that included the performance of Ariosto's *Lena*. This folk actor-dramatist had achieved fame throughout Italy.[102]

All through his life Angelo Beolco was close to the countryside. As an adult he administered the estates of his brothers at Motta di Montagnana and Pernumia. He rented a farm at S. Angelo di Sacco. His summers were spent at Cornaro's villas. He thus had many opportunities to become acquainted with peasants, and carefully studied their character traits and language. In the Venetian area peasants were not always the object of scorn for cultured city dwellers, because town and country had joined together in the

102 For centuries Beolco's unique importance in the history of the Italian Renaissance theater was forgotten until Maurice Sand in *Masques et Bouffons* (Paris, 1860), 2:77-118, rescued the Paduan dramatist from near complete obscurity. The Ruzzante that Sand presented was a romantic outcast who established the Commedia dell'Arte since his plays were originally supposed by the critic to have been entirely improvised and only afterward written down. Sand is often quite inaccurate, as he for instance overemphasizes the multiplicity of dialects in Beolco's dramas. A true scholarly evaluation came with the work of Emilio Lovarini, who from 1888 to 1953 applied the methods of a genuine folkorist and philologist to Beolco's writings. Unfortunately Lovarini never produced a synthetic study on Ruzzante. Lovarini's writings on Beolco are to be found in *Studi sul Ruzzante e la Letteratura Pavana* (Padua, 1965), in an admirable edition by Gianfranco Folena, who has gathered the fragmentary studies of the critic. In "Ruzzante a Venezia," pp. 81-107, Lovarini describes Beolco's career at the Venetian carnivals and the scandal that the often obscene language of his plays created; a positivist in method, Lovarini used Sanudo's diaries. For more biographical information see Lovarini's article, "Profilo di Ruzzante," pp. 369-76, originally written for *La Lettura* (July, 1942), pp. 493 ff., to commemorate the dramatist's death. Also consult Antonio Cataldo, *Il Ruzzante* (Milan, 1933), pp. 44-59; and for Beolco's acting career cf. M. Baratto, "L'Esordio di Ruzzante," *Revue des Etudes Italiennes* 3, nos. 2-3 (1965):93, 97. Burckhardt, *Renaissance in Italy*, 2:332-33, speaks of Cornaro's contributions to Renaissance culture.

military struggle to keep the nation independent of foreign control. There was considerable sympathy for the peasants, and Beolco expressed his feelings by taking the stage name *Ruzzante*. In the sixteenth century there were families of that name among the farmers at Pernumia. He doubtless also had in mind the verb *ruzzare* (to romp or sport, often with animals). Ruzzante saw the comedy inherent in the peasant's attitude toward life.[103]

During the late fifteenth century and the opening years of the following century a folk poetry had developed in the Po river valley region. This generally anonymous body of literature described the daily life of the area, picturing peasants fighting for their land against war, famine, and pestilence. There are scenes of young country lovers and rustic weddings. War, which lays waste to the farmland, is the most recurrent theme of this essentially pictorial literature. The *mariazo,* a farcical picture of domestic strife, is an important genre. Peasants trying to fight poverty and keep their farm animals are the heroes of these poetic compositions, while rapacious civil authorities like judges and police agents are satirized. Following this folk tradition, Ruzzante made the peasant the central figure of his works.[104]

Early in his career Ruzzante programmed his poetic ideas. The prologue, or *sprolico,* to his comedy *Betìa* (written ca. 1521 or 1524) explains his belief that people should always act naturally. He despised academic affectations, seeing the "natural" as the basic value of art. For Ruzzante the "natural" effect that an artist should try to achieve comes from picturing life at a simple, instinctive level, as it is found among peasants. He does not argue abstractly; instead he draws lively examples of the countryside: "Among men and women the natural is the finest thing there is, and consequently everyone ought to proceed naturally and honestly; for when you remove anything from the natural it becomes confused. Why indeed do birds never sing so well in cages as they do under the willows? And why do cows never give so much milk in towns as they do out of doors in the open dewy pas-

---

103 Baratto, "Ruzzante," p. 113, discusses famine and war's devastations among the peasants of the Venetian realm. In Act II of the comedy *Anconitana* the character Ruzzante explains his name: "My given name is Perduocimo; but when I was a child and I used to lead about the farm animals, I always played with the mares and cows and ewes and sows. And besides I used to have a dog that I had trained, which I used to lead on a leash just like a little ass. I constantly teased it; I used to tap it on the nose and then go behind some bush to play with it some more. And that's why they gave me the name Ruzzante the tease because I used to tease the animals."
104 Carlo Grabher, *Ruzzante* (Milan, 1953), pp. 24-40, describes the literature of the Po valley area. Raffaello Viola, *Due Saggi di Letteratura Pavana* (Padua, 1949), *passim,* also comments on that background.

tures? Why? Because you take the thing away from the natural."[105] The artist ought also to be faithful to nature linguistically; Paduan authors should write in their native dialect and not attempt to use the acquired literary Tuscan. Ruzzante was proud of his Paduan birth, scorning those who affected the speech of Florence. He states that he would not trade birthplaces even with Jesus Christ, for being Paduan is to him a beautiful thing. Once again the *questione della lingua* is raised. Since the characters of his works were mainly peasants of the Paduan area, Ruzzante felt he would be falsifying his art with Tuscan. Later, when he wrote comedies according to the classical pattern, Ruzzante continued to uphold his view about the "natural," making language fit character.[106]

The influence of the Erudite Comedy can already be noticed in his *Moscheta* (1526-28), in which he abandons verse, employed in his first two dramatic works, in favor of prose. This play is in five acts like regular comedies, and the peasant characters are transported to the city environment of Padua. Ruzzante and his friend Menato have kept their peasant outlook, but Ruzzante's wife Betìa has taken on a city sophistication. Menato came to town to seduce Betìa, and his complaints about her resistance to his advances are expressed in coarse peasant language. Ruzzante and his wife quarrel throughout the play, making the comedy a lengthened *mariazo*. But one of the peasant characters is a braggart warrior: the soldier Tonin, who speaks in the dialect of his native Bergamo (the traditional land of blockheads), would like to possess Betìa, in revenge for Ruzzante's cheating him out of some money. She actually comes and gives herself to the soldier. Beolco reshapes the braggart's role to fit contemporary conditions in northern Italy, for Tonin is a poor recruit, not like the opulent mercenary captains described by Plautus. But he is a born boaster and coward, who claims that the chief reason he avoids a fight with Ruzzante is that he does not want to lower himself to combat with a peasant. He is also a love-stricken warrior, and he admits that love makes idiots out of sane men and cowards out of the brave, thereby hoping to excuse his unwillingness to fight. The only time he threatens Ruzzante is when he is safely in his house looking at the enraged husband from a window. Then Tonin states that his own mirror re-

105 Translation by Herrick, *Italian Comedy,* pp. 43-44. For superb French translations of Beolco's works see Alfred Mortier, *Un Dramaturge de la Renaissance Italiene: Ruzzante (1502-1542)* (Paris, 1926), vol. 2. Bibliographical material to be found in S. Romagnoli, "Rassegna di Studi Ruzzantiani," *Belfagor* 7, no. 4 (July, 1952): 438-47; and G. Pullini, "Rassegna Ruzantesca," *Lettere Italiane* 6, no. 1 (1954):90-95.
106 Grabher, *Ruzzante* pp. 61-70, examines his poetics

flection frightens him with its ferocity. Despite his anger, Ruzzante is no more daring than the soldier; yet by accident he succeeds in wounding Tonin and putting him to flight. Although Beolco uses the classical character-type of the braggart warrior, he never forgets his desire to be true to nature. Tonin becomes ridiculous and grotesque when he tries to be anything more than he really is. These characters in the *Moscheta* act according to their elemental passions. The husband Ruzzante is greedy and sensual, jealous about his wife but also interested in cheating Menato and Tonin. Beolco sought to portray simple, instinctive human emotions in conflict in a tense domestic situation.[107]

Generally critics consider Beolco's *Parlamento de Ruzzante,* called the *Reduce* (one of his *Tre Dialoghi in lingua rustica*), his masterwork. The hero is another braggart, like Tonin, but is less professional in his pose. After the character Ruzzante went off to war hoping to make a fortune, his wife Gnua became a prostitute, taking hoodlums for her main clients and protectors. Because of a disastrous battle Ruzzante deserts the army. He declares to his friend Menato that Gnua will come back to him, but when his wife enters she is angered to see that Ruzzante is even poorer than he was before going soldiering. He is not at all scarred by his military service. Ruzzante pleads with his wife, but one of her protectors appears and beats him to the ground. When Gnua goes off with the hoodlum, Ruzzante gets up, asserting that more than a hundred men attacked him. He claims that Menato must have been under a spell if he did not see that many.

As a dramatic character the Ruzzante of the *Parlamento* is a peasant braggart warrior who ends up a cuckold because of his ambitions and his cowardly inability to pursue them. He never truly fights; instead he points out to Menato that military art is fleeing or feigning death. He fails as a soldier and as a husband. Even after deserting military service he is afraid of the idea of war. Ruzzante, the peasant-soldier, is a shabby wretch. Both he and his wife are dominated by their poverty, which pushed him into military service and her into a prostitute's career. Gnua's character has its psychological coherence: her husband's economic condition is the deciding factor for her. Love, the theme which is usually dominant in the comic theater of

107 Text of the *Moscheta* in Borlenghi, *Commedie del Cinquecento,* vol. 2. For texts of Beolco's earlier plays see Lovarini's critical editions of the *Betìa* (Padua, 1894) and *La Pastorale* (Florence, 1951). The *Betìa,* though in verse, is a five-act play. Boughner, *The Braggart,* pp. 101-2, describes Tonin as the peasant braggart warrior. Apollonio, *Storia,* 2:122-23, talks of Beolco's transferring the peasants to a city environment in the *Moscheta.* Herrick, *Italian Comedy,* pp. 46-49, analyzes the *Moscheta* and its characters.

the sixteenth century, is fully attenuated by economic circumstances. Beolco avoided showing these characters as sunk in total desperation. Sympathetically viewing them in their weaknesses, he created a farce about human illusions in the midst of severe realities.[108]

L'Anconitana

This dramatist turned definitively to the classical scheme with his comedy *L'Anconitana,* written perhaps between 1529 and 1532.[109] Although Beolco seemed to have mocked academicism in literature, he should still be regarded as a writer of culture. In deciding to employ the regular comic formula, he was fulfilling a need to structure his works in a firm architectonic form, one that could provide him with greater opportunities to resolve theatrical motives. He hoped to discipline his dramatic talents. Moreover, Beolco's works were performed before aristocratic circles; the classicizing culture of this "theatrical public" probably influenced his decision to employ the scheme of the regular comedy. After the *Moscheta,* his stage works started to show signs of strain, in that certain weaknesses, like his repetitiousness, were not always compensated for by humorous dialogue and situations.

108 For more information about the *Parlamento* see Boughner, *The Braggart,* pp. 101-2; Herrick, *Italian Comedy,* pp. 45-46; and Grabher, *Ruzzante,* pp. 95-120. Also note Viola, *Due Saggi,* pp. 63-65; and F. Angelini, "Saggio su Ruzzante," *Arena 2,* no. 4 (1954): 63-64.

109 This dating is highly debatable. Ludovico Zorzi, "Lettura del Ruzzante," *Lo Smeraldo 7,* no. 6 (1953): 24-31, insists that the *Anconitana* is an early work. Zorzi, who has translated this play into Italian, holds that Beolco was always a cultured man of letters. He denies the cultural evolution in the playwright's works that Grabher asserts. To prove his point, Zorzi notes that the second prologue of the *Anconitana* mentions the Turkish menace to Cyprus. In 1522 Rhodes was taken by the Turks, with Cyprus being placed in an extremely dangerous situation. Zorzi also points out that the plot of the *Anconitana* has nothing in common with the ancient Roman comedies, whereas Beolco's plays *Piovana* and *Vaccaria* are derived directly from Plautus. But Grabher, "Sulla datazione dell'*Anconitana,*" *La Rassegna d. lett. ital.* 7, no. 1 (January-March, 1954): 62-68, states that the Turkish menace remained strong in 1529; as late as 1537-38 Cyprus was barely saved from Soliman II. For Grabher this play is too refined to have been composed in Beolco's early period. Nino Borsellino, "La Datazione dell'*Anconitana,*" *Giorn. Stor. d. lett. ital.* 139 (1962): 246-55, however, holds a nonevolutionary opinion. He points out that Beolco does not enter into the polemic of the "natural" in this play. Also the character Ruzzante is a young man in the *Anconitana;* the explanation of the name "Ruzzante" is given here, seemingly as an indication that the actor-author is at an early point in his career. Borsellino feels that Beolco must have been present at the performance of the *Calandria* at Venice in 1522; Bibbiena's classical structure and novellistic plot would then have inspired the writing of the *Anconitana.* For hypothetical dating of Beolco's works see Borsellino, "Ruzzante," *Enciclopedia dello Spettacolo* 8:1342-50.

By working in the classical form, Beolco wanted to develop dramas in a wider range than he had covered in his purely peasant comedies.[110]

There are two prologues to *L'Anconitana*. The first is in Tuscan, in which the all-conquering force Time proclaims that the comedy's story is new and modern and that its events actually took place in Padua, the setting for the play. These are the usual assertions to be found in the prologues of Renaissance comedies. The play, as Time points out, is arranged according to ancient usage. By contrast, the second prologue is in the Paduan dialect with the peasant Ruzzante pronouncing a hymn to love. The inspiration for this apology for love may come from Boccaccio's *Filostrato* (III, 75 ff.).[111] Ruzzante declares that men of different dispositions become expert in the fields that interest them most; his specialty is love. According to Ruzzante, the god of love has left Cyprus for fear of the Turks and has come to Padua. Love saves everyone by renewing the earth; his spirit enters into all trees and penetrates the rivers to warm fish and cause them to multiply. Without love there would be no songbirds. Since love makes life possible, the play will be all about love. The language of the second prologue is often rustic, using examples drawn from plant grafting. Beolco contrasts two worlds in these prologues: one is "literary" and expressed in a dialect foreign to the author; the other is rustic and expressed in his native tongue. The author attempts in the play to unite those two worlds.

Although this comedy is divided into five acts, there is no subdivision into scenes. Each act is continuous, interrupted only by stage directions like these: "Ginevra and Isotta go indoors; Ruzzante, at the window of Madonna Doralice's, sings; and Messer Thomao walks under the window and speaks with Madonna Doralice" (Act IV); "Besa opens the door and Ruzzante enters; then Messer Thomao leaves and speaks to himself" (Act V). The scene is always a public square with streets leading off from it. Beolco was particularly sensitive to the grouping of characters as the stage directions indicate; he never forgot the spectacular use of the stage.

Like other erudite comedies *L'Anconitana* combines motives from the ancient Roman comic theater with novellistic themes. This play includes an old man, Sier Thomao, in love with the courtesan Doralice; two females (the widow Ginevra and Isotta) disguised in men's clothing; a tender recovery scene; passionate desires awakened by the disguise in men's clothing; the mention of Turkish pirates. The comedy even concludes with a

---

110 Grabher, *Ruzzante,* p. 186, and Angelini,"Saggio su Ruzzante," p. 60, discuss the maturing of Beolco's style.
111 Grabher, *Ruzzante* p. 188, refers to the *Filostrato*.

double wedding for one of the two main groups of characters. Some of the characters' names recall Boccaccian novelle: Tancredi, Teodoro, Ginevra, Isotta. It seems that *L'Anconitana* is a standard comedy with type characters.[112] But there are other elements. The courtesan's maid Besa and, above all, Thomao's servant Ruzzante are quite distinct from characters like Tancredi or Isotta, since they are drawn from the world of peasants Beolco described in his earlier works and are not modeled after the slaves in Roman comedies. The author clearly sets them off from the group of lovers linguistically; Ruzzante and Besa speak in the Paduan dialect while the lovers Tancredi, Teodoro, Isotta, and Ginevra, as well as the courtesan Doralice, use Tuscan. Sier Thomao is in the middle speaking Venetian. Beolco was a master at creating nuances of style and language, effecting tonal contrasts not only between the groups of characters but within the groups. The young lovers belong to an idealized, "literary" world, like that in Boccaccio's novelle, while the two servants are molded more realistically and speak in a fairly true-to-life manner. The characters of the literary world participate in a sentimental, melodramatic plot, whereas the servants take part in a lively farce. Doralice can move in both worlds, speaking in an "ideal" style to the three youths or bargaining for a high fee from Sier Thomao.[113]

The entire first act is given over to Tancredi, Teodoro, and Gismondo-Isotta as they wander about Padua in search of a patroness. On meeting Doralice, whom they take for a great lady, they describe their talents. Tancredi claims to be able to compose any kind of verse in the Tuscan dialect. Doralice, who is a cultured courtesan like Talanta, approves of his talent, pointing out that Petrarch's poems have made him and Laura immortal. Whereas Tancredi speaks in a polished manner that echoes Petrarchan verse, Teodoro recalls descriptions in Boccaccio's *Corbaccio* as he pictures the vain efforts of ladies who adorn themselves to ward off the ravages of time. He claims to be able to produce beauty products that are not harmful to any lady, by creating an entire program of beauty-aid work. In making his gallant homage to fair ladies Teodoro weaves phrases with an extravagant imagination. Gismondo-Isotta offers to embroider and design ladies' clothing. All three youths present themselves as cavaliers ready to serve a noble lady according to their talents. The spirit of the first act is refined.[114]

---

112 Apollonio, *Storia,* 2:131, speaks of the novellistic themes and characters.
113 Grabher, "Sulla datazione," pp. 65-68, talks of the juxtaposition of different worlds.
114 Grabher, *Ruzzante,* p. 192, contrasts the *Corbaccio.* Baratto, "Ruzzante," p. 148, fails to see Boccaccian grace in the play.

Sentimentality and melodrama become evident in the third act when Ginevra arrives in town, and this mood is carried through the following act. Ginevra becomes the dominant figure with her quest for Gismondo, while Ruzzante stands on the sidelines laughing to himself, since he knows that Gismondo is a female. Ginevra suffers from jealousy on hearing that Gismondo has been hired to work for Sier Thomao's wife. Ruzzante agrees to bring Ginevra together with Gismondo for a fee, but even the servant, who has the peasant's cunning for always seeking his own good, marvels how the force of love compelled the young lady to travel from Ancona to Venice and then to Padua in search of Gismondo. The tender spirit of the third act continues when Ginevra is offstage. Teodoro and Tancredi regret that Gismondo may be separated from them, since the ransom of the two youths is to be paid by some Paduan gentlemen, and permission given for them to return to Sicily. Gismondo must stay in Sier Thomao's service. Tancredi, still not knowing Gismondo's true sex, feels a strange attachment for his friend.

This comedy of sentiment reaches a high point in Act IV at the happily tearful moment when Ginevra and Isotta are reunited as sisters. Later they decide to marry the two young men, and in the final act there is a tender love scene when the sisters meet their future husbands. In words pierced with sighs Tancredi asks Isotta why she never revealed her true identity during the three years of captivity they spent together, because their love could have begun much sooner. All the lovers salute the city of Padua before starting home to Sicily. Their joy is complete, for after years of suffering these noble-hearted characters see their dreams of happiness fulfilled.

Alongside the idealized love story is the folk drama, but its characters do not speak in crude, down-to-earth language like the peasants in Beolco's earlier dramas; Ruzzante and Besa have a certain city sophistication. The whole second act is devoted to setting the mood of the folk action, in artistic and linguistic counterpoint with the first act. Sier Thomao opens the act with a monologue. His Venetian is not very refined; it fits a broker who has enriched himself. He is close to his eighties, and yet he is not satisfied with a beautiful young wife but has to have the courtesan. He is so vain that he thinks Doralice will come to love him; Beolco caricatured Sier Thomao's senile passion. Ruzzante plays on his master's feelings, although he never exploits them as slaves in an ancient comedy would do; instead this rustic servant delights in mocking Sier Thomao. The peasant is a ladies' man, as he shows in a scene with Besa. He is talkative, and he is bursting with joy after Besa leaves: "Boy, am I lucky! She has fallen in love with my dancing and singing, indeed she has. I've won over other women the same way, by faith. *Tandaran, Tarirondon, Tarirondon.* Let's see if we know how to make pirouettes and turns like the style of Padua. *Tiro, tirodon. . . ."* Devoted to singing and dancing, Ruzzante joins his master in singing both elevated and rustic songs. The old man sings Giustinian's strambotto *Quattro suspiri te vorria mandare;* the author here contrasts the peasant's naturalness with the literary artificiality of the old man. Throughout the act Ruzzante jumps about and dances, like the Zanni and Arlecchino of the later Commedia dell'Arte.[115]

A scene in the fourth act illustrates how Ruzzante enjoys working Sier Thomao into a rage. The old man wants news of Doralice's intentions, but Ruzzante is absorbed in his love for Besa. Pretending to be naive, the servant starts to tell how, when he was a little boy in love with a peasant girl, one night he met a wolf with big eyes that kept menacing him. Sier Thomao tries again and again to interrupt the tale, calling the servant a silly ass. But Ruzzante continues, in his mischievous fashion, accompanying his tale with pantomine and starting again after every interruption with the comic refrain: "com a ve dego rivar de dire." Ruzzante excels at this subtle and ironic teasing.

With malicious irony the author chose Arquà, where the master love-poet Petrarch died, as the site for the promised assignation between Doralice and Sier Thomao and their servants. The last act basically belongs to Ruzzante and his master. In the opening scene Ruzzante and his friend Menato, who is introduced only at this point, sing some duets together. Ruzzante is dreaming of the happy time he will have with Besa. The servant has accumulated many coins from his master and Ginevra, and in a comic scene he piles them up and plans to buy new clothes and perhaps a sword. But Sier Thomao, who is a strange sort of lover, orders the servant to go and fetch his nightshirt and slippers for the trip; the gouty old lover is painfully meticulous and does not let romantic thoughts prevent him from providing for his comfort. Ruzzante drops and loses some of Sier Thomao's articles when the old man's wife pushes him out of the house in her haste to receive her own lover, but he lies to his master so they can depart. At last the folk characters can meet in the country, the area most beloved by Beolco.

Love, from Ruzzante's prologue on, is the power that moves the characters of the comedy, whether on the "literary" or the folk level. It is, however, an ironical presentation of the force of love that distinguishes the play,

---

115 Mortier, *Ruzzante,* 1:142-43, makes character sketches of Sier Thomao and Ruzzante, Angelini, "Saggio su Ruzzante," pp. 71-72, comments on the contrast between Sier Thomao's "literary" song and Ruzzante's "natural" folk song.

since the characters indulge in comic ecstasies because of their amorous interests. Unfortunately, the author failed to develop the "literary" figures as true human types with individual personalities as he did with Sier Thomao and Ruzzante, and so the play is somewhat off balance. The mood and time of the play are modern, with references to Turkish pirates and Padua's university life. *L'Anconitana* succeeds best with its kaleidoscopic presentation of different groups of characters, each one speaking the dialect that properly suits it. Beolco broke away from his strictly peasant and dialectal style to fashion a unique form of the Erudite Comedy.

La Piovana

In his first attempt to write a comedy according to the classical pattern, Beolco combined novellistic themes and characters with peasant servant types, without any particular ancient source for either the characters or the plot of *L'Anconitana*. But in February 1533 two new comedies, the *Piovana* and the *Vaccaria*, were performed at Cornaro's town house in Padua. Here Beolco grew very close to classical models, with Plautus' *Rudens* and *Asinaria* influencing respectively the *Piovana* and the *Vaccaria*. The Italian dramatist tried to infuse a new spirit into the ancient material.[116]

Beolco starts off the prologue of the *Piovana* with a bold declaration. The actor delivering the prologue warns the spectators not to be surprised to hear on stage a language other than Florentine, for the prologue, like the whole play, is in the Paduan dialect. To rework an ancient play in any dialect but Tuscan is a daring effort by the author. In this prologue Beolco justifies the use of his native dialect for a classical-type comedy on the grounds that the Paduan dialect is the most "natural" to him. Beolco will always return to the principle of the natural to defend his dramas. As the prologue continues, the reciting actor admits that although the comedy was recently written, it has an ancient model. It is made out of "old wood," thereby being well aged. The actor mentions that his parish priest told him that we all once existed before just as we are now and that in the far future we shall return as at the present; consequently the actions in an ancient play can be repeated in a modern comedy. Machiavelli referred to a similar cyclical view of history in the prologue to the *Clizia* to justify his reworking a Plautine comedy.[117] The reciting actor goes on to state that this comedy is not a stolen play. The situation is like finding an old suit in a chest; the

---

116 Sanesi, *La Commedia*, 1:477, provides details on the first performance.
117 Marisa Milani, "L' Educazione Letteraria e *L'Oratoria* del Ruzzante," *Miscellanea di studi offerta a Armando Balduino e Bianca Bianchi per le loro nozze* (1962), pp. 53-54, discusses the cyclical view of history.

cloth is good, but the fashion is outdated and requires retailoring to please the tastes of living persons. The modern author has taken up an ancient play, left the dead words to the ancients, and transferred their sense into a living language.

This actor explains that the dramatist is opposed to many theatrical devices common to the period; along with excluding Florentine, the author has avoided mixing in other languages like French or German. The confusing babbling of different languages and dialects, as in Piccolomini's *L'Amor Costante,* is not to be found here. Beolco will not even contrast literary language and folk dialects as he did in *L'Anconitana.* In this second classical-type comedy he will also avoid presenting kidnapped girls, gallant lovers, cunning servants with distorted Latinized names like Firantibus, greedy old men, or gluttons. Obviously the dramatist wanted to stay away from the banal themes overworked by too many contemporary playwrights. The prologue goes on to point out that since the countryside existed long before the cities, there is no reason for the author to give way to city-type comedy. The scene will be Chioggia on the Adriatic coast, where there are orchards all around from which the characters will step. Even while modeling his comedy on an ancient source, Beolco has been able to keep a country setting.

Yet Beolco did not fulfill all the aims proposed in the prologue. Old Tura's daughter Nina has been kidnapped; she was born in the Piove region, thus giving the comedy its title *La Piovana.* Subsequently there is a recovery scene between father and daughter. The plot also includes a gallant lover, Maregale's son Siton, and the conclusion has the usual plans for a double wedding: for Siton and Nina as well as for the servants Garbugio and Ghetta. In following the Latin model of the *Rudens* the Paduan dramatist sometimes almost translated Plautus. At other times he reworked the Latin text by changing peasant values for ancient ones, as in the scene of Act IV in which the fisher Bertevello finds a chest owned by the procurer Slavero in a fishing net. The servant dreams of taking the money in the chest to buy a large farm. In a similar scene of the fourth act of the *Rudens* the fisher-slave Gripus grows ecstatic about becoming a mighty lord with the fortune he has found in a chest he fished out of the sea. The situation and the stimulus to dreaming are the same in the *Piovana* and the *Rudens,* but the character in the modern play has the mentality of a sixteenth-century peasant. At one point Beolco completely departed from the Plautine model. Whereas the prologue to the *Rudens* is given by Arcturus, who indicates the intervention of the gods by a storm at sea, in the *Piovana* the prologue does not mention supernatural forces, but makes clear the author's stand on several artistic questions. From the prologue onward it was obvious that Beolco was going to do something new with the plot imitated from Plautus.

One of the most necessary changes is in the setting. The *Rudens* is set near Cyrene, in Africa, not far from the seashore; in the scene, one of the most elaborate for a Plautine play, are a cottage and a temple of Venus. In shifting the scene to the Adriatic coast, chosen because of the shipwreck, Beolco had to explain why persons speaking the Paduan dialect were living near Chioggia. Tura had retired there after the wars, and his friend Maregale was resting from the misfortunes of Siton's departure. Instead of the temple of Venus there is a rustic church. Later, during the Catholic Reformation, the church was struck from editions of the play. The time is the sixteenth century: Slavero was sailing away to the New World of spices and gold when a storm struck his ship. Beolco did not approach the ancient comedy with academic stiffness. For him Plautus was a source of laughter.[118]

The *Rudens* was not the only comedy by Plautus that influenced Beolco in writing the *Piovana;* the *Mercator* provided him with models for the members of Maregale's family. The languishing youth Charinus in the *Mercator* set the pattern for Siton, while the relationship between Lysimachus and his shrewish wife Dorippa in the Plautine play is exactly like that of Maregale and Resca. Maregale, just like Lysimachus, married a woman with a large dowry and later regretted it, since his wife was forever nagging him. The fourth act of the *Piovana* particularly borrows from the *Mercator*. In the Plautine comedy Lysimachus is hiding a young girl in his home for his friend Demipho when Dorippa, who was supposed to be passing some days in their country home, arrives in town suddenly just as a cook is preparing a banquet in Lysimachus' house. The lady is enraged, believing that her husband has a young mistress. Similarly, in the *Piovana* the girls Nina and Ghetta are lodged in Maregale's house at Tura's request. The servant Garbinello has informed Resca about the presence of the girls and hinted that Maregale has more than a protective interest in them, thereby gaining some money from the greedy old woman in order to help Siton. After Resca chases the girls from her home, she is starting to scold Maregale when a fisher arrives to get a banquet ready. In both plays the shrewish wives come to know the truth and become reconciled with their husbands. Beolco was not the only playwright of his time who borrowed from more than one ancient comedy to fashion a play; this process is called "contaminatio," as

118 Apollonio, *Storia,* 2:131, talks of the modern approach to the subject.

Terence also used it when building a play from different Greek comedies.[119]

While the slaves in the *Rudens* are not major figures, the servants of the *Piovana* are important as a result of Beolco's interest in peasant types. Garbugio, a master at creating *garbugli* (entangled situations), is menaced by Slavero and an innkeeper early in the third act. Another servant, Daldura, has told the procurer that the two girls are hiding in a church. Garbugio orders the girls to turn the church upside down while he holds off the procurer and the innkeeper. Finally letting the two men into the church, Garbugio locks them in and starts screaming for help. Church bells begin to ring, and Tura comes on scene with a large group of peasants. All keep asking Garbugio what has happened, fearing a fire. The servant keeps talking without being specific, building up suspense in the crowd. At last he declares that two Lutherans are desecrating the church; during the early Protestant Reformation Lutherans were more hated in Italy than Turks. The peasants rush to the church, rescue the girls, and tie up the two "Lutherans." All these scenes, which take up the entire third act and the start of the fourth, are original with Beolco. In the *Rudens* the procurer and his accomplice succeed in breaking into the temple of Venus, and the procurer tries to drag the girls away, knocking down the priestess. He is stopped by the old man who corresponds to Tura and by the lover of one of the girls. Beolco has presented Garbugio's different intrigues as coming spontaneously to the servant, one after the other in a natural way. The whole third act builds momentum.

Garbugio's exploits are matched by Garbinello. In the *Rudens* the procurer Labrax recovers his chest with the money in it, and he is even invited to a final banquet by the father of the girl the procurer tried to hold as a slave. But in the *Piovana* Garbinello, Bertevello, and Daldura share the wallet found in the procurer's chest; afterward Garbinello frightens Slavero away by telling him that Nina's relatives are gathering a little army to seize the procurer and kill him for mistreating her. The servant points out a road by which Slavero can escape the region. Later Garbinello closes the play with a brief envoi in which he urges the audience to cry out and applaud so the procurer will think Nina's relatives are in hot pursuit and be so terrified that he will never show himself again. Beolco makes even the envoi

---

119 Mortier, *Ruzzante,* 2:360, examines the borrowings from the *Mercator.* A. Salza, *Delle Commedie di Lodovico Dolce* (Melfi, 1899), pp. 140-47, mentions the possible influence of Terence's *Heautotimorumenos* in the sorrow of Maregale on losing his son; the father in the Terentian play drove his son away because he did not want the youth to marry a lowborn girl.

more than a formal part of an erudite comedy; it contributes to the cunning servant's scheme.[120]

Not only in the actions but in the speeches of the *Piovana*, Beolco departed from the Plautine text to infuse a Ruzzantian spirit of rustic comedy. In the third scene of Act I, Tura reflects on old age, comparing it to a dog bitten by flies. The author's poetic gifts are evident here, capturing youth and old age with concrete images while preserving delicate nuances. Youth, flowers, and songbirds in contrast with a thin dog—all are part of the pictorial style that Beolco took over from the folk traditions of his native region.

In the prologue the author promised there would be no gluttons in the play. This did not include characters who have the peasants' love of gorging themselves on festive occasions. Garbinello goes into ecstasies (Act V, sc. 10) describing how he intends to rejoice during the week-long wedding festivities: ". . . eating good things is the king of pleasures. . . ." He makes a burlesque hymn to the joys of eating. Garbinello delivers an anatomical lecture on the effects of good food on the various parts of the human body. This peasant servant exhibits an animalistic joy in food, accompanying his words with comic gestures. His speech is in the same class as the sturgeon scene of the *Talanta*. The author was not thinking of any Plautine glutton when he described this folk rejoicing in the pleasures of the world, for Garbinello is not a flattering glutton imitated from an ancient comedy but a peasant who loves good fare.[121]

In reworking a Plautine comedy, Beolco tried for the maximum scenic effects. For this dialectal writer the stage was action. Act III with its animated rush of the peasants to the church reveals his sensitivity to spectacular stage movement. His greatest weakness is repetition; during the fourth act four monologues come in a row. Just as Plautus had taken his plots from the Greek New Comedy and forged a Roman comic theater, with the *Piovana* Beolco was seeking to fashion a modern dialectal drama from the material provided by the ancient Roman playwright.

La Vaccaria

From its very title the *Vaccaria* seems to be a comedy of the classical type. As in *L'Anconitana*, there are two prologues, one in Tuscan and the other in the Paduan dialect. A sprite delivers the Tuscan prologue, claiming that

120 A. Böhm, "Fonti plautine del Ruzzante," *Giorn. Stor. d. lett. ital.* 29 (1897): 101 f., examines the original way Beolco developed Plautus' *Rudens*.
121 Grabher, *Ruzzante*, pp. 223-27, discusses the Beolchian spirit as felt in this play.

Plautus has sent him from the other world to announce the performance of a comedy that evening. The audience should not be offended if the play is not in Latin, not in verse, and not in the refined Tuscan language. If Plautus were living today, the sprite reports, he would make comedies like the one the audience is about to behold. The sprite warns everyone not to judge this new play by the Plautine comedies that have come down from antiquity; he asserts that ancient comedies were performed in a manner very different from their appearance in printing. Many things that are written down look good but have a bad effect on the stage. These last statements indicate Beolco's awareness of theatrical values, for he did not regard the Plautine plays in terms of academic pomp. In writing a comedy based on Plautus' *Asinaria,* the Paduan dramatist wished to restore to the ancient author's work the comic style that was lost in humanistic editions of the play. Beolco hoped to make the Plautine comedy seem "natural" to the modern audience, not distorted and boring like most Renaissance translations. He was less interested in translating than in infusing a modern spirit into the ancient comedy. He is unique in his ability to distinguish between the written page and the theatrical scene, for he had a genuine sense of the theater.[122]

The servant Truffo comes on stage to give the Paduan prologue, declaring that he will do his best although his real job is merely being a servant. He explains that the sprite's arrival on a cloud has taken away the voice of the actor who was supposed to deliver the prologue. Truffo promises not to inflate his speech but to proceed naturally. This play is different from its ancient model in that Plautus' play was about asses and this one is about cows, animals that are useful and pleasing. It is evident from what Truffo says that a play on the word *vacca* is intended, since it also means a woman of easy virtue.[123] Truffo adds that the comedy is set at Padua. Onstage is an ancient coliseum.

Like the *Anconitana* this comedy has some characters who speak the Paduan dialect and other characters who use Tuscan. The servants Truffo, Vezzo, and Betta, the parasite Loron, and the minstrel Piolo speak in Paduan while all the other characters use the literary language. It seems strange that characters like a merchant, a steward, and the procuress Celega speak in Tuscan, since they seem to be folk characters. Here, unlike the *Anconitana,* there is no contrast between a "literary" novellistic world and a realistic

122 Borlenghi, *Commedie del Cinquecento,* 2:565-66, and Grabher, *Ruzzante,* pp. 211-12, analyze the prologue with an aim to demonstrate Beolco's theatric sense.
123 Mortier, *Ruzzante,* 1:149, discusses the play's meaning.

folk world; in the *Vaccaria* there is only a slight tonal difference between two realistically portrayed groups.[124]

Generally the *Vaccaria* follows its Plautine model far more closely than the *Piovana* follows the *Rudens*. Although the setting is modern, with anti-clerical references to the way priests and monks talked rich women into leaving their dowries to the church, the first four acts of Beolco's comedy are carefully modeled on the *Asinaria*. But the fifth act of the Italian comedy is radically different from that of the ancient play because of the change of heart for the old shrew Rospina. In the fifth act of the *Asinaira* haughty Artemona surprises her husband, Senator Demaenetus, reveling with a young courtesan; she loudly abuses her husband and then leads him off-stage. Artemona remains a shrew throughout the Plautine comedy. Perhaps the transformation in Rospina's feelings was influenced by Terence's comedy the *Adelphi,* which describes two brothers. The one, Demea, has two sons and lets his brother Micio adopt one of the boys. Demea is a rigid person, completely unfeeling to the burning desires of youth, and rears the son he keeps with him strictly, while Micio does not exercise this restraint over his adopted son and does everything to gratify the youth's inclinations. But toward the close of the play Demea decides to change his ways, declaring that he will be kind and considerate in the future. Demea's new intentions are motivated by a desire to take vengeance on his brother, who has won the love of both boys; through Demea's conniving Micio has to spend a good deal of money and marry an old woman. Rospina's agreement to the wedding of her son Flavio with the girl Fiorinetta and the gifts she makes to Vezzo could be imitated from the metamorphosis in Demea, but in Beolco's comedy Rospina does not change out of ulterior motives for revenge. She merely wants to be loving and pleasant. The novella tradition provides numerous examples of such a complete and sudden metamorphosis. Dramatically the last act change in Rospina is unsuccessful.[125]

Except for his handling of the repentant shrew, the author excels in portraying the characters, even giving a new spirit to traditional types. Celega and her adopted daughter Fiorinetta have a rather shaky relationship, for Celega is a cynical creature guided by an implacable logic of always seeking her own advantage. Unlike Ariosto's Lena, she does not inspire compassion from the spectator; Celega fits in the same class as the ruthless procuress Canthara of the *Chrysis*. In the third scene of Act I this procuress fights with Flavio because he cannot produce fifty florins to pay for the girl. She com-

124 Grabher, *Ruzzante,* p. 210, examines the linguistic question.
125 *Ibid.*, pp. 208-9, raises the question of Terentian influence.

pares herself to a fowler who uses the girl as bait to lure lovers like birds; her speech is, of course, taken from that of the procuress Cleaereta in the *Asinaria,* which was also imitated in plays such as the *Chrysis* and the *Cassaria.* Only money or expensive gifts can satisfy Celega.

But Fiorinetta wishes to remain morally pure despite the corrupt environment in which being an orphan has forced her to live. As a dramatic character she combines the budding courtesan Philenium of the *Asinaria* with the orphan Silenium in Plautus' *Cistellaria.* She loves only Flavio and has never yet given herself to anyone other than him, preferring an honorable marriage to a lucrative career as a courtesan. She is a sixteenth-century Gigi. The second scene of Act III, wholly original to Beolco, shows the clash of temperaments between Fiorinetta and the procuress. Although the girl respects Celega as her adoptive mother, she does not wish to sell herself for the sake of the woman's greed. The procuress loses patience in her efforts to teach the girl how to milk men of money and gifts. She tells her that if men know that Fiorinetta is friendly with a penniless youth, they will expect her favors for nothing. Instead the girl should put a high price on herself: if one man gives her a necklace or a ring, she ought to show it off to others so that one will surpass the gift with another of greater value. This scene has a marked realism, as Beolco reveals his accurate knowledge of human traits. Celega's profession thrives by competition among rivals for a courtesan's favors. Beolco describes here a conflict between an older woman with her experiences of harsh economic facts and a girl who tries to protect her true love in the face of strong pressures.[126]

Flavio's main rival Polidoro is an effeminate ladies man who hopes to control Fiorinetta through his opulence. The girl despises him and makes fun of his features, which have been scarred by syphilis. His important scene is the third of Act IV, in which he meets with a notary to draw up a contract that will guarantee him the favors of Fiorinetta for a year. Plautus wrote similar ridiculous contract scenes in some of his comedies. Polidoro wants Fiorinetta for a year not out of romantic ardor but out of fear of not getting his money's worth; he has the notary add one clause after another to protect his rights. Fiorinetta is to be confined indoors away from others; and if for some reason, including a physical one on Polidoro's part, he is deprived of her for a day or a night, she will be obligated to compensate

---

126 Cataldo, *Il Ruzzante,* pp. 96-97, speaks of Fiorinetta's purity. Apollonio, *Storia,* 2:132, points out the conflict between the procuress and the girl. Mortier, *Ruzzante,* 1:151, treats of the derivation from the two Plautine courtesans. Grabher, *Ruzzante,* p. 212, compares Celega with Canthara.

him even after the year's expiration. Legal terminology has always been an object of satire because of its general stupidity, and the language of the contract in this comedy makes clear how fatuous Polidoro is. It also explains Fiorinetta's unwillingness to follow the career of a courtesan.[127]

As usual, Boelco channeled his creative energies into molding folk characters. Even the parasite Loron is a folk figure who speaks in the Paduan dialect. His unsuccessful efforts to secure steady meals for himself recall the parasite Ergasilus of Plautus' *Captivi,* for indeed Loron admits that his only trade is eating. He is not a cultured figure like some of the parasites in the Roman comedies. Truffo calls him a buffoon ready to twist his face and humiliate himself at banquets to please others and have a free meal, but Loron describes himself as a "yes-man" for his pretentious patrons. The author combined traditional traits from the Roman Comedy with more down-to-earth folk features in shaping this parasite.[128]

Truffo and Vezzo correspond to the slaves Libanus and Leonida of the *Asinaria,* but they are free servants of peasant origin. Their country background explains their wily character, which has saved them in many tight situations. One such situation develops in Act II after Truffo meets a merchant who has come to buy some cows from Rospina's estate. They are at an inn, and Truffo describes Vezzo as Rospina's steward. Vezzo, on encountering the merchant, tries to speak a pure Florentine but ends up speaking very incorrect Italian. When the real steward comes on scene, Truffo holds him off by claiming that the merchant is a diviner who is seeking to defraud Rospina by saying that a treasure is hidden in her house. The servant adds that the diviner is willing to leave a money deposit, and asks the steward's help in carrying out the deception on the "diviner." If the steward hands his wallet with ten ducats in it to Vezzo, then the "diviner" will believe that Vezzo is the real steward; the steward falls for the ruse and turns over the wallet. Plautus' comedy had no similar scene in which the deception was worked right in the steward's presence. It is also in the second act that Truffo and Vezzo declare that they are equal to city-born persons. Even though they are considered ignorant peasants, they assert that educated persons are in no way superior to them. Truffo points out that man's weapon is intelligence: "Thinking works for men as claws and teeth and horns for the other animals, for animals defend themselves with these weapons from the harm that can befall them; and men defend themselves by thinking." Peasants easily outsmart city-dwellers. According to

127 Grabher, *Ruzzante,* pp. 217-18, describes Polidoro.
128 Mortier, *Ruzzante,* 2:559, discusses the parasite.

Vezzo, the only advantage that city-dwellers have over peasants is wealth, because poverty is the chief reason the qualities of peasants are not recognized. Beolco did not have any protosocialistic theories; but he was aiming at a moral evaluation of the peasant.

These two peasants are very fond of Flavio. In the *Asinaria*, before the slaves turn over money to their young master they make him humiliate himself, and his courtesan has to kiss Leonida. Then Libanus rides horseback on his young master. But in the *Vaccaria,* when Truffo and Vezzo go, in the fourth scene of Act III, to deliver the money to Flavio, they find him and Fiorinetta expressing to each other their sorrow at having to separate. She is ready to kill herself rather than go with Polidoro, and even faints from her emotion. The servants look on with typical peasant humor during this dramatic love scene. Before handing over the money, the servants tease the lovers without malice by telling a nonsensical story of how they obtained the funds. This is the same device of trying a person's patience that Ruzzante used on Sier Thomao in *L'Anconitana.* Plautus was interested in arousing laughter with slapstick action, but Beolco wanted to portray the peasant with his unadulterated folk humor.

One of the motives Boelco added to the Plautine plot is the love between Vezzo and Betta. Their major scene is the sixth of Act IV, which shows a fresh, delightful peasant love. Vezzo compares men to vine-sticks and women to vines, using rustic images. Betta feels closed-in, suffocated by the city surroudings, especially since her mistress keeps such a strong hold over her that she is out of practice in singing folk songs. The gift of a farm and a dowry from Rospina later make it possible for Betta to return to her beloved countryside. Although the love story of Betta and Vezzo occupies little of the comedy, it contributes to the general rustic atmosphere that the servants create in an urban environment.

Beolco's peasants are always at work, since activity makes the folk scenes more natural. With his keen theatrical sense, the author does not let the action slow down for a minute. After Rospina's metamorphosis early in the final act, Truffo and Vezzo prepare for the wedding and start to decorate the walls with ivy. The wandering Bohemian singer Piolo arrives, always ready to snatch a free meal at a celebration. He is a creature who trusts blind Fortune; although he is poor, he is happy. The servants ask him to choose a song from his repertory, and Piolo sings passages from several folk songs in an effort to decide on one, finally selecting a song that starts "La Deveosa, quando l'è in casa." With these songs the joyous spirit of the peasant characters bursts out. The frame of the Plautine plot has for a second time given Beolco the chance to represent the world of peasants.[129]

Beolco's Unique Role

After 1533 Angelo Beolco stopped writing comedies. His family had suffered several disasters. One of his brothers was imprisoned in Venice for life and another brother had gone into exile, since both had been involved in political conspiracies. Because he was illegitimate, Beolco had never had the opportunity for a political career. During those difficult years the members of his family entrusted him with the administration of their country estates, and in this way he remained amid the peasants. Some of his enemies hinted that he was practicing usury at that time, but the literary theorist Speron Speroni came to Beolco's defense in the *Dialogo dell'Usura*, in which the allegorical character Usury fails to tempt Ruzzante. Beolco had won a position of esteem in the literary world. On March 17, 1542, the Accademia Patavina degli Infiammati was to perform Speroni's play *Canace* in Padua at the home of Giovanni Cornaro. Angelo Beolco, Alessandro Piccolomini, and Luigi Cornaro were to preside at the event, which included a costume ball and a banquet for 150 persons. But all preparations were cut off when the news of Beolco's death arrived.[130]

Regular, classical structure was doubtless a point of arrival in Beolco's artistic career, as it became his personal task to strike a balance between free inspiration and formal culture. Even at the start of his career as a playwright in 1520 with the farce *Pastorale*, he echoed—if only in a mock fashion—the eclogue tradition of Sannazzaro and Poliziano. In his peasant works he showed himself totally free of intellectual prejudices and thus able to eliminate the barrier between aristocratic culture and peasant psychology.

---

129 Böhm, "Fonti plautine del Ruzzante," p. 103, mentions the folk element in the *Vaccaria*. Grabher, *Ruzzante*, pp. 213-19, points out Beolco's moral evaluation of the peasants. Mortier, *Ruzzante,* 1:151, notes changes from the *Asinaria*. Cataldo, *Il Ruzzante*, p. 96, details the similarities between the slaves in the antique play and the servants in the *Vaccaria*, Angelini, "Saggio su Ruzzante," p. 72, feels that Piolo with his songs helps to bring life to the play, transforming it from mere imitation of Plautus.

130 Cataldo, *Il Ruzzante*, pp. 45-49, discusses the last years of Beolco's life. Lovarini, "La Prima Stampa e il Cornaro," *Studi*, pp. 112-15, states that Beolco had received permission from the Venetian Senate to publish the *Piovana* and the *Vaccaria*, but the dramatist was too modest to have his works printed. After Beolco's death Cornaro took charge of the manuscripts and was eventually responsible for the first printing in 1548.

He stood between two worlds. Beolco's career has been viewed by some critics along evolutionary lines; others have seen his classicizing comedies as the fruit of his years of decline. It can be noted how he progressed, making his dramatic characters more refined and admitting the influence of Boccaccio and the ancient comic theater, and finally uniting the regular comedy with folk comedy. For Beolco there was no antithesis between those two dramatic forms; he came to see that he could use a novellistic or Plautine plot and still be true to his ideal of the natural.[131]

Beolco's theatrical works are often regarded as anticipating the Commedia dell'Arte. Although from comedy to comedy many characters have the same names, like Ruzzante, Vezzo, Menato, or Bettìa, they are not mere masks. A mask is by its nature unchanging. Arlecchino is always the same, no matter what the situation. But the character Ruzzante is a greedy and suspicious husband in the *Moscheta,* a poor cowardly braggart in the *Parlamento,* and a wily ladies' man in the *Anconitana;* he is never fixed in a mask. The same is true of other recurring characters. Beolco came closest to the Commedia dell'Arte in repeating situations like quarrels and beatings from one comedy to another, in using pantomine, and in providing a chance for the actor to improvise.[132]

The plays of Angelo Beolco are more than an example of regional, dialectal literature. For him his native dialect was the only genuine way of representing a certain level of character. But his peasant characters have more than folkloric interest; the actor-playwright Ruzzante succeeded in portraying man's elemental passions.[133]

131 Viola, *Due Saggi,* pp. 61-62, holds that the period of classical imitation is one of definite decline for the author. Baratto, "Ruzzante," pp. 118 and 154, mentions the idea of two worlds in Beolco's works and career.
132 Grabher, *Ruzzante,* p. 205; and Cataldo, *Il Ruzzante,* p. 144, point out that there are no masks in Beolco's plays. Herrick, *Italian Comedy,* p. 211, indicates the ties to the Commedia dell'Arte.
133 Beolco's works have enjoyed considerable revival in the twentieth century. Bruno Brunelli, "Il Ritorno di Ruzzante," *Rivista di Studi Teatrali* 1, no. 1 (1952): 12-21, describes the theatrical resurrection of Beolco's comedies. In the late twenties Jacques Copeau produced *L'Anconitana* at the Vieux-Colombier and carried it to Switzerland, Holland, and Belgium. In 1940 A. G. Bragaglia directed the *Reduce* in Rome. In 1942 there were several Beolchian productions to commemorate the four hundredth anniversary of the playwright's death. For Brunelli there are three technical obstacles to successful performances of Beolco's works: (*a*) the limited number of his works and their fragmentary nature; (*b*) the rustic Paduan dialect which often seems obscene but merely corresponds to the author's theory of the natural; (*c*) the difficulties of selecting a correct acting style that allows for a certain degree of improvised gesture within a carefully delineated character. Also, Brunelli emphasizes that Beolco's dramas must be given in a small, intimate theater. M.

THE VARIETIES OF THEATRICAL EXPERIMENTATION

Within its formal pattern the Erudite Comedy permitted dramatists a wide range of experimentation. Several playwrights openly set themselves up as rebels and ridiculed adherence to strict classical canons. Aretino and Beolco, despite the Tuscan background of the first, are surprisingly close to each other. Some of Aretino's plays are lengthened farces, with folk elements in the characterization of servants and the use of folk songs. Both Aretino and Beolco launched polemics against literary custom in the narrow academic sense. Yet with all their railing, Aretino borrowed motives both from the novellistic tradition and from ancient comedy and Beolco showed an erudite influence even in folk works like the *Moscheta* and the *Parlamento*. Neither dramatist remained untouched by the cultural atmosphere of the period.[134] An even bolder departure from dramatic norms is evidenced by Agostino Ricchi's *I Tre Tiranni*. Although his play was produced in the strongly academic environment of Bologna with all the pomp of an imperial celebration, the author's imagination was not strangled. Ricchi not only attacked various classical conventions in his prologue, but he actually violated the unity of time. In his youthful rebellion he sought bizarre dramatic effects.

Even in Siena the sharp distinction between folk drama and the erudite

---

Baratto, *"La Moscheta," Théâtre Populaire*, no. 43 (1961), pp. 81-89, reviews the Paris performance of the *Moscheta*, which the touring Teatro Stabile of Turin had just given. Baratto demonstrates that Beolco's theater is the product of a postwar period, following the devastation of the battles fought by the League of Cambrai (1508-18). According to Baratto, the Ruzzantian drama hinges on a contradiction between the content of the plays (reality as viewed by peasants) and the aristocratic audience to which Beolco addressed his works. This critic asserts that the vitality of Beolco's theater lies in the confrontation between the naturalness of peasant characters and the historical power of the elite who patronized the author. Baratto feels that the period of creative growth for Beolco was 1524 to 1529, an essentially antiliterary phase of his writing. Beolco broke with conventions to portray the bitter struggle of peasants to survive in unnatural environments like the city. The hero of Beolco's grim comedy is a victim. With his Marxistic opinions, Baratto concludes that the three erudite comedies attest to an artistic compromise which Beolco made for his cultured audiences. Lucio Ridenti *"L'Anconitana e Bilora," Il Dramma*, nos. 343-44 (April-May, 1965), pp. 114-16, reviews the success of the Teatro Stabile in interpeting the *Anconitana* and the *Bilora*. Ridenti notes the ways in which Beolco anticipated the Commedia dell'Arte; Sier Thomao prefigures Pantalone. Beolco's theater is a universal one, in Ridenti's evaluation, that presents the eternal conflict between city and country, culture and violent instinct.
134 Herrick, *Italian Comedy*, p. 85, talks of the similarity between Aretino and Beolco.

theater did not cause a stifling academic atmosphere. Alessandro Piccolomini and the creator of the *Ingannati* did not take stands against following classical conventions, and Piccolomini ended his literary career as an Aristotelian commentator. But neither the *Ingannati* nor the *Amor Costante* is a strict imitation of a sepcific Roman comedy, especially when compared with Beolco's close adherence to Plautine plots in the *Piovana* and the *Vaccaria*. Aretino himself drew from the *Menaechmi* for both the *Ipocrito* and the *Talanta*. The Sienese erudite dramatists were interested instead in representing youthful love, the aristocratic cult of fair ladies, and the satire of Spanish conquerors and corrupt clergymen. Piccolomini, with his portrayal of sentimental love, created the same type of serious romantic comedy that Aretino later sketched out in the *Ipocrito*. The productions of the Accademia degli Intronati possess qualities wholly original to the Renaissance period, without any dependence on ancient comedy.

This second phase of the Italian Erudite Comedy was scenically more varied than the earlier formative phase, since the picture of contemporary society was filled out by the works produced at that time. A theme of romantic love and tender sentiment that was to be significant for the rest of the century developed, although no high point like the *Mandragola* was reached. It was during this period that the whole gallery of character types was completed. The dramatists of those years established a theatrical pattern which later playwrights chose not to modify. In the second half of the sixteenth century the Erudite Comedy found a favorable environment in Naples, with imaginative authors like Giordano Bruno and Giovanni Battista Della Porta. Complicated comedies of intrigue and sentimental plays became the fashion of the day, with the taste for spectacle growing all the more overwhelming. At the same time literary critics were codifying the unities into strict canons, thus restricting the freedom of dramatists to experiment. By the close of the century two theatrical tendencies were dominant. Formal theater turned into the pure spectacle of music and ballet that was the early Italian opera, while the Commedia dell'Arte reached out for a wider popular audience than the Erudite Comedy had ever attracted.

Conclusion: The Creation of a Modern Comic Theater

EUROPE'S DEBT TO THE ITALIAN COMEDY

Italy contributed more than any other nation to the founding of the modern European stage. The Latin plays written by Italian humanists had gained renown throughout Europe. Although learned comedies never played to vast audiences in Italy, since productions were usually given by amateurs in a courtly environment, even before the middle of the sixteenth century playwrights in other countries were imitating the *Commedia Erudita;* for traveling companies of professional Italian actors had begun to diffuse comic material in one land after another. The exact origin of the Commedia dell'Arte is debatable. One theory traces it back to the ancient Atellan farce with its grotesque masked characters like Maccus and Buccus, but there is no evidence for a continuous tradition up to Renaissance times. During the Middle Ages performances of sacred dramas featured mimes, jugglers, and tumblers, especially in the role of devils, whose spontaneous buffoonery clearly seems to anticipate the capers of Arlecchino and the Zanni in the Commedia dell'Arte. Throughout the medieval and Renaissance periods

233

carnival festivities always included acrobatic dancing and slapstick acting by gaily costumed clowns with type masks. By the early years of the sixteenth century professional buffoons were appearing not only in public squares but also at the banquets of the bourgeoisie and nobility. The most famous clown of that era, the Venetian Zuan Polo, often entertained in the same patrician homes where Ruzzante's company performed. Zuan Polo led public processions, improvised his own comedies, and dazzled his audiences with witty remarks. These buffoons finally came to take part in the spectacular intermezzos during amateur productions of learned comedies. This encounter between cultured amateurs and professional entertainers led to a refinement in the tastes and acting style of the improvisational performers. Having won for themselves both academic recognition and noble patronage, the actors soon felt ready to return to the general public. Their guilds evolved into wandering companies like the Gelosi, Confidenti, Uniti, Accesi, Desiosi, and Fedeli, all of which flourished during the second half of the Cinquecento.[1]

The Commedia dell'Arte was never the antithesis of the Erudite Com-

---

1 Our intention is not to present a detailed history of the Commedia dell'Arte but just to sketch the transition from Learned Comedy to popular, professional comedy. An early, polemical discussion of the acting profession can be found in Tommaso Garzoni, *Piazza universale delle professioni del mondo* (Venice, 1595), pp. 734-41; although Garzoni expresses admiration for the craft of certain actors, he generally regards improvised theater as a perversion of the ancient histrionic art. Francesco Bartoli, *Notizie istoriche de' comici italiani che fiorivano intorno all'anno 1550 fino ai giorni presenti* (Padua, 1782), presents an alphabetical listing with biographical description of the acting profession from 1550 to the author's own day; his book mentions major figures like Francesco Andreini, the master braggart of *Le Bravure del Capitano Spavento*. Bartoli chose 1550 as the starting point since women began to act on the stage at that period; he classes earlier Italian actors as mimes and buffoons. Francesco Bertelli, *Il Carnevale italiano mascherato ove si veggono in figura varie inventione di capritii* (Venice, 1642), provides illustrations that point out the early iconography of the masked figures. Emilio Calvi, *Il Teatro popolare romanesco nel medio evo* (Rome, 1907), pp. 3-17, studies the Roman dialect dramas of the medieval period. Enzo Petraccone, *La Commedia dell'Arte* (Naples, 1927), provides documentary material on the history and technique of the improvised theater along with a collection of scenarios. Vito Pandolfi, *La Commedia dell'Arte* (Florence, 1957), 1:9-16 and 30-33, emphasizes the Goliardic plays like the *Janus sacerdos* and folk songs with a clownish figure as their subject to have exerted an influence on the arising of a national theater. Pierre Louis Duchartre, *The Italian Comedy*, trans. R. T. Weaver (New York, 1966), pp. 24-29, upholds the descent of the improvised comedy from the Atellan farce; but Constant Miklascefsky, *La Commedia dell'Arte* (Paris, 1927), pp. 208-34, rejects the Atellan theory and asserts that a decline in princely patronage forced actors in the second half of the sixteenth century to turn to a wide audience. Kathleen M. Lea, *Italian Popular Comedy* (Oxford, 1934), 1: 223-54, traces the antecedents and origins of the popular theater and mentions the activities of Zuan Polo.

edy. Comic formulas that had been tried in the learned plays were repeated again and again by professional actors. Lovers with their Petrarchan language, pedantic doctors of law, strutting but cowardly Spanish captains continued to make up the cast of characters. The employment of different dialects on stage remained a standard device to arouse laughter. Many of the scenarios used by the actors of the Commedia dell'Arte were adapted from regular comedies. As well as deriving plots from the learned theater, the professionals acquired the art of dramatic construction. For the new class of actors no longer consisted primarily of mountebanks but included members of the nobility like Flaminio Scala, the troupe director who eventually published a collection of fifty scenarios. Scala's plot constructions used devices from the erudite comedies like the disguise of lovesick heroines in masculine attire to be near the objects of their affection. With his knowledge of classical characterization this actor-director transformed the antics of Zanni clowns into the astute stratagems of servants. In his desire for a high professional standard Scala also adhered to the three unities. Academic honors and titles attest to the esteem which Scala and other actors such as the versatile Francesco Andreini and his wife, the poetess Isabella Andreini, enjoyed among the literati. To a great extent the Commedia dell'Arte results from a compromise between a popular desire for spontaneity and an academic demand for classical culture. The success of the improvised comedy over the learned was due to its richer theatrical nature, with its reliance on comic action, visual effects, acrobatics, and often vulgar humor while admitting classical material in the dialogue. Through its quest for variation and innovation along with fixed masks and pantomime, the professional theater could appeal to every class. The actors of the Commedia dell'Arte adapted the Erudite Comedy for popular needs and carried it to an international audience.[2]

In France medieval morality and mystery plays were supreme until the middle of the sixteenth century. Momentous events occurred in 1548 which determined the future of the French theater, for in that year parliament

2 Winifred Smith, *The Commedia dell'Arte* (New York, 1964), pp. 67-102, analyzes the give and take between the improvised comedy and the learned theater. Also cf. Mario Apollonio, *Storia del Teatro Italiano* (Florence, 1951), 2:264; and Marvin T. Herrick, *Italian Comedy* (Urbana, Ill., 1960), p. 215. Michele Scherillo, *La Commedia dell'Arte in Italia* (Torino, 1884), pp. 117-34, asserts that Giambattista Della Porta composed scenarios for the professional troupes in addition to writing erudite comedies; but L. G. Clubb, *Giambattista Della Porta Dramatist*, (Princeton, N.J., 1965), pp. 302-7, denies Scherillo's theory and demonstrates that the actors of the Commedia dell'Arte often used the dramatist's plays to derive their plots.

forbade the further performance of mysteries, which had slipped into buffoonery. In September of the same year a group of Florentine actors under the direction of Cardinal Ippolito d'Este presented the *Calandria* at Lyons in honor of the French monarch Henry II and his queen Catherine de' Medici. Just five months later Joachim du Bellay brought out his *Deffence et Illustration de la Langue Françoyse,* in which he urged the production of comedies and tragedies on ancient models and the abandonment of farces and morality plays. The Italian Erudite Comedy, along with ancient plays, was the model to which French playwrights turned.[3]

Even before 1548 some playwrights had translated Italian comedies into French. Ariosto's *I Suppositi* was a favorite. During the century P. de Mesme, Jacques Bourgeois, and Jean Godard translated or adapted this comedy. In the second half of the century Jean de la Taille translated the *Negromante.* Nardi's *I Due Felici Rivali,* as well as its source in *Decameron* V, 5, provided Jean de la Taille with material for his *Les Corrivaux.* He admitted his debt to "quelques nouveaux italiens." His translations even preserved some of the original Italian words. Some French authors were servile imitators of the Italian playwrights rather than of Plautus and Terence. The productions of the Sienese *Accademici Intronati* appealed to the French with their theme of youthful love. As early as 1549 Charles Estienne translated the *Ingannati* with his *Les Abuséz,* leaving out the figure of the braggart Giglio. In 1560 Jacques Grévin reworked Estienne's play in his own *Les Esbahis,* restoring the braggart with the Commedia dell'arte character *Panthaleoné.* By this time the influence of the Erudite Comedy had already been contaminated by that of the Commedia dell'arte. Then Louis le Jars imitated the *Amor Costante* in his tragicomedy *Lucelle.* The tendency of the Sienese school toward political satire was muted in favor of sentimental values. French playwrights generally cleared up the complicated plots that prevailed in the Italian comedies. They relaxed the sharp satire of contemporary abuses that Italian authors excelled at; a character-type like the braggart warrior usually became fairly likeable. With the comic characters and devices of the Italian Erudite Comedy, French playwrights were able to produce a new theater.[4]

3 Details on the Lyons performance of the *Calandria* and on Du Bellay's work are in Gilbert Highet, *The Classical Tradition: Greek and Roman Influences on Western Literature* (New York, 1957), pp. 133-34.

4 Antero Meozzi, *La Drammatica della Rinascita Italiana in Europa Sec. XVI-XVII* (Pisa, 1940), pp. 13 and 17, discusses the imitations of Ariosto's play in France. The possible influence of Nardi's *I Due Felici Rivali* on Jean de la Taile is taken up by Daniel C. Boughner, *The Braggart in Renaissance Comedy* (Minneapolis, Minn.,

Spain had influenced the development of the learned comedy in Italy, as the braggart was generally a Spaniard. The Spanish control of most of Italy made it possible for the conquerors to know and appreciate the culture of the Italian Renaissance. Early in the century Bartolomé de Torres Naharro, one of the initiators of the Spanish theater in the Renaissance, arrived in Italy. From the Italian scene, at Rome where a Chigi nobleman was his patron or at Naples where he worked for Fabrizio Colonna, Torres Naharro acquired a sure knowledge of stage technique. Besides observing customs, he used novellistic devices in his plays. A scene in the fifth *jornada* of his *Calamita* is drawn from Act II, scene 9, of the *Calandria,* in which Calandro learns how to die. Torres Naharro was ready to borrow from the Italians' comic themes without becoming a slavish imitator.

Not every playwright possessed Torres Naharro's originality. Juan Pérez of Toledo rendered Ariosto's *I Suppositi* in Latin and later did the same for the *Negromante* and the *Ingannati*. The author who actually introduced the sophisticated comedy of intrigue according to the Italian model was Lope de Rueda. He was to a certain extent the Spanish Ruzzante, being an actor-playwright who produced both learned comedies and folk plays. His important innovation was the use of prose. Lope de Rueda reworked the *Ingannati* with his *Engañados,* in which he eliminated the braggart, since a satirical portrait like that of Giglio would have been highly displeasing to a Spanish audience. Lope de Rueda's friend, editor, and in part imitator Juan de Timoneda also shared his appreciation of Italian culture. For his *Farsa Trapacera* he used Ariosto's *Lena* without even changing the names of the characters. Various passages from Ariosto's *Negromante* inspired his *Comedia llamada Cornelia.* The "primitive" period in the history of the Spanish theater bore the mark of Italian influence.

Spanish playwrights displayed far greater independence from Italian and classicizing influence than did French authors, since national tradition always remained strong in Spain. By the height of the Golden Age theater with Lope de Vega, there was a drama considerably different from the Italian Erudite Comedy. Even with a limited influence, the Italian learned

---

1954), p. 257. Information on the vogue of the *Ingannati* can be found in Boughner, *The Braggart,* pp. 254-56, and P. Toldo, "La comédie française de la Renaissance," *Revue d'histoire littèraire de la France* 5 (1898): 582. Robert C. Melzi, *"Gl'Ingannati* and its French Renaissance Translation," *KFLQ* 7 (1965): 180-90, demonstrates how Estienne infuses more pathos into the character of Lelia so that the French play is not a reworked classical comedy or a typical learned drama; Melzi also provides more information on Castelvetro's authorship of the *Ingannati.*

comedy suggested modern plots and characters to the Spanish writers.[5]

Elizabethan authors were often drawn to Italian literature in spite of themselves. The plots of intrigue, the devices of disguises and mistaken identities, and the witty dialogue in the Italian comedies fascinated English playwrights. There was something unchaste, irreligious, and definitely salacious in the Italian works that commanded the attention of Elizabethan authors. Italian Renaissance life as it was portrayed in the learned comedies seemed exotic to them, and several were to place their dramas in an Italian setting. Throughout the Elizabethan and Jacobean periods the British became directly acquainted with the stage technique of the strolling Italian companies, which performed not only in London but as far north as Scotland. Italian musicians were influential in court circles, and several distinguished Italians like the philosopher-playwright Giordano Bruno sought refuge in England. On the continent English actors competed in Vienna, Paris, and Madrid against their Italian rivals in the theatrical arts. The comic repertoire which Italian companies brought to the British Isles consisted not only of improvised plays but also of regular erudite comedies like those of the Neapolitan Giambattista Della Porta, whose works were widely imitated in university circles and on the London stage during the Jacobean era. Although the English frequently expressed disapproval of the bawdy subject matter of the Italian pieces and the vulgar gestures of many actors, the Italian influence on the dramatic technique and writing of the Elizabethan-Jacobean theater was far from negligible.[6]

---

5 Meozzi, *Drammatica,* pp. 133-40, describes the various Italian influences during the "primitive" phase of the Spanish theater. Francesco Flamini, *Il Cinquecento* (Milan, 1903), pp. 314-18, mentions the imitation of Italian learned comedies by Torres Naharro and Lope de Rueda. Ireneo Sanesi, *La Commedia,* 2d ed. (Milan, 1954), 1:429 and 431, discusses the work of Pérez. Boughner, *The Braggart,* p. 204, speaks of the *Engañados* and the absence of a braggart.

6 Herrick, *Italian Comedy,* p. 226, describes the attitude of the English toward Renaissance Italy. John W. Cunliffe, "The Influence of Italian on Early Elizabethan Drama," *Modern Philology* 4 (1907): 597-604, speaks of the complex development of English theater and the contribution of Italian literary models for comedy and tragedy. Winifred Smith, "Italian and Elizabethan Comedy," *MP* 5 (1908): 555-67, lists three kinds of evidence for Italian influence in England: (*a*) the presence of Italian actors in the English theatrical scene, (*b*) internal proof of Italian influence in the texts of English comedies, (*c*) tracing of certain plays to Italian originals. Smith feels that the rhymed couplets closing scenes in English plays were derived from the *chiusette* of Italian comedies; this critic believes that the English debt to Italian comedy was as great and perhaps greater than to Italian novelle. Smith, *The Commedia Dell'Arte* pp. 170-99, talks of the activities of traveling Italian troupes in Elizabethan and Jacobean England. Lea, *Italian Popular Comedy,* 2:339-455, assesses the Italian

Disguise plots were among the Italian imports which most deeply impressed British playwrights. Along with the exchange of roles between master and servant, two popular devices were the girl-page and the boy-bride disguises. In 1556 George Gascoigne produced his comedy *The Supposes,* which is a skillful translation of Ariosto's *I Suppositi* along with additions from Terence's *Eunuchus* and Plautus' *Captivi. The Supposes* is the first English comedy in prose; it develops the usual character types like the pedantic lawyer, the amorous dotard, and cunning servants. This play, with other sources, may have inspired the episode of Bianca and Biondello in Shakespeare's *Taming of the Shrew.* The Shakespearean drama heightens the romantic element, moving from the disguise intrigue to place emphasis on character and ethical overtones. Gascoigne's work was paralleled by that of John Jeffrey, who during the same period adapted some elements of the *Ingannati* in a verse rendering in his *Bugbears.* The comedies of the *Accademici Intronati* enjoyed such a vogue throughout Europe that later in the sixteenth century George Chapman imitated Piccolomini's play *Alessandro* in his *May-Day* as well as borrowing from the *Ingannati.* So striking was the vivacious, enterprising heroine of the *Ingannati* that a Latin version of the Italian play, with the title *Laelia,* was performed at Queens College, Cambridge, in 1590 and 1598. The disguise entanglement of the *Ingannati,* in which the heroine masquerades as a boy and acts as the messenger between the man she loves and a rival mistress until the return of the twin brother offers a solution, was to be repeated in the Viola-Orsino-Olivia story of Shakespeare's *Twelfth Night.* Shakespeare may also have been influenced by the *Gl'Inganni* and *L'Interesse* of Niccolò Secchi, a dramatist writing toward the middle of the century, as well as by Della Porta's comedy *La Cintia.* With his theatrical genius the English playwright subordinated the story of the twin brother to focus on the poignant drama of Viola, with its delicate shades of feeling. Pedestrian realism yields in *Twelfth Night,* making it a sentimental comedy about the Force of Love. Disguise plots from

---

contribution to English drama and finds it to be superficial. Daniel C. Boughner, "Italian and English Comedy," *Renaissance Drama Supplement* 7 (1964): 6-8, discusses Machiavelli's blending of skillful Terentian structure with Plautine comic material and the giant stride toward modern comedy which the Italian playwrights prepared for the English. David Orr, "The Influence of Learned Italian Drama of the XVI Century on English Drama before 1623" (unpub. diss.; North Carolina, 1960), rejects the theory of strong Italian impact on Elizabethan-Jacobean drama. Clubb, *Della Porta,* pp. 273-95, points out how several of Della Porta's comedies were adapted in England during the early seventeenth century—four of them in Trinity College at Cambridge with performances before King James I.

Italian plays enabled British authors to create idyllic and romantic comedies.[7]

One of the waves of Italian influence in Elizabethan England was Machiavellianism. For the English, Machiavelli and Aretino were cynical, heartless creatures who symbolized the vices of Italy. Although Elizabethan authors disparaged the two Italian writers and sometimes pictured Machiavelli as a satanic figure in English plays, the literary influence of the Italian writers was profoundly felt. In 1588 John Wolfe published Aretino's first four comedies. Aretinesque plot situations, dramatic devices, and verbal reminiscences can be detected throughout Shakespeare's comedies. Both Aretino's *Marescalco* and Machiavelli's *Clizia* seem to have exerted an influence of Ben Jonson's *Epicoene (The Silent Woman)*, which is structured upon the disguise of the boy-bride in feminine garb and his eventual surprise revelation. This boy-bride device lent itself ideally to farcical situations in which the disguised character courted a male lover, mingled with female companions, and swindled money from victims. The skill that Machiavelli and Aretino both possessed at portraying human eccentricities captured the imagination of Jonson and other English writers.[8]

Italian influence on the Elizabethan-Jacobean drama can be noted in the Mediterranean settings of many plays, in the use of Italian names for the characters, and in the weaving of plots. But Elizabethan stage technique

---

7 Piero Rébora, *L'Italia nel Dramma Inglese 1558-1624* (Milan, 1925), pp. 37-41, treats Ariosto's influence in England. K. F. Thompson, "A Note on Ariosto's 'I Suppositi,'" *Cl* 12, no. 1 (Winter, 1960): 42-46, compares Gascoigne's version with Ariosto's original and finds the English play to be far more "modern" and in tune with the rising romantic tendencies. Geoffrey Bullough, *Narrative and Dramatic Sources of Shakespeare* (New York, 1958), 1:66-68, discusses the originality of *Taming of the Shrew*. Lea, *Italian Popular Comedy*, 2:408-10, mentions the standard disguise plots. Also see Victor O. Freeburg, *Disguise Plots in Elizabethan Drama* (New York, 1915), pp. 73-74 and *passim*, for a discussion of *Twelfth Night*. Although the *Laelia* comedy was never printed in Elizabethan times, see the modern edition by G. C. Moore (Cambridge, Eng., 1910). Bullough, *Sources of Shakespeare* 2:269-372, presents the sources of *Twelfth Night* with a translation of *Gl'Ingannati* and summaries of Secchi's plays; for Bullough the *Ingannati* is devoid of poetic fancy and suffers from cumbersome exposition. Helen A. Kaufman, "Nicolò Secchi as a Source of *Twelfth Night*," *SQ* 5 (1954): 271-80, examines Shakespeare's possible debt to the Italian dramatist. Melzi, "From Lelia to Viola," pp. 75-79, analyzes the parallels between *La Cintia* and the Shakespearean comedy. Boughner, *The Braggart*, p. 27, gives details on imitations of the *Ingannati*.

8 For Machiavellism consult Daniel C. Boughner, "*Clizia* and *Epicoene*," *PQ* 19 (1940): 89-91. Also see O. J. Campbell, "The Relation of *Epicoene* to Aretino's *Il Marescalco*," *PMLA* 46 (1931): 752-62. Freeburg, *Disguise Plots*, pp. 101-20, studies the device of the boy-bride.

generally remained independent of the Italian adherence to the classical three unities. Jonson was the only major playwright who attempted to structure plays on the classical pattern; yet even his stage technique is far more free of academic imprint than most of the Italian erudite comedies. Usually Elizabethan dramas move from one setting to another, over a period of time that often exceeds twenty-four hours; there are subplots. The English borrowed heavily from the Italians but preserved their national character.

Not only the major Italian writers of comedies exerted their influence abroad; numerous minor dramatists produced works that were imitated in France, Spain, and England. The Italian learned comedy helped introduce Europe to the classical theatrical technique. It offered models of political and religious satire to writers in other countries. Italian playwrights were the first modern European authors to develop a serious romantic comedy. In France the model of the Italian regular comedy encouraged writers to break with medieval dramatic traditions. Although the influence of the Italian Erudite Comedy did not arrest the evolution of the theater in Spain and England from earlier dramatic forms, it suggested new subject matter and characters.

The Originality of the Erudite Comedy

Classical imitation was not a crippling factor in the development of comedy in Renaissance Italy, since the leading Italian dramatists did not approach the comedies of Plautus and Terence like reverent, solemn academicians. They were ready to alter the plots of the ancient comedies for their own needs. Often a playwright like Ariosto carried on the practice of *contaminatio*, combining elements from several antique comedies in one dramatic work. For the Italians the plays of the ancient Roman dramatists were a proved model of comic action. But though they payed homage to the excellence of the Roman dramatists, the Italian authors announced their determination to create a theater for modern times.

Italy's novellistic tradition furnished dramatists with motives that had never been tried on the ancient stage. Boccaccio, perhaps even more than Plautus and Terence, inspired the growth of comedy. Italian dramatists, with the example of novelle, explored domestic relations more deeply than the Roman playwrights had ever dared to attempt. Before the rise of the vernacular Erudite Comedy, the humanistic authors of Latin plays like *Conquestio uxoris Cavichioli* and the *Cauteriaria* had used novellistic themes of dissatisfied wives and negligent husbands. Marital infidelity, a theme that was avoided by the Roman playwrights, became a favorite subject for the Italian authors. Perhaps the arch dramatic figure of the Erudite Comedy is the deceived husband. Sometimes he is too old to satisfy the sensual urges of his young wife; sometimes he is too preoccupied by pedantic activities to take any interest in her. He rarely succeeds in punishing his adulterous wife, for often he has to proclaim his wife's innocence and conjugal virtue before her enraged relatives. Messer Nicia in the *Mandragola* and Calandro in Bibbiena's one comedy are victimized husbands. The Italian dramatists, like the authors of novella collections before them, did not let respect for the institution of the family deter them from picturing adultery.

Yet many of the erudite comedies end with plans for a wedding. The dramatists were following an amorous tradition established by the writers of novelle. Adulterous wives in novelle and later in comedies declared their rebellion against social restraints in the name of Love, but the institution of marriage could be considered as the culmination of a love affair. The girls who become heroines in the Italian comedies are rarely slaves. They are usually freeborn of middle-class families, eager to taste sensual pleasures even without the socially ordained bonds of marriage. The modern heroine, as portrayed in the *Decameron,* resents the social conventions and family upbringing that deny her the chance to enjoy sexual pleasures before marriage. The Latin humanistic comedies *Philogenia* and *Poliscena* had anticipated the portrait of the young heroine in the Italian regular comedies. This heroine, aided by the power of Love, is capable of doing anything to be with her lover, as when she plots with her nurse to receive him in her home. Like many novellistic heroines, she leaves home disguised as a male. The lover, also impelled by the force of Love, will try every trick against jealous husbands or cautious parents to meet his beloved lady; he sometimes hides in a chest so he can be transported to the girl's bedchamber. Even if he is wealthy and wellborn, the lover is willing to become a servant in the girl's household just to have some contact with her. When necessary, he puts on women's clothes for an assignation. Both lovers stubbornly oppose family plans for an odious marriage, despite the offer of a large dowry. Along with the force of Love is the power of Fortune, that aids or impedes the desires of the lovers. Although most of the love affairs between young couples are consummated outside legal matrimony, as in Ariosto's comedies, they usually conclude with a wedding, so love is upheld by a social institution.

Most of the authors of comedies chose to set their dramas in modern times. This choice compelled the playwrights to portray modern customs and environments, even in comedies whose plots were taken from ancient dramas. In the prologue to the *Clizia,* a play derived from Plautus' *Casina,* Machiavelli justified his setting the play in contemporary Florence and not ancient Athens. Aretino proclaimed in the prologue to the second version of the *Cortigiana* that the comic style had to be altered to suit the changed living conditions of modern times. Italian dramatists were careful to relate the plots to the political events of the day, adding fierce satire on corrupt officials and decadent courts to a portrait of contemporary life. Adherence to the unity of place established the setting of a public square, and this scene, with the streets that led into it, recaptured the life of a city, as in the *Lena* or in Aretino's Roman plays. Even the cries of itinerant salesmen and the folk songs chanted by urchins echo city sounds. The Italian dramatists succeed admirably in reproducing the movement and color of the contemporary scene.

Onto this scene come characters that never appeared in the ancient Roman comedies. Many members of the clergy, such as priests, friars, and nuns, are leading dramatic figures. Like the authors of novella collections and humanistic Latin comedies, the Italian authors of erudite comedies did not hesitate to point out the hypocrisy of the clergy. Latin-spouting pedants wrapped up in their studies, pompous physicians, and strutting lawyers come onstage. A whole class of charlatan magicians, necromancers, astrologers, and procuress-witches, never portrayed by Plautus or Terence, participates in several learned comedies. The *Sacre Rappresentazioni* and the humanistic Latin plays had anticipated the learned comedies in introducing types from the life of Renaissance Italy like professors and students, innkeepers, policemen, or peasants come to the city. The braggart warrior, a character-type definitely taken from the ancient Roman comedies, ceased to be an opulent captain and became a pretentious Spaniard giving himself a noble title in spite of his poverty. A whole new cast of characters, drawn from real life, takes part in the actions of the erudite comedies.

Italian playwrights turned to Roman antiquity to find a dramatic technique, but they combined literary traditions and the contemporary reality of their own country to create a comic theater that helped determine the course of modern European drama.

APPENDIX 1

Plots of Latin Plays

VERGERIO: *Paulus*

The hero Paulus reveals from the start his weak, vacillating character. In the first scene he is brusquely awakened by the noise his servant Herotes makes setting the table. Paulus relates a beautiful dream he has just had: he had won his doctorate, returned home, and married a virgin more beautiful than the sun. In the dream all the leading citizens of his home town kept running to him, asking his advice in interpreting the old laws. Sad reality makes Paulus confess to himself that he is only in the fourth year, scarcely well-equipped for studies. But if he were to make a heroic effort to change his way of life, and stay up nights reading his texts without any regard for health, then he would one day succeed in acquiring wisdom and glory. Herotes sneers and asks him why he should renounce his pleasure when there is always time for study. Above all he ought not to wear out his fresh, healthy body by staying up all night to study. The servant easily persuades carefree Paulus to abandon his studious ambitions.

In the course of events Paulus wavers between Herotes, the tempter, and the faithful servant Stichus. While Herotes leads Paulus from one dissipation to another, Stichus tries in vain to open his master's eyes; but he ends up scolded by Paulus and brutally beaten by Herotes. While Stichus is lamenting to his devoted comforter Titus, Herotes is busily at work with schemes to corrupt Paulus. As the play proceeds, Herotes grows diabolical, persuading Nicolosa to prostitute her own daughter for Paulus' pleasure. Before turning her over, Herotes enjoys the girl first and then with his usual boldness passes her off as an unblemished virgin. He laughs at the skill with which the girl Ursula makes Paulus pay a high price for her virginity. The negative triumphs.

Sicco Polenton: *Catinia*

Five characters carry on the dialogues: Catinius, an itinerant salesman of kitchenware; Lanius, a wool-carder; Cetius, a fisher; Bibius, an innkeeper; and Quaestius, a friar of the order of St. Anthony. They pass their time eating and drinking, since only those things that men have eaten and drunk can really be called their own. At first the play seems a hymn to bodily pleasures, but the author reveals a moral aim in the major part of the dialogues, which consist of an argument and a mock learned discourse. On seeing that sunset is near, Catinius starts a dispute after he has asked for the bill so that everyone can pay his part and leave. Bibius is offended, thinking that Catinius wants to deceive him. Quaestius is chosen to judge the argument and decide who is guilty. In a long discourse, interrupted by the other members of the group, Quaestius demonstrates that Catinius has broken both biblical and Julian laws with his inopportune demand: the biblical laws forbid innkeepers to ask for payment when there is no more wine in the glasses, and Catinius asked his question just at the moment all the glasses were empty. According to Julian law one cannot disturb the peace of a republic, and Catinius' demand has upset their tranquil company, which constitutes a perfect miniature republic. He sentences Catinius to pay the bill for all of them. Into the discourse go many subjects, such as the meaning of the Epicurean life, the hazards of a military career, the role of philosophy, the importance of medicine, and the lives of emperors. The high point is a discussion of the trivium and quadrivium.

Conquestio uxoris Cavichioli

A woman complains of being left in perpetual virginity by her husband Cavichiolus; she wants to be a wife and not just a housekeeper. For some time she has been making excuses to herself about the boys who visit her husband, telling herself that they were relatives or young priests. Now she is ready to leave, no longer willing to deceive herself. Cavichiolus, despite his preferring "pueros aureos" to peevish females, is not eager to lose his wife, as she is an excellent homemaker. Realizing that his sweetly-phrased defenses are no help to him, Cavichiolus holds onto his wife by promising to share the best of his boys with her. Young Aurelius comes into view to visit Cavichiolus, but the husband runs off to the noisy forum so his wife can enjoy the boy.

Commedia Bile

Bila, a rather greedy woman who hardly understands what hospitality is, is about to set dinner on the table when she sees the jolly student Episcopus approaching. She hides some big fish under a chair so she will not have to offer any of them to Episcopus, to whom her husband Aristancus then gives some small fish. The student, out to enjoy the larger fish of far better quality, thinks up a stratagem. He pretends to speak with the small fishes, making them answer him. Both husband and wife are astonished on hearing fish talk. Claiming that the fish have not answered him satisfactorily, Episcopus explains to the couple that his father disappeared in a shipwreck. Since fish are dwellers of the deep, he asks every one he meets if it knows anything about his father. These little fishes have told him that they cannot possibly know anything at all as they are entirely too young, and that he would do best to question the big ones under the chair, who are older and far more knowledgeable about those who live in the sea. Aristancus is delighted by the little show and hands Episcopus the big fishes, saying they are the fathers of the little ones he was questioning.

ALBERTI: *Philodoxus*

The young Athenian Philodoxus, noble in spirit, loves the Roman citizen Doxia. His rival is the unscrupulous Roman Fortunius. Philodoxus seeks advice from his friend Phroneus. Fortunius, on seeing that his attempts to win Doxia are fruitless, decides to use his servant Dynastes in a kidnap plot. He breaks into the girl's home, but by mistake he carries away her sister Phemia. Finally Chronos, the *magister excubiarum,* settles the conflict by declaring that Fortunius must marry Phemia while Philodoxus can have Doxia as his wife.

Janus sacerdos

On Holy Friday, the priest Janus is wandering about trying to decide whether he should rejoice that day for Christ's redemption of mankind or whether he should lament for Christ's agony on the cross. Young Dolosinus enters to make confession. As soon as a group of ladies leave the confessional area, the priest entreats the boy to gratify his pederastic desires. Shocked by Janus' words, Dolosinus succeeds in breaking away from the priest's embrace. Later he tells of his near escape to the students Savucius, Filanius, and Riancus. Savucius, the leader of the group, decides to punish Janus. He goes to the church and tells the priest how much he hates women. Believing the student, Janus agrees to go to Savucius' home. Just as the priest is about to satisfy himself, the other students burst into the bedroom. Pretending to be ashamed and afraid, Savucius flees, while the others take hold of the priest. Filanius is appointed supreme justice, while Fabius and Crispinus discourse on the gravity of the offense. But since Janus is one of townspeople, who are always complaining that the students are troublemakers, Fabius points out that the students have no jurisdictional right over a clergyman. Filanius decrees that Janus will be forgiven on swearing never to commit his crime again.

Here direct representation makes it appear that the priest has escaped with no more than a scare and a humiliating mock trial. But soon afterward Janus encounters Savucius, who is still out to fool the priest with his pose as a woman-hater. The priest informs the youth that the band of students dragged him down into the cellar and started beating him up, kicking him in the stomach and tossing him up and down. They threw him into a room and bound him securely. Besides making him swear to give up his homosexual pursuits (which the priest admits to Savucius that he plans to continue as his natural tendency), the students took away all his money to treat themselves to a grand banquet.

BRUNI: Poliscena

Young Graccus, given to a life of pleasure, is intent on seducing the girl Poliscena. First he turns to his servant Gurgulio for help. When Gurgulio fails, Graccus enlists the aid of the old woman Tharatantara. She first tries to buy the consent of Calphurnia, the girl's mother, to letting Graccus have his way. The mother, not the type to be bribed into prostituting her daughter, throws the old woman out. Tharatantara decides to seek out the girl when her mother is not home. She describes to Poliscena how much Graccus adores her and how he is wasting away for love of her. For some time the girl has been in love with Graccus, and she soon agrees to meet him. Calphurnia is enraged when she becomes aware that Poliscena has given herself to the youth. She rushes to his father, Macarius, and threatens to have Graccus punished by the city magistrates if he does not marry the girl. Macarius consents to the wedding.

Pisani: *Philogenia*

Epiphebus, the hero, ardently desires Philogenia. One night he goes to her window and passionately addresses her. She tries to appear indifferent, holding back the love she long has felt for him. But Epiphebus is skillful in pleading how sincerely he worships her, even threatening suicide if she does not give way. Overcome by his apparent agony, Philogenia agrees to flee with him. He rushes her to his home and violently consummates their love. That night her parents become aware of her disappearance and seek aid from the authorities. After a few days it is generally known about town that Epiphebus is holding the girl. Warned of the imminent danger of a police raid, the youth hides Philogenia with his friend Emphonius. Epiphebus realizes that he cannot keep transferring the girl from one friend to another forever. Since he is wealthy, he decides to grant her a dowry so she can marry Gobius, a stupid peasant who can easily be made a cuckold. He wins over her objections, pointing out that marriage with the peasant is the only means for the lovers to continue their relationship. Gobius is told that she was reared by Epiphebus' maternal aunt. To make the story more convincing, Epiphebus hires two procuresses, Servia and Irtia, to pose as the aunt and as the girl's nurse. The girl is presented to the peasant as a modest virgin. Prodigius, a greedy priest, is engaged to confess Philogenia and absolve her of sin. The following day Gobius arrives with his brother Zabinus and a group of peasants. After the ceremony the newlyweds leave for the country with the whole peasant train following them to the tune of bagpipes.

Frulovisi: *Corallaria*

The "knight" Miles wishes to swindle the rich elderly widow Claudipotis, and he pretends to intercede on her behalf to persuade the old noble Facetus to marry her. Cleobula, Miles' wife, tells her friend Johanna that she has feigned an illness so her husband can obtain from Facetus a string of corals credited with having curative powers. By now Claudipotis has broadcast about town her love for Facetus, and two of her relatives are fiercely objecting. Heuclio, a senile creature, is determined to marry her to steal her fortune, as he confesses to his son Pecuphilus. In his household Facetus has two German servants, Henricus and Sigismondus (really the girl Hernia disguised as a young man). Facetus' daughter tries to seduce the false Sigismondus, and on failing she claims that the youth has attempted to rape her. When Henricus tries to defend Sigismondus, the ruthless police-officer Ascalaphus arrests him. Miles lures Facetus and Claudipotis to the Franciscan church, where the thief secretly passes the string of corals to the widow as an engagement gift and obtains a large sum of money from her, claiming he will later give it to Facetus. Then Cleobula and her husband flee from town. Facetus denies the engagement, and Claudipotis marries Heuclio. When Hernia's identity is established, Facetus decides to marry her.

FRULOVISI: *Claudi duo*

Plusipenus of Ravenna is a reformed profligate. He turns to his friends, who comfort him with commonplace maxims. Another student, Philaphrodita, is a healthy young beast; he has tried unsuccessfully to get money from his wealthy mother so that he can purchase the favors of the prostitute Porna. His tutor, a crippled humanist and physician, had warned his mother about him, but the gods in heaven are considering the fate of the young men. Jupiter commands Plutus, the lame god of wealth, to fly back to Plusipenus with Mercury as his escort. Plutus decides to help Philaphrodita by arranging for his mother to die first and for the tutor to be beaten into becoming the boy's assistant. Mercury and Plutus start to argue with the Virtues who reside with Plusipenus and Poverty. At last Plutus is able to serve Plusipenus.

FRULOVISI: *Emporia*

Euthymus, a young Austrian commoner, has made pregnant Adelphe, daughter of the Venetian patrician Paraphron, while her brother Leros has exhausted all his funds on the courtesan Aphrodite. When their father confronts Euthymus over the seduction, the youth angrily threatens the entire family. Leros' skillful friend Loedorus and the loyal slave Chrisolus intercede to put Euthymus out of the way and enable Leros to enjoy the courtesan. These two tell the Spanish merchant Emporus that Euthymus is Leros' gifted but excitable slave. After some lively bargaining they succeed in selling the youth and call the police to push him on board Emporus' ship. Leros can now return to Aphrodite's good graces, with the money paid by the Spanish merchant. Soon messengers arrive from Euthymus' father Symulus looking for the youth. Other messengers appear on the scene and report that the ship has been wrecked and that Euthymus has escaped safely to Austria. Euthymus intends to revenge the sale and has sent a letter to the Council of Ten, but Leros intercepts the letter. Just before Euthymus' return, Adelphe gives birth to a son who can proclaim past, present, and future. Euthymus reconciles himself with the girl's family and marries her.

FRULOVISI: *Symmachus*

Courageous young Symmachus, a commoner, flees to Syria after killing the cowardly patrician Alazo, his rival for the love of Piste, daughter of the patrician usurer Danistes. The girl, determined to find her lover, robs her father and sets sail for Syria disguised as a male. But pirates have taken the youth prisoner, carrying him to Salonika as a slave. The noble Eubulus steps forward to comfort the boy's weeping father Gerseus by offering to ransom Symmachus. But the liberal gesture is not necessary, as it soon becomes known that Symmachus has won the Sultan's favor by his bravery in a war between the Turks (Friges) and Mamelukes (Assyril) and has gained the post of Despot of Salonika. The Turkish ambassadors entreat Danistes to allow his daughter to marry Symmachus. Danistes has learned that Piste is now a well-to-do merchant in Syria, and he pretends that she is sick but is ready to marry the youth upon her recovery. News arrives that the girl has fallen prisoner to Turkish pirates. After a while Symmachus and the girl return together. She had been taken to Salonika, where Symmachus was able to release her. Throughout the comedy the scene remains at Venice. There is a subplot in which Piste's friend Agape is out to find someone to love her; she finally marries the youth Hippeus. Some of the liveliest scenes are between the spirited Piste and Alazo's angry aunt Stigna.

FRULOVISI: *Oratoria*

The Neapolitan count Exochus has dreamed about Hagna, daughter of the Venetian patrician Omus. Wishing to find her, he describes her to several artists and then sends slaves all over Italy with copies of her portrait.

The painter Grapheus arrives in Venice and pretends to be selling pictures in the Dominican church. Hagna, disobeying her father, comes to make confession. The friar Leocyon, instead of confessing the girl, tries to seduce her, and she runs away screaming. Exochus rushes to Venice after hearing from Grapheus that the lady of his dreams is there, but is impeded in his search by not knowing her identity. Omus is angry because his daughter has devoted herself to religion and commands her to marry. She is finally persuaded to take a foreign husband, knowing well how much her father hates foreigners. The procuress Cypris counsels Leocyon to disguise himself as a Roman noble and to serenade Hagna from under her window. The procuress then reports him to the authorities, and the bishop orders his arrest. Omus learns of Exochus' search and grants his marriage to Hagna, happy to find a wealthy and titled suitor for his daughter. Meanwhile Leocyon has escaped from prison.

Frulovisi: *Peregrinatio*

Young Clerus arrives in Rhodes with his tutor Aristopistes. They are looking for the youth's father Rhistes, a Cretan who years before had traveled to Britain and married Erichia, the boy's mother. Just before Clerus' birth his father had deserted Erichia. She has always refused to tell the boy his father's native country, lest he leave her. Clerus decides, nevertheless, to search the entire Mediterranean. In Rhodes the tutor is put in prison on a false charge. Having turned all their cash over to the tutor, Clerus steals a prostitute's cloak and sells it to sail to Crete. His father lives in Crete, where he has married a widow. Bothered by his conscience, he has ordered his servant Presbites to go to Britain to find out about Erichia and their child. Presbites returns to announce that Erichia has died because Clerus went away. Meanwhile Aristopistes has come to Crete with his jailer Lorarius, claiming that he is of a wealthy noble family. Clerus, keeping his name and parentage hidden, enters Rhistes' service as a steward. The youth almost contracts an incestuous marriage with his half sister Anapausis, who has fallen in love with him at first sight. The British youth Evangelus arrives in Crete to identify Clerus, stop the wedding, and release the tutor. At last the father and son are united.

Frulovisi: *Eugenius*

Eugenius dedicates himself to literature with the aid of his mentor Synetus. The youth's father, Endoxus, is a tyrant who is determined to make his son marry. After explaining all the disadvantages of marriage, Eugenius agrees to wed when his father returns from a trip to bring home his orphan ward Stephanus. While his father is away, Eugenius weds Macrothyma (Patience), daughter of Eunus (Goodness) and Penia (Poverty). When Endoxus comes back, he forces his son to secure a divorce and marry Erichia (Wealth), daughter of Mataeus (Vanity) and Hyperiphania (Pride). Macrothyma accepts everything with patience. Endoxus comes to despise Erichia and her parents and on Synetus' advice arranges for Eugenius to obtain a second divorce and remarry the kind Macrothyma. Penia must not be allowed to enter their home.

A. S. Piccolomini: *Chrysis*

This play, which has no true plot, represents in a crude but striking manner the life of prostitutes skilled at coaxing money from young men: Antiphila takes Archimenides as her lover; Cassina and Chrysis offer their favors to Charinus and Sedulius, while making Dyophanes and Theobulus maintain them. Chrysis' married sister Pythias hates the tyranny of a husband and enjoys herself with young Lybiphanes. The leader of the group is the procuress Canthara. Aeneas Sylvius carefully reveals the falseness of this corrupt society. He places a scene in a *bagno,* which functions as a bordello. Cassina and Chrysis have sworn to Dyophanes and Theobulus that they are the first and only men to have touched them. In one scene, in which the two prostitutes know that their lovers are listening, the girls declare to the procuress that streams would have to flow backward and the stars would have to fall before they would ever be unfaithful. Chrysis later asserts that every new sun should bring her another lover.

Comoedia sine nomine

Philostrates, queen of the Carilles in Thrace, is dying and asks her husband King Emolphus not to marry any other woman except one who resembles her perfectly. Upon her death the king launches a massive search for the late queen's double. The three painters Fidus, Calys, and Myron are sent all over the world to find the right woman. Finally all three return to the capital city with a large number of portraits made during their journeys. All the paintings are placed before the king for his approval, but the work has been in vain. Although many of the portraits show beautiful women, not one satisfies the king with a perfect resemblance to his late wife. There is only one creature in the world who unites in herself all the beauties of

Philostrates: their daughter Hermionides. So greatly does she resemble her mother that her nurse, on seeing the girl at her embroidery work, almost thinks she is the queen. Emolphus is determined to marry his daughter and reveals his designs to the nurse, who is supposed to resign the girl to the wedding. First the nurse tells the king to consult the oracle of Apollo and Minerva before going ahead. She warns the girl, and they both flee to the shore and set sail. After a stormy trip they land on the shores of Phocis, just opposite the isle of Lemnos. Here they live in poverty doing embroidery. One day the handsome young king Orestes chances to pass by and falls in love with the girl. In spite of the objections of his mother Olicomestra, he marries the girl and makes her queen at the capital city of Phocais.

Olicomestra abandons the court and withdraws to her castle at remote Rutella. Soon Orestes goes to Athens for the great tourneys and jousts. A messenger stops at Rutella to pay homage to the king's mother. She lets him become drunk so she can change the contents of a letter from the seneschal Coelius to the king. During Orestes' absence, Hermionides has given birth to a son, but Olicomestra changes the letter to say that a terrible monster has been born. On receiving this news, Orestes answers the seneschal, telling him to continue to respect the queen and not to harm the monster until his return from Athens. Once again Olicomestra intercepts the letter and alters it to command the seneschal to kill Hermionides and the child. Coelius shrinks from the deed, but he does not wish to disobey his king. He leads the two away to a desert place near the sea and leaves them. Upon his return to the capital, Orestes is enraged by his mother's actions. Anxious for revenge, he gathers his army and goes to besiege Olicomestra in her castle. But when he learns that his wife and child are still alive, he rushes away from the battle to find them. He finally locates them near the temple of Apollo at Delphi. Hermionides' days of persecution are at an end, for her father has died repentant, leaving her the throne. Olicomestra has killed herself.

Electoral Comedy

At the University of Padua the time is drawing near for the foreign students to elect one of their number as public reader for the professor of law. Parties are being formed, and intrigue is in the air. Glokengisser asks Rudophus to aid his "praeceptor" Jacobus against Conradus Schutz, who has already declared his candidacy. Rudophus then appeals to Pirchemer, who assures him that Jacobus will receive the votes of their fellow students from Nuremberg but that it might be advisable for Jacobus to confront Conradus personally and try to persuade him to withdraw from the election and concede his promised votes. Jacobus follows this advice, but he approaches Conradus with so little diplomatic skill that he can get nowhere with him. He tells Conradus brusquely that he will use his hands and feet to win the election. Jacobus says that everyone hates Conradus, and that those who have promised him votes are now sorry about it. The best thing he could do would be to concede now and save face. Angered by Jacobus' brutal words, Conradus points out that he is Jacobus' senior in years and studies; thus the greater right is on Conradus' side. According to Conradus, his desire to be public reader is Pirchemer's fault. When Pirchemer won the post of reader, he wrote home to his father and the news went around all of Nuremberg that Pirchemer was a professor at Padua. Conradus feels that acquiring the post will gain for him the same kind of fame in Nuremberg.

Now that he understands his rival's position, Jacobus entreats more mildly. All Conradus has to do is turn over the votes already promised to him. But Conradus cannot be turned away from his determination to run for the readership. When Jacobus leaves, Conradus admits to himself how difficult his position is. The Nuremberg students despise him, as he is not a native of that town; his father was an itinerant map-painter. His fellow students also envy his intelligence, while the Italian students naturally cannot be trusted. The best thing for him to do is seek rest in the embrace of his beloved girl friend. Pirchemer and Jacobus enter and declare that Conradus will never succeed with his bullheaded attitude. The election is all but won by Jacobus.

BARZIZZA: *Cauteriaria*

Act I opens with Scintilla's lament that her husband Brachus, worn out by drinking and woman-chasing, has not been able to satisfy her sensual urgings during the year they have been married. She is attracted to the young, manly priest Auleardus. Her maid Salamina suggests that her mistress pretend to be dying so the priest can be called to confess her. The maid promises to keep the jealous husband out of the room. Salamina goes out and meets Bacharinta, the priest's mother. Informed by the maid, Bacharinta goes to her son, who is distracted and keeps rejecting his mother until she implores in Scintilla's name. In the second act Brachus starts to take counsel from his servant Graculus. He is suspicious about Scintilla's strange actions: she has not been sleeping; her eyes are red; she withdraws to herself. For Brachus all women are evil. Later in the act he becomes angry with his wife. Salamina skirmishes with him and shames him by pointing out how industrious he once was; he is now a drunk. Momentarily repentant, he tries to be reconciled with Scintilla, who refuses. He recites the virtues of wine. When she swears her constant fidelity, he counterattacks by urging her to take a lover. He recounts his cruelties to his first two wives, who died from his brutal treatment of them. He married Scintilla because prostitutes cost too much. Scintilla makes her position clear; a chaste wife cannot be made adulterous with gold or silver, but a wife inclined to infidelity is harder to hold down than an army of flies in the sunshine. She confesses that she has hidden her illness so as not to worry him and agrees never to do so again. Shortly afterward Graculus questions Salamina, the other maid Socratina, and the porter Calmarus, and concludes that Scintilla is faithful. Brachus ends this act with a rhetorical flourish in which he praises his wife's faithfulness an immediately falls melancholy, believing that nothing good can last.

Brachus is right in his suspicions, for in the third act Calmarus tells Graculus that a young man was earlier hanging about the door. Graculus spies on the women on the way to church. Salamina instructs the priest's secular assistant during the sermon while Graculus overhears. Returning home, Scintilla pretends to faint, and Salamina rushes out to fetch the priest. Auleardus arrives immediately and is closeted with Scintilla. The husband is made to withdraw while she confesses. Graculus reports to his master, but before Brachus can break into the bedroom, Salamina warns Auleardus to escape. Scintilla screams that she would rather die unconfessed than have Auleardus near her. She claims that Auleardus has long been after her, and that he has corrupted Graculus. Brachus is again won over by his wife; he goes to punish Graculus. Auleardus is called back, but this time Brachus surprises the lovers and there is no question of their acts. Auleardus again flees. Despite their pleas for forgiveness, Brachus is determined to punish Scintilla and Salamina. In Act IV he discusses with Graculus the ways of inflicting punishment. Scintilla is led into Brachus' room. Graculus is hiding under the table and jumps up to grab her while Brachus applies a brand to that part of her body which sinned. Salamina is bound and flogged. Scintilla withdraws to a basement prison.

In the fifth act there is counteraction from Auleardus and his friends. They storm the house and capture Brachus and Graculus. On learning the means of vengeance, Auleardus gets ready to use the same torture on the husband and servant. Brachus tearfully pleads with Auleardus to show mercy, offering money and a splendid banquet for all. Auleardus is unmoved until Scintilla says she will not be vindictive as long as she and the priest can continue their love. Brachus is grateful and prepares the banquet. Victory is in Auleardus' hands.

Mezzo: *Epirota*

Antiphile had left Epirus with her father to live in Syracuse, but he died during the journey. On her arrival she was welcomed by the youth Clitiphones, who has given her a house and maintained her at his expense. She returns his love. Clitiphones wants to marry her, but the girl has neither a dowry nor relatives. While continuing to promise marriage to Antiphile, he encourages rich old Pamphila, who is hopelessly in love with him. A gentleman arrives from Epirus, the Epirotan who gives the play its title. He is Antiphile's uncle and is searching for her. On finding her and learning of her relations with Clitiphones, he agrees to her marriage and provides a large dowry. Clitiphones would like to have still more money. He tells Pamphila to marry the Epirotan so both couples can live in the same house, holding all their wealth in common. Clitiphones overcomes the Epirotan's objections to marrying Pamphilia.

Slyterhoven: *Scornetta*

Blanchinus' maid Lolla, who is old and inclined to heavy drinking, loves the elderly shepherd Corydon distractedly. The servant boy Codrus teases her by waking her up at night and keeping her from housework during the day; the boy also pretends to be in love with her so he can insult her obscenely. Lolla does not want Codrus' love, as she thinks that he is out for her savings. She calls out to her beloved shepherd, who is far away tending his flocks; Lolla describes the beauty and fertility of villa Scornetta. Then she says angrily that she will no longer love Corydon, since he has abandoned her. From now on she will attend to her household duties and please her lovely mistress Corynna, who has been scolding her for neglecting her work. Suddenly Lolla grows confused; Corydon is calling her, but her mistress is present. Trying to overcome her embarrassment, Lolla calls to her shepherd. Corynna, amused by their love, lets the two go off.

ARMONIO: *Stephanium*

The setting is Athens. Years before, the girl Stephanium, along with her servant maid Amphelisca, was kidnapped from Lesbos after the death of her parents. The girls were sold at Megara to a certain Mnesilocus. Upon his death they were set free. Coming to Athens, Stephanium fell in love with the youth Niceratus, son of the miserly merchant Aegio. He has been keeping the two women without his father's knowledge. His father, always intent on acquiring more wealth, insists that the boy sail away on a commercial journey, but Niceratus keeps postponing the day of his departure. His father suddenly falls ill and is forced to stay in bed. The youth's servant Geta, who has been aiding him in the love affair, takes advantage of Aegio's illness and steals a purse filled with gold coins. Besides keeping some of the money for himself, Geta enables his master to support the girls longer. Later, Stephanium's uncle Philodocus arrives from Lesbos with his servant Palestrio. He has long been searching for his niece. It happens that he is an old friend of Aegio's. By granting a dowry to his niece, he makes possible her marriage with Niceratus.

ZAMBERTI: *Dolotechne*

Old Polycrisis would like his son Mononius to marry as soon as possible and not lead a dissolute life. The father orders the servant Sfalerus, who has long been the youth's pedagogue, to persuade Mononius to agree to marriage and recognize it as in his best interest. The youth is already in love with the lovely Rhodostoma, who has been kidnapped from her parents and sold to the procurer Crisophagus. This girl would by now have been forced into prostitution if the procurer's drunken wife Merophila had not realized that Rhodostoma's commercial value would be much higher with her virginity preserved. Crisophagus has set a price of three hundred mine for the girl. Learning that Rhodostoma and Mononius love each other, Merophila tells the youth to gather the money in any way possible.

Mononius has long excited the passion of rich old Bdeliria, an extremely lascivious woman. She is ready to purchase his love at any cost. Sfalerus is charged by his young master to raise the funds to release the girl. He goes to Bdeliria and explains to her that Mononius desires her affection but cannot come forward because of financial embarrassment. Easily believing that she has won the youth's love, Bdeliria immediately hands over three hundred mine. Rhodostoma is freed, and the young lovers consummate their affection. But when Polycrisis learns of the affair, he angrily sends Sfalerus to the prison workhouse. He feels that his son has disgraced their household by taking up with a common prostitute. An Athenian friend of Polycrisis arrives in search of his daughter. This friend, Alitologus, recognizes Rhodostoma as his lost daughter, for whom he has searched the whole Mediterranean. Sfalerus is called back from the workhouse to take part in the wedding between Mononius and the girl, who will have a large dowry.

MORLINI: *Comoedia*

Leucasia greets Protesilaus affectionately, while Orestes runs away screaming that he will drag everyone to his own ruin. The gods descend from the Heavens to hail the greatness of Protesilaus. Pallas calls him "noster dux inclytus"; Mars proclaims him as "decus armipotens" and "sanguen Dis oriundum"; Mercury salutes him as "inclyte bellorum ductor." Pallas and Mars promise their aid to Protesilaus in all the wars he will fight. Mercury encourages him to strike his enemy immediately now that all signs are favorable. The hosts of Spain, Germany, Britain, and Italy are ready to serve Protesilaus, and the hour of triumph is at hand. Leucasia, just before surrendering herself to the delights of love, declares that she is willing to cross the rivers of France to fight for her beloved and defeat Orestes. The play closes with a love duet between Leucasia and Protesilaus, who embrace and kiss while serenely waiting future battles.

Aetheria

The penniless noble Paurea claims to be in his forties but is really in his fifties, as his servant Margippus reveals. To save his farm from a greedy banker, Paurea has resolved to marry a young commoner with a rich dowry. The wealthy old Caridemus, regretting his low origin, wants to ennoble his family by marrying off his fourteen-year-old daughter Clarimena to the impoverished nobleman, but she loves young, timid Archites, son of the honest blockhead Deritus. Archites has a very beautiful sister, Aetheria, who captures the love of her brother's enterprising friend Faliscus. Margippus is the most active figure in the comedy. Disguised as a merchant and speaking in a mock Ciceronian manner of "O tempora, o mores" he succeeds in swindling both Deritus and Caridemus of large sums. Margippus saves Paurea's farm with twenty mine, freeing Clarimena to marry Archites. The servant gives Faliscus another twenty mine to marry Aetheria even though she has no dowry.

Plots of Italian Plays

MANTOVANO: *Formicone*

Barbaro has to leave on a long sea journey. Being very jealous, he entrusts his wife to the care of his servant Formicone, who is warned to be strict in supervising his mistress's activities. Justifiably frightened by Barbaro's words, Formicone determines to be more vigilant than Argus; but some time afterward he finds himself in need of five ducats to ransom a girl friend from the power of a merchant. Formicone lets himself be overcome by the bribes of handsome Filetero and allows the youth to enter Barbaro's home and keep assignations with his mistress. Meanwhile, bad winds have forced Barbaro to disembark at the same port from which he had set sail. Filetero has just enough time to flee from his beloved's bedroom on hearing Barbaro return home unexpectedly. But in his haste the youth leaves his slippers by the lady's bed. They are a mute but convincing testimony to Barbaro of the zealous guard maintained by the servant. Enraged, Barbaro orders the other servants to bind Formicone and drag him outside to be punished. Filetero has been waiting with a stratagem to remove all suspicion. He runs about angrily, and upon seeing Formicone he yells out that the servant is a thief, accusing him of stealing his slippers from the public baths. Formicone realizes at once that this is his only chance to save himself and confesses to the imaginary theft, begging for forgiveness by saying that his act was intended as a joke. Filetero pretends to be merciful. Thanks to the youth's quick playacting Barbaro ceases to doubt his wife's fidelity.

Ariosto: *Cassaria*

Two youths of Metellino, Erofilo and Caridoro, are in love with Eulalia and Corisca, who are held by the procurer Lucrano. To free the girls, Erofilo first gains the keys to his home during the absence of his father Crisobolo. He and the servant Volpino devise a plot whereby the rogue Trappola will disguise himself as a merchant and purchase the slave Eulalia with a chest full of rich cloth. The merchant Aristandro has left the chest on deposit with Crisobolo. After enjoying Eulalia, Erofilo will go and report the "theft" of the chest to Caridoro's father Bassà, Captain of Justice, accusing Lucrano of the crime. Upon the procurer's arrest Caridoro will be able to possess Corisca, as the procurer will be happy to have the youth's favor with Bassà.

After Trappola carries out his part, the other servants (Corbacchio, Negro, Gianda, Nebbia, and Morione) seize Eulalia so that they can carry her to their young master, thinking that the rogue really is a merchant. Volpino's master plan has fallen apart. Crisobolo suddenly returns home, as he has not had to sail for Negroponte. Volpino acts quickly and makes Crisobolo think that Nebbia (at the play's start the only servant loyal to the older master) is guilty of handing the chest over to Lucrano. Crisobolo gathers some friends and raids the procurer's establishment to carry away the chest. Volpino's success is ruined because of one mistake: he has left Trappola, dressed as a merchant in one of Crisobolo's suits, back in the house. Trappola is forced into confessing the entire plot, and Volpino is bound at Crisobolo's order.

Another servant, Fulcio, takes command of the dangerous situation by terrifying Lucrano into hiding and turning Corisca over to Caridoro. He frightens Crisobolo into paying for the procurer's departure because of the raid on the house of prostitution. Erofilo obtains his father's forgiveness and Volpino's release. Now the two youths will be able to enjoy the girls without any trouble from the procurer.

Ariosto: *I Suppositi*

The Sicilian youth Erostrato, son of Filogono of Catania, loves the Ferrarese Polinesta, daughter of Damone. Erostrato came to Ferrara to study.

He soon spied the girl and fell in love with her; in order to consummate his love he changed name and clothes with his servant Dulippo. For the last two years Dulippo has been attending the university, while his master Erostrato has been working as a servant in Damone's house and having illicit relations with Polinesta. Erostrato's love affair has been threatened by talk about Polinesta's marrying the old doctor of laws, Cleandro, who has offered to provide her with a rich dowry. To counter that offer, Dulippo (the false Erostrato) asks Damone for his daughter's hand, promising the same special dowry.

As the false Erostrato is a minor, he must have his father with him to vouch for the dowry. He frightens a Sienese gentleman into playing Filogono's part, but just at this moment the real Filogono arrives in Ferrara. Determined to take his son back home, Filogono knocks at the door of the house indicated to him as that of Erostrato. When he identifies himself the servants chase him away, believing that the Sienese is Filogono. The old man is puzzled. He encounters Dulippo, dressed as a student, and at once recognizes him as Erostrato's servant. Dulippo pretends not to recognize Filogono and denies that he is anyone other than Erostrato of Catania.

Afraid that his son has been murdered, Filogono decides to take legal action to prove his identity. The lawyer recommended to him is Cleandro. Through a long talk with the lawyer, Filogono reveals that the false Erostratro must be Cleandro's son who was kidnapped as a baby when the Turks took Otrando. Meanwhile Damone has had Erostrato bound to wait punishment for seducing Polinesta. On finding that the false Dulippo is the son of a wealthy Sicilian merchant, Damone readily consents to his daughter's marrying Erostrato.

ARIOSTO: *Il Negromante*

Before the play's represented action begins, the youth Cintio (adopted son of the rich Cremonese citizen Massimo) has already secretly married Lavinia, ward of the Florentine Fazio. Fazio permitted the secret wedding, feeling powerless to oppose the reciprocally violent passion of the two lovers. The marriage had to be kept secret so as not to anger Massimo over his son's marrying a girl without a dowry, since the youth could have been disinherited. But at the moment when the play opens Cintio has been married publicly for a month to Emilia, daughter of the well-to-do Abondio. Cintio was too weak-willed to resist his father's command to marry Emilia. But this second wife is still a virgin because Cintio pretends that he is physically unable to consummate the marriage, hoping that it will have to be annulled.

Massimo has hired the magician Giacchelino to cure Cintio of his impotence. But at the same time Fazio has doubled Massimo's offer to the magician so he will bring about an annulment of Cintio's marriage to Emilia. A new party enters in Camillo Pócosale, a youth passionately interested in Emilia. Camillo hires the magician to enchant Emilia so she will surrender to him. All the threads of the plot thus come into the magician's hands. This scoundrel plans to escape with his fees and rob Camillo. He tells the credulous youth to hide in a chest so he can be transported to Emilia. While Camillo is a prisoner in the chest, the magician plans to flee Cremona with the youth's valuable possessions; but the chest is intercepted and placed in Lavinia's room. Camillo overhears Lavinia and Cintio and finds out they are married. He reveals everything to Massimo and Abondio.

Fortunately for Cintio, Massimo learns that Lavinia is his daughter by a woman he had married under the assumed name of Anastagio of Alexandria. Cintio can stay with her, as both of the lovers are Massimo's heirs. Emilia will be married to Camillo. The magician has had to flee for his life.

Ariosto: *Lena*

Young Flavio of Ferrara is determined to possess Licinia and has been appealing to Lena, who gives lessons in domestic arts to the girl, to arrange an assignation. Lena is willing to play procuress for twenty-five florins and tells the young man to send his servant Corbolo to a Jewish moneylender to pawn the youth's fine cap and hood. While Flavio is eagerly awaiting Licinia's arrival, a surveyor appears to measure the house. The youth hides in a barrel that has been lent to Lena's debt-ridden husband Pacifico. Soon Bartolo, one of Pacifico's creditors, and Giuliano, owner of the barrel, arrive at the house and start a fight over the right to confiscate the barrel. Fazio, Licinia's father and Lena's lover, intervenes and has the barrel placed in his home until Giuliano and Bartolo settle their argument. Flavio is carried away in the barrel, straight to the arms of his beloved. Later one of Fazio's servants discovers Flavio and Licinia together and reports everything to his master. Through the quick acting of Ilario, Flavio's father, wedding plans are made for the lovers.

Ariosto: *I Studenti*

The Veronese student Claudio has had to flee to Ferrara after being accused of murder in Pavia by Professor Lazzaro, who was angry because of the youth's love for his daughter Flamminia. Claudio's close friend Eurialo was also studying at Pavia, where he became the lover of Ippolita, a countess's maid. Eurialo has had to return to his home in Ferrara at the command of his father Bartolo. Lazzaro has meanwhile lost his position at Pavia and is going to take another post at Padua. At first he had intended to stop off and meet Bartolo, with whom he has been corresponding, but then he decided to go to Padua by way of Venice. Claudio wants to head the professor off at Venice. Just at that moment Ippolita and an older servant woman arrive in Ferrara, having fled the countess. Acting on the advice of his servant Accursio, Eurialo brings the women into his home as the daughter and wife of Professor Lazzaro. Claudio, hearing that Flamminia and her mother are in town, thinks his friend has betrayed him. The situation grows more complicated when Bartolo, who had left to journey to Naples, comes back to Ferrara after hearing news about the arrival of Lazzaro's family.

Next Riccio, an agent of Ippolita's countess, arrives in Ferrara with letters to the duke asking for help in recovering the fugitive servants. To add further to Eurialo's problems, the real Lazzaro reaches Ferrara with his family, as he has decided not to go by way of Venice. To avoid a meeting between Bartolo and Lazzaro, Accursio enlists Claudio's landlord Bonifazio to pose as Bartolo and receive Lazzaro into his home.

At this point Ludovico Ariosto's work ends. Bartolo had been entrusted by a friend with a fortune intended for the man's mistress and illegitimate daughter. Both Gabriele and Virginio Ariosto saw in Ippolita that friend's daughter. Gabriele's *Scolastica* shows Bartolo soon surprising Bonifazio in his disguise. Revealing himself to Lazzaro, Bartolo orders Accursio to be bound and held prisoner. Claudio meanwhile discovers Flamminia in Bonifazio's home, and they consummate their love. Once Ippolita's identity is established, she can marry Eurialo. Flamminia and Claudio are also to wed; Eurialo is not seen in Act V. Riccio appears only at the very end. The complex intrigue is lessened as the characters are withdrawn.

Virginio adds new characters to his version, the *Imperfetta*. Agnola, a stranger, comes to Ferrara looking for Lazzaro to consult him on a business venture that has failed; he serves to misdirect the servant Fromba. Eurialo had told Fromba to inform Bartolo that Lazzaro's wife and daughter (really the old servant woman and Ippolita) were supposed to leave town so they could meet the professor in Padua. Following Agnola's bad directions, Fromba encounters Lazzaro at Bonifazio's house and states that he wishes to lead away the professor's wife and daughter. Lazzaro screams out in horror. Riccio and Eurialo are seen in this version throughout the fifth act.

Bartolo shrewdly allows Eurialo to marry Ippolita, thus keeping the girl's fortune in the family.

NARDI: *La Commedia di Amicizia*

An Athenian renounced his marital rights so that his Roman friend Lucio would not perish from his passion for the woman who had been destined as the Athenian's wife. The bride is accordingly deceived on the wedding night as she gives herself to Lucio believing he is the Athenian. Although this woman is eventually granted as wife to the Roman, her family takes revenge on the intended husband by depriving him of his wealth and imposing perpetual banishment from Athens. Going to Rome where Lucio lives with his wife, the Athenian loses all hope when Lucio passes him by without even noticing him. The Athenian wanders away to a cave to sleep. Afterward two thieves arrive and start fighting over their loot; one of them is killed. The Athenian decides to take the blame, as life is meaningless for him. Condemned to crucifixion, the Athenian is recognized by Lucio, who declares his friend's innocence and confesses to the murder. The true murderer is so touched by this sacrifice that he comes forward and also confesses. A full pardon is granted to all three. The Athenian is married to Lucio's sister and receives half his friend's wealth.

NARDI: *I Due Felivi Rivali*

Two youths of Athens fall in love with the ward of a well-to-do citizen. Despising each other, they separately corrupt servants in the gentleman's household in the hope of carrying off the girl. On the same night both youths, Carino and Callidoro, arrive at the girl's home, each accompanied by an armed band of friends. During the kidnap attempt the two groups start fighting and make so much noise that the authorities arrive. Both rivals are arrested and put in prison. The girl in question is discovered to be the sister of Carino; she was believed to have perished in a fire years before. The girl is therefore given as wife to Callidoro. Since Callidoro's sister has been seduced by Carino, the comedy ends with plans for a double wedding.

MACHIAVELLI: *La Mandragola*

Though born in Florence, Callimaco Guadagni has spent most of his life in Paris, but the renowned beauty of Madonna Lucrezia, wife of the lawyer

Messer Nicia Calfucci, has drawn the thirty-year-old Callimaco back to his native city. He is determined to win her love. Unfortunately for him she is a faithful wife. To achieve his aim, Callimaco hires the services of the parasite Ligurio, who often visits the lawyer. The parasite tells Callimaco to play the role of a physician from Paris ready to provide Nicia with a draught that will enable Lucrezia to conceive and thus provide the lawyer with an heir. According to Ligurio's fiction, there is danger that the first man to possess Lucrezia once she has taken the draught will die shortly afterward. To protect Nicia it would be best to kidnap some youth who could take the poison of the mandrake draught upon himself.

Once Nicia is persuaded to accept this scheme, Callimaco and Ligurio enlist the aid of Frate Timoteo, the confessor to Nicia and Lucrezia. The friar, Nicia, and Lucrezia's mother Sostrata all exert so much pressure that the lady yields to their demands to lie with a stranger. The youth turns out to be Callimaco, who had disguised himself as a strolling musician. The comedy concludes happily for everyone. Nicia and Sostrata look forward to the birth of a boy, after six years of waiting. Callimaco has won Lucrezia's love. The parasite receives a large sum of money, while Frate Timoteo is to gain three hundred ducats.

MACHIAVELLI: *Clizia*

The Florentine merchant Nicomaco wishes to possess his ward Clizia. To forward his scheme he plans to marry her to his depraved servant Pirro, who will allow his master to enjoy the girl in exchange for a home and shop that Nicomaco will purchase for him. But Nicomaco's wife Sofronia is aware of his plot and is determined to stop him. The old man's son Cleandro is also in love with the girl. Sofronia hopes to keep both her husband and her son away from the girl by marrying her off to the farm-steward Eustachio. After several battles with his wife and son, Nicomaco proposes to decide between Pirro and Eustachio by drawing lots. He wins and orders the wedding to be held at once. Wedding preparations are delayed for a short while when the bride goes mad from grief and threatens to kill Pirro and Nicomaco with a dagger. But once the girl is led to the nuptial chamber, Nicomaco takes Pirro's place in bed. Instead of the girl he finds that the "bride" is his strong male servant Siro, who soundly beats up his master. Nicomaco repents and surrenders to Sofronia's control. Just then a Neapolitan gentleman arrives and claims Clizia as his daughter. Cleandro will be able to marry her.

Bibbiena: *Calandria*

Sometime before the beginning of the action, the twins Lidio and Santilla lived with their father Demetrio in the Greek city of Modon. During a Turkish raid on the city Santilla was dressed as a boy and carried away to safety by her nurse and the servant Fannio. They thought Lidio had been killed. While fleeing from the city all three were captured by the Turkish pirates. Carried off to Constantinople, they were ransomed by the Florentine merchant Perillo, who took them to Rome. Several years have passed during which Santilla has used the name Lidio and has let Perillo continue to' believe that she is a male. By the time covered in the comedy the merchant is pressing Santilla to marry his daughter Verginia. Her brother Lidio, however, had been rescued by the servant Fessenio. Living in Tuscany, the youth acquired the language and customs of that region. Upon his arrival in Rome, he falls in love with Fulvia, Calandro's wife. Fessenio enters Calandro's service to aid his young master, since Lidio wants to become Fulvia's lover despite the pleadings of his preceptor Polinico for the youth to take the way of reason. Following Fessenio's advice, Lidio dresses as a female and calls himself Santilla so he can make assignations with Fulvia. Calandro is so stupid that he does not see through the disguise. Instead he is fired with love for Lidio, believing that Fessenio is going to procure the girl for him.

Fulvia hires the magician Ruffo to enchant Lidio so that he will never desert her. The only Lidio that the magician knows is the one who lives with the merchant Perillo; Ruffo therefore goes to approach Santilla. Fulvia's maidservant Samia meets Santilla on the street and tries to lead her to Fulvia. Santilla declares, truthfully, that she knows no Fulvia. Shortly afterward Fessenio warns Fulvia that Lidio is going to leave Rome to search for his sister, but that he will visit the lady before starting his trip. Fulvia is easily upset, fearing loss of her love. Fessenio informs Calandro that Santilla will meet him, and the older man agrees to be enclosed in a chest so he can be carried to his new love. Fessenio meanwhile has hired a prostitute who will pretend to be Santilla when she greets Calandro in a darkened room. On the way to Lidio's home Fessenio and the porter carrying the chest are stopped by customs officers. On opening the chest, the officers are told that Calandro is a corpse dead from the plague, and that he is to be thrown into the river. Calandro starts to scream out, frightening away the officers. Fessenio makes Calandro carry the chest the rest of the way to Lidio's house.

Worrying about her lover, Fulvia disguises herself in men's clothes and goes out to find him. She plays the jealous wife when she discovers Calandro in Lidio's home. Meanwhile Fannio and Santilla arrive at Calandro's house to meet Ruffo, who is informed by the servant that Santilla is a hermaphrodite with the ability to appear male or female as the occasion demands. But when Fulvia thinks that her lover is a female, she accuses the magician of altering Lidio's sex. Ruffo claims that he can make Lidio reassume his male sex. Santilla does not want any magic applied to her, but Fannio assures her that he will take her place in Fulvia's darkened bedroom. When Samia relates to Fessenio that Lidio has been enchanted by the magician, the servant begins to admire Ruffo. While wandering about the street, Samia beholds the twins. At first astonished, the maid concludes that Fulvia ought to be able to distinguish the real Lidio. Shortly afterward Fessenio encounters Santilla, and on finding out her name and sex he realizes that she must be Lidio's sister. Fannio and the real Lidio come on stage. A family reunion occurs.

A little later Lidio joins Fulvia, but Calandro's brothers discover them and go off to find Fulvia's husband. Samia thinks that the magician should be called in to switch Lidio into a female. This suggestion inspires Fessenio to substitute Santilla for Lidio. When Fulvia is found alone with a female, no one can attack her for adultery. Now all complications have passed. Fulvia wants her son Flamminio to marry Santilla, and Lidio is going to save his sister from the embarrassing situation in Perillo's household by marrying Verginia. The comedy closes with plans for a double wedding.

Aretino. *La Cortigiana*

Messer Maco da Siena arrives in Rome hoping to become a cardinal. He is under the impression that one must become a courtier in order to rise to the rank of cardinal. Wandering about the city, he falls in love with Camilla Pisana. Maco's ambitions and amorous interests lead him to the swindling painter Maestro Andrea, who promises to instruct the Sienese in the art of courtiership and to arrange for a meeting with Camilla. Maco ends up letting Andrea place him in a kettle, where he is to take on the mold of a courtier. Meanwhile Parabolano, a Neapolitan noble who carries on a parallel plot in the play, has become the victim of his own treacherous servants. His servant Rosso has joined forces with the procuress Alvigia to substitute a prostitute for Parabolano's beloved Livia, wife of Luzio Romano. After paying a high fee, Parabolano is placed in a darkened room with Togna, wife of the baker Arcolano. The Neapolitan becomes aware of the substitution. But by the play's end the deceived and the deceivers have made peace with each other.

ARETINO: *Il Marescalco*

The Duke of Mantua has decided to play a trick on his official farrier and other members of the court. It is announced that a beautiful, well-to-do girl is to be married to the farrier, a woman-hater. Several characters attempt to persuade the farrier to marry, such as the old nurse who sings the praises of married life as a terrestrial paradise. The farrier is obdurate to her pleas as well as to the warnings and threats he hears from the boy Giannicco, Messer Jacopo, Count Nicola, a knight, and the official pedant. His stubborn resistance is supported by Ambrogio, a bitter old man who describes all the sorrows and pains of married life. Finally the farrier yields when he sees that the Duke is unrelenting in insisting on the marriage. The wedding is held. But when he kisses the "bride" the farrier realizes that it is the page Carlo da Fano. By order of the Duke, the page has disguised himself in the wedding dress. The farrier is overjoyed to see that he has married a boy. Everyone present starts to laugh. All the members of the court have fallen for the Duke's trick.

ARETINO: *Ipocrito*

Liseo Rocchetti of Milan is weighed down by domestic and financial responsibilities, since his family includes an independent-minded wife, Maja, and five daughters. He is also afraid that a missing twin brother may one day return to add new problems to the already crowded household. Liseo's one comfort is his friendship with the Hypocrite, who has the run of the house and advises him on every important decision. The eldest of Liseo's daughters, Tansilla, was married to the youth Artico; but her husband left to travel about the world. Now she is to wed Tranquillo. Her sister Porfiria was engaged to Prelio, and to test his love Porfiria sent Prelio on a quest to bring back the feathers of the phoenix. Meanwhile the youth Zefiro has been seeking the favors of Annetta, another of Liseo's daughters.

A day of calamities develops after Brizio, Liseo's twin, returns to Milan. The Neapolitan soldier Rodalosso had carried him away when he was a baby and reared him as his own son, finally leaving Brizio his whole estate. Liseo and Brizio resemble each other so closely that the other characters keep mistaking one for the other. Brizio is handed a string of pearls meant for Tansilla's wedding, but Brizio's servant Tanfuro gives them to Liseo, confusing him with his master. Then Prelio comes home with the required feathers. Porfiria has, however, fallen in love with another youth named Corebo. She and Corebo seek to escape their obligations by taking rat poison. In the meantime Artico is back, announcing his intention to keep Tansilla as his wife. Annetta has run off with Zefiro.

Fortunately, disaster is avoided. The Latin-spouting Dr. Biondello has substituted a sleeping potion for the rat poison, and Prelio afterward frees Porfiria of her obligation so she can marry Corebo. The daughter Sveva will be wed to Prelio instead, while Tranquillo is consoled by marriage with Angizia, still another daughter. Zefiro also has decided to make his relationship with Annetta legitimate. Brizio's wealth will solve all the financial problems. The comedy closes with plans for multiple weddings.

ARETINO: *Talanta*

Three lovers are fighting for the Roman courtesan Talanta: the youth Orfinio, the braggart Captain Tinca, and the wealthy Venetian Messer Vergolo. To win her love each one presents an expensive gift. Orfinio hands her a golden chain. The captain presents her with a Moorish slave girl who has been the close companion of his daughter Marmilia. In his turn Vergolo gives a male Saracen slave, whom he had treated with such kindness as to let him sleep with his son Marchetto. But the slave girl is really the youth Antino, who has enjoyed intimate relations with Marmilia. The Saracen slave is a female and the beloved of Vergolo's son. The two slaves do not remain long with Talanta, for they flee her establishment to meet their lovers. The arrival in Rome of Messer Blando of Castro in the company of his servant Fedele and his daughter Oretta (disguised as a male) solves all difficulties. Antino and the girl Lucilla are his children, born at the same time as Oretta. A Turkish raid had separated the family. The disguise of sex and the use of a dye to change the skin color were devices aimed at fooling the Turks. This prose comedy concludes in the typical fashion: Antino and Lucilla are properly married to Marmilia and Marchetto. A certain Armileo, who pretended love for Talanta to be close to the false slave girl, is wed to Oretta, who is identical to Antino. Vergolo and Tinca surrender their claims on Talanta to their younger rival Orfinio.

ARETINO: *Il Filosofo*

The jewel merchant Boccaccio arrives in Siena from his native city Perugia and meets an old family maid, Mea. Later the prostitute Tullia approaches the maid to learn Boccaccio's family background so that she can pose as his lost half sister and rob him of fifty florins. She succeeds in luring him to her establishment. Once Boccaccio puts down his moneybelt, Tullia sets a trap so he falls out of her house. On the street Boccaccio encounters a group of thieves, who lower him into a well to wash himself off, deserting him when the officers of the night patrol pass by. But Boccaccio climbs out and rejoins the thieves in an attempt to loot the tomb of a recently buried wealthy citizen. When he refuses to turn a ruby over to the others, Boccaccio is left in the tomb. Fortunately, another group of thieves breaks in and releases him. Boccaccio now has a ruby to compensate him for his lost florins.

Paralleling this tale is one about the pedantic philosopher Plataristotile, who buries himself in his metaphysical studies to the neglect of his young wife Madonna Tessa. She plots with her maid Nepitella to receive the archlover Polidoro into her home, but her husband overhears the plan. Plataristotile locks Polidoro in his study after the lover arrives at the house. While the philosopher is going to fetch his mother-in-law Monna Papa, Polidoro's servant Radicchio releases him. As Plataristotile confronts his wife and mother-in-law with his accusations, Polidoro's voice is heard from down the street singing a serenade. Tessa complains that her husband has not fulfilled his marital duties. Instead of a lover they find an ass in the philosopher's study. Tessa angrily leaves with her mother. Later Plataristotile and his wife become reconciled in the hope of having a son. The philosopher has awakened from his metaphysical dreams, and promises to act like a husband.

RICCHI: *I Tre Tiranni*

Three men are fighting to possess Lúcia: old Girifalco, the youth Filocrate, and the rich noble Crisaulo. Girifalco never gets anywhere, falling victim to the fraudulent schemes of the parasites Pilastrino and Listagiro. He ends up marrying the girl's mother, Calonide. Cruel Fortune persecutes Filocrate until he has to renounce his claims for the girl and go as a pilgrim to Santiago de Compostella. When he returns almost a year later, Filocrate sneaks into Lúcia's house at night and by mistake possesses her maid Fronesia, who takes him for the noble Cricaulo. Filocrate decides to marry the maid. The only one who succeeds in seducing Lúcia is Crisaulo, who at first intends to abandon her but later marries her. Plans for a triple wedding close the play.

Intronati: *Gl'Ingannati*

Old Virginio is beset with financial problems. Four years before, he lost his fortune in the Sack of Rome. His rich, elderly friend Gherardo would like to marry Virginio's daughter Lelia, who is supposed to be staying at the convent of San Crescenzio. But Lelia has fled the convent with the aid of a nun. Disguised as a man, she calls herself Fabio and works for the young noble Flamminio, with whom she fell in love some years before at Rome. Flamminio, however, is passionately interested in Gherardo's daughter Isabella. Fabio-Lelia has had to carry Flamminio's love messages to Isabella, who has been fired with love for the beautiful page. Virginio's daughter has taken advantage of this difficult position by persuading Isabella to reject Flamminio's advances.

Meanwhile Lelia's identical twin brother Fabrizio has arrived in Modena in the company of his servant Stragulcia and his preceptor Messer Piero. Fabrizio had fallen prisoner in Rome to a Captain Orteca. The youth was shipped to Siena and then to a Spanish army camp. After the captain died at the battle of Correggio, Fabrizio was freed. Knowing about Lelia's flight and disguise, Gherardo and Virginio come upon Fabrizio; thinking him a female, they confine him in Isabella's room. Isabella and her maid strip the confused youth to see if the page really is a female. Fabrizio surrenders himself to the search and afterward to Isabella's love. Flamminio has learned about Isabella's interest in the page and that Lelia-Fabio has kissed the girl. He sets out to mutilate the page. But once the page's true sex is discovered, Flamminio agrees to marry Lelia. Isabella will wed Fabrizio.

A. Piccolomini: *L'Amor Costante*

Ferrante di Selvaggia and Ginevra were secretly married and had to flee from their relatives in Spain. On the voyage to Italy Turkish vessels intercepted their ship and took them prisoner. The lovers were divided: Ginevra was ransomed by a Spanish knightly order and given to Guglielmo da Villafranca, a resident of Pisa, while Ferrante remained a prisoner in Tunis until imperial forces liberated that area from the Turks. He then went to Florence and worked in its city guard; but one night during carnival time he went to Pisa and saw Ginevra. He entered Guglielmo's service under the name of Lorenzino. Ginevra was using the name Lucrezia so that her family could not find her. She failed to recognize Ferrante because of a thick beard he had grown since his captivity.

When the play opens, the young priest Giannino is desperate because of his unrequited love for Lucrezia. He has been in Pisa for three years under the pretext of studying there, but his real reason is to win the girl's affections. He is not at all interested in Margarita, the daughter of the physician Guicciardo, although she has let Giannino know of her delirious passion for him. Margarita is sought after by the Neapolitan poetaster Ligdonio, who is interested in her dowry.

Lorenzino has tested the faith of his beloved by trying to seduce Lucrezia without revealing his identity. When he is fully convinced of her fidelity, he lets her know who he is. Ferrante-Lorenzino has pretended to act as Giannino's go-between with the girl. The lovers plan to flee. Fearing to tell Guglielmo their story, they are prepared even to kill him if the old man opposes their flight. But their plot is exposed. Disgusted by such ingratitude, Guglielmo has the lovers locked up and orders Dr. Guicciardo to get a poisonous drink ready for them. Giannino, to rescue his beloved Lucrezia and his go-between, rushes on the scene with a group of school friends.

A street brawl develops when Guglielmo comes out with a crowd of servants and supporters. The Spanish police captain, Francisco Marrada, arrives but fails to keep peace. Finally the Spanish nobleman Consalvo comes on the scene and offers to arbitrate the dispute. Through all the questioning it becomes clear that Guglielmo really is Pedrantonio, Consalvo's brother. Pedrantonio had to leave Castile years before as a rebel. Lucrezia is his daughter Ginevra, left in the custody of her uncle; and Giannino is Ginevra's brother Ioandoro, who was sent to Italy as a page of the de' Medici cardinal, later Pope Clement VII. Pedrantonio is overwhelmed with grief, fearing that he has killed the lovers, but fortunately Guicciardo had prepared a harmless drink. Ferrante and Ginevra will be able to make their marriage public. Ioandoro is to wed Margarita, giving up his priestly benefices to Lidgonio. As usual, the comedy ends with wedding preparations.

BEOLCO: *L'Anconitana*

Three youths arrive in Padua seeking their fortune. Two, Tancredi and Teodoro, are from Sicily while the third, who goes under the name of Gismondo but is really a girl, is from Gaeta. All three were prisoners of Turkish pirates, who sold them to a Moor. Later a Venetian merchant ransomed them and took them to Venice. They gave him their promise that they would not leave the Venetian realm until the ransom price was paid back. He allowed them to leave Venice to go and raise funds. They went to Padua to find a noble lady in whose service they could enlist. While the three are addressing the courtesan Doralice, the wife of the broker Sier Thomao falls in love with Gismondo and persuades her husband to pay the youth's ransom price. Sier Thomao is seeking the favors of Doralice, and his servant Ruzzante loves the courtesan's maid Besa. The broker is willing to let his wife have the youth in her service so she will be too occupied to spy on his activities.

Ginevra, a widow from Ancona, appears in Padua disguised as a male. She is looking for Gismondo, whom she saw at Ancona and wishes to marry. But Ginevra learns about Gismondo's true sex. The two turn out to be sisters. Gismondo's real name is Isotta. She and Ginevra have been separated for eight years. The family fortune will enable Gismondo to repay Sier Thomao the money he advanced for the ransom price. Isotta is to wed Tancredi, and Ginevra will marry Teodoro. Sier Thomao has succeeded in arranging for an assignation with Doralice. The courtesan has skillfully made the greedy broker agree to a high price for her favors. Ruzzante is to accompany his master to a villa at Arquà, where Besa will be waiting for him. Master and servant depart together in high spirits.

BEOLCO: *Piovana*

As the play starts, two old friends, Tura and Maregale, are complaining of their misfortunes. Tura's only daughter was stolen from him during a war. Maregale's son Siton fell in love with a girl named Nina, who was in the power of the procurer Slavero. Siton's mother Resca kept insulting the youth because of his passion for the slave girl until finally he could no longer tolerate her nagging and left home. Maregale has temporarily separated from his shrewish wife.

Siton is in the vicinity of Chioggia searching for Nina. The youth had paid the procurer for her ransom, but Slavero sailed away on the advice of an innkeeper from Apulia who suggested that the procurer might obtain higher prices for his merchandise elsewhere. When a storm breaks, Slavero's ship sinks. Nina and her fellow slave girl Ghetta manage to reach shore in a skiff, afterward begging the protection of Tura.

But Slavero and his innkeeper friend were not killed. During most of the play the procurer tries to recover Nina and Ghetta. Slavero is frustrated, thanks largely to the efforts of the servants Garbugio and Garbinello. Another servant, Bertevello, fishes up a casket that belongs to the procurer. In it are family relics that identify Nina as Tura's lost daughter. She will now be able to marry Siton, even with the blessing of his mother Resca, who has arrived in the area. Garbugio is to wed Ghetta. Everyone rejoices at the procurer's defeat.

BEOLCO: *Vaccaria*

Placido is an indulgent father who understands the impetuous nature of young men. He prefers being loved to being feared by his son Flavio. The youth is intensely in love with Fiorinetta, the charge of the procuress Celega. Unfortunately Placido is at the mercy of his rich wife Rospina. This woman is a shrew who is completely indifferent to the desires of her husband and son. Two servants, Truffo and Vezzo, come to the aid of their young master. With the help of Placido they cheat a merchant of the fifty florins Flavio needs to purchase Fiorinetta. Vezzo pretends to be Rospina's favorite steward when the merchant arrives to pay for some cows that he has purchased from Rospina's estate. With Placido's support the scheme succeeds, and Flavio is able to defeat his rival Polidoro.

Placido lent his support on the condition that he could enjoy Fiorinetta for a day. Loron, Polidoro's parasite, learns that Flavio and his father have gone to a victory banquet at Celega's establishment. The parasite runs to Rospina and reveals everything that has happened. She invades the banquet, but suddenly she is overcome by the scene of happiness, realizing how she has alienated herself from her husband and son. Rospina approves of a wedding between Flavio and Fiorinetta. She also gives Vezzo a farm and a dowry so that he can marry the peasant girl Betta. In this mood of repentance for past wrongs Celega promises to change her way of life, and Rospina joins the party. The wandering singer Piolo enters to close the play with some folk songs.

Bibliography

TEXTS OF LATIN PLAYS

Aetheria, ed. Ezio Franceschini. *Atti e Memorie d. R. Accad. di scienze, lettere ed arti in Padova* 56 (1939-40): 107 f.

Bartholamei Zamberti Veneti Comedia Dolotechne (no indication of city or date).

Beutler, E. *Forschungen und Texte zur Frühumanisten Komoedie*. Hamburg, 1927.

Bolte, Johannes. "Eine humanistenkomoedie," *Hermes* 21, no. 2 (1886): 316-18.

————. "Zwei Humanistenkomoedie aus Italien," *Zeitschr. f. vergleich. Litteraturgesch. und Renaissance-Litteratur* 1 (1888): 79 f.

La Catinia, Le Orazione e le Epistole di Sicco Polenton umanista trentino del Secolo XV, ed. A. Segarizzi. Bergamo, 1899.

Chrysis, commedia, ed. Ireneo Sanesi. Florence, 1941.

Franceschini, Ezio. *Due Testi latini inediti del basso medio evo*. Padua, 1938.

Frulovisi, Tito Livo. *Opera hactenus inedita,* ed. C. W. Previté-Orton. Cambridge, 1932.

Hieronymi Morlini Parthenopi. Novellae, fabulae, comoedia. Paris, 1855.

Johannis Harmonii Marsi Comoedia Stephanium urbis venetae genio publice recitata (no indication of date).

Muellner, Karl. "Vergerios *Paulus*, eine Studentenkomoedie," *Wiener Studien* 22 (1900): 236-57.

277

Opere Volgari di L. B. Alberti per la più parte inedite e tratte dagli autografi, ed. A. Bonucci. Florence, 1843.

Pierantoni, Amalia. *Pier Paolo Vergerio seniore.* Chieti, 1920.

Roy, Emile. *Études sur le théâtre français du XVIᵉ et du XVᵉ siecle.* Paris, 1902.

Teatro goliardico dell'Umanesimo, ed. Vito Pandolfi and Erminia Artese. Milan, 1965.

Teatro umanistico, ed. and trans. Alessandro Perosa. Milan, 1965.

Texts of Italian Plays

Aretino, Pietro. *Le Commedie e l'Orazia,* ed. Camerini. Milan, 1879.

Ariosto, Ludovico. *Le Commedie,* ed. M. Catalano. 2 vols. Bologna, 1933.

Beolco, Angelo. *Oeuvres Complètes,* trans. A. Mortier. Vol. 2. Paris, 1926.

———. *La Pastorale,* ed. E. Lovarini. Florence, 1951.

Commedie del Cinquecento, ed. Aldo Borlenghi. 2 vols. Milan, 1959.

Commedie del Cinquecento, ed. Nino Borsellino. Milan, 1962.

Commedie del Cinquecento, ed. Ireneo Sanesi. 2 vols. Bari, 1912.

Formicone Comedia di Publio Philippo Mantovano. Venice, 1534.

Machiavelli, Niccolò. *Commedie e Belfagor,* ed. Luigi Russo. Florence, 1943.

———. *La Mandragola, ed. Roberto Ridolfi.* Florence, 1965.

Nardi, Jacopo. *Comedia di Amicizia* (no indication of city or date).

———. *I due felici rivali,* ed. Alessandro Ferraioli. Rome, 1901.

General Studies

Agresti, Alberto. *Studii sulla Commedia Italiana del Secolo XVI.* Naples, 1871.

Apollonio, Mario. *Storia del teatro italiano.* Vol. 2. Florence, 1951.

Bahlmann, P. *Die lateinischen Dramen.* Muenster, 1893.

Baratto, Mario. *Tre studi sul teatro (Ruzante, Aretino, Goldoni).* Venice, 1964.

Bartoli, Francesco. *Notizie istoriche de' comici italiani che fiorivano intorno all'anno 1550 fino ai giorni presenti.* Padua, 1782.

Bond, Richard Warwick. *Early Plays from the Italian.* Oxford, 1911.

Boughner, Daniel C. *The Braggart in Renaissance Comedy.* Minneapolis, Minn., 1954.

Bullough, Geoffrey. *Narrative and Dramatic Sources of Shakespeare.* Vols. 1 and 2. New York, 1958.

Burckhardt, Jacob. *The Civilization of the Renaissance in Italy.* 2 vols. New York, 1958.

Campanini, Naborre. *Lodovico Ariosto nei prologhi delle sue commedie.* Bologna, 1891.

Catalano, M. *Vita di Ludovico Ariosto ricostruita su nuovi documenti.* Geneva, 1931.

Cataldo, Antonio. *Il Ruzzante.* Milan, 1933.

Cerreta, Florindo. *Alessandro Piccolomini, letterato e filosofo senese del Cinquecento.* Siena, 1960.

Clubb, Louise George. *Giambattista Della Porta Dramatist*. Princeton, N. J., 1965.

Creizenach, Wilhelm. *Geschichte des neueren Dramas*. Halle, 1901.

Crescimbeni, Giovanni Mario de'. *Comentari intorno alla sua Istoria della Volgar Poesia*. Rome, 1702.

Croce, Benedetto. *La Spagna nella Vita Italiana durante La Rinascita*. Bari, 1949.

D'Ancona, Alessandro. *Origini del teatro italiano*. 2 vols. Turin, 1891.

De Amicis, Vincenzo. *L'Imitazione Latina nella Commedia Italiana del XVI Secolo*. Florence, 1897.

De Sanctis, Francesco. *Storia della Letteratura Italiana*. Vol. 2. Bari, 1925.

D'Orso, Libero. *Gli Studenti di Ludovico Ariosto*. Padua, 1929.

Duchartre, Pierre Louis. *The Italian Comedy,* trans. R. T. Weaver. New York, 1966.

Duckworth, George E. *The Nature of Roman Comedy*. Princeton, 1952.

Flamini, Francesco. *Il Cinquecento*. Milan, 1903.

Freeburg, Victor O. *Disguise Plots in Elizabethan Drama*. New York, 1915.

Garzoni, Tommaso. *Piazza universale delle profesioni del mondo*. Venice, 1595.

Gaspary, Adolf. *Geschichte der Italienischen Literatur*. Vol. 2. Strasbourg, 1888.

Ginguené, Pierre Louis. *Histoire Littéraire d'Italie*. Paris, 1813.

Grabher, Carlo. *Sul Teatro dell'Ariosto*. Rome, 1946.

———. *Ruzzante*. Milan, 1953.

Graf, Arturo. *Studi Drammatici*. Turin, 1878.

Greco, Aulo. *La Vita Romana nella Commedia del Rinascimento*. Rome, 1945.

Grismer, R. L. *The Influence of Plautus in Spain before Lope de Vega*. New York, 1944.

Herrick, Marvin T. *Comic Theory in the Sixteenth Century*. Urbana, Ill., 1950.

———. *Italian Comedy in the Renaissance*. Urbana, 1960.

Kennard, Joseph Spencer. *The Italian Theater*. Vol. 1. New York, 1932.

Lea, Kathleen M. *Italian Popular Comedy*. 2 vols. Oxford, 1934.

Lovarini, Emilio. *Studi sul Ruzzante e la Letteratura Pavana*. Padua, 1965.

Lowe, J. E. *Magic in Greek and Latin Literature*. Oxford, 1929.

Luzio, A. *Pietro Aretino nei primi suoi anni a Venezia e la corte dei Gonzaga*. Turin, 1888.

Maffei, Giuseppe. *Storia della Letteratura Italiana*. Naples, 1864.

Malkiel, María Rosa Lida de. *La Originalidad artística de la 'Celestina.'* Buenos Aires, 1962.

Meozzi, Antero. *La Dramatica della Rinascita in Europa Sec. XVI-XVII*. Pisa, 1940.

Miklascefsky, Constant. *La Commedia dell'Arte*. Paris, 1927.

Momigilano, Attilio. *Storia della Letteratura Italiana dalle origini ai nostri giorni*. Milan 1960.

Moncallero, Giuseppe L. *Il Cardinale Bernardo Dovizi da Bibbiena umanista e diplomatico*. Florence, 1953.

Mortier, Alfred. *Un Dramaturge de la Renaissance Italienne: Ruzzante*. 2 vols. Paris, 1926.

Napoli-Signorelli, Pietro. *La Storia dei teatri antichi e moderni*. Naples, 1777.

Pandolfi, Vito. *La commedia dell'Arte: storia e testo*. 3 vols. Florence 1957-58.

Pellizzaro, Giambattista. *La Commedia del Secolo XVI e la Novellistica Anteriore e Contemporanea*. Vicenza, 1901.

Petraccone, Enzo. *La Commedia dell'arte: storia, tecnica, scenari*. Naples, 1927.

Petrocchi, Giorgio. *Pietro Aretino tra Rinascimento e Controriforma*. Milan, 1948.

Piromalli, Antonio. *La Cultura a Ferrara al Tempo di Ludovico Ariosto*. Florence, 1953.

Quadrio, Francesco Saverio. *Della Storia e della ragione d'ogni poesia*. Vol. 3. Milan, 1744.

Rébora, Piero. *L'Italia nel drama inglese (1558-1642)*. Milan, 1925.

Reinhart-Stoettner Karl. *Spaetere Bearbeitungen plautinischer Lustspiele*. Leipzig, 1886.

Riccoboni, Luigi. *Histoire du théâtre italien*. 2 vols. Paris, 1730-31.

Ridolfi, Roberto. *The Life of Niccolò Machiavelli*. trans. Cecil Grayson. Chicago, 1963.

Rossi, Vittorio. *Storia della Letteratura Italiana*. Vol. 2. Milan, 1903-4.

Russo, Lugi. *Commedie Fiorentine del Cinquecento*. Florence, 1939.

Sand, Maurice. *Masques et Bouffons*. 2 vols. Paris, 1860.

Sanesi, Ireneo. *La Commedia*. 2 vols., rev. ed. Milan, 1954.

Scherillo, Michele. *La Commedia dell'Arte in Italia*. Turin, 1884.

Settembrini, Luigi. *Lezioni di Letteratura Italiana*. Vol. 2. Naples, 1870.

Sismondi, Sismondo de'. *Historical View of the Literature of the South of Europe,* trans. Thomas Roscoe. Vol. 2. London, 1823.

Smith, Winifred. *The Commedia dell'Arte*. New York, 1964.

Spingarn, Joel E. *A History of Literary Criticism in the Renaissance*. New York, 1924.

Stoppato, L. *La Commedia Popolare in Italia*. Padua, 1887.

Storia del Teatro italiano. Vol. 1., ed. Silvio D'Amico. Milan, 1935.

Symonds, John Addington. *Renaissance in Italy*. Vol. 2. New York, 1935.

Tiraboschi, Girolamo. *Storia della Letteratura Italiana*. Vol. 7. Milan, 1824.

Viola, Raffaello. *Due Saggi di Letteratura Pavana*. Padua, 1949.

Wallace, H. W. *The Birth of Hercules with an introduction on the Influence of Plautus on the Dramatic Literature of England in the Sixteenth Century*. Chicago, 1903.

Weinberg, Bernard. *A History of Literary Criticism in the Italian Renaissance*. 2 vols. Chicago, 1961.

Wellek, René. *Concepts of Criticism*. New Haven, 1963.

Zecca, Giovanni. *Dell'Influenza di Terenzio nelle commedie di Ludovico Ariosto*. Milan, 1914.

Index of Names

Index of Plays